Mary S. Lovell began writing in 198... her to take a sabbatical from a successful business ... major biography was the international best-seller *Straight on till Morning*, a life of the intrepid aviatrix Beryl Markham. Since then she has built upon her reputation with a succession of acclaimed biographies, the research for which has involved travel all over the world. She lives in Gloucestershire and is currently writing a dual biography of Sir Richard Francis Burton and his wife Isabel.

The Belle of Almacks 1824. The Slater Portrait of Jane aged 17, made at the time of her marriage to Lord Ellenborough.

By Mary S. Lovell

STRAIGHT ON TILL MORNING
The Biography of Beryl Markham

THE SPLENDID OUTCAST
(with Beryl Markham)

THE SOUND OF WINGS
The Life of Amelia Earhart

CAST NO SHADOW
The Biography of Betty Pack

A SCANDALOUS LIFE
The Biography of Jane Digby

A Scandalous Life

The Biography of Jane Digby el Mezrab

MARY S. LOVELL

FOURTH ESTATE · London

First published in Great Britain in 1995 by Richard Cohen Books
This paperback edition first published 1996 by
Fourth Estate Limited
6 Salem Road
London
W2 4BU

A catalogue record for this book is available from the
British Library

ISBN 1-85702-469-9

5 7 9 8 6 4

Printed in Great Britain by
Clays Ltd, St Ives plc

This book is dedicated to
Joan Williams
to whom I owe a great deal;
she knows why.
And also to my aunt
Winifred Wooley
who is a great lady.

Contents

	Author's Note	xi
	Preface	xiii
1	Golden Childhood 1807–1823	1
2	The Débutante 1824	11
3	Lady Ellenborough 1825–1827	21
4	A Dangerous Attraction 1827–1827	36
5	Assignation in Brighton 1829–1830	49
6	A Fatal Notoriety 1830–1831	63
7	Jane and the King 1831–1833	76
8	Ianthe's Secret 1833–1835	96
9	A Duel for the Baroness 1836–1840	107
10	False Colours 1840–1846	120
11	The Queen's Rival 1846–1852	134
12	The Road to Damascus 1853	149
13	Arabian Nights 1853–1854	172
14	Honeymoon in Palmyra 1854–1855	185
15	Wife to the Sheikh 1855–1856	201

Contents

16 Return to England 1856–1858   215

17 Alone in Palmyra 1858–1859   231

18 The Massacre 1860–1861   242

19 Visitors from England 1862–1863   256

20 The Sitt el Mezrab 1863–1867   266

21 Challenge by Ouadjid 1867–1869   278

22 The Burtons 1870–1871   287

23 Untimely Obituary 1871–1878   300

24 Sunset Years 1878–1881   313

25 Funeral in Damascus 1881   322

    Epilogue   327

    Appendix: Last Will and Testament of
    the Hon. Jane Digby   335

    Notes   337

    Bibliography   351

    Acknowledgements   355

    Index   359

'How could this Lady Ellenborough, whose scandalous life is known to all the world, have deceived you, Your Majesty?'

Letter to King Ludwig I from his mistress's maid

Author's Note

Spelling of Arabic words

During research for this book I very quickly noticed considerable inconsistencies in the spelling of Arabic names and words when written in English. For instance Jane Digby might describe an acquaintance as 'Mohammed ebn Dukhy of the Wuld Ali tribe', while Anne Blunt wrote it 'Mehemmed ibn Dookhi of the Welled Ali tribe', Isabel Burton wrote 'Mohammed Dukhi of the Wuld Ali tribe' and Charles Doughty 'the Wulled Aly tribe'. The name Medjuel was pronounced Midgewell, and written variously – Miguel, Michwell, Midguel, etc., by English visitors.

These discrepancies (and there are too many to list) are easily explained by the fact that only three vowels are recognised in the Arabic language, and that some of the consonants have no equivalent in English. Each writer in English was therefore constrained to write what he or she heard, using phonetic spelling, and this naturally varied from person to person and town to town, just as pronunciation differs in our own regions, for example bath: baath or barth. Nor is the problem confined to the previous century. T. E. Lawrence had much the same experience when writing *Seven Pillars of Wisdom*.

To avoid confusion and irritation I have adopted a standard spelling of proper names and used them throughout the book, so that names such as 'Beyrouth' appear as the more familiar 'Beirut', etc. The standard is of my own devising and I make no claims as to its superiority over anyone else's spelling. I have merely used a version which seems to coincide with the way words are pronounced by the majority of contributors, avoiding accents where possible. This has sometimes necessitated my changing spellings used in original source material, but since – in many cases – the spelling was inconsistent within a single document I feel I can justify my decision.

Translations

Apart from Arabic, the original material used as sources for this book came in a variety of languages. This not only applies to published material: Jane and her contemporaries frequently employed foreign phrases to make a point in their letters, diaries, journals and memoirs. Assuming that not all readers will be multilingual, and for the sake of expediency, I have taken the liberty of translating these so that most quoted texts appear entirely in English. The translators who assisted me in this context are mentioned in the Acknowledgements section.

Preface

Friends often ask me how I choose my subjects. The answer is that my subjects usually choose me, and so it was with Jane Digby.

This book began at a cocktail party at the RAF Club in London in the spring of 1992 when Jane Digby's name and her story came up in conversation. I had never heard of her, so I made a mental note to do some research and rapidly found myself in the early stages of an obsession that was to last several years. Who was Jane Digby, and why should she cast such an appeal?

Born into the English aristocracy with every conceivable advantage in physical beauty, social position and wealth, Jane spent the final years of her life married to a desert prince. The Palladian mansions and gilded Mayfair salons of her youth made way for low black goat-hair tents and rugs spread upon wind-washed sands. Even now, with jet travel and motorised transport, the Syrian desert is one of the few lonely places left on earth. What unlikely circumstance, I wondered, had led Jane Digby there a century and a half ago?

Barely out of the schoolroom, already regarded as one of the most beautiful women of her day, Jane had married an ambitious politician, Lord Ellenborough, who was twice her age. In achieving his desire for a Cabinet post, Ellenborough neglected his bride and she soon sought consolation elsewhere. Before she was twenty-one Jane's love affair with an Austrian prince precipitated her into one of the most scandalous divorce cases of the nineteenth century. In April 1830, to the astonishment of its readers, *The Times* cleared its traditional front page of classified advertisements to carry a sensational news story –

a verbatim report of the Ellenborough divorce hearing in Parliament which included intimate details about the beautiful peeress and her prince.

Jane did not dispute the charges. Head over heels in love, she had already run off to Europe. But her story did not end there. Subsequently, for over twenty years Jane was to have a number of love affairs with members of the European aristocracy including a German baron, a Greek count and the King of Bavaria, as well as an Albanian general from the mountains. During this time she also married twice and travelled from the royal courts of Europe to the wilder regions of Turkey and the Orient. After a succession of scandals and betrayals, she made a journey to Syria. By then she was almost fifty and feared her life was over. Astonishingly, the most exciting part of her story still lay ahead of her.

The Arab nobleman who had been engaged to escort her caravan to the ruined city of Palmyra fell in love with her. He was young enough to be her son, was of a different culture and already had a spouse; indeed, he had recently divorced a second wife but he asked Jane to marry him. Although she was doubtful at first, she was soon deeply in love and, ignoring the entreaties of British officials, placed herself willingly in the power of a man who could divorce his partners on a whim. Sheikh Medjuel el Mezrab was the love of her life, and he brought her all the romance and adventure she had ever dreamed of.

Inevitably, because of the years she spent in Arabia, Jane's story invites comparisons with that of Lady Hester Stanhope, the niece and confidante of William Pitt who became the self-styled 'Queen of the Desert' a generation before Jane. But Hester Stanhope ended her life in Syria in abject poverty as an eccentric recluse, robbed, abused and eventually deserted by her Arab servants. Jane Digby lived as a respected, working leader of her adopted tribe, spending months at a time in the Baghdad desert, sharing the spare existence of the bedouin.

So astonishing was Jane Digby's career to her contemporaries that no fewer than eight novels based on her character and various elements of her story were written during her lifetime – one for every decade of her life. From 1830 until her death in Damascus in 1881 her name was rarely out of the newspapers as she featured in one outrageous tale after another.

Was it possible, I wondered when I embarked upon this project, to discover the rationale of such a person who even as a young woman

married to an eminent Cabinet Minister refused to concede to convention by hiding her illicit love affair? Who a century ahead of her time
was completely free of any form of racial or cultural prejudice? Who
saw travel to exotic destinations as a *raison d'être* second only to sharing
her life with a great all-encompassing love (though she showed
remarkably little regard for the immense difficulties involved in both)?
Who had, even prior to her desert expeditions, carelessly abandoned
the comfortable life of a royal mistress to live with an Albanian chieftain who was virtually a legitimised brigand?

Over a hundred years had elapsed since her death, but I knew
that, in common with many contemporaries, Jane kept diaries all her
life. Her first biographer, E. M. Oddie, who wrote *A Portrait of Ianthe*
in 1935, had access to some of them; but several subsequent biographers (such as Lesley Blanch and Margaret Schmidt) declared that
the diaries were lost. Since E. M. Oddie had quoted from the diaries
hardly at all, this seemed especially tragic. So I set out to discover
what had happened to them in order to learn about Jane through her
own voice. I also decided to try to locate the diaries and correspondence of people who met or were friends with Jane, not only to see
what more could be learned about her, but to give a three-dimensional
perspective to her story.

I contacted Lord Digby, a direct descendant of Jane's brother,
Edward, and in April 1993 at his invitation I drove down to Minterne
House in Dorset one morning to see his collection of Jane's watercolours. Over lunch I told him about my work and, after a pause, he
looked at me, seemed to come to a decision, and said, 'Um, we do
have Jane's diaries here. But we've never shown them to anyone.'

Within a short time I was seated at a writing table with objects
that had once been Jane's; her notebooks and sketchbooks, and her
diaries which covered more than three decades, principally those years
she spent in the desert. All would need to be transcribed and indexed
to be easily accessible. Some sections written in pencil were badly
faded; many entries were written in code and there were passages
written in French and Arabic. I realised too that the code, once
broken, might translate into any of the many languages that Jane
spoke; it would be a mammoth task. Five days later I was due to
leave for Syria to research Jane's life there. I asked to be allowed to
return to Minterne at some date in the future for a very long time.

Somewhere there must be a patron saint of biographers, to whom
I owe much. On my second visit Lord Digby showed me a small

portrait of Jane which hangs in the great hall at Minterne. 'We believe from portraits that she had the same colouring as my sister Pamela ... we've always thought they were probably quite alike.' The Hon. Pamela Digby, later Mrs Randolph Churchill and now US Ambassador Mrs Averell Harriman, shares a great deal with Jane: intelligence and charm, an unselfconscious sexuality, a disregard of the mores that accept (even admire) polygamy in men but deprecate similar behaviour in women. Mrs Harriman is widely regarded as a nonpareil among US Ambassadors to France and her ability to attract and fascinate is as legendary as that of her ancestor. Several portraits of Jane bear a remarkable likeness to Pamela Digby Harriman.

One memorable day I received a package from a descendant of Jane's brother Kenelm, a branch of whose family moved to New Zealand some decades ago. It contained letters written by Jane to her family and others over a thirty-year period. Together with her diaries and other papers, they provide a unique insight into a remarkable life.

During my trip to Syria I encountered the seductive spell of the desert that so bewitched Jane. With the enthusiastic help of my guide and interpreter Hussein Hinnawi, I was able to locate the remaining traces of her residence in Damascus; her home with its celebrated octagonal drawing-room and the high cupola ceiling, its curved alcoves for books and china, and its treasury of gilded woodcarving; her grave and – not least – Jane's lingering legend. Even after I left Syria, Hussein continued to research the story, purely out of interest, and his contribution to this book has been invaluable.

Had I simply copied all the information amassed during research, including relevant excerpts from over 200 books and scores of newspapers, parliamentary records, Jane's own diaries, letters and sundry papers, and those of her many friends such as Lady Anne Blunt, Isabel Burton and Emily Beaufort, the result would have been many thousands of pages of text. However, the job of a biographer is not merely to unearth and assemble facts; one must also dissect, compare, confirm and analyse; then hone the result in order to present to the reader a historically accurate, digestible and, I hope, enjoyable account of the subject.

Here, then, is my portrait of Jane Elizabeth Digby.

I

Golden Childhood
1807–1823

When Jane Elizabeth Digby was born at Forston House in Dorset on 3 April 1807 her parents had hoped for a son. However, she was such a beautiful child that her family were soon besotted with her. After all, there was time for sons and, as Jane's aunt wrote, 'providing the little girl is well and promising we must not hold her sex against her'.[1]

Later, with her large violet-blue eyes and pink-and-white complexion, little Janet (as her family called her then) was a pretty sight. Her waist-length golden hair, curling free from the prescribed banded and ringleted style, glistened halo-like in the sunshine. Her cheeks glowed: 'a picture of health,' local villagers said. As curious and agile as a kitten, as intelligent and eager as a puppy, she seemed to want to take the world by the coat-tails, and there was about her, even then, an irresistible charm.

This alert vitality captivated her grandfather, who was called 'Coke of Norfolk' throughout the country and 'King Coke' by everyone in Norfolk. Widely regarded as the most important and powerful commoner in England, Thomas Coke might have had a peerage for the asking; indeed, King George III was eager enough to bestow one. Yet this would have meant Coke giving up his independence and his seat in the House of Commons where he represented the county of Norfolk. He saw no merit in doing so.

Thomas Coke had three daughters, Jane, Anne and Elizabeth. They were all acknowledged beauties and all well educated; his late wife had seen to that when it became obvious there would be no male heir.[2] In addition to these advantages, Mr Coke had dowered his girls generously so that their eligibility in the marriage market was assured, though, in the event, all three married for love.[3] Since their sex prevented them from inheriting a title from their father, he therefore resisted ennoblement – once to the extent of openly rebuffing the King – spoke his mind freely and often bluntly, and owed allegiance to no man he felt had not earned his respect.

Coke's home in Norfolk was Holkham Hall, a Palladian mansion more like a palace than the home of a country squire. Here, in the great house where her mother had grown up, Jane spent much of her childhood.

Jane's mother, Thomas Coke's eldest daughter Jane, was known as Lady Andover, a form of address she used for the remainder of her life. The title was retained from a previous (childless) marriage which had ended in tragedy when she was twenty-one. Her husband Lord Andover had been killed as the result of a shooting accident that she had accurately foreseen in a dream. She had rushed out to him upon hearing the news, and almost his last words to her were: 'My dear, your dream has come true!'[4] It was not her only successful prediction and, curiously, her second husband had a similar ability, claiming that he owed his first success to a voice in a dream which told him to change the direction in which his ship was headed and even the course to steer.[5]

Captain Henry Digby, Jane's father, was a fair, handsome and much decorated naval hero. Prior to his marriage to Lady Andover he had distinguished himself at Trafalgar as commander of HMS *Africa*. In a letter to his uncle, the Hon. R. Digby (later Lord Digby), at Minterne he wrote of his part in the battle:

> HMS *Africa* at sea off the Straits
> November 1, 1805
>
> My dear Uncle,
>
> I write merely to say I am well, after having been closely engaged for 6 hours on 21st October. For details, being busy to the greatest degree, I have lost all my masts in consequence of the action and my ship is otherwise cut to pieces but sound in the bottom. My killed and wounded number 63, and many of the latter I shall lose if I do not get into port . . .
>
> After passing through the line in which position I brought down the fore masts of *Santisima Trinidad* mounting 140 guns, after which I engaged with pistol shot *L'Intrépide* 74 guns, which afterwards was struck and burnt, *Orion* and *Conqueror* coming up. A little boy that

stayed with me is safe. Twice on the poop I was left alone, all about me being killed or wounded. I am very deaf.[6]

Before Trafalgar he had been posted aboard the frigate *Aurora* and in less than two years had captured six French privateers (thanks to the voice in his dream) and one corvette, *L'Egalité*, making a total of 144 guns and 744 men, besides 48 merchant ships taken or sunk. In command of the *Leviathan* he assisted in the capture of the island of Minorca. Later he captured two French men-of-war, *Le Dépit* and *La Courage*; and in 1799 two Spanish frigates *Thetis* and *Brigide*, which carried between them 3 million dollars in gold. Fifty military wagons were needed to convey the spoils from Plymouth Dock to the Citadel. By the time he was thirty, Captain Digby had earned himself over £57,000 in prize money alone, and another £7,000 over the next five years.[7]

At the time of Jane's birth Captain Digby owned Forston House, a pleasant country property in Dorset. It overlooked the famous Cerne Abbas giant and was close to his uncle's estate, Minterne. It was because of her father's frequent absences at sea, and her mother's natural wish to spend time 'at home' at Holkham while he was away, that Jane and her two younger brothers, Edward and Kenelm, were often at their grandfather's house and, like their mother, came to regard Holkham as a second home. Here the eleven children of Lady Andover's sister Anne and her husband, Lord Anson, were also educated in the capacious schoolroom. Jane was particularly close to her Anson cousins Henry and Fanny who were nearest to her in age.

Those first decades of the nineteenth century were a golden era for the rich. Vast country houses surrounded by shaved lawns and pleasure gardens, with artificial lakes, follies and deer parks, stables full of hunters, hacks and work-horses, and coach-houses full of elegant equipages, provided work and livings for hundreds of servants indoors and out. Holkham was no exception.

Tom Coke could not be described as extravagant; he spent shrewdly enough, but no visitor ever walked through the deliberately unpretentious front entrance of Holkham Hall without being stunned at what lay within. The massive entrance hall, modelled on a Roman temple of justice, is an extravaganza of marble, alabaster and carved stone. Fluted Ionic columns support the domed Inigo Jones roof, a gilded crown for this masterpiece of light and space. Around the walls are bas-relief and marble sculptures, and the classical theme continues throughout the house. Holkham was – and remains – richly endowed with Greek and Roman statuary, but it is also famous for its art collection, its rich and rare furnishings and sumptuous Genoese velvet hangings, and its incomparable library. It is still regarded, along with Chatsworth, Blenheim, Badminton and Burghley, as one of the truly great houses of England.

Such grandeur, however, was not the brainchild of Jane's grandfather. The property was bought in 1610 by Edward Coke, the famous jurist, who became Lord Chief Justice. The first Earl of Leicester built the present house in 1734 and, when the direct line failed, the estate, but not the title, passed to Thomas William Coke. If Thomas Coke ever was inclined towards prodigality, the money was spent on his lands rather than his house. Politically he was a staunch Whig, but first and foremost he was a dedicated agricultural reformer, who spent a fortune[8] transforming a rugged wasteland 'where two rabbits fought over a single blade of grass' into a fertile, productive, 'scientifically controlled' region famous for its barley soil.[9] He convinced men of substance to invest in long-leases of farms and to 'induce their sons, after [reading] Greek and Latin in public schools, to put themselves under the tuition of well-informed practical farmers to be competent for management.'[10] It is no exaggeration to say that this far-sighted man was the architect of modern farming methods throughout the world.

His livestock, particularly sheep, were selectively bred for meat, breeding stock and wool. His annual sheep-shearing, known as Coke's Clippings, became a sort of four-day county fair which attracted thousands of sightseers from all over the country, and overseas. Exhibitions of every aspect of rural industry, from animal husbandry to flax weaving and the building of agricultural cottages, were presented. Conferences were held during which papers were given on agricultural matters such as crop rotation and stock-breeding, and these were a magnet for the guests assembled at Holkham for the Clippings, almost all of them titled.[11] The autumn and winter shooting parties at Holkham included royalty and top political figures of the Whig Party, as well as sporting squires, and Mr Coke's hospitality was legendary.

Despite his leaning towards outdoor pursuits, Thomas Coke did not neglect the arts. Educated at Eton (where on one occasion, to avoid being caught poaching on the neighbouring royal estates, he swam the River Thames with a hare in his mouth),[12] he spoke both Greek and Latin. He inherited the vast library of classical literature and manuscripts at Holkham, considered to be a national treasure (when he took over Holkham he found hundreds of rare books from Italy still unpacked in their crates), but he continued throughout his life to purchase rare books, and works of art by such contemporary geniuses as Gainsborough, to add to those by Titian, Van Dyck, Holbein, Rubens and Leonardo da Vinci.

It was in this atmosphere that Jane spent much of her youth. She was encouraged by her grandfather to ride, to take an interest in the active management of horses and small farm animals, to read the classics and to be aware of the ancient civilisations represented at Holkham, as well as modern politics. She lived the privileged life of a cosseted only daughter, surrounded on all sides by love and admiration, and the constant companionship of her two brothers and numerous cousins. In turn she worshipped her hero father, adored her lovely mother, who was called by all three children 'La Madre', and loved and revered her aunts.

We have mere glimpses of Jane in those days. A family friend who peered round the door of an upper-floor room saw through the dust motes of an early summer morning that 'the schoolroom was nearly full . . . there was Miss Digby – so beautiful – and the two Ansons, such dear and pretty children'.[13] Another noted Jane's vitality and grace of movement, but judged that 'her chief glory was her hair, which fell, a rippling golden cascade, down to her knees.'[14] An aunt recollected that as a child Jane used to refer to annoying incidents with the impatient phrase, 'it is most provocative and bothersome.'[15] In later years, Jane's own diary recalls the wonderful, rumbustious, 'old-fashioned' Christmases at Holkham, with all the traditions of feasting and mummers and laughter and games, and the annual servants' party. We also know from the diaries of her relatives, and visitors to Holkham, of the gargantuan dinners of dozens of courses for scores of appreciative diners from the Prince of Wales (a frequent visitor before he became Regent) to scholars, to which the children were sometimes invited. Again, we learn from her own diary that Jane's chief delight was to beat her brothers in their frequent mock horse-races.[16] She had no time for dolls and girlish toys but preferred riding and playing with dogs and the numerous family pets.[17] Totally fearless, she could ride anything in the Holkham stables, and was as at home looking after a sick beast as riding one – which must have especially endeared her to her grandfather.

That she was frequently wilful is enshrined in family legend, as is the further characteristic that she was so prettily mannered and always so abjectly apologetic at having offended that she was instantly forgiven. It was a happy childhood, but her natural high spirits led her into many 'scrapes', as she called them, and a picture emerges of a highly intelligent, active, perhaps somewhat spoiled little girl who instinctively threw up her head at any attempt to check her. She was not unfeeling in her pranks, however; her anxious cajolery shines through the tear-stained and ink-blotted note of apology that she wrote to her mother at the age of about eight:

Dearest Mama,

I am very sorry for what I have done and I will try, if you will forgive me, not to do it again. I wont contradict you no more. I've not had one lesson turned back today. If you and Papa will forgive me send me an answer by the bearer – pray do forgive me.

You may send away my rabbits, my quails, my donkey, my monkey, etc., but do forgive me.

I am, yours ever,
JED

P. S. Send me an answer please by the bearer. I will eat my bread at dinner, always.[18]

It was perhaps hardly surprising that Jane was a beauty. Her looks were inherited from her maternal grandmother – a woman of almost fabled loveliness and charm. Jane's mother was herself described by the Prince Regent as 'without doubt, the handsomest woman in England'.[19] However, it was unusual that Jane was given the same education as her brothers and male cousins, so that in addition to the practical basic education which naturally included French, a little German and Italian and a knowledge of the arts, she also had a thorough grounding in classical languages and acquired a love of history both ancient and modern. Nevertheless she managed to emerge from the schoolroom at the age of sixteen reasonably unspoiled and without undue vanity. Credit for this must go in large part to Miss Margaret Steele, the sober, fair-minded and determinedly moral governess recruited when Jane was ten years old.

The daughter of a scholarly but impoverished clergyman, Margaret Steele had been discreetly educated as a lady. She never married and when, on the death of her father, it became necessary to find a way of supplementing the meagre income bequeathed by her late parent the role of governess was one of the few acceptable occupations open to her. Her family was well known to Lady Andover and Lady Anson, and Lady Andover had no hesitation in offering Margaret Steele the position of governess to her daughter; not as a £40-a-year drudge at the mercy of the household but as a social equal who commanded the respect of the pupil's family and whose opinions were heard.

Miss Steele took very seriously her duty to impart the behaviour and skills that Jane would require for her adult role in the highest ranks of society. These skills included a thorough training in music, needlework, the Bible, social deportment and other accomplishments not normally dealt with by the male tutor who had been engaged at Holkham for the young men of the family, who would later be shipped off to public school at the age of eleven or twelve to finish their education.

The governess had an apt pupil in Jane when Jane wished to attend. She quickly displayed, in common with her mother and aunts, a remarkable talent for painting. Margaret Steele – already irreverently called 'Steely' by her young charge – was not artistically gifted; however, Margaret's elder sister Jane, who painted watercolours of a professional standard, gladly consented to tutor Jane Digby in this subject. Between them the two sisters had a great influence on Jane's upbringing, and a deep affection developed between mentors and child which would last into the old age of all three. Steely's nickname was apt: she was uncompromising in her steadfast obligation to duty and industry. She had a firm belief in Christianity and adhered strictly to the tenets of the Church of England, striving always for self-improvement. In the louche era of the Regency she was almost a portent of the Victorian ideal to come; in an earlier age she might have been a Puritan. However, Steely's forbidding nature was offset by the presence of her gentler sister, who was soft and kind, and forgiving of the sins of others. Moreover, Steely had one failing of her own, a slightly guilty enjoyment of popular literature of a 'non-improving' variety such as the novels of Mrs Radcliffe, which the sisters used to read aloud to each other.

Jane's lifelong delight in travel was fostered early. Her father rose quickly to the rank of rear-admiral and was often absent for long periods of duty with the fleet. In 1820, when it was necessary for him to visit Italy, Lady Andover accompanied him on the overland journey, and Jane and the Misses Steele went also, attended by Admiral Digby's valet and Lady Andover's French maid. They travelled in a convoy of carriages and luggage coaches, calling at Paris and Geneva.

7

While they were in Italy thirteen-year-old Jane, obviously totally confident of her father's love for her, engagingly requested an advance on her allowance. Her coquettish use of punctuation and heavy underscoring, sometimes teasing, sometimes firm, reflects their close relationship:

Rear Admiral Digby
Casa Brunavini
Florence, Italy

Florence, Thursday

Dearest Papa,

I *write* because I have a favour to ask which I am *afraid* you will think too great to grant; but as *you* at Geneva *trusted* me with [a] littler sum I am not ashamed, after you have heard from Steely my character, to ask a second time.

It is to ... to ... to advance me my pocket money, two pounds a week for *20 weeks* counting from next Monday and I'll tell you what for! If *you approve* I'll do it *but* if not I'll give it up!!!

Remember at Geneva after you advanced me *12 weeks*, I never teased you for money until the time was expired. I promise to do the same here. Do not tell anyone but give me the answer. I will not ask for half a cracie until the time is expired. Think *well* of it and remember it is *20* ! ! ! *weeks*; I ask *40 pounds* ! ! ! ! Not a farthing more or less. *40 pounds*.

Goodbye and put the answer at the bottom of this [note]. I have long been trying to *hoard* the sum but I find that I want it *directly* and then I should not have it till we were gone. If you repulse me I will not grumble and if you grant it me '*je vous remercie bien*'. *Pensez y* and goodbye, *mon bon petit père*, I remain your very affectionate daughter.

Jane Elizabeth Digby[20]

Unfortunately the surviving note lacks Admiral Digby's response, and it is impossible to guess at the childhood desire that prompted such a request, or whether it was granted.

At the age of fifteen Jane was sent off to a Seminary for Young Ladies near Tunbridge Wells, Kent, for finishing. Here, in the traditions of English public school life, Jane fagged for an older girl, Caroline 'Carry' Boyle, during her first year.[21] She missed her family but not unusually so, and to compensate she became a frequent correspondent, especially with her brothers, of whom she was very fond. Their notes to each other were partly written in the 'secret' code which she would use freely in her diary throughout her life.[22]

There was a good deal to write about. Their grandfather Coke, only a year short of seventy, decided to remarry in February 1822. His bride, Lady Anne Keppel, was an eighteen-year-old girl, the daughter of a family friend, Lady Albemarle (who had died at Holkham in childbirth some years earlier), and god-daughter to Mr Coke. Furthermore, since Lady Anne's father married a young niece of Mr Coke's at the same time, there was a good deal of speculation that Lady Anne had married merely to escape from home.

Soon afterwards, Coke's youngest daughter, Elizabeth (Eliza), who had reigned at Holkham as chatelaine while her father was a widower, married John Spencer-Stanhope and finally left the family home.

When Jane Digby left school at Christmas 1823, she was – as the French writer Edmond About wrote – 'like all unmarried girls, a book bound in muslin and filled with blank white pages waiting to be written upon'.[23] She was also a lively, self-confident young woman who adored her parents and was not above teasing her papa with humorous affection when she came upon a 'quaint' tract on his desk entitled 'Hooks and Eyes to keep up Falling Breeches'.[24]

It had already been decided by 'dearest Madre' that Jane would make her début in the following February when the season started, rather than wait a further year. There is an unsubstantiated story that Jane was romantically attracted to a Holkham groom,[25] and that an attempted elopement precipitated her early entry into society; however, according to her poems, Jane had thoughts and eyes for no one during these months but her handsome eldest cousin George Anson. It is doubtful that George, one of the most popular men about town, gave Jane more than a passing thought, for he was busy sowing his wild oats with married women; the hero-worship directed at him by his cousin was totally unrequited. Besides, there was a family precedent for early entry into society. Jane's Aunt Anne was betrothed at fifteen, and made her début a year later.

Though no longer required in the role of governess, Steely remained as Jane's duenna, to chaperon her during her forthcoming season when Lady Andover was engaged elsewhere. Miss Jane Steele continued to provide drawing lessons.

Had they been told that Jane would hardly be out of her teens before she would appear in one of the most sensational legal dramas of the nineteenth century, making it impossible for her ever again to live in England; that she would be so disgraced that her doting maternal grandfather Coke would cut her out of his life, and her uncle Lord Digby would cut her brother Edward (heir to the title Lord

Digby) out of his will; that she would capture the hearts of foreign kings and princes, but would abandon them to live in a cave as the mistress of an Albanian bandit chieftain; that in middle age she would fall in love and marry an Arab sheikh young enough to be her son, and live out the remainder of her life as a desert princess, the Misses Steele could not possibly have believed it. Yet all those things, and much more, lay in the future for Jane Digby.

2

The Débutante

1824

Unlike many of her contemporaries, Jane was not a stranger to London. Her parents owned a house on the corner of Harley Street 'at the fashionable end',[1] so she would not have arrived wide-eyed at the bustle and noise noted by so many débutantes. However, as a girl who had not yet been brought out into society, the time she had previously spent there would have been very tame.

When not in the schoolroom Jane would spend her days shopping with her mother in the morning, if the weather permitted walking. In the afternoon she might walk in Hyde Park, chaperoned by Steely, and paint in watercolours or practise her music at other times. Jane and her brothers would have eaten informal meals with their parents, but for dinners and parties they would have been banished to the nursery – a far cry from Holkham, where the children often mingled with the adults. In town it was not possible for Jane to walk round to the stables and order her horse to be saddled for an invigorating gallop. It was necessary to appoint a given time for the horse to be brought round to the house, and it would be a solecism if a girl not yet out in society or even one in her first season went for a gallop in the park.

But all this changed when she took London by storm. The change to her life was an intoxicating experience. Now she breakfasted late with her parents and, while she might still shop with her mother in the mornings, it was for clothes and fashionable fripperies for her town wardrobe: new silk gloves or satin dancing slippers, an embroidered reticule for walking out, a domino for a masked rout, white ostrich feathers for her presentation, some ells of white sprigged muslin. Now she attended lessons in the cotillion and the waltz, given by a dancing master under Steely's watchful eye. Now she rode her neat cover-hack in the park at the fashionable hour of 5 p.m., or rode with her mother in the chaise in Rotten Row, nodding to acquaintances, stopping for a chat with friends. Now the florist's cart was never away from the door with small floral tributes from admirers.

The years of instruction by Steely at last bore fruit. Jane's natural ear for languages enabled her not only to infiltrate foreign phrases into her conversation and correspondence – the outward sign of a well-rounded education – but also to converse in Italian, French and German with foreign visitors. All those music lessons that Jane had found a dreary bore were now justified, for after a dinner party she might be called upon to perform for her fellow guests. She was a good pianist, and played the guitar and lute; she also had a sweet singing voice. She acquired a wide repertoire of foreign love songs, which generally delighted her listeners. She was not slow to recognise when she captivated her hearers, and was feminine enough to enjoy doing so.[2]

At sixteen, however, Jane was younger than the average débutante and had little experience of life. But she realised quite quickly that what was acceptable behaviour in the country was not so in London. A young lady might never venture abroad alone, on foot without a footman, or on horseback or in a carriage without a groom in attendance. She might, by 1824, have shopped with a girlfriend in Bond Street without raising eyebrows, just; but no lady would be seen in the St James's area where the gentlemen's clubs were situated. A young unmarried woman could never be alone with a gentleman unless he was closely related, and, while she might drive with a gentleman approved by her mama in an *open* carriage in the park, it must be a safe gig or perch phaeton and not the more dashing high-perch phaeton affected by members of the four-horse club, nor the newest Tilbury driven tandem. Either of the latter would have branded a girl as 'fast', even with a groom acting as stand-in for a chaperone. At a ball she must not on any account stand up to dance with the same man more than twice. The merest breath of criticism against a girl or her family was enough to prevent her obtaining a voucher from one of the Lady Patronesses of Almack's.[3]

Despite the high standards they set for patrons of Almack's it would be fair to say that the private lives of most of the Patronesses would not stand close examination, for with one exception they all had famous *affaires* with highly ranked partners ranging from the Prince Regent himself to several Prime Ministers; however, they maintained a discreet appearance of respectability – a pivot, as it were, between the open licentiousness of the Regency and the rapidly approaching hypocrisy of Victorian morality.

Not to be seen at Almack's branded one as 'outside the *haut ton*', so that, in effect, the Patronesses constituted a matriarchal oligarchy to whom everyone bowed, including the revered Duke of Wellington, who was turned away one evening for not wearing correct evening dress. Captain Gronow, the contemporary social observer, wrote: 'One can hardly conceive the importance which was attached to getting admission to Almack's, the seventh heaven of the fashionable world. Of the three hundred officers of the Foot-Guards, not more than half a dozen [Captain Gronow was one of those] were honoured by vouchers.' Almack's was a hotbed of gossip, rumour and scandal, and the country dances were dull. Matters improved somewhat after Princess Lieven and Lord Palmerston made the waltz respectable, though it was still regarded by many parents as 'voluptuous, sensational . . . and an excuse for hugging and squeezing'.[4] Alcoholic drinks were forbidden, and refreshments consisted of lemonade, tea and cakes, and bread and butter.

Why entrance to so prosy a venue should excite such passion, when the London season offered dozens of more exciting and enjoyable occupations every evening, can be explained by the fact that Almack's was the most exigent marriage market in the Western world,[5] and marriage was what the whole thing was about. It was *desirable* for a young man of decent background and respectable expectations to attract favourable connections through marriage, and if the wife had a good dowry so much the better. But it was *essential* for a young woman to contract an eligible match with a man who could provide all the social and financial advantages that she had been reared to take for granted. The lot of an unmarried woman past her youth in that milieu was unenviable – thrown, as it were, on to the charity and tolerance of her relatives. Jane Austen's heroines exemplify, with a touching contemporary immediacy, the importance of a woman 'taking' during her début.

Vast wardrobes of morning dresses, afternoon dresses, walking-out dresses, ballgowns, riding habits and gowns suitable for every conceivable occupation were necessary. But cloaks and gowns were only the start. Accessories, such as collections of hats ranging from the simple chipstraw to high-crowned velvet bonnets, were indispensable. Gloves of silk, lace, satin and kid for every occupation that might be fitted in between rising and retiring, from walking to riding to dining and dancing, were essential. Sandals, reticules, shawls, tippets, fans, chemises, camisoles and undergarments such as stays were obligatory. All of this, with luck, would form the basis of a girl's trousseau in due course. Further expenditure included the cost of a good horse for riding in Hyde Park (a prime shopwindow in the marriage market) and the use of a carriage, since it was no use expecting a girl to travel everywhere by sedan chair. If the parents had no town-house of their own, and no relative with whom to stay, they must also bear the cost of hiring a house for the season as well as organising several smart dinner parties and soirées, and at least one ball. It was a huge investment, and this can only have served to heighten the pressure on the girl to fix the interest of a suitable man.

Jane made her début at a royal 'Drawing Room' in March 1824, when Lady Andover introduced her daughter to King George IV and the fashionable world. Henceforward Jane was an adult, free to attend adult parties and dances. With her background, connections and appearance, it was inevitable that she would be an immediate success. Her aunt, Eliza Spencer-Stanhope, wrote to the family that her sister, Lady Andover, was 'graciously' anticipating imminent conquests.[6]

Vouchers for Almack's were, of course, forthcoming for Lady Andover and her fledgeling, and Jane was subsequently to be seen at every ball, soirée, rout and dinner party of note. Young admirers wrote poems to her eyes, her shoulders, her guinea-golden curls; and she replied by telling 'her wooers not to be "so absurd"'.[7] No new entry truly made an impression unless a nickname attached itself to her; 'the Dasher', 'the White Doe' and 'the Incomparable' were typical. Jane became known as 'Light of Day'.

The pencil and watercolour sketch made of Jane in 1824 shows her hair springing prettily from her high forehead, curling naturally into small ringlets around her face and coiled into a coronet. Large eyes fringed by thick dark lashes gaze serenely at the viewer and the sweet expression which might otherwise be serious is lifted by curved full lips. What the sketch does not convey is Jane's colouring; oil portraits show that her hair was a rich tawny gold, her eyes dark violet-blue, and her fine clear skin a delicate pink. The sketch does not portray her figure (described by many diarists as 'perfect . . . instinctive with vitality and an incomparable grace of movement)',[8] nor that when her pink lips parted her teeth were like 'flawless pearls'.[9] She had a roguish smile, a soft light voice and a pleasing modesty which gave way to lively animation once initial shyness had been overcome.

George IV was no longer the handsome Prince Regent of yesteryear but a tired and corpulent old man who walked with a stick. Nevertheless Jane must have enjoyed the thrill of the occasion. She wore the uniform white silk gown of simple cut, high-waisted with tiny puff sleeves, a sweeping train falling from her slim shoulders, long white gloves, and the *de rigueur* headdress of three white curled ostrich feathers. Small wonder that within days of her daughter's presentation Lady Andover was so certain of a conquest that it was being noted in family correspondence. Small wonder that within a matter of weeks the youthful admirers who shoaled around Jane were scattered by a shark attracted into Jane's pool of suitors.

Edward Law, Lord Ellenborough, was no stranger to Jane. She had met him at least once some four years earlier when he had sided with Thomas Coke in opposing the King's wish to divorce. As a consequence Ellenborough had visited Holkham, though at that time Jane was a mere twelve-year-old occupant of the schoolroom. Now, creditably launched into society, although very young she was considered by many to be one of the catches of the season.

Ellenborough was thirty-four, a widower, childless, and by any standards eligible in the marriage market. He was rich and pleasant-looking, with a polished address, having been educated at Eton (where he was known as 'Horrid Law', and generally regarded as 'prodigious clever'),[10] and Cambridge. He had wanted a military career but his father, a former Lord Chief Justice in the famous post-Pitt 'All the Talents' coalition government, forbade it, so he entered the world of politics. By 1824 Edward, who succeeded to the title in 1819, had every anticipation of a Cabinet position. His late wife Octavia had been sister to Lord Castlereagh – Ellenborough's political mentor – and *The Times* report of her funeral reflects their status:

> At an early hour yesterday, the remains of Lady Ellenborough were removed from his Lordship's house in Hertford Street, Mayfair. The cavalcade moved at half-past 6, and consisted of four mutes on horseback, six horsemen in black cloaks etc.
>
> The hearse, containing the body enclosed in a coffin covered with superb crimson velvet, elegantly ornamented with silver gilt nails, coronets etc. and with a plate bearing the inscription; 'Octavia, Lady

Ellenborough, daughter of Robert Stewart, Marquis of Londonderry died the 5th of March 1819, aged 27'; was followed by five mourning coaches and four, with several carriages of the nobility etc.[11]

Five years had passed since Lady Octavia's untimely death. Meanwhile her brother had become the most hated politician of the day, and ended his life in 1822 by slitting his throat with a penknife. Probably England's forty years of peace after Napoleon's downfall owed much to Castlereagh's period as Foreign Secretary,[12] yet he was so despised that his coffin was greeted with shouts of exultation as he was borne to his grave in Westminster Abbey. Some of that odium still clung to Lord Ellenborough. Further, Ellenborough's championship in 1820 of the former Queen Caroline's cause, and a major speech in 1823 during a debate on the King's Property Bill seeking to reduce George IV's powers to dispose of Crown property, had permanently alienated his sovereign and made him *persona non grata* at court. Nevertheless Lord Ellenborough was a rising power in the land, despite whispered hints and rumours that he had some murky secrets in his private life and that he had been refused by several respectable young women.

Jane and Lord Ellenborough met in early April around the time of Jane's seventeenth birthday, possibly at Almack's. Less than eight weeks later Ellenborough sought permission from Admiral Digby to address Miss Digby (he always called her Janet) and a week later, on 4 June, Coke's friend Lord Clare was writing to a mutual acquaintance, 'I hear Ellenborough is going to be married to Lady Andover's daughter.'[13]

They were a handsome couple and each had much to offer a partner, but there was an obvious disparity in age and experience. Ellenborough was twice as old as Jane and a friend of her father, though at thirty-four he was hardly the raddled ancient roué that some Digby biographers have implied.[14] The difference in years is anyway of questionable importance when within Jane's own family there was ample evidence that April could successfully marry December. However, Ellenborough was an ambitious and mature politician who had little time to spare for social obligations unless they might further his work or career, and even less to cherish and instruct – let alone amuse – a child bride. Here was a man who, when obliged to entertain, would inevitably fill his table and his guest rooms with minor members of the royal family, ambassadors and senior politicians.

Jane was a young girl who only a few weeks earlier would have needed her governess's permission even to ride her horse. This marriage would place her at a stroke in charge of an elevated domestic establishment, hostess to the country's leaders and responsible for dozens of servants. Jane's family connections were considerable, but Ellenborough had no need of them to further his career. Perhaps he fell in love with the enchanting girl, or at least was so charmed with her that he was willing to overlook her lack of experience. He desperately wanted an heir and her family had a record of healthy fecundity. It was said that he 'courted her with the impatience and persistence of an adolescent boy'.[15]

That Jane chose to marry Lord Ellenborough when, to judge from her family's correspondence, she might have chosen a bridegroom nearer her own age is equally surprising. Previous biographers have speculated that Jane was compelled to marry Ellenborough by her parents, but there is no evidence to substantiate this. Jane could twist her father – whom she called 'darling Babou' – round the proverbial little finger, as surviving letters show, and it would have been out of character for either of her doting parents to coerce Jane into an unwanted marriage. Furthermore, Jane was so young that, even had she not found a match she liked in her first season, she could have returned again – as many girls did – for a second shot, still not having reached her eighteenth birthday. It seems far more likely that she was flattered by the attentions of an older, experienced man and that she romantically concluded that she was in love with him. This is borne out by poems that the couple sent each other, and by subsequent entries in Jane's diaries. One of Lord Ellenborough's poems tells of Jane's love for him:

> O fairest of the many fair
> Who ruled, or seemed to rule my heart
> The first I have enthroned there
> Without a wish my bonds to part.
> The thought that I am loved again
> And loved by one I can adore,
> That I have passed through years of pain
> And found the bliss I knew before.
> O 'twould have ta'en away my mind
> But thy sweet smile a charm has given
> And love's wild ecstasy combined
> With deepest gratitude to heaven.[16]

17

His Lordship's other poems spoke of 'joy in the present day' because of her and the bliss of knowing that 'the next will be yet happier than this . . . Oh! this is youth and these the dreams of youth . . . And heaven itself is realised on earth.'[17]

During their whirlwind courtship society found a synonym for Jane's sobriquet 'Light of Day.' 'Aurora' was a name with which Jane could not have found fault in view of the fact that her father had once captained a ship of the same name, and it had a pretty sound. However, it was almost certainly intended to be less flattering to her suitor, Jane being cast in the role of Lord Byron's sixteen-year-old heroine Aurora Raby, with Lord Ellenborough as the debauched, ageing, eponymous subject of the best-selling *Don Juan*:

> there was indeed a certain fair and fairy one
> Of the best class and better than her class,
> Aurora Raby, a young star who shone
> O'er life, too sweet an image for such glass.
> A lovely being, scarcely formed or moulded,
> A rose with all its sweetest leaves yet folded.[18]

It was not to be supposed because of the speed of the courtship that the marriage could be held with similar haste. During June the engaged couple enjoyed the last days of the season with its military reviews, balloon ascents, race meets and ridottos. As his fiancée Jane could ride publicly in Lord Ellenborough's glossy phaeton, with his groom in attendance. She must be introduced to her prospective in-laws, Edward's sister Elizabeth and his brothers, Charles and Henry. There were also the Londonderrys, his former in-laws, a valuable relationship he wished to maintain. When Lady Andover received a letter from Lady Londonderry congratulating her upon Jane's betrothal and eulogising Lord Ellenborough,[19] it must have been comforting to know that her cherished daughter was to marry such a paragon.

At the end of July, Edward visited Holkham, where he met the Cokes, Digbys, Ansons and Spencer-Stanhopes.[20] It was not his first visit, but Jane must have derived immense pleasure from showing him some of the treasures of the great house, and riding with him in the parkland bordering the beaches. However, Edward and Mr Coke, having once been allies, had now moved apart politically; consequently his future visits to Holkham, and eventually Jane's own, were few.

Shopping and fittings for the bridal clothes were time-consuming, and Jane must be taken over her future homes – an elegant pillared and porticoed town-house in Connaught Place, whose rear windows today overlook Marble Arch, and Elm Grove, Lord Ellenborough's country house at Roehampton near Richmond.[21] Yet somehow, during this time, Jane must have been instructed in her duties as chatelaine, for, although she would have had domestic instruction as she grew up, she would have had little reason to put such knowledge to practical use. Her mother wrote a treatise, which subsequently served as a model for other brides-to-be within the Coke family, upon the qualities requisite for 'members of the household', including that most valuable servant, the Lady's maid:

Essentials for a Lady's maid

She must not have a will of her own in *anything*, & always be good-humoured and approve of everything her mistress likes. She *must not* have an appetite . . . or care when or how she dines, how often disturbed, or even if she has no dinner at all. She had better not drink anything but water.

She must *run* the instant she is called whatever she is about. Morning, noon and night she must not mind going without sleep if her mistress requires her attendance. She must not require high wages nor expect profit from old clothes but be ready to turn and clean them . . . for her mistress, and be satisfied with two old gowns for herself. She must be a *first-rate* vermin catcher.

She must be clean and sweet . . . let her not venture to make a complaint or difficulty of any kind. If so, she had better go at once.[22]

Few of Jane's papers from this period survive and her journal is not among them. We know, however, that her parents were delighted with the match, and that Steely approved also. But there were some dissensions, notably among Ellenborough's political opponents. One could not accuse the Duke of Wellington's *chère amie*, Harriet Arbuthnot, of political bias, however, when she wrote that 'Ellenborough having flirted and made himself ridiculous with all the girls in London now marries Miss Digby . . . she is very fair, very young and very pretty.'[23] The diarist Thomas Creevey, who was a close friend of Jane's aunt Lady Anson and knew Ellenborough well, wrote:

Lady Anson goes to town next week to be present at the wedding of her niece, the pretty 'Aurora; Light of Day' Miss Digby . . . who is going to be married to Lord Ellenborough. It was Miss Russell who refused Ld Ellenborough, as many others besides are said to have done. Lady Anson will have it that he was a very good husband to his first wife, but all my impressions are that he is a dammed fellow.[24]

Lady Holland wrote to her son that Ellenborough 'has at last succeeded in getting a young wife, a poor girl who has not seen anything of the world. He could only snap up such a one . . . she is granddaughter of Mr Coke *who has another son!*'[25] Thus she broke the news that Jane's grandfather had the felicity of a spare for his cherished heir. However, Lady Holland's views on Lord Ellenborough were politically jaundiced; she disliked him intensely and openly held the opinion that he was impotent.[26]

In August, Ellenborough noted in his diary that he had 'dined with Janet at the Duke's'. The Duke of Wellington's London home was Apsley House, near Hyde Park. It was a huge formal dinner with many notables present, all much older than Jane. Ellenborough was clearly pleased at the manner in which Jane conducted herself in such august company.[27]

The day designated for the marriage was 15 September 1824, some five months after their meeting in London. The venue was not, as might be supposed, the chapel at Holkham; with a new son only three weeks old, Jane's step-grandmother could not accommodate a wedding party. Jane was married to Edward at her parents' London house, as an entry in the register of the Parish of St Marylebone shows:

> The Right Honourable Edward Lord Ellenborough, a Widower, and Jane Elizabeth Digby, Spinster, a minor, were married by Special Licence at 78 Harley Street by and with the consent of Henry Digby Esquire, Rear Admiral in His Majesty's Navy, the natural and lawful father of the said minor, this fifteenth day of September.[28]

It was not unusual for a society marriage to be conducted in a private home. Slightly more unusual, perhaps, was that it was performed in a secular venue by a bishop, Edward's uncle, the Bishop of Bath and Wells. The court pages reveal that the happy couple sped off to Brighton for the honeymoon where, as Jane recalled many years later, a wholly satisfactory wedding night followed.[29]

3

Lady Ellenborough
1825–1827

The honeymoon in Brighton lasted a mere three weeks and Lord Ellenborough was back at work in October. During the following period, though busy with affairs of great moment, he still found time to write poetry to his bride. The epithet 'Juliet' was only used in the first months of their marriage, probably as an allusion to Jane's youth. Jane had a pet name for her husband – 'Oussey' – but in all surviving correspondence between the two she signed herself 'Janet', except in the following exchange:

> Oh Juliet, if to have no fear
> But that of deserving thee,
> To know no peace when thou art near
> No joy thou can'st not share with me
>
> If still to feel a lover's fire
> And love thee more the more prospect,
> To have on earth but one desire
> Of making thee completely blest!
>
> If this be passion, thou alone
> Canst make my heart such passion know.
> Love me but still, as thou hast done,
> And I will ever love thee so.
>
> Ellenborough, 12 November 1824

To which his bride of two months readily replied within twenty-four hours:

'To love thee still as I have done'
Say, is it all thou ask of me?
Thou has it then, for thou alone
Reign in the soul that breathes for thee.

Edward, for thee alone I sigh
And feel a love unknown before
What bliss is mine when thou art nigh
Oh loved one still, I ask no more

As thou art now, oh ever be
To her whose fate in thine is bound
Whose greatest joy is loving thee
Whose bliss in thee alone is found.

And she will ever thee adore
From day to day with ardour new
Both now and to life's latest hour
With passion, felt alas! . . . by few.

Juliet, 13 November 1824

Those words 'whose greatest joy is loving thee' hardly reinforce the image of a girl coerced into an unwanted marriage, nor charges that the marriage was a failure from the day of the wedding, and these facts are important in view of what was to follow. Visitors to Elm Grove found the couple happy together and living in terms of open affection.[1] They rode out together most mornings when Edward was at Roehampton, often across Richmond Park.[2] Joseph Jekyll, who visited the Ellenboroughs just before Christmas, wrote: 'I dined and slept . . . at Roehampton to be presented by Lord Ellenborough to his bride. Very pretty, but quite a girl, twenty years younger than himself[3] . . . The general subject was his lordship's lamentation at being called away so frequently from his beautiful wife by debates and politics.'[4]

The poetry and literary love-making during Ellenborough's absences continued for months, whenever Ellenborough was away from Jane, and some, such as the following extract from a poem written on New Year's Day 1825 while he was staying at Boldrewood in Hampshire with Lord Lyndhurst, the Attorney-General and a close friend, is illuminating:

My bride! For thou art still a bride to me
And loved with all the passion of a soul
Which gave itself at once, nor would be free . . .

Yet I have had a roving eye, till now,
And gazed around on every lovely face
And still would, all enthralled to beauty, bow

But ne'er in fairest features could I trace
The sympathetic smile, and winning grace
Which beam aloft on thy illumined brow

And every thought of others is effaced
In dreams of bliss which heaven's behests allow
So wedded truth alone, and love's unbroken vow,

Ellenborough

Unless this poem came as a shock to her it seems that Jane was aware of Ellenborough's reputation as a womaniser; he freely admits that he is still a potential rover were he not in love with his wife and her sympathetic smile and winning grace.

During her husband's many absences Jane was initially content to get to know her new homes and learn the ordering of them. Steely was a visitor to Roehampton several times, as were Lady Andover and Lady Anson. Nor was Roehampton far from London, should Jane have felt the want of company. Once the 1825 season started, though, Jane removed to town and immediately her name featured regularly in the court page of the *Morning Post* as guest of socially prominent hostesses, often – but not always – accompanied by her husband, and also as the hostess herself of several formal dinners and a ball.

As the year wore on, however, hairline cracks began to appear in the fabric of the marriage. Lady Londonderry had earlier commended her former son-in-law for the five years of happiness he had given her late daughter, and Ellenborough's biographers claim that the first Lady Ellenborough, Octavia, was the love of his life. Ellenborough is on record as saying that in his opinion whatever good he had done in his life was due to his first wife.[5] Perhaps it is not surprising, then, that Jane, feeling rejected by her husband's frequent absences and hurt by his apparent coolness, attributed the neglect not to his work but to his love for the dead Octavia.

In a poem to him, written about the time of the first anniversary of their wedding, answering Edward's comment on her 'lack of gaiety', she asked his forgiveness for her jealous fears that Octavia 'thy love of former years still reigns, while every thought and wish of mine is breathed for thee alone'. Beyond doubt she believed herself in love with her husband when she asked plaintively, 'did her passion equal mine? Her joy the same when thou art near? And if not present did she pine?'

> And here I am the fond, the young,
> The blest in all that earth can give,
> By men beloved, by lovers sung,
> Yet silent, loveworn do I grieve.[6]

Why did this marriage, which had begun so well, run into trouble so quickly? On the face of it Jane had everything most women of her world could have wished: love, wealth and social position. At least Edward's poetry proclaimed love, and whatever his faults he was always generous. Jane had a 'pin-money' allowance that her female relatives regarded with envy,[7] and on their marriage he presented her with a green leather box of family jewels. Even a year after their marriage he habitually returned from short absences with a costly gift of jewellery such as the emeralds for which Lady Ellenborough became envied. However, it becomes clear from her diary in later years that these gifts were not appreciated by Jane as much as would have been a display of warmth from her husband.[8]

During the London season it was inconceivable that she would not attract the attention of admiring young men prepared to offer a solace her husband could not or would not give. Ellenborough might have smiled at the stir his wife created whenever she appeared in company, indeed basked in the thought that he possessed what other men so desired. Or he may have been so preoccupied and immersed in his work that he did not notice that the only time his bored young wife came to life was when she was the adored centrepiece of a crowd of young men.

Perhaps it is not surprising that Jane began to move away from her husband, in fantasy if not in deed. The next poem is almost certainly about George Anson, and was written after the visit of a horseman whom, at first sight from a distance, Jane mistook for her cousin. She recalled his winning look and had to 'quell each rebel sigh' at the thought of him. But then loyalty to Edward overtook her fantasy:

> I may not think, I will not pause
> One look behind my faith to shake.
> Henceforth must buried be the past
> Nor in my heart shall e'er awake
> Its echo, for dear Edward's sake.[9]

So far as one can take this surviving written work as evidence of the pattern of their marriage, it is possible to conclude that Jane felt neglected by her husband and believed he no longer loved her. Given Ellenborough's age and disposition, and Jane's lively but romantically inclined personality, such a situation was always probable. Had she confided in her mother or Steely, she would undoubtedly have been advised to accept that Edward must be about his business. It would be wrong, however, not to produce another piece of the jigsaw at this stage. Edward had a mistress, and within six months of the marriage Jane apparently discovered a portrait of this woman in their home.[10]

At this point, although the couple clearly had problems, the marriage survived a potential crisis. The Ellenboroughs spent some weeks in Paris during the autumn of 1825,[11] and, at least to observers who would later testify to the fact, all seemed perfectly normal. In the following April, when seen by a member of the family at an early season ball, she was 'on the arm of her Lord looking devastatingly handsome in black velvet and diamonds'.[12] Two nights later she was noted by Mrs Arbuthnot at a Spanish ball held at the Opera House, where the company '*Polonaised* all around . . . Lady Ellenborough looked quite beautiful . . . it was altogether as magnificent a fete as I ever saw.'[13] No event of any note, it seems, was held without the presence of this lovely young woman. And she was never without her crowd of male admirers. At the end of the season the couple spent several weeks in Brighton, staying at the Norfolk Hotel in a suite which they habitually engaged for regular visits to the seaside town.

The appearance of serenity was, however, a front. The eighteen-year-old Jane, still more child than woman, left more and more in her own company, was inexorably sucked into the glittering and sophisticated world of the European diplomatic set, to whom she had first been proudly introduced as Ellenborough's fiancée. They were Edward's friends and now they were hers too. She was intelligent enough to see that their rules on behaviour were not those of her own family, but it seemed to her that if these highly regarded people behaved in such a manner then she too could play by their rules. Her husband's infidelity may have caused the new note of defiance in her conduct.

Jane's activities were remarked by friends of the family, who were concerned that the young woman should be given a hint in order to correct any danger of being thought 'fast'. Predictably, when her parents remonstrated with her, Jane defended herself vigorously, provoking an estrangement with her father which lasted some months.[14] Steely spoke to her and, receiving no satisfactory response, took the matter up with Lady Anson. This conversation caused George Anson to be charged with keeping an eye on his young cousin, escorting Jane about town and guarding her reputation. It was an unfortunate commission. That summer, only two years after her marriage, Jane embarked upon a romantic liaison that had been waiting in the wings, so to speak, for several years.

George Anson was ten years older than Jane, yet they had known each other for ever. Perhaps he had not recognised the hero-worship of his pretty cousin that had begun when he returned as a handsome eighteen-year-old subaltern from the battlefield of Waterloo. Three years later, when Jane was still only twelve, Anson had just been elected to Parliament as the Member for South Staffordshire.[15] He quickly became acknowledged by men of character as a likeable sprig and 'a top sawyer', despite a well-earned reputation for womanising.[16] 'George Anson is to have all the married women of good character in London this year,' wrote one to another good-naturedly. 'And so he ought, for he is the best looking man I know.'[17]

In fact, in his first years in town George was in one scrape after another, tipping a boatload of cronies into the Thames near Kingston, getting drunk, behaving outrageously with older women.[18] He was believed to be the organiser of the famous quadrille at Almack's in which both George and the lady he would later marry danced together all evening, to the irritation of many matrons:

> I went two nights ago to a costume ball at Almack's. It was all very brilliant and there was a quadrille that was beautiful. All the prettiest girls in London were in it . . . the men were in Regimentals and each wore a bouquet. The quadrille, however, gave great offence for they danced together all night and took the upper end of the room which was considered a great impertinence.[19]

But Anson's pranks were conducted with such innocent good humour and unselfconscious charm that he was instantly forgiven, particularly by women, who fell at his feet in droves. He was a cracking horseman and could drive a carriage 'to an inch'; he was also one of the best shots in England.[20]

Jane had been a pretty schoolgirl with a schoolgirl crush on him, but, as they both grew older, on two counts – her being a virgin and a member of his own family – she was strictly forbidden territory to

George. He was used to tougher meat, his name being linked by both Creevey and Mrs Arbuthnot with the fastest women in town: in particular, the young Duchess of Rutland and Mrs Fox Lane, who, though the latter was considerably older than he, were both said to be his lovers.[21]

In the summer of 1926 it was a different matter. Jane was a married woman and therefore a 'safe' target by the code of the day. She was among the most desirable women in London, her virginal sweetness having given way to a slim voluptuousness guaranteed to turn men's heads. It was perfectly acceptable for George to escort his first cousin Jane to functions in the absence of her busy husband. George, as well as serving in several political posts, was now a colonel in the Guards, and Jane was delighted to have such a handsome and personable chaperon.

They were seen together often, at Almack's, at the races, at a fireworks party. Almost certainly the affair began perfectly innocently with the touch of hands or a snatched kiss; but at some point it became something else. Two handsome young people, both with a healthy libido – 'Oh it is heaven to love thee,' she wrote, and 'rapture to be near thee.' If he only felt half the joy she experienced, then, 'what ecstasy is thine!' He swore undying love; she countered that he might – at some time in the future, when her beauty had gone – be seduced by others. Still, she claimed, she would be true to him, for 'though all righteous heaven above, / Forbids this rebel heart to love, / To love is still its fate.'[22]

Gone now was all her resolution of quelling her 'rebel sighs, for Edward's sake'. She flung herself into the affair with passionate involvement. Such a remarkable couple could not escape attention; indeed, they were frequently mentioned in contemporary correspondence, and featured on the same guest lists of court pages, but at this stage there were no raised eyebrows and no gossip, because the pair were reasonably discreet. At Roehampton there was a side-door to the house from the garden which was little used and consequently kept locked. Jane gave the key to George so that he could come and go at night during Edward's absences, without the servants seeing him.[23]

At the same time, in a more public manner, and to the sustained disapproval not only of her parents but also of Steely (who visited Roehampton every two months or so as a friend of the family), Jane infiltrated deeper into the set of cynical, worldly men and women who, while considered by many to constitute the *haut ton*, the people of high fashion, were not at all suitable companions for a girl of nineteen. They included at least a brace of Almack's Patronesses – Princess Esterhazy, the wife of the Austrian Ambassador, and Princess de Lieven, the haughty and imperious wife of the Russian Ambassador – as well as other leading members of the diplomatic set who were also the intimates of the King in the so-called 'Cottage Clique'.[24] All were regular dinner guests at Lord Ellenborough's London house and at Roehampton, and their reciprocated hospitality was accepted by both Edward and Jane.

The Digbys' distress at Jane's behaviour was increased on the publication of a novel which, under the title *Almack's*, could hardly fail to be a bestseller. It was a *roman-à-clef* in which the anonymous author provided only paper-thin guises for the real-life characters that populated its pages. The beautiful Lady Glenmore was widely identified as Lady Ellenborough. Jane was amused, not recognising the damage it would inflict upon her reputation. It was no comfort to her family that the book, in fact written by a member of the family (Eliza Spencer-Stanhope's sister-in-law Marianne), presented as fiction several true incidents in Jane's life.

During one of her visits to Roehampton, having been primed by Lady Andover, Steely delivered a stern lecture on the importance of a woman's reputation. Jane appeared to listen, but several days later, in a letter to her former governess, she brushed Steely's concerns aside on the grounds that the persons to whom she and her parents objected were Edward's friends and must therefore be perfectly acceptable.[25] By now Steely was so concerned about Jane that she overrode any personal sensibilities and went to see Lord Ellenborough. Her case was that Jane was mixing too freely with associates who, she insisted, were 'gay and profligate'. Significantly she did not include George Anson in her list.[26] Ellenborough clearly did not know whether to be angry or amused at such an approach from a woman who, though undeniably gently bred, was, when all was said and done, a former employee of his wife's family. In the end his sense of humour got the better of him; he laughed and told Steely that he thought she was being 'too scrupulous', stating that he had 'unlimited confidence in Lady Ellenborough'.[27]

It is surprising that Ellenborough did not connect Steely's warnings with what was happening at home, for when he wrote to Jane in September from Stratfield Saye (the Duke of Wellington's country seat in Hampshire) he spoke of her recent 'coldness and indifference' towards him. 'But all is now forgotten,' he continued.[28] Her 'want of gaiety' had certainly disappeared as she went about town on her cousin's arm. Indeed, Edward misread all the signs that would have been obvious to a more concerned husband. Even Jane's style of dressing should have alerted him. She set off to perfection the high velvet bonnets with huge upstanding pokes that framed her little heart-shaped face, and on Jane the modish high-waisted narrow gowns, worn with a short, demurely fastened spencer for walking out, looked exceptionally elegant. But the deep *décolletage* of her evening dress, though fashionable in that the edges of her nipples could be plainly seen, was thought unseemly by a visitor from Paris, who reported himself entranced with Lady Ellenborough but 'sickened by her dress'.[29]

But among the smart set it was considered neither stylish nor particularly commendable to be faithful to one's spouse. Despite Steely's stern moral teaching Jane was impressionable and looking for justification that her behaviour with Edward was acceptable. She had only to look at her peers to conclude that it was. The women with whom she was most often seen were the subject of open gossip. One gentleman wrote: 'My whole time for the past week has been devoted to the Belgrave's Chester committee. I am very thankful for a violent cold which came to my assistance on Saturday and has prevented my further attendance. There can be nothing in life so disagreeable, not even sleeping with Mme Lieven.'[30] While Princess Esterhazy had been the subject of scurrilous gossip for years, 'said Esterhazy has been in Cheltenham for three weeks, where the people, being a moral race, were shocked at her having a fresh lover for every week. The order ran thus: 1st week Castlereagh; 2nd Viner; 3rd Valerfrie.'[31] So Jane's liaison with the handsome and universally popular George Anson undoubtedly did her no discredit in their eyes. Her other intimates were George's former lovers, the Duchess of Rutland and the notorious Mrs Fox Lane. If the approbation of these high-flyers should be insufficient, her husband's affair with the pretty daughter of a confectioner in Brighton was common knowledge and provided justification enough.[32]

There was, however, nothing calculated in Jane's affair with her cousin, no deliberate attempt at retribution. She believed that the frothy romance with Edward was true love. A degree of ingenuousness would explain an incident which occurred the following spring, when

Jane visited Holkham to see the latest addition to her grandfather's growing new family.[33]

As usual Holkham was full of guests during March and April, including Jane's parents, her maternal aunts – Anne, Lady Anson and Eliza Spencer-Stanhope – as well as sundry other family members who came and went, an archdeacon, a Captain Greville, various neighbours who called in casually and the diarist Thomas Creevey. There was also a man described by Creevey as 'a young British Museum Artist who is classing manuscripts'.

He was Frederick Madden, aged twenty-six, an academic who specialised in and spoke Norman-French and Anglo-Saxon, and who was also a noted scholar in ancient manuscripts. In the spring of 1827 Madden was working in a freelance capacity with Mr William Roscoe of the British Museum, cataloguing Mr Coke's manuscripts and hoping it might lead to a permanent position. Paid employment would enable him to marry his fiancée Mary, about whom Madden wrote each day, longingly, in his diary. Mary lived in Brighton with her widowed mother, who disapproved of Madden, having no wish to see her daughter married to an impecunious man, no matter how scholarly he might be.

It is Madden's diary, rather than the more famous one of Creevey, that provides the clearest surviving description of Jane at that period, and also of the daily routine at Holkham. Frederick Madden was a conscientious man, and, as he meticulously recorded, he spent each day, from 10 a.m. until 4 or 5 p.m., working hard in the library. This was his second visit to Holkham; like the first, it would last a month or so. Everything went on as usual until Wednesday, 14 March, when something occurred to change his routine:

> *Wednesday 14th.* In library from ten until five and went over some of the Greek Fathers which will, as before, prove the most tedious.
>
> Lady Ellenborough, daughter of Lady Andover, arrived to dinner and will stay a fortnight. She is not yet twenty and one of the most lovely women I ever saw, quite fair, blue eyes that would move a saint, and lips that would tempt one to forswear heaven to touch them.[34]

One look and the sober scholar was smitten. It was completely normal for someone on meeting Jane to note before anything else her beautiful appearance; this started when she was in the cradle and would continue until she was over seventy. But Madden was infatuated. He found it impossible to concentrate on his work, and within two days he was finding excuses to finish work at noon to spend time with his host's granddaughter. 'Lady Ellenborough is such a charm that I find the library become a bore, and am delighted to be with her, and hear her play and sing, which she is kind enough to do.' A day later he recorded: 'From four till half past five with Lady Ellenborough in the saloon; she sings to me the most bewitching Italian airs, the words of which are enough to inflame one, did not the sight of so lovely a creature sufficiently do so.'[35]

Poor Madden. 'Dearest Mary' appears to have been forgotten and instead his diary is filled each day with Lady Ellenborough: tête-à-tête walks around the mile-long lake with her; sitting in the salon while she plays the guitar and sings to him; strolling in the garden with her past the bronze lions that guard the house's entrance, to the extravagant fountain depicting Perseus and the Medusa; rides to the nearby fishing village of Wells-next-the-Sea, and back along the sweeping sandy beaches in her company; heads bent together over her sketchbooks; playing écarté in the drawing-room with her each evening. Madden was furious when a visitor, Captain Greville, called and robbed him of an opportunity to be alone with her.[36]

Ten days after her arrival Madden's diary entry has degenerated into a hurried scrawl:

> *Saturday 24th.* In library till 4 o/c. Then out. In the evening drew pictures for Lady Anne Coke and Miss Anson. Also played whist and won. Lady E. lingered behind the rest of the party and at midnight I escorted her to her room——Fool that I was!——I will not add what passed. Gracious God! Was there ever such good fortune?

> *Sunday 25th.* Chapel in the morning. In the afternoon, walked out with Lady E. She pretended to be very angry at what had passed last night, but I am satisfied that, she——!

Satisfied that she what? Satisfied that she was at least as much to blame as he? Satisfied that she was as eager as he? Satisfied that she intended it to happen? We shall never know. Madden's irritating slashes across the page convey only that he was emotionally overwrought.

Jane cold-shouldered him for a couple of days, advising her family that she intended to leave as planned in three days' time. The day before her departure she relented her cool behaviour to the bewildered scholar:

Wednesday 28th. In library till 2 o/c then went with Lady E. tête-à-tête around the lake, and remained in one of the hermitages with her until 5 o/c. We have completely made it up. She is a most fascinating woman! Whist in evening. Won. Afterwards drew pictures in Lady E's album, cupid on a lion.

Thursday 29th. To my infinite regret Lady E. left Holkham this morning. Since I parted with dear M[ary] I never felt more melancholy or vexed. Whist in the evening. Won.

Madden stayed on for a further fortnight, but, as quickly as he could decently escape, he returned (as he had come) by Mr Coke's gig to Fakenham, then an uncomfortable seventeen-hour stage-coach journey to the Golden Cross Inn at Charing Cross and a hackney coach to his modest lodgings near the British Museum.[37] He was, it is obvious, still upset and bewildered, though whether he was suffering from Jane's absence or a severe attack of guilt he failed to say. Madden was a hardworking young man, but he often felt life was unfair to him and spent a lot of time justifyng himself. When he failed to obtain hoped-for positions of employment, for instance, he would justify the selection of a candidate he believed inferior to himself as being due to his own lack of important connections. On the subject of his short relationship with Jane, though, he is surprisingly silent. There is no suggestion that he was seduced; no hint of self-justification for his betrayal to Mary.

When he posted down to Brighton a few weeks later to visit 'dearest Mary', Madden booked into the newly opened Albion Hotel. He walked disconsolately on the pier for an hour, and ascertained that Lady Ellenborough was not in town. Nor was Lady Anson, from whom he thought he might obtain news of Jane. His hopes dashed, he returned his heart to Mary. His diary entries become happier and, as the days pass, linger once more on his fiancée: 'In a new white satin bonnet . . . she looked lovely . . . How very kind has fortune been to me . . . her I love more than all the world.'[38]

Madden and Jane never met again, and it is difficult to place the incident in context. It is unlikely that Jane set out deliberately to seduce him. Perhaps she was simply dejected and, enjoying the young man's obvious admiration, allowed a simple flirtation to get out of hand. Or maybe she was miserable and hurt and, having been inexplicably rejected by both her husband and her lover, needed reassurance that she was still desirable.

For her affair with George Anson was in trouble. Indeed, there was no possibility that it would prosper in the long term, even supposing George had wished such a thing. Marriage to Jane was out of the question. The average divorce-rate was two a year at that date, and the publicity and expense surrounding such a course was usually sufficient to ruin the applicants and their families, socially as well as economically. A divorce would have finished George's career in the army, and both cousins would have been aware that the closely linked Anson, Coke and Digby families would never countenance their union.

There is no evidence, however, that George ever regarded the affair as anything more than a light-hearted romance with his pretty cousin. It was Jane who elevated it to a more serious level. Her poetry implies no thought of divorce, nor indeed what might come of such a relationship, but in her romantic and impractical way she expected things to continue, and George to be faithful to her. Too late Colonel Anson recognised that this affair was not like his others and that Jane was not an experienced woman-about-town who could insouciantly treat a liaison for what it was, but a still-naïve girl who was bound to be emotionally hurt. His way of handling the problem was to stay away from Jane, trusting she would recognise the implication of his actions. There is a strong possibility, too, that a senior officer or member of the family warned George that his behaviour would not do. Whatever the reason, there came a time when George was forced to tell her that their affair must end.

So when Jane made her visit to Holkham in March 1827 she was desperately unhappy. Unseasoned in the art of sophisticated dalliance, she had believed George when he had sworn to love her no matter what. She had never been refused anything, and could not believe the hurt occasioned by George's rejection. Reared in the age of Byron, when strong emotions were often channelled into verse, she wrote a series of poems to George, attempting to convey her feelings. The following was written when she retired to her room on 19 March. According to Madden's diary, she had spent that evening playing the guitar and singing Italian love songs.

> . . . is passion's dream then o'er
> Is tenderness with love then fled?
> So soon cast off, beloved no more.

Yes! Nought of all I've done for thee
   Will e'er awake a pitying sigh
Or should my name, remembered be
   E'en friendship's tear thou wilt deny.

Twas then a crime to love *too* well!
   Ah when did man e'er grateful prove
To her whose heart has dared rebel
   Against the laws of man and God?[39]

There are more poems in this vein, written during the weeks that followed. They spoke of 'love betrayed by a soft voice and sweet accents'; of how easy it had been for her to forget 'in one wild, thrilling kiss' that ultimately it would have to end. And now the man she adored 'though chill neglect has snapped the silver cord . . . in the heart in which he reigned'.[40] With her cousin, Jane found a sexual joy and companionship that was perhaps missing in her relationship with her husband. She had mistakenly believed her first love affair to be the love of her life.

Yet this makes the interlude with Madden all the more surprising. There were a few other occasions in her life when Jane indulged in casual sexual encounters, and it is obvious from diary entries in her middle age that she had a frank enjoyment of sex that was unfashionable in a world where brides-to-be were advised that sex was meant to be not enjoyed but endured. Her attitude has somewhat predictably led two (male) biographers to suggest 'nymphomania', but in fact her views on sex were similar to those of most women of the late twentieth century. Under normal circumstances Jane was faithful to the man with whom she was in love because, quite simply, each time she fell in love she believed the man to be the centre of her existence. Each time she thought that this man, this love, was the one she had been seeking. Between partners, however, she experienced no guilt in occasionally seeking 'rapture'.

Madden made no secret of the admiration he felt from the moment she arrived. Jane was flattered and tempted. Her sexual mores were already established. Had her relationship with George been stable, she would never have looked at Madden, but given the situation that prevailed she accepted his admiration and the solace of his obvious desire. On the following day she recalled Steely's moralising and was remorseful. The pattern would repeat itself occasionally in the future.

That visit to 'dear old Holkham' was to be almost the last. Many years later she would recall it in a letter to her brother Kenelm and explain how 'Lord Ellenborough's politics at that time prevented Holkham intimacy, which I always regretted.'[41]

Jane's twentieth birthday passed and suddenly, to her joy, George was back in her life for a few weeks, but by 23 May they had parted again, this time – as he made clear – permanently. The danger of discovery by their families and the potential damage to George's military career were too great. He left London and ignored her notes to him, returning them unanswered. Jane continued to pour out her distress in poetry. She accepted the reasons for which he said they had to part, but his instruction to her at their last meeting to 'forget him' she could not obey. She could never forget him, she wrote in anguish – even if they were never to meet again.[42]

However, it was not to be as simple as that. Although she was not aware of it when she wrote her poem in May 1827, Jane was pregnant. And, as she would later confide to a friend, the father of her child was not her husband but George Anson.[43]

4

A Dangerous Attraction
1827–1829

Jane's state of mind as she parted from George Anson and discovered that she was pregnant is not a matter for speculation, for she was still using poetry as a sort of psychiatric couch, much as she used her diaries years later when there was no one in whom she could confide. Her pregnancy and subsequently the safe arrival of her child are mentioned briefly in surviving family correspondence, but from Jane herself there was a series of forlorn compositions written at Cowes, when she and Edward visited the Isle of Wight in August for the annual regatta. George Anson was also at Cowes and had returned to his former wild living. He was rarely seen there without a pretty woman on his arm and, as cartoonists noted, he was involved in a duel. Jane's verse reveals her misery at the broken relationship and Anson's present, hurtful, attitude towards her. Tormented by his calculated indifference, she found it hard to accept that he now regarded her as just another of the 'host' of pretty women who loved him.[1] All her life she had known only unconditional love and approval. George had sworn he loved her but clearly he did not, at least not as she had interpreted his declarations. As her body thickened she felt herself unattractive and deserted.

Of her pregnancy she wrote nothing. She was a married woman enjoying a normal sex-life with her husband; the manner in which her love affair had been conducted had provoked no gossip. There was apparently no reason why Edward, or anyone else, should suspect the child was not his. Indeed, until her confinement confirmed the date of conception she may not have been entirely sure herself whose child she was carrying. Meanwhile her emotions were centred around the hurt she felt. She wrote despairingly of how, like many other women, she had succumbed to George's 'specious flatteries, breathed by lips none could resist'. Who could have refused to listen to George's softly spoken words of love, she asked.

> Not I, alas! For I have heard and drank
> Delicious poison from those angel lips,
> And listening first believed, then tempted, fell
> By passion wrought to madness. I can see
> No shame in infamy, no hell beyond
> The doubts and jealous fears that rack my soul
> Lest thou should e'er forget her who has loved
> With more than woman's love, and given thee all
> She had to give; a spotless name, and virtue.[2]

For him and for his love she had risked everything: her marriage, hurting Edward, family honour and public contempt. Out of superstition, rather than penitence, she ceased to attend church as a communicant, lest she should provoke divine vengeance. George had taken her innocence and her unquestioning love and, it now seemed to her, tossed them in her face. She felt utterly betrayed. Her family saw none of this; she was, outwardly at least, the same sweet, smiling, brilliant Janet. Family letters to her are chatty and congratulatory.[3]

Jane's first child, a boy, was born on 15 February 1828. Ellenborough, who had longed for a son, was elated. Only a month earlier he had achieved his primary ambition, a Cabinet post; he was made Lord Privy Seal in Wellington's new government. It was not a universally popular appointment. Lady Holland is said to have 'nearly killed' the messenger who brought her the news.[4] A fellow member of the Upper House wrote of the new administration:

> and indeed, were it not for *one blot*, there is not a name I object to. The blot is Ellenborough. It is miserable and unworthy to stop his teasing babble by [giving him] one of the great offices of State and his appointment is an indignity to the memory of Canning which I regret was advocated in the House of Lords. He will be nothing; though he might be a worrying opponent and as a member of the cabinet will be unpractical and unmanageable.[5]

Even Princess Lieven, whom, together with her husband, Ellenborough regarded as a friend, was less than happy, writing to Earl Grey, 'You will imagine that I am not highly delighted at seeing Lord

Ellenborough, a rabid Turk, in the Ministry.'[6] And, though there were some who felt that Ellenborough had earned his appointment, clearly the King was not among them. He met the new Lord Privy Seal only once, out of courtesy. He was charming and polite but Ellenborough was never again invited into his presence.

Ellenborough did not allow his monarch's dislike to worry him. He wrote a triumphant personal note in his political diary:

> Janet has brought me a boy. I put this down as a political occurrence because I shall make him, if he lives and I live, a political Character. I shall ask the Duke of Wellington and Lord Dudley to be his Godfathers. Princess Esterhazy is to be his Godmother. A good diplomatic introduction to the world.[7]

One must assume from this that Ellenborough accepted the child as his. The baby was named Arthur Dudley after his illustrious godparents. Evidently the birth was an uncomplicated one, for the smart christening party was held only a fortnight later, and within two months or, as one biographer cheerfully put it, 'as soon as she could get her stays fastened again', Jane was back in circulation apparently in glowing good looks.[8] Lord Ellenborough was now more preoccupied than ever with his work of national importance, though Jane accompanied him to several state functions at this time.

She was a poor mother, which is surprising, for she was a warm and caring person by nature. But she was unable to form any maternal bonds with her baby. It was not that she did not love him, but it was as though the child belonged to someone else. This disappointed her, but, as she wrote to her brother, she was as a child 'never *naturally* fond of babies, never played with *dolls*, if you recollect, but was much fonder of animals etc.'[9] Her inability to bond may also have been rooted in the fact that her lifestyle did not allow a great deal of contact with her 'darling boy'.[10] It was the established custom of the upper class to have children cared for by servants, thus enabling the mother to regain her place in society quickly. Moreover, London with its winter palls of smog from coal fires, and its summer plagues of typhoid, was considered unhealthy; the mortality of infants was high enough (hence Ellenborough's remark 'if he lives'), without exposing a child to additional risks. It was considered almost a duty to have a child professionally cared for in a quiet, healthy place. In little Arthur's case this care devolved initially on a wetnurse and nursemaid in the country.

Despite her glowing appearance, Jane was deeply unhappy in the weeks and months following her confinement. Edward was tolerant but remote, and her relationship with her child was conducted at arm's length. She pined, according to her poetry, for the days of love and laughter, and the 'magic' she had shared with George.[11]

The Ellenboroughs' close friendship with the Russian and Austrian ambassadors and their wives meant that Jane was a frequent guest at embassy balls. It was at one such ball at the Austrian embassy, in May 1828, shortly after her twenty-first birthday, that Jane's life was changed for ever. Her son's godmother, Princess Esterhazy, introduced her on a warm early-summer evening, when the lilac trees in London squares were drenched in rain and heady scent, to Prince Felix Schwarzenberg, the newly arrived, darkly handsome attaché and secretary to Prince Esterhazy.

Prince Felix Ludvig Johann Friedrich zu Schwarzenberg was a member of one of the great aristocratic families of Europe. Born the fourth child and second son of a happy marriage, he grew up at Schloss Krumlov, one of the most beautiful and romantic castles in Bohemia, situated amid dense forests on rocks overlooking the River Vltava. His father's holdings of land amounted to half a million acres over which the family ruled in an almost feudal manner.[12]

The name Schwarzenberg was already familiar in London and Paris for the exploits of Felix's uncle, Field Marshal Karl Philipp Schwarzenberg, Commander-in-Chief of the Austrian forces ranged against Napoleon at Leipzig; and no less for the tragic story of Felix's mother Princess Pauline who died at a state banquet given in Paris to honour Napoleon and Marie-Louise in 1810. When the building caught fire everyone was successfully ushered to safety, but a false report that her daughters were trapped in their bedchambers sent Princess Pauline flying back inside to rescue them. When they found her body next day, crushed by a fallen roof beam, all that was recognisable in the charred remains was her diamond necklace.[13]

By the age of twenty-one, Felix had attained the rank of captain in a cavalry regiment bearing his family name (the Schwarzenberg Uhlans). After catching the eye of the self-appointed kingmaker, Prince Metternich, Felix joined the Austrian Diplomatic Corps. His first assignment was to the legation at St Petersburg where the Tsar was a friend of his father.[14] Unfortunately, he became innocently involved in the Dekabrist revolt of army officers attempting to overthrow the Tsar's government – a minor embarrassment which made it politically expedient to transfer him to another post. He was sent to Portugal to prepare for the arrival of Dom Miguel, Metternich's choice for King. Dom Miguel was not the choice of the people, however, and Prince Felix subsequently found himself very unpopular, on one occasion being stoned by a mob from which he was lucky to escape without serious injury. He stuck to his post, regardless of unpopularity and, once Dom Miguel was safely installed in 1826, Felix was sent via Paris to London, where he took a ship for Rio de Janeiro on a special mission.[15] He was subsequently appointed as attaché to London in May 1828.

At the time he met Lady Ellenborough, Prince Felix was twenty-seven years old, handsome, dashing and accomplished. Highly intelligent, he was an excellent linguist, speaking fluent German, Czech, French, English, Latin and Spanish. He studied anatomy and, to judge from remarks by his biographer, it is probable that he was a natural healer.[16] Felix was a music lover with a good voice, who wrote musical comedies to entertain his friends.[17] 'He was', wrote one contemporary, 'artless . . . and kind and friendly,'[18] and according to his friend Count Rodolphe Apponyi, the Hungarian-Austrian diplomat and diarist, he was witty and amusing to be with.[19] On that night at the Russian embassy ball Jane knew only that the prince smiled down into her eyes with uncomplicated admiration, waltzed as only someone who had learned to waltz in Vienna could, and held her attention to an extent that made her forget, for a while, her wretchedness over George Anson.

Even Schwarzenberg's biographer, who had no good word for Jane, admitted grudgingly that, as soon as the prince laid eyes on Jane, 'it was love at first sight in the Byron style.'[20] Jane was attracted but not smitten. It was the prince who laid siege to Jane with flowers, poems and notes. Wherever Jane went, the prince managed to be, and soon she was seen in his company, as she had previously been seen in George's, riding with him in Rotten Row, in his cabriolet at the races, waltzing at Almack's, in his box at the opera, walking round the Zoological Park on his arm.[21] To find herself so courted and so desired after her lover's seemingly callous desertion and her husband's indifference was balm to Jane's wounded spirit. Despite initial discretion it was quickly apparent to interested members of society that Lady Ellenborough had exchanged her regular escort, Colonel Anson, for the handsome foreign prince. It suited Jane's hurt pride that society assumed the change was by her own choice, but her poetry confirms that she was not yet in love with the prince.

The 1828 Derby, held shortly after Jane met Felix, was narrowly won by the Duke of Rutland's Cadland, with the King's horse, The Colonel, which started favourite, finishing in second place. It seemed excruciatingly amusing when Felix suddenly acquired the nickname 'Cadland', because, as the fashionable world tittered, 'he had beat the Colonel' out of Jane's affections. Later Cadland was shortened to 'Cad'. In that form it has been passed down to the present day as a synonym for ungentlemanly behaviour – not surprisingly, given the prince's subsequent conduct.

In June, several Harley Street residents noted a striking girl visiting number 73, a house that had been taken by Prince Schwarzenberg and Count Moritz Dietrichstein,[22] two young attachés from the Austrian embassy. There was no reason why Jane should not be seen walking in Harley Street. Her parents' home at number 86 was a mere hundred yards away at the opposite end of the block. The Ellenborough town-house at Connaught Place was a fifteen-minute stroll along Oxford Street, or a five-minute drive by horse and carriage. Jane's carriage was an elegant small green phaeton, drawn by two long-tailed black horses which, being an able whip, she habitually drove herself. She was always accompanied by a groom, a fifteen-year-old boy dressed in Lord Ellenborough's livery of drab olive with blue-lined facings and a top hat with a band of silver lace. This boy often stood about in the afternoon, holding the horses while he waited for his mistress, who visited a house a few steps away on the corner of Queen Anne Street and Harley Street.

One resident who lived opposite saw the young woman several times through the window of the first-floor drawing-room. As the summer wore on, her visits became more frequent, often three or four times a week, and the neighbours noticed with heightened interest that sometimes she came on foot, and started wearing a veil. Her phaeton was spotted in adjacent streets, sometimes Wimpole Street, sometimes Portland Place. Several times she left her carriage in Cavendish Square and walked past her parents' house to number 73, and on a few occasions she came by hackney coach.[23]

But it was not until many months later that Jane would be able to write of recovery from the depression over what she called George's 'betrayal', though it is difficult to see what he could have done given their situation. Even then she could not accept that George could apparently forget her so finally and transfer his affections so quickly. At length she came to realise that their youthful love had been perhaps no more than 'the bright creation of a heated brain', and that her 'idolisation' of him had been misplaced. 'Now', she wrote, 'another love inflames my lonely heart', and this new love promised 'far, far higher ecstasy'. At last, she wrote, there was 'sun in a breast which else were cold'.[24]

Prince Felix courted Jane hotly throughout the summer. In the early part of their relationship it was he who set the pace, he who fretted when she could not meet him or went away with her husband. At the end of July, when society decamped to the country, Jane was due to leave town for a short stay at Roehampton before a visit to Cowes in early August. The diplomat diarist, Count Rodolphe Apponyi, wrote of dining with Felix at the Esterhazys' and finding the prince very preoccupied because Jane was due to leave town within a few days. 'This did not suit him and consequently he was in a very bad humour.'[25]

But the prince was to see Jane several times before she left, once in the park, where they rode their horses together, and again on the evening of the same day at a masked ball given by Lady Londonderry, Ellenborough's former mother-in-law.[26] The Londonderrys' townhouse was very grand and had formerly belonged to the late Queen Caroline. It was here, among a vast glittering throng, that Count Apponyi was to meet for the first time the lady whose imminent departure was causing his old friend Felix Schwarzenberg such dejection. Guests were dressed magnificently in historical costume. As they were announced, each had to curtsy or bow to their hostess, who, in the guise of Queen Elizabeth I, graciously inclined her head in greeting. To some the hostess showed individual favour and, since she had met Apponyi in Paris, Lady Londonderry went to some pains to introduce the count to as many people of influence as she could:

> among all these people, one lady in particular attracted my attention. It was Lady Ellenborough, one of the most beautiful women I have ever seen. Nineteen years of age [*sic*], with fair hair, a magnificent complexion, large blue eyes and the figure of a nymph, she is everything that is desirable. It is she whom Schwarzenberg adores, and I lost no time being introduced. I was not overawed by her intellect, it is true, but one cannot have everything. The expression on her face is sweet, as is her voice, and her whole personality exudes an indefinable air of modesty and decorum which I found ravishing.

The coldness and formality of first acquaintances did not last long between us. She spoke to me very freely about her husband, whom she accuses of being jealous, and of not understanding her. This is what she likes to say, but in reality I think that Lord Ellenborough, preoccupied with the duties of his position, has no time to give good advice to his young wife.

. . . I had already danced with Lady Ellenborough when Schwarzenberg arrived. Madame did not reveal that she had danced with me and instructed him to engage me with her for the first waltz which I accepted with great pleasure. I was so preoccupied with dancing and with my partner that I had to endure reproaches from all the ladies I know whom I had not yet approached.[27]

It is strange that Jane complained to Apponyi of Edward being 'jealous' when his coolness towards Jane was so marked that it was noticed by a number of writers, contemporary and later, with the added explanation that he was totally dedicated to his work. But despite Apponyi's excuses for Jane's husband it would be fair to say that Ellenborough too had his share of extramarital diversions. He had at this time two mistresses that are known about and contemporary gossip speaks of another. One was the Countess St Antonio, an aristocratic member of the set to which Jane's parents so objected. The other, 'a very pretty girl', according to Joseph Jekyll, was 'the pastry-cook's daughter at Brighton who Ellenborough preferred to his bride'; she was also referred to in *The Times* as a 'confectioner's daughter'.

The latter allegedly had a child by him and, being cast off in disgrace by her family, might have starved had not Lord Ellenborough finally been shamed into providing support for the mother and child under threat of exposure – or so said the equivalent of today's tabloid press.[28] Since Jekyll's gossip was written in 1829 after the birth of Jane's child, it is probable that the term 'bride' was being used figuratively rather than literally. Whoever she was, the 'pastry-cook's daughter' was the *on dit* in London that winter and there is even evidence that Jane may have met this young woman. In her notebook Jane wrote the first line of a poem, 'Ah! Wert thou, love, but all thou seemed . . .' She got no further than the first line but she scribbled underneath, in the 'secret code' she had used since her childhood, the explanation that she had written it 'on meeting the poor woman who called on my lord'.[29]

The Ellenboroughs officially 'quit town' at the end of the season, but Edward continued to use the town-house as a base when he was detained in London for reasons of work. Jane, in summer residence at Roehampton, was therefore free to meet Felix by prior arrangement. Each morning she rode out with her young groom, William Carpenter. Sometimes she rode as far as Wimbledon Common, and there, at the old windmill, she met Felix. One wet and windy day when the prince could not keep his appointment he sent his groom, who handed Jane a letter. The two grooms watched from a distance as Jane read the letter and placed it back in the envelope with a red rose which she had brought with her. She handed the envelope to the prince's groom and told him to return it to his master.[30]

Given Jane's immature romanticism and her self-confessed rebellious nature, these illicit trysts, so eagerly sought by the inflamed Prince Schwarzenberg, must have in themselves been a major attraction to her. Thwarted lovers, a handsome prince and a beautiful girl, meeting in secret, with all the sweet sadness the frequent partings inevitably brought about, was the stuff of the romantic novels that Steely loved. Sometimes when they met and rode together they stopped at inns and hotels, such as the Castle at Richmond.[31] Jane had the utmost confidence in her youthful groom, for he was always present to see to her horse. By the time summer slid into autumn she had ceased to think of the relationship as a flirtation; she was deeply, passionately in love, and this time she had the delight of knowing that her chosen partner loved her equally. Jane had fought the feeling at first, not because of Edward – she had already released her hold on that relationship – but fearing to let go of her girlish adoration of George Anson. But it dawned on her that the glow she felt whenever the prince was near was love. Gradually her affair with George became as a candle to the sun of the emotions she began to experience. When she was with Felix she felt whole and alive; at other times she looked for him everywhere she went, and thought only of him and the next time they would be together. Gone was any thought of the discretion she had employed in her affair with Anson; she spoke openly of her love to anyone who cared to listen. According to one acquaintance,

> Lady Ellenborough . . . tells everybody she meets the whole history, and it is a long one, of her and Schwarzenberg. Any indifferent person by whom she sits at dinner is sure to get up intimately acquainted with every circumstance related to their intercourse. How she drives to Schwarzenberg's lodgings, and how Dietrichstein, who lodges with him, sees her.

44

What they do together, how often they have been in Schwarzenberg's cabriolet to the White House in Soho Square etc. How she meets Ellenborough, as she walks the streets, who intent on high matters does not know her.

And then she concludes with most amiable naïveté by exciting indignation against George Anson who is so 'uncivil and unkind. Do you know he is gone out of town without giving me up the key to the secret door at Roehampton though I asked him so often for it.'[32]

What Jane related to her cronies was that on most weekday afternoons when she was in town she called at 73 Harley Street in her carriage. If Dietrichstein was at home he quickly made his excuses and left. The lovers would spend an hour or two together. Several times she rode there accompanied by her groom, who returned her horse to the stables off Portman Square; when Jane and Felix subsequently left his house they drove off together in his cabriolet.

Sometimes they called on friends such as Princess Esterhazy upon whose discretion they believed they could rely. On at least one occasion they drove together to the house of Felix's colleague, the Count St Antonio, whose wife was widely rumoured to be Lord Ellenborough's mistress. Jane's carriage had been ordered to meet her fifty yards from the countess's gate, where she transferred to it and drove up the drive to the entrance. Felix 'arrived' five minutes afterwards. When they left at ten o'clock that night Felix drove out and waited for her carriage to catch up. Jane then joined him in his closed chaise and they travelled to within a short distance of Elm Grove, where he handed her out and she returned home in her own carriage, while he continued on to London.

But mostly, unless they met in public, their meetings were confined to 73 Harley Street, when always, whether clothed in a walking dress or riding habit, she wore a light veil over her face. This was not regarded as unusual; many fashionable women lowered veils to protect their complexions. Indeed, a lady's magazine of the day warned its readers that the complexion could be discoloured by moonlight as well as sunlight.

Towards the end of 1828, an observant neighbour glanced across the street into the house opposite and saw the veiled visitor in Prince Schwarzenberg's arms. A door behind them had been left open, letting in light behind them. How long the neighbour stayed glancing across the street he did not say, but it was long enough to notice that the prince was dressing himself, and subsequently laced up the lady's stays.[33]

It would be easy to write off Jane's behaviour as that of a promiscuous woman deceiving her busy husband. But to sit in judgement one must also take into consideration that her conduct was no better or worse than that of her husband and their closest friends of both sexes. Jane regarded the attachment as more than a casual love affair, which was, for her, sufficient justification. That she did not choose to conceal her relationship with Felix, indeed that she broadcast her feelings so openly that it was almost guaranteed to get back to her husband, was certainly a departure from the norm. But Jane went even further. Her love for Felix had now made sexual intercourse with Edward abhorrent. So, giving as her reason the fact that she did not care to have another child, she told Edward that in future she wished to sleep alone.[34]

Her poems to 'F.S.' passionately denied that her feelings for him were a passing fancy, as he had suggested to her; 'Oh say not that my love will pass . . . my love is not the love of one who feels a passion for a day.'[35] Felix had already been warned by his ambassador to be more discreet. Prince Esterhazy was visiting Dietrichstein one day when Jane called at 73 Harley Street and, seeing her husband's friend in the hall, chatted to him 'without a shade of embarrassment' before going up to Felix's rooms.[36] After an informal admonishment Felix moved from the house in Harley Street to a similar one in nearby Holles Street, and the meetings between the lovers went on as before.

By this time everyone, except – apparently – Edward, was talking about 'Ellenboriana'.[37] Joseph Jekyll, who took a puckish delight in reporting scandalous gossip to his sister-in-law Lady Sloane Stanley, was a little behind with the news when he wrote, 'Torrents of scandal afloat! They call Schwarzenberg "Cadlands" because he beat the Colonel out of Lady Ellenborough's good graces. It is added that she talks openly of her loves.'[38] From their correspondence, on the other hand, it seems certain that the Digbys, Cokes and Ansons found the situation between Jane and the prince not amusing at all.[39]

However, at this point another family matter removed Jane from centre-stage. Earlier that year George Anson's younger brother Henry, accompanied by his friend John Fox Strangways, had set out on an extended Grand Tour of Europe, the Holy Land and the Near-Middle East. With only three years separating them, Henry was the cousin to whom Jane had been closest in the years growing up at

Holkham. She was as anguished as anyone in the family when news came that the two men had perished of the plague in Syria.

In fact Fox Strangways survived. The two young men had entered a mosque in Aleppo disguised as Muslims, but foolishly neglected to remove their shoes. They were set upon and beaten by a mob who deeply resented the intrusion by Christians into their sacred place. The two Englishmen were then flung into a prison, where they languished in appalling conditions before diplomatic persuasion was able to effect their release. Their incarceration in a cell below ground with only a pinprick of light was at least cool during the worst of the day's heat, but the prisoners were given the barest of rations, and water whose source was dubious. Sanitary arrangements were non-existent, and many of the inmates were ill.

Their eventual release came too late for Henry Anson, who having contracted the plague was already a dying man. Strangways assisted him from the prison and they walked as far as a field on the outskirts of Aleppo, where Anson lay down, unable to move further. Strangways did what he could for his stricken friend, but Anson died before medical aid arrived. The manner of his death was rendered more horrible to all the family by virtue of its being in such a far-off place. Syria might have been on a different planet, so far removed from their lives was that alien country. More than a quarter of a century later Jane would stand at the site of Henry's death, recalling her childhood friend.

The tragic news at least effected a reunion between Jane and George when she went to pay a duty call on her Aunt Anson, who was staying at Holkham. The cousins had seen little of each other during the past months, for Felix was jealous of George.[40] He had no cause for jealousy, as Jane's final poem to George Anson shows; it was written while she and her parents stayed at Holkham over Christmas, and he at his parents' home in the neighbouring county.

> I'll meet thee at sunset, but not by the bower
> Where with thee I've gathered love's gory, torn flower,
> Since that would be only recalling to mind
> Bright visions of pleasures now left far behind.
>
> What tho' the cold stoic proclaim it as mystery
> The feelings of youth are as lasting as history
> And the rays with which love has once lit up the heart
> May fade for a while but they cannot depart.

> Then come, but come not with the accent of love,
> I would not its echo reply from the groves
> Oh! Come as if all, save old friendships, were o'er
> And, – I'll meet thee at sunset once more.[41]

They were bound to each other now more by grief for Henry than by their child. For Arthur was undoubtedly George's son and not Edward's. Jane openly said so, as a friend wrote to a correspondent in the country:

> The other day Belfast was riding with Lady Ellenborough and said to her 'Do you see much of your child?' 'No,' was her answer. 'It would grieve Felix if I was to see much of George's child . . . ! ! !'[42]

Nine-month-old Arthur had been poorly with a respiratory complaint. In November he had been sent off to Brighton with his nursemaid and nanny for three months' convalescence. His parents visited him in January and a month later, having been advised that her son was doing well, Jane decided to drive down and spend a night there before bringing the little boy home to Roehampton.

She reserved a suite at the Norfolk Hotel, where she and Edward always stayed when in Brighton. Felix also reserved a room there. The opportunity to spend a night together was irresistible. The date was carefully chosen; Ellenborough's day was fully committed to a parliamentary debate, and furthermore he had a dinner engagement that evening.

On 6 February 1829, Jane travelled down to Brighton in a closed chaise, accompanied by her maid Anna Gove; Felix was only a short distance behind. The going was heavy on the unmade-up road because of the seasonal heavy rains, so it took longer than usual. By prior arrangement, the horses were changed at the halfway point and left at a livery stable for collection on the return journey.[43] Every mile of that journey took Jane inexorably closer to ultimate disaster.

5

Assignation in Brighton
1829–1830

Jane arrived at the Norfolk Hotel just as the winter light was fading at about five o'clock. She was shown to the suite of apartments in the east wing which she and her husband often used. Entrance from the main part of the hotel was by a private staircase which led nowhere else other than to some staff quarters. Arthur was brought to her and, as babies will, having not seen his mother for some weeks threw a tantrum. A little later Jane dashed off a quick note to Ellenborough at Roehampton:

> Brighton, Friday night
> [postmarked 7 February 1829]

To Lord Ellenborough
Connaught Place, London

Dearest Oussey,
   I am just arrived, and will only write you one line as I am tired to death with my journey, the roads were so very heavy. I found Arthur looking *really* pretty – you may believe it if I say so – and appears to me much improved in strength, but he greeted me with such a howl!! We shall improve upon acquaintance.
   If you go to Mrs Hope's tonight, have the thought to make my 'scuses to save me the trouble of writing them.
   The post is ringing –

> Good night, dearest
> Janet[1]

Felix arrived at the hotel between six and seven o'clock in a hired yellow-bodied chariot driven by a post-boy. He alighted from the coach carrying his cloak and a carpet-bag which bore his coat of arms and initials, and was shown to a room in the west wing. This room was approached by the centre stairway from the main hall of the hotel. Having settled in and had his luggage unpacked by a member of the hotel staff, he took dinner in his private sitting-room and as the waiter was clearing away he asked casually who else was staying in the hotel at this unseasonal time of year. He was told that Lady Ellenborough was in residence. 'Is that the dowager Lady Ellenborough?' the prince enquired. 'No,' was the answer. 'It is the young Lady Ellenborough.'[2] The prince asked the waiter to take his card to the lady with his compliments.

Within a short time the waiter returned to the prince with the message that the lady would be delighted if, after the prince had dined, he would take tea with her in her room. The waiter personally served tea to Lady Ellenborough and her guest and noted that they remained together until half-past ten, when the prince left to return to his sitting-room. Requesting the waiter to fetch a bedroom candle and light it, Felix said goodnight and went up to his bedroom.

At about midnight the hall porter, Robert Hepple, who was sitting in his pantry awaiting the late return of a family who had gone out for the evening, heard someone coming down the main stairs. He walked across the hall foyer, which was illuminated by gas lighting, and saw the prince descending the stairs. As soon as the prince saw the porter, he retreated back up the stairs.

Hepple was 'anxious to know what a person at that time of night was wishing to do . . . and kept out of sight' for a while. To ensure that he was not seen, he put out the light in his pantry. His vigil was not long. Within ten or fifteen minutes the prince, still wearing the 'frock coat, trowsers and boots' in which he had dined, softly descended the stairs, crossed the hall and went along the passage leading to the east wing's private stairway. Mr Hepple followed him and watched as the prince entered Lady Ellenborough's bedroom without knocking. The door was closed and the key turned in the lock. After peering through the keyhole and listening for some fifteen minutes at the door, Mr Hepple formed his own opinion of what was happening within. He returned to his pantry. When he retired at 3 a.m., the prince had not yet reappeared. Next morning Hepple was summoned to the prince's room and asked to press some clothes.

At about 9.30 a.m. the prince descended to the hotel sitting-room, where he joined Lady Ellenborough for breakfast. Although it is not possible to say for certain what Jane and Felix spoke of over breakfast, it is possible to guess that one subject under discussion was an unpleasant incident which had occurred in Jane's bedroom earlier that morning. Mr William Walton, the proprietor's brother, who was responsible for waiting on the suite of rooms in the east wing, took it upon himself to tell her ladyship that his colleague, Mr Robert Hepple, had confided in him what he had seen and heard the previous night. Mr Hepple felt that the information ought to be communicated to Lord Ellenborough, a frequent guest in the hotel.

Jane was taken by surprise but did not panic, relying upon her ability to charm the opposite sex. She admitted 'that what she had done was wrong' and said she did not wish anyone to learn about what had transpired. Begging Walton not to repeat what he had told her to anyone, especially not to her maid, she then gave him 'a present' of £20. Not surprisingly, Walton promised his silence in response to such generosity. It was not often that he received a tip that equalled half a year's wages, even though he subsequently gave Hepple £5 of it.

The prince watched Jane depart at eleven o'clock with her small retinue before he also left at about noon in the hired chariot to post back to London.

Within weeks Jane discovered she was pregnant. There was no doubting the paternity of her second child, since, although she had a bed in the marital bedchamber, she and Edward had not enjoyed sexual relations for some months at her own request. A miniature, painted by James Holmes at this time, shows Jane reclining in gipsy-style *déshabillé* on a couch draped with an Eastern rug. She has lost the wide-eyed innocence of earlier portraits and despite the slimness of her hips appears voluptuous. The diarist Thomas Creevey met her in the same month at a party held by Lady Sefton. Present were 'Mrs Fox Lane, Princess Esterhazy, Lady Cowper . . . Lady Ellenborough and the Pole, or Prussian or Austrian or whatever he is . . . anything as imprudent as she or as barefaced as the whole affair I never beheld . . . in short by far the most notorious and profligate women in London.'[3]

Meanwhile, reports of Jane's flagrant behaviour had finally begun to make an impression on Edward, especially when his brother Henry related gossip which reflected unfavourably upon her. Too late, Ellenborough accepted the sense of Margaret Steele's warnings and the letter he had received from Lady Anson strongly urging he spend more time with his young wife. At first his concern showed itself in requests for Jane not to visit those very people to whom he had introduced her.[4] At length he received a letter from one Robert Hepple, a former employee of the Norfolk Hotel in Brighton. Unfortunately £5 had not seemed sufficient reason for Mr Hepple to keep his lordship uninformed about Lady Ellenborough's delinquency; he felt his knowledge might be worth more to her husband. The letter contained information which, though he was reluctant to believe it, Lord Ellenborough could not ignore.

When Ellenborough confronted his wife with the contents of the letter Jane confessed, but only partially. She admitted her attachment to Felix, though not the full extent of it, and she denied the act of adultery at Brighton. This was foolishness taken to an absurd degree, for she could not have hoped to hide her condition indefinitely; and at the date of this discussion she must at least have suspected her pregnancy. Probably because of Ellenborough's political commitments the matter was left hanging bitterly between them.

Jane's first thought was to rush to Felix and lay her problems upon his broad shoulders; but she got little comfort from him. Apparently realising for the first time the predicament in which he was now placed, the prince was appalled. He saw clearly that the matter could cause a major diplomatic incident and the end of his promising career. He immediately reported the matter to his ambassador and was given forty-eight hours to put his affairs in order, pack and leave for home, pending an imminent transfer to the Paris embassy. Ambassador Esterhazy knew that here was a man marked out by destiny for greater things than a life spent as secretary to the Ambassador at the Court of King James; the great Metternich himself took a keen interest in Schwarzenberg's progress. Esterhazy decided to place the young man out of harm's way and ride out any resulting unpleasantness.

On 11 May 1829 Felix left for Europe, telling Jane he had no alternative but to accept his new posting and suggesting that, since she could not confess her pregnancy, she should attempt to obtain Ellenborough's permission to go abroad to be confined in secret.[5] He would, of course, do all in his power to assist her in this delicate matter. His suggestion was not made coldly; he was, according to his letters, still very much in love with Jane. Yet, whatever protestations of love Felix made to her, the fact remains that he rode off leaving his pregnant young mistress to face public condemnation and the wrath of her husband, for the sake of his career. Jane blamed the Esterhazys for transferring Felix and quarrelled with them, and also with Princess Lieven, who was furious that Jane had endangered the prince's career.

With no alternative, Jane did as Felix suggested, choosing the evening of 22 May to make her request to Edward. But Edward refused to allow her to go abroad to 'reflect on her feelings' for Schwarzenberg. The entire matter seems to have culminated in a quarrel in which Jane said she could not live without Felix. The outcome was that Edward proposed a formal separation in which they would each go their separate ways, but leaving little Arthur in his custody. Edward would, he said, make adequate provision for Jane's future needs, and before leaving for an important dinner party with Lord Hill to discuss a military matter he arranged for her departure for Roehampton with her personal servants. The following morning, before attending a Cabinet meeting, he found time to write to his mother-in-law, Lady Andover, suggesting she join her daughter immediately at Roehampton.

All her life Jane hated to quarrel with anyone, and the fracas with Edward unnerved her. However, the thing was done. Naïvely, she thought the worst was now behind her, and her sole ambition was to leave immediately and join Felix. The explanatory note she wrote to her Aunt Anson must have come as a relief to Lady Anson, for Jane's former relationship with George remained the subject of gossip. Since Jane made no mention of her pregnancy, Lady Anson was inclined at first to think the matter was a storm in a teacup, an affair that, with careful management of Ellenborough's natural anger, might be smoothed over and the couple brought together again. She called on Ellenborough later that day as a peacemaker and later wrote to her niece, no doubt pointing out the impossibility of her travelling abroad without her husband's permission. The following letter from Jane was the result:

Lord Ellenborough,
Connaught Place

Roehampton,
Saturday night

Dearest Edward,

Forgive me if I do wrong in writing to you, a note just received from Lady Anson seems to imply that you have expected it. I had begun a letter to you this morning, thanking you from the bottom of my soul for your unbounded kindness in act and manner – it was *far* more than I deserved, and I am deeply grateful.

I again renew all the assurances I gave you last night, that in *act* I am innocent. I hardly know what or how to write to you; I daren't use the language of affection, you would think it hypocrisy, but though my family naturally wish all should be again as it once was between us, those feelings of honour which I still retain *towards you*, make me still acquiesce in your decision. I continue to think it *just* and *right*

I have not been able to speak to them on the subject I confessed to you last night; I have spoken little today but have never for an instant swerved from my own original opinion. I write this to you, if it is possible for you to keep what I have said from *them*, do, as they would only set it down as another proof of unkindness on my part.

Could you write me a line through Henry; were it only to tell me your opinion, be assured I should think it right. But Oh! Edward, *dear* Edward! ought not time, solitude, and change of scene to be tried by me, to conquer or obliterate sentiments so inimical to our mutual peace? *Pray* write to me, tell me all you think upon the subject, all you wish me to do. I shall now answer you candidly, and without a shade of deception.

> God bless you, dearest Edward,
> Janet

If my Aunt has misunderstood any expression and you did *not* expect or wish to hear from me personally, forgive me, for although I longed to tell you how gratefully I feel towards *you* yet I confess I should never have ventured to write.
Ever Yours. J.

Were it not for two short declarations, 'that in *act* I am innocent' and 'my family . . . would only set it down as another proof of unkindness on my part', this would be a straightforward letter. Yet she could hardly profess to be innocent in act without lying. And surely the act of infidelity merited a word stronger than merely 'unkind'? Not that it made a scrap of difference; the extent of her relationship with Schwarzenberg could not be concealed for much longer.

On Sunday, 24 May, Miss Margaret Steele received a hand-delivered message from Lady Anson. It asked her to go immediately to Elm Grove, where Lady Andover and Lady Ellenborough were in need of support. Steely was living with her sister and a friend in Stanhope Terrace in London's Regent's Park, so it took her only a few hours to arrange a chaise and travel to the Ellenboroughs' house at Roehampton. There, in place of the normally relaxed household presided over by Jane, she found a strained atmosphere.[6] In residence, as well as Jane and her mother, was Henry Law – Edward's brother – whom Jane disliked at the best of times and who now wore a face of self-righteous gloom.

It took only a short time for Steely to discover the reason her presence had been requested and the news came as a thunderclap to her, for despite her reservations about Jane's companions she was under the impression, as she was shortly to state under oath, that the Ellenboroughs had always lived together 'most happily'. Jane was tearful but obstinately determined, ultimately, to join Schwarzenberg. Lady Andover was distraught but equally determined that her daughter should not leave the country. For a week the unhappy quartet shared Elm Grove, during which time arrangements were made for Steely to take Jane to the West Country. There they were to join Jane's brother Edward, by now a twenty-year-old subaltern in a cavalry regiment, in a rented cottage at Ilfracombe. Jane's parents must have hoped that a holiday in rural surroundings, miles from any social diversions, would bring Jane to her senses. At the very least it might stay the gossip which was already on everyone's lips, and faithfully recorded within forty-eight hours by Mrs Arbuthnot, close companion of the Duke of Wellington and a frequent guest of the Ellenboroughs:

> There has been an explosion at last in the house of Lord Ellenborough. He has found out all or at least a part of the improprieties of her conduct. Her lover, Prince Schwarzenberg, is gone back to Austria &, at just the same time, Lord Ellenborough took her to her father & refused to live with her any longer. She has been boasting of her own infamy & ridiculing Lord Ellenborough's blindness; but now she protests that, however foolish and indiscreet she may have been, she is not a criminal. I understand she has gone down to Roehampton where he has allowed her to be for the present. What will be the end of it I do not know.[7]

Jane and her companions remained at Ilfracombe for a month during which Miss Steele wrote at Jane's request to Lord Ellenborough, asking once again for permission to take Jane abroad for a period of reflection. He replied in a kindly manner but refused. During this entire period Jane was somehow receiving letters from Felix at the rate of two a week and she was presumably responding.[8] On 1 July the two women left Ilfracombe and travelled to Minterne, where Admiral Digby and Lady Andover arrived for a prearranged visit with Lord Digby.

Jane was then five months pregnant. Two days after arriving at Minterne her condition became apparent to the straitlaced Steely and, 'much agitated', she broached the subject. By then Jane was relieved to be able to discuss the matter that had been at the forefront of her mind for so long. Admitting her condition, she broke down and sobbed, 'God knows what will become of me, for the child is not Lord Ellenborough's but Prince Schwarzenberg's.' She then confessed the entire circumstances of her adulterous relationship, including the overnight stay in Brighton. When questioned about how she could be sure the child was not her husband's, Jane admitted that they had not slept together for some time prior to her becoming pregnant.[9] Only a few weeks earlier, Steely had remarked to Jane that her sleep was troubled and that she spoke in her sleep. On that occasion Jane had answered lightly that Edward said the same thing to her. From this Steely had supposed that they slept together, but Jane subsequently explained that they had two beds in the same room.

Miss Steele was not only a spinster but, according to Jane, a 'gloomily severe' Christian. Nothing could have prepared for her such news from her former pupil. She had hardly started to gather her thoughts together before Jane, who had recovered her composure and did not wish her plans to be thwarted, was beseeching her not to divulge what she had been told to Lord Ellenborough, her parents or her aunts. Steely reluctantly agreed not to do so without Jane's permission. However, before the month was out Jane consented to share the appalling secret with Lady Anson.

Meanwhile Edward, acting on the strong recommendation of his brothers and cousin, had contacted a solicitor and produced certain papers alleging infidelity by his wife, including the letter from Hepple. The solicitor felt initially that, though damaging, there was insufficient evidence to warrant an investigation. Who would take the word of a hotel waiter against that of a peeress? However, some weeks later in early July, Ellenborough's cousin again contacted the solicitor and suggested that he begin private investigations into Lady Ellenborough's behaviour during the past twelve months, starting at number 11 Holles Street where Prince Schwarzenberg had most recently lived until his precipitate departure for Europe.

Within a short time all was discovered. A routine call at the Holles Street address led the detective inevitably to the prince's former address in Harley Street and the many eye-witnesses to Jane's indiscreet conduct. Next he visited Robert Hepple and William Walton, both of whom had been dismissed from the Norfolk Hotel for their part in the affair. Their testimony, however, led first to the post-boy who had driven the prince to Brighton, and then to the hirer of the yellow chariot. In attempting to make Jane's groom betray his employer, the solicitor hit his first difficulty. The boy was as uncooperative as could be without telling any untruths, and gave evidence as near to 'no comment' as he could manage. There was no mistaking where his sympathies lay.

It made no difference, of course. Ellenborough 'appeared to be amazed' at the evidence, according to his legal advisers. Surprisingly – or perhaps not so, bearing in mind his behaviour towards his wife – Ellenborough's diary entries at this date betray no personal emotions, minutely detailing instead the daily meetings and committees and conversations at formal dinners that he attended. His manner was not one of outrage: indeed he made it clear to his legal advisers and Jane's family that his wife was always to be treated with all the courtesies to which her rank entitled her. He arranged for a generous allowance to be paid to her, and, though he asked for the return of heirloom items, he insisted that she keep the magnificent jewellery which he had given her during their marriage. His generosity prompted Jane to write dispiritedly:

> My dearest Edward,
> I hope you will believe me when I say that I feel myself utterly unequal to writing to you today. I *cannot* thank you enough for your kindness but entreat you will not think of making me such an allowance. Indeed it is more than I can possibly want. I will send back the green box tomorrow.
>
> Ever, ever yours,
> Janet[10]

In a letter written from his father's palace, Frauenhof, near Vienna, Felix advised Jane to leave England as quickly as possible for the address in Basle which he had indicated in a previous letter, where she would be cared for during her confinement. He instructed her not to come to him, as he suspected (incorrectly) that all his movements were being watched by agents of Lord Ellenborough. He bitterly regretted the position she had lost because of their affair, and the more so, he said, because it would be impossible for the sake of his future, as well as hers, that they should ever marry. Nevertheless, he swore, he loved her, and his life would be devoted to her happiness and that of their child.[11]

Soon after receiving this letter Jane left England in the face of all entreaties from her distraught mother to remain. She could not bear to be separated from Felix and believed that he would find some way of joining her if she went, as he advised, to Basle. Her father told her that if she went ahead with this plan Ellenborough would have no option but to divorce her. Her reputation, he said, though damaged, might yet be partly restored if she were to remain in England and lead an exemplary life. Furthermore, it was not impossible that Ellenborough might be persuaded to reconsider; no man in his position would wish to be involved in a divorce. Gossip about the affair was confined to her own class and, after a time, would be overlooked if not forgotten. But the inevitable consequences, if she ran away now, were that she would never be permitted to resume her place in society. Nor could she depend upon marriage to the prince; his Catholic faith precluded it. What she was contemplating was lifelong exile from her country and her family, and total disgrace.

For anyone but Jane, with her entire family pleading for her to give Felix up and remain in England under their protection, there would surely have been some wavering of resolve at this point. She adored her parents and her brothers, and the feeling was reciprocated, as letters and diaries would show. But her love for Felix was transcendent. His frequent letters to her, swearing eternal devotion if not promising marriage, bolstered her insistence that there was no future happiness for her without him. She must join him whatever the cost.

Edward Digby accompanied Jane and Steely to the east coast, where they took the packet ferry to the Continent. Steely travelled as far as Brussels and then returned home. Jane continued on with her maid to Basle, where she assumed the name of Madame Einberg at the accommodation arranged by Felix. By then she was six months pregnant.

Rumours had already started to swirl in London, and the ripples quickly spread outward to Jane's greater family in Norfolk.[12] With the open intelligence that Jane had fled to Europe to have Schwarzenberg's child, Ellenborough's original plan of a formal separation was dropped in favour of his seeking a legal divorce. This was the man who had once alienated the King by expressing disapproval when George IV attempted to divorce Caroline of Brunswick. He was also, and remained long afterwards, a friend of Jane's father. The two men met and reached an amicable agreement; obviously they decided to make the best of a bad business.

News of Ellenborough's intention to seek a divorce spread like a bushfire. Some tried to excuse Jane – 'but think of being very pretty and very young and just finding oneself married to such a monster of odiousness as Lord Ellenborough, and then discovering that he wanted the only quality for which women ever forgive monsters'.[13] These allusions to Ellenborough's lack of sexual ability, or alternatively his extreme licentiousness, were common, and summed up by one correspondent: 'Ellenborough's divorce is going on – so we shall soon know, I hope, whether he is as Lady Holland says, impotent, or as others say given to bad women and blessed with a family of natural children.'[14]

Meanwhile, Jane was quite alone in Basle apart from her servants. Contrary to legend, her family did not abandon her but stayed in constant touch by letter. There is a report that her husband visited her, and indeed Ellenborough made a visit of several weeks to the Continent in early September 1829.[15] There is no way of verifying this rumour, for such a visit would have been the subject of greatest secrecy to avoid any accusations of collusion between the divorcing parties. However, in view of what followed it is more than likely that Ellenborough visited Jane to ensure that she fully realised how the mechanism of divorce worked.

By now Admiral Digby had realised that there was no hope of a reconciliation. Jane wanted the divorce as much as Ellenborough; she could not bear the thought of being married to any man but Felix. Therefore she agreed not to offer any defence. A few weeks later she received another visitor, a Mr Wigram, who presented her with a 'Copy of a Bill for the Divorce to be Heard in the House of Lords'. She instructed him to refer the matter to her solicitor in England.

As the last stages of her pregnancy, coupled with the winter weather, confined her to her apartment, Jane felt increasingly lonely, bored and desperate. If only Felix would come to her, everything would be well. But her only relief from the continuous misery lay in the regular letters from Austria, promising that he would try to be with her in time for the birth of the child. It was not until 10 November, more than two months after her arrival in Basle, that Felix managed to visit Jane en route to his new appointment at the Austrian embassy in Paris. She had longed for this moment for months, but she was soon to suspect that his former feelings had undergone a subtle change, doubtless influenced by his family.

Their daughter was born two days later – nine months and one week after the fateful night spent in the Brighton hotel.[16] They called the baby Mathilde (after Felix's favourite sister), which was shortened to 'Didi'. Seeing Jane's distress when the time came for him to leave five days later, Felix promised to visit again within weeks and this time kept his promise, for he spent a further few days in December with Jane and his daughter. During this visit he promised to make arrangements for her to join him in Paris as soon as she and the child were well enough to travel.

Four weeks later tragedy struck the house of Ellenborough. Little Arthur Dudley Law, just a month short of his second birthday, had again been ill with a childish infection, and Ellenborough had sent him in the care of his nurse, Mrs Mowcock, to the seaside in the belief that the fresh air would help alleviate the symptoms. All seemed to be under control on 27 January:

> My Lord,
> Master Arthur is in very good spirits but his tonsils have been very [troublesome] . . . Mr March has been to see him today and says it is his teeth and he will bleed him tomorrow to correct it. He will be all the better for it but is much fawling [sic] away. The weather is so very wet so he could not go out today.[17]

The next letter, from Mr March himself, only two days later, must therefore have come as a shocking blow. Ellenborough noted on the envelope that he received it as he returned home from a Cabinet meeting:

> Worthing 29th January 1830
> My dear Lord,
> I am distressed beyond description to be compelled to relate the melancholy fact that your dear infant has ceased to exist. He was attacked this morning by a convulsive fit which caused his extinction in a few minutes. Everything was done judiciously by the nursery assistant who was on the spot instantly but so violent was the attack that all was over before I could get to him.
> He passed a tolerably quiet night till about 5 . . . up to the time of the fit which seems to have been immediately caused by some accidental noises, there was no reason to consider the child in the slightest danger as everything was going well.[18]

It was distressing news for all concerned, the Digby grandparents as well as the father. The black-edged mourning letters expressing shock and grief, as well as concern for Ellenborough, carefully folded back into their original envelopes, still exist in a pathetic stack neatly tied with deep-purple ribbon among Lord Ellenborough's papers.[19]

It might be assumed, because of the history of the marriage and the fact that the child had spent a lot of his time away from his parents, that his death was of no great moment to them. But Ellenborough, whose ambitions for his son now lay in ruins, mourned him with genuine grief. Like Jane he found consolation in writing poetry throughout his life, and on this occasion wrote:

> Poor child! Thy mother never smiled on thee
> Nor stayed to soothe thee in thy suffering day!
> But thou wert all the world to me,
> The solace of my solitary way.

Despite any bitterness he might have felt towards Jane, Ellenborough wrote to her, as always in a kindly manner, to break the news and thoughtfully enclose a lock of Arthur's soft, fair hair. A messenger delivered the letter to her personally, under Ellenborough's seal. She kept it with her, through all her travels, until her death.

A week later Jane set out for Paris with her baby daughter. It is clear, from a poem written in December 1830, when fresh tragedy struck, that she was distressed about Arthur's death. She was also depressed after the birth of Mathilde, and worried about her future. Just as her father had warned, Felix had confirmed that his religion would not allow him to marry her and, further, her reputation could damage his career. Jane optimistically believed that once she joined Felix their former love would reassert itself and he might find a way. Meanwhile, at least they would be together.

In England, Ellenborough too was concerned for the future. The forthcoming divorce hearings would, he knew, be extremely unpleasant. Jane would not – could not – contest the charge of adultery. However, it was important that his own behaviour did not come under close scrutiny, for under the prevailing laws a divorce could not be granted if both he and Jane were found equally guilty to adultery. Yet with the death of his son and heir it was even more important, now, for him to obtain a divorce in order to remarry.

Jane decided to keep the name of Madame Einberg when she arrived in Paris. Felix had rented an apartment for her in the fashionable quarter of the Fauberg Saint-Germain,[20] and she lived there for some weeks while she searched for something more suitable for herself and her child. Primarily, though, simply being with Felix was all she asked. It was perhaps just as well that she chose to live quietly under an assumed name. Within weeks she was to become the most notorious woman in England.

The Norfolk Hotel at Brighton where Jane and Prince Felix
spent a night together.

6

─────────

A Fatal Notoriety
1830–1831

─────────

Until comparatively recent years *The Times* newspaper was renowned for its front page which consisted of classified advertisements. In May 1966, when the front page was changed to a news format, there was an outcry of protest. However, there was a precedent: 136 years earlier, in April 1830, the editor broke with tradition and placed the Ellenborough divorce case on the front pages.

On 1 April the entire right-hand column of the first page and two-thirds of the second page were given over to the story. It was a sell-out. On 2 April virtually the entire front page and part of page 2 were given over to a complete transcript of the Ellenborough divorce hearing. For weeks the name of Lady Ellenborough was in every newspaper and Jane's misdemeanours became the breakfast-table tittle-tattle of the entire country, causing her name to become a byword for scandalous behaviour for generations. Indeed, for decades small news items continued to appear (they were often incorrect) about her adventures, always referring to her as Lady Ellenborough, though after 1834 she never again used this name.

The preliminary hearing by the Consistory Court, held in relative privacy on 22 February, readily established from the assembled evidence that Jane was guilty of adultery. That was the easy part. But Ellenborough's application for his marriage to be dissolved then had to be examined, under law, by both Houses of Parliament, in public. Divorce was a difficult and highly complicated legal matter. As a lawyer Ellenborough knew that only too well. The social ignominy and sheer cost of obtaining a divorce meant that few were applied for.

On 9 March 1830, in the House of Lords, the Clerk read out the Order of the Day:

> being the Second Reading of the Bill entitled, 'An Act to dissolve the marriage of the Right Honourable Edward Baron Ellenborough with the Right Honourable Jane Elizabeth Baroness Ellenborough his now Wife, and to enable him to marry again; and for other purposes therein mentioned', and for hearing Counsel for and against the same, and for the Lords to be summoned.[1]

The witnesses were called, gave their evidence and were cross-questioned at length by Lord Ellenborough's counsel and subsequently by any member of the House who wished to query the facts. Jane was not represented and offered no defence; no attempt was made to mitigate her actions. Ellenborough's counsel, Mr Wigram, began calling staff from the Norfolk Hotel, who detailed the couple's movements during their overnight stay in Brighton. Robert Hepple, the night porter on the evening of 7 February 1828, was questioned minutely about what he had heard after watching the prince go into Lady Ellenborough's room at midnight:

Q: Did he lock the door after him?
A: He did.
Q: Did you still watch him?
A: I waited a short time at the door . . . a quarter of an hour the first time: then I went again . . . and remained there, I daresay, nearly an hour . . .
Q: How near to the door?
A: Quite close . . . I heard two persons talking, a man and a woman in the room . . . the language was foreign to me, it was not a language I understood at all.
Q: Did you hear anything more?
A: I heard him get into bed . . . and I heard them kissing.

The entire performance was repeated again in early April in the House of Commons, where radical members were not inclined to allow an easy passage of the reading to accommodate Lord Ellenborough. Not surprisingly, Jane's grandfather did not take his seat for the hearing. On this occasion Robert Hepple was constrained to take his answer at the same point in the proceedings a step further:

Q: What did you hear then?

A: I could hear them kissing, and a noise that convinced me that the act of cohabitation was taking place.

A word-for-word transcript of the Commons hearing was reproduced in *The Times*. Thus respectable ladies might sit in their own drawing-rooms or boudoirs and learn the shocking nature of Lady Ellenborough's guilt from Mr John Ward, the prince's neighbour in Harley Street. Mr Ward testified that Jane was a frequent visitor to the house opposite, disguised with a white veil. Sometimes he saw her in the upper-floor room which faced this drawing-room:

Q: Have you ever observed anything in particular passing between them?
A: On one occasion I saw Prince Schwarzenberg assisting in dressing the lady.
Q: In what state was the lady at this time?
A: The Prince was lacing her stays.

Jane's groom, William Carpenter, was as economical with his answers as could possibly be while remaining truthful under oath. For his loyalty to his mistress he was told that he was the most difficult and unwilling witness it had ever been counsel's misfortune to examine. Yet even young William had to admit that he had accompanied Lady Ellenborough when she went to the Castle Hotel, Richmond, one afternoon with the prince. Yes, he had put the horses up there, and yes, he had lied to the head groom about where he had been that afternoon. Was there another similar occasion at Highgate? Yes. And yes, he had ridden out with his mistress on many other occasions when she met the prince. Yes, he had looked after her horse on many occasions while she visited a house in Harley Street. No, he did not know which house; he presumed it was her father's house. Why should she ask him to wait so far from her father's door? He did not know the reason why. Yes, she had left him in charge of her carriage after they left the Countess St Antonio's house; Lady Ellenborough travelled with the prince in his closed chaise until they were within sight of Elm Grove at Roehampton where she transferred back to her own carriage again.

As William Carpenter stood down, a Member of the House intervened in the hearing. Mr Joseph Hume, Member for Montrose, bravely objected *per se* to the entire case on the grounds that

in this country a woman is punished severely for faults which in the husband are overlooked. For a single slip she is banished from society.

And yet if justice is to be done to Lady Ellenborough, can anyone overlook the gross neglect on Lord Ellenborough's part that has led to the unhappy events of the past couple of years? Ought not the charge to be read as one of criminality against Lord Ellenborough, who had permitted and even encouraged his wife's association with the persons responsible for her downfall, rather than one of marital infidelity against an unfortunate lady whose youth and immaturity ought to have been safeguarded by her natural protector? What is a young lady to do who is neglected by her husband? Is she to stop at home all day long?

Touching upon the present line of questioning, in which the prosecution were clearly suggesting that while in the closed chaise together Lady Ellenborough and the prince indulged in a sexual encounter, Mr Hume asked seriously: 'would anyone believe that a lady dressed to go out to dinner could be guilty of anything improper?' Indeed, with the stays and panniers, wigs and feathers of a decade earlier, impropriety might have been difficult. However, fashions had changed in recent times, and the ribald laughter and sallies which greeted the Honourable Member's final remarks left no one in any doubt that a number of members of the House had experienced little difficulty in misbehaving under similar circumstances.

Next the prince's maid provided evidence that on the frequent occasions when Jane had called on her master the couple had usually spent the afternoon in bed together. How could she tell, asked the prosecutor? By the rumpled and marked bedlinen, replied the maid.

Miss Margaret Steele's evidence served to damn Jane completely. She gave her answers quietly, so quietly that *The Times* journalist in the gallery missed some of her answers and complained about it indignantly in his column. She acknowledged that she was a personal friend of Lady Andover and Lady Anson and that for six years she had taken responsibility for the upbringing of Lady Ellenborough prior to her marriage. She told how she had been summoned to Roehampton on the occasion of the couple's separation, how she accompanied Jane to the West Country, of her discovery that Jane was pregnant and of Jane's confession that she had spent the night with the prince at the Norfolk Hotel:

Q: Did you ask Lady Ellenborough any questions as to why she supposed the child was not Lord Ellenborough's?

A: When she first disclosed the circumstances of her guilt to me, I was told to keep it a secret. I think I made no further inquiry, and seeing me much agitated, and being very much agitated herself, she merely said to me, as I have stated, 'God knows what I shall do, for the child is not Lord Ellenborough's but Prince Schwarzenberg's.' That is to the best of my recollection. At that time I asked her no further questions. She was always very modest in her manner to me.

Miss Steele explained that Jane had asked her husband if she might sleep alone, having told him that she did not wish for another child. Questioned on the state of the marriage generally, Steely said she thought the couple had always appeared very happy together. 'You do not recollect seeing Lord Ellenborough ever treat her with harshness, either in word or manner?' On the contrary, replied the witness, 'he was always remarkably kind and attentive to her.' Indeed, she said, she had found Lord Ellenborough to be an unfailingly kind and considerate husband in every way. Indulgent? Very much so, indeed! She had been astonished when the separation occurred.

Her memory failed her only when it came to the conversation she had had with Lord Ellenborough a year earlier on the subject of his wife's behaviour. She recalled that Lady Ellenborough had been 'indiscreet, giddy and very regardless of consequences'. She could not recall exactly in what manner, nor from whom she had heard the report. Her answers were weak, and she knew it, and so did her interlocutor:

Q: What particular acts were indiscreet?
A: I heard of her riding a good deal.
Q: Was there anything indiscreet in a lady riding?
A: I think in her riding alone there was.
Q: Did she ever ride without a servant?
A: No, with a servant. I thought it very indiscreet.
Q: Is that all the acts of indiscretion you ever heard of?
A: . . . I cannot recollect.

She did, however, recollect that she had advised Lord Ellenborough about some of the friends to whom he had introduced his wife before their marriage, and who were frequent guests of the Ellenboroughs. Making it clear that she placed the full blame for Jane's behaviour on the example set by these unnamed persons, she nevertheless hedged and weaved for what must have been some twenty minutes of questioning. When asked directly for names she murmured a short reply which was drowned in loud cries of 'No! No!' by angry members.

Q: Were these associates men or women?

67

A: Both . . . I thought them very bad companions . . . I cannot mention names, it might implicate many persons.

Q: Were they persons universally accepted at respectable houses in London?

A: At houses *called* respectable. (*Laughter.*)

Q: In the best society in England?

A: In fashionable society. (*Laughter.*)

Q: Can you recollect what answer Lord Ellenborough made to your warning?

A: He laughed.

Several times during the long interrogation Miss Steele asked to be allowed to sit down and sip at a glass of water. Later the men and women she alluded to were identified by the broadest of hints in the newspaper leaders, and they would complain loudly that their behaviour had been judged by a person they thought their social inferior.

It was undoubtedly an ordeal for Steely. This modest and moral woman elected to stand up before several hundred men and discuss the sexual behaviour of her former pupil, knowing that it would be widely reported in the newspapers. No one would have forced her to do so, but Lady Andover had begged it as a favour and Steely complied, knowing that her evidence would clinch Lord Ellenborough's case. She must have known that this would ensure a decision that would provide the freedom Jane wanted, but only at the cost of Jane's reputation.

The last of the twenty-one witnesses (many were called twice or three times during the Commons' exhaustive hearing, the rest consisting of prying neighbours and hotel staff, post-boys and coachmen, maids, grooms and lawyers' clerks) was Thomas Kane, the Ellenboroughs' butler. He testified that as far as he and the other servants could see their master and mistress lived in happiness and affection, they generally called each other Edward and Janet, and had until two years ago frequently gone out together in the evening, less often after that. Prince Schwarzenberg had never been a guest at either house. All the servants (there were many) knew that the Ellenboroughs latterly slept in separate beds. Yes, it had been discussed in the servants' hall but no one had taken it to mean that the couple were estranged.

After Kane stood down, the Honourable Members debated the matter. The arguments raged back and forth. Jane had many champions who said that Ellenborough ought to have been more vigilant, that an experienced and worldy man ought not to have left his young wife so alone and unprotected that she had opportunity to behave so badly. Besides, said several, she had behaved no better nor worse than her peers, people who were also personal friends of her husband. And how had this husband reacted when warned by those closest to his wife that she was in moral danger? He had laughed. When one speaker asked what arrangements had been made to secure Lady Ellenborough's future he was advised by Ellenborough's barrister that Lord Ellenborough had made arrangements which ensured 'she should not want for any of the comforts and conveniences which her rank in life required'. The barrister then produced what he described as a letter written by Lady Andover to Lord Ellenborough absolving him of responsibility for the break-up of the marriage, but the members of the House refused to allow it to be admissible.

Those who supported Ellenborough argued that a husband could not possibly watch over his wife every minute of the day. There was no man in the House, said one Member, whose wife and daughters did not go out during the fashionable hours of the afternoon. Where did they go? Did the Honourable Members know every move of their womenfolk? Of course not. Were they then to suspect them of being false?

The newspapers had their say too. *The Times* stated that there was little doubt about Jane's adultery. However, it pointed out that there were other facts to be proven before a divorce might be granted. The editor hoped that there was no 'collusion or connivance with the wife, [or] gross negligence of her morals or comforts . . . or gross profligacy on his part which might prevent the divorce going through'[2] – especially, said the editorial suspiciously, in view of the fact that Lady Ellenborough had made no attempt to contest the divorce, nor offer any defence for her behaviour.

Denying the rumour that Prince Schwarzenberg had offered marriage to Lady Ellenborough if she obtained a divorce, the editor pointed out that in Austria, a Catholic country, such a thing was impossible. However,

> as there has been no opposition by Lady Ellenborough or her family to this bill, we must conclude that neither she nor they have any objection to let the divorce be completed
>
> Now this is a state of things which naturally begets the idea of collusion between the parties . . . the party seeking relief must come into court

with clean hands. An adulteress cannot lawfully divorce her profligate husband. Nor can an adulterer his adulterous wife.

... it seems to us, from reports that are current that an enquiry might be advantageously directed to what might be called 'the Brighton affair'.[3]

The open reference to the 'Brighton affair' – widespread reports of Ellenborough's affair with the daughter of a confectioner from Brighton – was astonishing unless there was some evidence to back up the accusations. Yet it was mentioned in several papers, including *The Times*, and the word 'collusion' was raised a great deal by many in the debate.[4] At one point it looked as though George Anson's name might be brought into the proceedings, but to the relief of the family this dangerous ground was skated over.[5]

The cheaper papers were less circumspect than *The Times*. The *Age*, having questioned a former servant, claimed that Jane had found a portrait of Ellenborough's current mistress 'within six months of their marriage' which 'insulted the delicate sensibility of an affectionate wife'. Openly accusing Ellenborough of neglecting Jane not because of his work, but because of other women, the editor asked his lordship to answer publicly certain statements being made by many people, namely:

you have been an adulterer yourself, you have seduced and intrigued with females, more than one or two in humble life, one of whom has a child of which you are the father, and whom you refused to aid in her poverty and misery until fear of exposure tempted you to grant her a pittance ...

The Times says boldly that there was an affair with a confectioner's daughter at Brighton. Now this is downright slander or downright truth. Lord Ellenborough is bound, in justice to the public, to deny *in toto* the verity of such a charge.[6]

The same paper continued the attack a week later, referring also to an alleged relationship with another young woman, which led to a '*recontre* in Portland Place and even to a personal conflict' between Ellenborough and a young doctor.[7]

Ellenborough loftily ignored the press, and so apparently did his peers, for after a third reading in the week of Jane's twenty-third birthday, on 7 April, the bill was passed. Royal Assent was duly granted and the Clerk of the House gravely announced, in time-honoured fashion, '*Soit fait comme il est désiré.*'[8] *The Times*, seeing the end of its best lead story since the King's attempt to brand Queen

Caroline an adulteress in order to divorce her, contented itself with a huffy statement:

> As we hinted yesterday, such a result was all but inevitable; seeing in the first place that the chief opponent of the bill proceeded on the absurd ground that adultery was not proved, and secondly that nobody had the courage to take the true ground – the alleged conduct of Lord Ellenborough with respect to other women.[9]

There was a beneficiary of the publicity surrounding the Ellenborough divorce case. Advertised in *The Times*, as often as not alongside the daily reports of the hearings, was 'A Satirical Novel of Fashionable Life', entitled *The Exclusives*. The publisher's blurb proclaimed: 'This extraordinary production continues to be the leading topic of conversation among the higher circles. The astonishment felt at the details connected with a certain system of London Society is indescribable.'[10] Although appearing under the shelter of anonymity this book was written by a lady-in-waiting to Queen Adelaide, and the leading character was unmistakably Lady Ellenborough. Just to ensure that her readers were not left wondering, the author boldly plagiarised the name 'Lady Glenmore', the same name as that used for the character based on Jane in *Almack's*. *The Exclusives* ran to three editions in a month while the hearings lasted, and the publishers could not keep it in print. Covering the period 1827–8 the story told how Lord Glenmore, a Minister of the Crown, was cuckolded by a man bearing a remarkable resemblance to Colonel George Anson. It was the second of eight novels that would be written, during Jane's lifetime, using her character or story.

Given the weight of evidence against Jane – publicly self-admitted, one might say, through Miss Steele – one might have expected *some* sympathy for Ellenborough. After all, he was the proven injured party and had recently been bereaved of his only son and heir. However, virtually no one believed that he had not behaved badly himself on the two counts of adulterous behaviour and neglect of Jane.

There is no doubt from the surviving evidence that an agreement was reached between Admiral Digby and Lord Ellenborough, which appears to be that, in return for Jane's matrimonial freedom and a financial settlement, no defence evidence would be offered. However, if blame must be apportioned for what happened to the Ellenborough marriage, and despite the decision of Parliament, it was clearly not one-sided. Jane was guilty of adultery, on two previous occasions as well as her affair with Schwarzenberg, but it was well known in their circles that Ellenborough was as guilty as Jane of marital infidelity. At that time, however, it was not possible for a woman to divorce a man on the grounds of his adultery.

Ellenborough's relationship with the Countess St Antonio terminated abruptly, and the Princesses Lieven and Esterhazy's activities were sharply curtailed by their respective husbands after *The Times* hinted broadly that they were the undesirable persons to whom Margaret Steele had alluded. Lady Holland, at whose home all those most involved had often met, openly stated that Jane had been corrupted by the Esterhazys. Count Apponyi claims that Prince Esterhazy locked his wife in her bedchamber for a week[11] and, according to Lord Clare, he 'threatened her with divorce if she did not mend her ways'. In the same letter, Clare touched on the current widespread rumour that Ellenborough was to marry Clare's sister Isabella. This 'absurd story' was swiftly denied: 'You who know her will acquit her of the indelicacy of forming an engagement with a married man. But in truth the [two] parties, which by the way have not met for more than a year, have not and never have had any thought of being mated.'[12]

In fact, Ellenborough was never to marry again. After a brilliant career during which he became a highly successful Governor-General of India, he died without a legitimate son to inherit his title, which then passed to another branch of his family. He was never socially ostracised as Jane was, but, though his career was never affected by the divorce, few decent families were prepared to risk a daughter to the dubious protection of a man over whose reputation so many questions hung. Instead, as the years passed, Edward lived with several mistresses (not of his own class), by whom he had a number of children, one of whom is said to have been Madame Hamilton, the 'petite Mouche Blanche' of King Victor Emmanuel of Italy.[13]

Although Lord Ellenborough subsequently had two natural sons, he left a large part of his fortune to his two natural daughters, apparently much loved, who lived with him at his Gloucestershire estate, called Elm Grove, like his house at Roehampton. His daughters were raised and educated as ladies.[14] At the chapel on the estate he erected a beautiful monument to his first wife Octavia. A brief note in his will acknowledges: 'Jane Elizabeth Digby and her assigns may receive yearly [the sum of] £360 clear of tax or duty . . . in satisfaction of a bond executed by me to the said Jane Elizabeth Digby . . . during her lifetime . . . on the first of April and eighth of October in every year . . . as shall happen after my death if the said Jane Elizabeth Digby shall by then be living.'[15] Apart from this, it was as though Jane had never existed.

Stories that Ellenborough had settled a large capital sum upon Jane, and that he had forced Schwarzenberg to contribute the sum of £25,000 to a trust account for Jane's future security, were widely circulated, even finding their way into respected reference books such as *The Complete Peerage*. It has not been possible to substantiate these rumours; however, it has been possible to confirm that, in the years that followed, Jane received monies far in advance of the annual £360 allowed by Ellenborough's bond, and the various legacies subsequently bequeathed by her parents and grandfather. These surpluses did not emanate from future partners, for in the main they were supported by Jane. A substantial sum (which will be discussed later) was undoubtedly settled upon Jane at the time of the divorce, providing the wherewithal for her lifestyle and adventures.

During the spring and summer of 1830, when Jane's shocked relatives were busy trying to live down her notoriety, Admiral Digby and Lord Londonderry (an emissary of Lord Ellenborough and a lifelong friend of Jane)[16] made separate abortive attempts to persuade Felix Schwarzenberg that he had an obligation to marry her. They entreated Jane to recognise 'the necessity of steady conduct and patient forbearance' towards the prince. This seemed especially appropriate when Jane discovered that she was again pregnant by him.

By the time she regained her marital freedom, Jane, still calling herself Madame Einberg, had found a larger apartment near the Palais-Royal in Paris.[17] Here she held her famous 'salons' which were, as Apponyi put it, 'much frequented'. Her first function, referred to by Apponyi as 'Lady Ellenborough's Ball', was well attended, though Apponyi stated that he was unable to dance since it was the season of Lent.[18] Despite her pseudonym it was clearly well known that she was the former Lady Ellenborough, and, glittering and entertaining as Jane's functions were, they were noticeably not attended by the English contingent in Paris. Instead of her former connections, Jane found herself hostess to Felix's unmarried friends, minor European royalty, and the slightly louche members of Paris's artistic and literary society.

One wonders what Jane had expected when she gave up her

husband, name and position to run into Felix's arms. She may well have assumed (despite her father's warning) that Felix would marry her, and it is doubtful that she suspected the reality which ultimately faced her. To have had a love affair with a dashing foreign prince when she had few responsibilities, and to conduct it while under the nominal protection of an aristocratic husband, with no doors closed to her, was one thing. It was quite another to live almost as a *demi-mondaine*, a woman disgraced and regarded as not quite acceptable in circles which had once clamoured to receive her. Jane held her head up and pretended to ignore slights, but she was deeply hurt.

She had plenty of invitations until her pregnancy began to show, but it was never possible for her to accompany Felix to state banquets and formal diplomatic functions. She was not received at court, and many houses were closed to her. Her days were spent visiting acquaintances, attending salons, riding in the Bois de Boulogne; notoriety hung around her and she knew that those who stopped to stare at her now were not merely admiring her beauty as in the past but identifying her as the disgraced divorcee.

As the heat of the summer settled upon Paris, revolution seethed, forcing the abdication of King Charles X in favour of the Duc d' Orléans. Felix became involved to an extent that later enabled him to produce a treatise called *The Revolution of 1830* which earned him praise in Austria for his analysis of the control of mobs. It was a way back to favour after the adverse publicity of the previous spring. His love for Jane was not strong enough for him to risk his brilliant career for it, let alone his security and reputation.

The relationship for which Jane had risked everything had already started to go wrong by the autumn of 1830, according to a letter written by Felix, which refers to frequent disagreements between them.[19] This friction almost certainly stemmed from the prince's refusal to agree to a marriage under French law as suggested by Jane's father, which would bypass the restrictions of his own country. At one point Felix had appeared to be giving the possibility serious consideration, though he was always aware that the illegality of such a move in his native Austria would affect his career. The story that Jane and Felix were to marry imminently was so widely accepted in Paris salons that it was reported in *The Times* and Jane received several congratulatory letters.[20] However, under pressure from his family and possibly Metternich, Felix finally rejected this solution to the problem.

In October, Jane received news from home about George Anson.

Her 'first love' was to be married to Isabella, daughter of Lord Forrester – a noted beauty who had been in love with George for years. Their betrothal had been delayed, undoubtedly because of the possibility of George being implicated in the Ellenborough divorce. Other news was not so happy: George's younger brother William, serving in His Majesty's Navy, had been killed aboard his ship; two of the young Anson boys who had shared Jane's lessons at Holkham were now dead.

Her teenage affair with George, and the misery it had caused her, now seemed as though it had happened to someone else. But the uncertainty in her relationship with Felix began to affect her health. In this unhappy state, shortly before Christmas, Jane gave birth to a son, whom she called Felix after his father. The child died ten days later.

Jane had hoped that a son might induce Felix to marry her, and for that reason she had welcomed his birth. Her poetry makes it clear that the death of her baby put an end to her 'bright vision' of marriage to his father. In an agony of guilt, loss and self-reproach she wrote of her worship of the prince and her sentiments that perhaps it was best the child had not lived 'to share [my] destiny of shame'.[21]

Two days later Felix sent her a note of consolation for her loss, regretting the many dissensions they had had during the past year.[22] It was not very consoling to Jane. Felix was hardly ever with her. She had begun to fear that there was little hope of ever becoming his wife and that even the likelihood of remaining his beloved mistress was far from assured.

7

Jane and the King
1831–1833

During the period of Jane's third confinement, and especially after
the death of their baby, one might have expected that Prince Schwarzenberg – in common decency – would spend more time with the
woman who had given up so much for him and who, lacking any
family support, was otherwise alone. However, on the good authority
of the wife of the British Ambassador in Paris, we know that his
thoughts were not with Jane. 'Poor Lady Ellenborough is just going
to be confined', Lady Granville had written to the Duke of Carlisle,
'and Schwarzenberg is going about flirting with Madame d'Oudenarde.'[1] Nor did his behaviour improve after the death of Jane's baby,
according to Schwarzenberg's friend and colleague, Count Apponyi,
who noted that 'Felix Schwarzenberg is paying court to Mme Hatzfeld, they are inseparable in the salons. Mme d'Oudenarde, to whom
our attaché paid his first homage, is very jealous and cannot believe
he would drop her for a red-haired German.'[2]

The defence offered by Schwarzenberg for his behaviour was his
suspicion that Jane was having an affair with a Monsieur Labuteau,
who until 1830 had been an officer in the élite royal Guarde du Corps
of the erstwhile Charles X, and was a scion of one of the great French
families.[3] That this young man was an admirer of Jane's may have
been true. Apparently he acted as an escort on several occasions; even
in Paris a woman could go nowhere alone, and during the late stages
of her pregnancy she had been glad of his arm. But that Jane had
betrayed Felix with him was untrue, and she indignantly denied the
charge;

If to gaze upon thee waking with love never ceasing
And fondly hang o'er thee in slumber when laid,
Each tender dear moment my passion increasing,
If this is betraying, thou hast been betrayed.

. . . if thy comforts by every fond art to enhance
Thy sorrows to lighten, thy pleasures to aid,
To guess every wish and obey every glance,
If this be betraying, thou hast been betrayed!

J.

Paris 1831[4]

At the bottom of the rumours concerning Jane's fidelity was the
prince's handsome sister, Princess Mathilde, whose ambition for her
much loved younger brother was boundless. She saw nothing but
disaster in his relationship with Jane and feared that if the couple
married in France, as suggested, his career was finished. Mathilde
enlisted the aid of a Schwarzenberg cousin (there were several Prince
Schwarzenbergs in Paris) to ensure that Felix heard of Jane's friendship with Monsieur Labuteau in an unfavourable light.[5] The seeds
of suspicion were well sown and provided Felix with self-justification
for his own shameless behaviour.

Jane was well aware that the Schwarzenberg family were ranged
against her and were almost certainly responsible for Felix's re-
scinding his earlier semi-agreements to marry her. But an interest in
Monsieur Labuteau was never even mentioned by Jane; not in her
poetry, nor in subsequent letters to close friends, in which she denied
the allegation, nor in her surviving diaries. She was accustomed to
having a court of admirers, and the young man clearly meant nothing
to her beyond a convenient and pleasant escort.

Immediately after Jane's confinement, Felix too appeared to believe
that there was nothing in the story he had been told. In a note to
Jane he confirmed that he had now 'entire faith in her', though for a
time, he wrote, he had believed her 'incapable of speaking a word of
truth'.[6] However, only a few months later, in May 1831, the couple
had a further violent disagreement on the same subject and they left
Paris, separately. Felix went home to Austria, Jane took little
Mathilde and fled to Calais. Shortly afterwards she travelled to Dover,
where she was met by Lady Andover and Margaret Steele; the three
women and Didi lived there for a while in a cottage rented by Jane,
using the name Mrs Eltham.

77

Jane wrote to Felix to try to heal the breach. His reply, from his father's castle in Austria, was frigid. She may have forgotten the events of that last fortnight in Paris, he said, but he could remember all too well. First, he said, 'there were my suspicions, which would soon have been laid aside had you not made such lame excuses for the unaccustomed hours you kept.' As a result he had had her watched until he knew all her movements, and there was no room left for doubt that the stories he had been told about her were correct. His old suspicions of her untruthfulness had returned, and now there was no possibility of 'the happy union to which I had looked forward' and by which he might have reinstated Jane 'in the position which you had lost'.[7]

To anyone but the besotted Jane, his reliance on this trumped-up case as an excuse to end their relationship would have said everything there was to say. But she had not been unfaithful, she knew there was no truth in the accusations, and therefore believed that if she could just see him and explain matters all would be as before. After talking it over with her mother and Steely, Jane, again rejecting their advice, decided to go to Felix to deny what his cousin had told him and to defend her behaviour immediately prior to their quarrel. She was still passionately in love with Felix, and she had a naïve belief that love, and the truth, would triumph in the end.

Lady Andover and Steely became agitated at this plan, believing that Felix was a thoroughly self-centred man whose personal ambitions were more important to him than Jane. His treatment of her to date was clear proof that this was the case, Steely said. She would never change her opinion of the man she saw as a complete bounder.[8] But Jane would have none of it, still believing that she and Felix could return to the heady early days of their love affair. In late July she left England for Europe, arriving during August in Munich, where she evidently expected to meet Felix.

In fact Felix was lying low at his family home in Bohemia. According to his biographer he was 'in low spirits and poor health because of the Ellenborough affair and the perpetual whirl of activity and excitement in Paris' which had 'left their mark.'[9] We must assume Felix believed that Jane had been unfaithful to him, which might have justified his anger had he been entirely faithful himself. But the fact remains that when he met her she was a respected and well-established member of the highest society in England, living in the utmost comfort and security; he had avidly pursued and seduced her, eventually enticing her away from her husband and family. He had fathered two children by her, one of whom (Didi) still lived, and yet because of rumours which could not truly be substantiated (though evidently he was satisfied of their veracity) he was content, apparently, to abandon her to the uncertain fate of an unprotected woman with a ruined reputation trailing around Europe with their illegitimate child. Although Schwarzenberg's supporters in England described him as 'very honourable and right, and ready to make every reparation in his power',[10] it is not surprising that his nickname 'Cad' became synonymous with ignoble behaviour.

One wonders why Jane chose to go specifically to Munich at this point. Of course, she had to go somewhere other than England, where her notoriety was such that she could never have been received in society. She was still not yet twenty-five, and beautiful. She had a comfortable income and a zest for life; she could not hide away in a rented cottage for the rest of her days. In Paris there was nothing for her as an unprotected woman with a reputation, and besides she now hated the city where her hopes had turned sour.[11] A previous biographer suggests that she chose Munich because the British Ambassador there was Lord Erskine, a good friend of Jane's grandfather.[12] Jane had grown up with the large family of Erskine sons and daughters who might be depended upon not to bar her from their home nor be too critical of the scandal surrounding her name.[13] There may have been more than one reason, however.

Diplomats are not normally at liberty to leave a situation merely because of a disagreement with a mistress (if such were the case, diplomatic legations could hardly continue to function). Since Felix had been openly keeping Jane as his mistress in Paris for over a year, it is doubtful that he was whisked away by his superiors to avoid another 'incident', as he had been in London. Clearly the disagreement between Jane and Felix coincided with the end of the prince's time at the Paris legation anyway; it had only been a temporary assignment for the sake of expediency. He was almost certainly aware that his next posting would be to Germany, and Munich was the most likely base.

Formerly a stolid provincial town, Munich was at that time enjoying a renaissance. Under the personal direction of the latest scion of the House of Wittelsbach, King Ludwig I of Bavaria, a new era of neo-classicism was in vogue. Determined to break the French stranglehold on German culture, and in a bid to achieve his dream of creating the perfect city, Ludwig ensured that German Gothic and rococo design gave way to Grecian friezes and clean rows of Ionic columns. Narrow tree-lined streets opened into broad thoroughfares and plazas with triumphal Roman arches; quiet squares were crowned with obelisks and monuments. Churches and basilicas, palaces and rotundas, museums, art galleries and libraries, public gardens and theatres sprang up around the city. As a result of this feverish activity Munich increasingly came to be regarded as an important centre for the arts; art galleries and libraries have to be filled.

However, after a period of seclusion at Krumlov, during which time he wrote his famous treatise on the 1830 Revolution, Prince Felix Schwarzenberg was appointed Legation Counsellor and posted, not to Munich, but to Berlin. But Jane had already rented a house in Munich. She wrote again to Felix begging him to meet her, anywhere, confident that if they could only meet she could convince him of the truth. There was no reason why she should not hope for this, since in his letters Felix insisted that he still loved her and their child, Didi. Presumably her relationship with the Erskine family meant that she was not friendless upon her arrival in the city, and her beauty and personality immediately ensured a number of eager escorts. However, she could not go into what she called 'society' – that is, the society of those she regarded as her peers.

For some weeks she was occupied in furnishing and decorating her new home and designing the garden; these were newly acquired interests that would remain with her for the rest of her life. Munich was exciting, and promised, once the many building projects were completed, to rival any city in Europe for architectural interest. Yet it was Munich's proximity to Felix's home, less than 200 miles away, that was its chief attraction for Jane. One of her first purchases must have been a good horse, for the first mention of her at this time is of her beauty and horsemanship.

Within a remarkably short time of Jane's arrival in the town, word of her reached the ears of the King. Ludwig was a man who worshipped beauty all his life: beautiful objects, beautiful buildings and beautiful women.[14] Either by design or by coincidence a meeting occurred between the two in early October 1832 at an Oktoberfest ball and so began for Jane a wonderful relationship with the man whom as friend, and in her personal estimation, she regarded as second only to the great love of her life, and the latter was as yet many years in the future.

Born in Strasbourg in 1786, King Ludwig I, a godson of King Louis XVI of France and Marie-Antoinette, and a somewhat unwilling protégé of Napoleon and Josephine, had ascended the Bavarian throne seven years earlier at the age of thirty-five.[15] The House of Wittelsbach had ruled Bavaria for almost a thousand years, and its latest head was the same age as Lord Ellenborough. He was an amiable and intelligent man, kind to a fault, and a workaholic.

At the age of eighteen Ludwig went to Italy. It is said that he saw the Colosseum by moonlight and fell deeply in love. In Venice he was further enthralled. And as he roamed the sun-baked Tuscan hill towns he gave his heart completely to southern lands. It was the one love in his life that was never to fade. As a result of the years he spent in Italy and his later travels in Greece, Ludwig formed a deep interest in ancient civilisations and subsequently became an acknowledged expert on the subject during a period of almost twenty years' study. His taste in art was, in fact, remarkably similar to that of Jane's grandfather. The decorations at Holkham and those in Ludwig's palaces might have been planned by the same person.

He married the former Princess Theresa of Saxe-Hildburghausen, 'the best-looking princess in Europe' according to Ludwig's biographer. Their wedding celebrations in October 1810 were so well received that the people of Munich repeated them again on the couple's anniversary; and the celebrations are still being held each year as Munich's famous Oktoberfest. Ludwig himself was then 'a fair young man ... with soft features, a flushed face, a proud full mouth and wide blue eyes. Allowing for the flattery expected by princes, he still must have been amazingly good-looking.'[16] The royal couple had seven children and the marriage was, despite Ludwig's many love affairs, an affectionate one.

When he ascended the throne of Bavaria, Ludwig used his classical knowledge and his philhellenism in the design of his new capital. He set in motion, at huge cost, many civic projects designed to turn Munich into the most beautiful city in Europe, a second Athens, a city to rival Florence and Paris. Excavations were commissioned in Italy and Greece to recover 'lost' works of art, the cities of Europe were combed to purchase classical treasures originally plundered by Napoleon's armies. One of his first actions as King was to commission a great art gallery (the Pinakothek) to house the royal art collection and make it available to the public. No expense was to be spared to achieve his objective, even though it reduced the members of his household to petty economies and Ludwig himself wandered around his many building sites dressed like a penniless artist.

The year that Ludwig met Jane was a landmark for him in that his eighteen-year-old second son, Otto, had been elected King of Greece by a self-selected mini-League of Nations headed by Metternich. Short of being made King of Greece himself, nothing could have pleased Ludwig more than that his son should become ruler of the country which had evolved what he considered to be the ideal culture. Coincidentally, Lord Ellenborough had been involved in the early discussions on a suitable candidate to fill this role,[17] and Jane knew something of the political background to the choice of Prince Otto. Although she was never interested in politics Jane still maintained a correspondence with, among others, the Princesses Lieven and Esterhazy and Lord Londonderry, so that she could not help but pick up news which undoubtedly made her an interesting conversationalist. She was an animated talker with a good sense of humour, and this shows in the surviving letters of her later years. From her upbringing at Holkham, Jane retained a basic knowledge of classical art, and she had travelled in Italy – which enabled her to talk on the subjects that most interested Ludwig. Had she been merely a pretty face, she would no doubt have gone the way of most of Ludwig's numerous beautiful mistresses in a very short time.

As it was, the two quickly forged a close friendship based on shared confidences, punctuated by a correspondence that would last for six years. In her letters and billets-doux she addressed him as 'My Dearest Friend' or 'Dearest Lewis', an anglicised version of his given name, Louis, used by his intimates.[18] In her diaries and between themselves, however, Jane and the King used names from the ancient world. She was 'Ianthe' (the Greek equivalent of the name Jane) while he was 'Basily' (from the Greek *basileus* meaning king).

Initially, Jane regarded the King as a friend and comforter. Within days of their meeting he had written a poem to her and she was writing to him on intimate terms. At the same time she confessed that she trembled to use his Christian name so freely, despite his *insistence* that she dispense with all formalities, and hesitated to give him her complete trust 'lest at some future date you will receive it as another did!'[19]

Ludwig was intensely attracted to this charming young woman, who seemed to him at times little more than a hurt child. She was recovering from a mild eye infection when he first met her and seemed fragile and forlorn.[20] The King found it difficult to resist the romantic story of Jane's ultimate sacrifice for love, of her continuing devotion to Felix and her determination to be reconciled to him. Undoubtedly he felt protective towards her. Jane was happy to have such a sympathetic and uncritical ear for her problems, and the King made daily visits to her home to listen and advise. She happily shared Felix's letters with him, already secure in the knowledge that Basily was her champion.

Meanwhile Jane was besieged by other admirers, and within several weeks of her arrival in Munich had already received several proposals of marriage, none of which she took seriously.[21] She now knew how to handle flirtations with charming expertise, refusing suitors in a manner which left them feeling complimented rather than rejected. Hence she received a diet of admiration which bolstered her spirits and kept about her a court of suitors which did her no disservice in the eyes of Ludwig. He became completely immersed in the romantic story of Jane and her prince, with its haunting Tristan and Isolde theme. The thought of this extraordinarily lovely child-woman, whose passions were apparently as strongly felt as his own, who was desired by so many yet rejected all to remain faithful to her one true love, enchanted him. He swore to do all in his power to help her achieve a reunion with Felix, and meanwhile was happy to dispense advice and offer warm affection.[22]

Their daily meetings were augmented by frequent notes, sometimes two or three times a day, hand-delivered by their servants.[23] Each evening the King called at Jane's home, and most days she called on him at the vast Residenz Palace. They exchanged gifts. He gave her an inscribed prayer book, and often sent her posies of violets which she told him were her favourite flowers; she embroidered a cap for him and sent him sketches she made of the countryside around Munich. From the beginning he warned her to be careful of the content of her letters to him, for his position made him vulnerable. His fears were prophetic, for he would ultimately lose his crown through the indiscretion of a mistress. Throughout their correspondence Jane was careful, sometimes advising him she was being so, for his sake.

One of the proposals of marriage rejected by Jane came from a more than usually attentive and eligible source. Baron Carl Theodore Venningen, whom Jane met one morning while riding in the Hofgarten, fell instantly in love with her, just as Felix Schwarzenberg had done. But in the baron's case Jane would remain his ideal while there was breath in his body. Unlike Jane's other suitors, Carl – or Charles as Jane called him – refused to be rebuffed and became too attentive for Ludwig's liking. This may have been because Ludwig was jealous on his own account, or because it spoiled his dream of a romantic reunion between Felix and Jane, the thought of which the King found irresistible.

However, it is obvious that Jane could not be singularly dependent upon her royal friend for friendship. She was not received at court, and the time the King could devote to her was, of necessity, limited. So Charles, who pursued her as tirelessly as Felix had once done, was Jane's diversion from loneliness. He was tall, red-haired and good-looking, an aristocrat of obvious Germanic stock who wore the dashing uniform of a cavalry officer of the King's Regiment.[24] He rode well, and wrote exquisite French in a small, neat hand. He spoke English and indeed had English connections too, for he was first cousin to Lady Granville, the wife of the British Ambassador in Paris during the time that Jane was living there with Felix Schwarzenberg. Left to himself, Charles was inclined to perceive life as a serious business; Jane was like a beautiful butterfly that had fluttered within his grasp. He was utterly fascinated.

At first she regarded him merely as an amusing and pleasant companion; his constantly repeated proposals became almost a joke between them, prettily parried by Jane. Indeed, Charles's devotion and frequently professed wish to marry her must have counterbalanced to some extent the pain of rejection by Felix. Yet she loved Felix so utterly that no man could even begin to be a substitute. She explained her feelings to Charles as she had explained them to the King, but Charles continued to press his suit. After all, he must have thought, he was here in Munich; Felix was not.

Felix continued to write to Jane, however, and though he resisted a meeting his constant declarations of love gave her reason to hope that their relationship could be resuscitated. In an attempt to assist in their reunion, Ludwig suggested that the couple might meet secretly at Schloss Berg, a Wittelsbach hunting lodge on Lake Starnberg, some forty miles south-west of Munich. There in romantic isolation they could discuss their differences and perhaps achieve a *rapprochement* without inviting further gossip. At the end of October 1831 Jane wrote to Felix telling him of the meeting proposed by the King. She begged him to join her and set out for Schloss Berg.

Full of anticipation, though Felix had not yet actually agreed to meet her, Jane waited for him. The poem she wrote upon her arrival wondered anxiously whether he would look at her 'as of old' or whether she must expect 'a change I never thought to see'. Convinced that he merely had to see her to know that she loved only him, regardless of what others told him and the deceitful 'breath of shrilling slander', she refused to believe he could receive her coldly after all they had meant to each other.

Her confidence in her ability to win Felix back was undoubtedly due to her experience that where men were concerned one look was all it usually took. Felix possibly knew this too; hence his attitude regarding a meeting. It must not be forgotten, either, that Felix was an unusual man with unique qualities. His official court biographer in Vienna insisted he had mystical powers: 'The excessive life-force of the Prince is illustrated by the fact that he had a magnetic influence over women – not in the romantic and figurative way, but actually and medically. His sister was supposed to come especially to visit him and touch his hand to acquire more strength.'[25] Perhaps this explains, in part, Jane's obsession.

Jane remained at Berg for several weeks in October and November 1831, wandering in the glorious woodlands alone, on horseback or on foot, willing her prince to come to her. One day her hopes soared when a visitor arrived, but it was not Felix. The persistent Charles Venningen had pursued her to her secret hideaway. Fearful that his presence might be misinterpreted by both the King and Felix, Jane insisted Charles return to Munich immediately and to ensure he did so made him the bearer of one of her frequent letters to the King. 'I am so glad, dearest Lewis, to have had this opportunity of sending you these lines by Monsieur de Venningen who came here today. By this means you will receive them sooner . . . as he returns this evening' – not, however, before he had made some ardent advances.

After ten days Felix wrote to advise that he could not meet Jane because of his commitments. As consolation the same post brought two letters from the King, a bouquet of violets and a book of his own poems preceded by the handwritten inscription:

> These poems show you, show you my innermost feelings
> You who became a victim of love, you will understand me
> As I understand you, dearest, whom the world has exiled.
> I will never judge you harshly, even if all the world does!
> I cannot condemn you, because I understand it all.

Jane replied: 'Do you really long for my return? Your wish shall be gratified . . . My first care shall be to sit for your picture. You are very impatient to have it finished, and that wish is sufficient for your Ianthe.'[26] She returned to Munich having written her own dispirited poem of disappointment: 'He comes not, 'twas but fancy's dream which mocked my hopes with visions bright.'[27]

It is difficult to explain Schwarzenberg's behaviour. If he did not wish the relationship to continue, why the constantly repeated avowals which kept Jane dancing to his tune? Had he simply told Jane that he no longer loved her it would have set her free, though painfully. The King sought to console his lovely young friend, and during the course of their conversation queried Baron Venningen's frequent attendance at Jane's home. When Jane confessed that his advances were becoming pressing, the King was alarmed. He begged her to discourage Charles and to be true to their shared ideal of love in its purest form.

One of Ludwig's minor self-indulgences had been to commission the Schönheits-Galerie (Gallery of Beauty) for the *Festsaalbau* (or assembly rooms) at the Residenz. Similar in concept to the Lely series of Charles II's 'Ladies of the Bedchamber', it consisted of a series of paintings by the court artist, Josef Stieler, of beautiful women. They were mainly members of Ludwig's court (some were his mistresses), but Ludwig's appreciation of pulchritude was catholic and women of every social rank were included, from the beautiful daughter of a Munich shoemaker to the wife of the British Minister, Lord Milbanke. In this gallery the royal connoisseur liked to wander each morning to contemplate in an inspirational communion of beauty. Ludwig asked Jane to sit for Stieler as an example of her type of beauty, and was present for most of the sittings.

It was a pretty compliment, but, just as Lely did before him, Stieler, though undoubtedly an artist of great talent, reduced some of his subjects to a contemporaneous ideal. Technically speaking, his portrait of Jane set against a typically classical background captures perfectly the sumptuousness of her clothes, the richness of her colouring, the transparency of her skin, the symmetry of her features. But the quicksilver quality which was Jane's real beauty eluded Stieler. At the time of this portrait Jane was in her mid-twenties and just coming into her full magnificence, and Stieler himself wrote that, of all the women in the Schönheits-Galerie, Jane was the only one who could rival in beauty the exquisite Marchesa Marianna Florenzi.[28]

Jane herself some time later nevertheless made the comment that it was not 'very like'. A white marble bust of Jane that Ludwig commissioned Josef Bandel to sculpt a month later confirms the slender voluptuousness hinted at in Stieler's portrait.

Arguably, her intelligent vivacity as much as her physical beauty attracted Ludwig, and also brought Charles Venningen back to her time and again. But it was her own physical needs that broke her sexual fast in November. It is not entirely clear whether this was with Ludwig or with Charles, but the reawakened desire provoked by the encounter created difficulties, as she told Ludwig in a letter:

> Forgive me, dearest Lewis, if our last night's conversation pained you, but your openness, affection and sincerity encourage mine.
>
> It is not to be denied that rapture, *untasted for six months*, has [now] reawakened passions I flattered myself were nearly if not quite extinguished. Still, dearest, I repeat my *intentions* remain unchanged . . . My word of honour I regard as a sacred vow and I dare not, dare not, give it lightly.
>
> What would [you] . . . think if after all my promises to the contrary I fell a victim? Do not be thus unhappy. I vow not to deceive you, I never will.[29]

In her latest letter to Felix she had begged him to allow her to come and live near him in Berlin. If he would not agree, she wrote, she would go into a convent and take Didi with her.[30] It is difficult to believe that Felix took this threat seriously, since a more unlikely nun would have been hard to find. But when, in fulfilment of her promises, Jane revealed to Ludwig her dilemma over the ever more pressing Charles, she found the King unsympathetic. It would be impossible for their relationship to continue, he told her, if she eventually succumbed to Charles's advances. This frightened her into agreeing not to take her relationship with Charles further, for 'to cut with *you*, I cannot, will not. Do not be angry with him for I am *sure* his intentions are good . . . Believe that I love and will love you for ever.'[31]

For a while Charles seems to have been kept in check, but he was a proud man, unused to being balked. He allowed himself to be played on Jane's line throughout January and February, during which time Jane told Ludwig that Charles was 'in a terrible state' at her treatment of him. 'I cannot doubt his . . . devoted love, but I cannot return it, at least not *now*.'[32]

One evening in March the baron called on Jane again. She knew in advance it would be a difficult interview and that the situation was becoming uncontrollable if she was to retain his friendship, which she valued. She had even rehearsed with Ludwig what she would say. She told Charles she had decided that she could not allow their relationship to become more intimate and that she would only continue to receive him if he gave his word of honour not to continue his proposals of marriage and his attempts to make love to her. Afterwards she wrote to Ludwig:

> It was in vain. Neither entreaties nor threats could prevail upon him. He answered that on such a subject it was *morally impossible* for him to give his *word of honour*; that all he could promise were his resolutions not to ask more, but a *vow* he could not, and would not, give.
>
> At the same time he told me that he could not help suspecting that you had more than friendship for me, as this last sentiment could be mixed with no jealousy. He added, too, that he plainly perceived that I was ever more ready to follow your advice in the slightest circumstances than to listen to his most earnest prayers. At the same time he felt that the greatest joys would have no value if yielded with regret.[33]

It is hard not to sympathise with the baron. Jane's close friendship with the King, whose reputation for extramarital amours was well known, was something of an enigma. Jane's letters reveal that they had discussed his relationship with Marianna Florenzi, for the King forbade Jane to be jealous of the love he bore the Marchesa.[34] Jane also complains of hearing that he has taken another lover and 'this', she said, 'gives me deep pain'. These hints at deep intimacy, even proprietorship, allied to the conviction at Ludwig's court that Jane was the King's mistress, are impossible to dismiss.

But Charles was not the only person immediately concerned that the 'true sentiments' of the pair were more than those of a platonic nature. Marianna Florenzi had recently refused to meet Ludwig, using the curt excuse that her health prevented it. 'Besides,' she added with false insouciance, 'I do not wish to bore you. I fear that I am no longer in exclusive possession of your love.'[35] It was left to Marianna's maid to explain to the King what lay behind this jibe. Her mistress was angry about the time he spent with Jane, the maid wrote to Ludwig. 'How could this Lady Ellenborough, whose scandalous life is known to all the world, have deceived you, Your Majesty?' she asked angrily.[36]

It was inevitable that Jane would eventually submit to her own physical needs, and unfortunate that she so quickly suffered the consequences. At the beginning of May 1832 Jane conceived her fourth child, though by the time she realised her condition Ludwig had already departed for his annual summer vacation with his wife and children. On the eve of his leaving he presented her with a puppy as a living reminder of their affection, and to reinforce his attachment to Jane despite his relationship with the Marchesa.[37] It seems clear that Jane was sure from the first that the baby was Charles's. Furthermore, Charles accepted the child as his and renewed his entreaties that she should marry him. Irritated at the fecundity that had placed her in such an unenviable position, Jane wrote to Felix telling him of Charles's desire to marry her, hoping that it would make Felix jealous. The plan backfired. The prince replied that, although he loved her and she would always be part of his life, if she had the offer of marriage with a good man she should accept it for marriage with him would never be possible.[38]

Jane was now in another of her so-called 'scrapes', for while she was undoubtedly fond of Charles she had no desire to marry him. She believed that it would signal the end of her relationship with the King, of whom she was far fonder, though, as Ludwig had already gently pointed out, her relationship with him could never lead to anything beyond close friendship. Furthermore, she was still convinced she was in love with Felix, though how she proposed to explain her pregnancy to him is a mystery. For both reasons she insisted to Charles that her pregnancy be kept a complete secret. Felix must never know; the world must never know. From the hint dropped in a letter to Ludwig that 'if I did not know from experience that all my letters are opened, there would be a thousand things I would give worlds to tell you'[39] it appears that she would have confided in him in person, possibly without damaging their intimacy.

After some consideration, Jane decided to go to Italy, find a remote place where she could stay under an assumed name, and have her baby secretly. All she could tell Ludwig openly was that she was planning a trip to Italy, but not that she intended to stay away until at least February of the following year. The remainder of her letter answered his questions about Felix. Her old friend the Princess Esterhazy had written that Felix's family would probably agree to their marriage.

Stieler called upon me on his return and told me that Felix's father often came to him at Vienna and spoke of nothing but me, asked a thousand questions of my manner of life here, whether *you* really took as great an interest in my fate as people said, and many other things . . .

. . . You ask if I love him still. Alas, yes, and I feel convinced I shall never be able to marry another. There exists something in a first passion, especially in one such as mine has been, *which has dared all and sacrificed all* for its object, that no time, no subsequent ill treatment can efface.[40]

During that summer she travelled south through the glorious scenery of the Alps with a small party consisting of her personal maid Emma, her daughter Didi and nursemaid, the little dog given by Ludwig which she called Tuilly and another puppy given her by Ludwig's mother. Behind her followed the luggage coach with all the comforts essential for enjoyable travel; fine bedlinen, crystal and plate, a full wardrobe, painting materials, a small library of books. These precepts had been instilled in her at an early age by her mother on a previous journey through Italy. Jane's letters to Ludwig, through a go-between called Monsieur Kreutzer, are full of rapturous descriptions of her travels, as well as news of Felix, who had 'once more created a sparkle of hope in my heart that one day he will return to love me. I have just received a letter in which he speaks of a future.' She was convinced that 'sooner or later I shall reap the rewards of patience in a union with him that I have so long worshipped.'[41]

In September she began to make excuses for her delayed return, relying on the King's own passion for Italy for his understanding, and assuring him in a letter from Naples that 'it was not my intention to go further than Genoa. There, however, as I still continued not very well, the physician ordered me to try a sea voyage, and as I dislike any undertaking without an object, I embarked in a vessel for Sicily.' At this point she felt she could no longer keep from Ludwig the fact that she was not alone.

And now I must tell you what greeted my arrival [at Genoa]. Baron von Venningen has followed me day and night, travelling under a different name . . . when he heard I had left or was about to leave Genoa for Sicily, he could no longer endure the separation, combined with the idea that I was now alone in Italy.

By abandoning his affairs he has added this proof of his devotion to all the rest. I confess that his unceasing love, in spite of all my refusals, touches my heart, without inspiring that *passion* it is in my nature to feel. I tell him that before I can give the least hope or answer to his constant prayer for marriage everything must be finally settled between me and

Felix, and that also I *must* see the latter once more. You are the only person to whom I shall mention these circumstances.[42]

The King received this information uneasily, suspecting that her journey with Charles had been prearranged. In her subsequent letter from Palermo in northern Sicily, however, Jane denied this: 'I give you my word it was not ... He begged to come, it is true, but I positively refused on account of the world, and principally of Felix [who writes] that he will see me as soon as he can leave Berlin.' However, she reiterated that the baron's devotion had touched her and disposed her to listen to his proposal that *should* she decide to marry, she would marry him. She reminded the King that he himself had told her that passionate love such as she had felt for Felix 'was not necessary in marriage'. She now accepted that principle, 'but the time for decision is not yet come. Should I marry, I would fain make him a good wife, and that I feel I am not yet prepared to do. Felix, in spite of all, is still too dear.'[43]

In fact Felix had just written in great irritation that she should 'bury herself' and his daughter in so remote a place as Palermo. Perhaps, after all, he believed there might be something in her threat of entering a convent. He said he had sent a draft of £400 to his bank at Naples in case she should want for money while there, and he would try to arrange a time when they could meet. Jane had received similar promises on previous occasions; she returned the money.[44]

Meanwhile, since there was nothing she could do about her condition and she was committed to remaining in Palermo for some months at least, she decided to enjoy her time there. She rented a house under an assumed name, though her identity was known to the Austrian consul, a friend of Felix Schwarzenberg. She spent her time sketching and taking lessons from a singing master. As usual she quickly attracted a small court of admirers and several proposals (to Charles's fury), one from a young French aristocrat and one from a Sicilian, who several times managed to enter her house disguised variously as a friar, a woodcutter, a travelling musician and a milk-seller. She insisted to Ludwig, however, that 'I have forgotten none of my promises, although temptation is not wanting here'.

The Baron is still at Palermo and intends remaining probably as long as I do. I must confess I have the greatest reason to praise his conduct towards me in every respect; he dreams of marriage and I should be ungrateful if I were totally insensible to such tried and constant devotion. But alas! in love I am not, and while Felix continues to write as he does, assuring me that he is not extinguished, I fear much I never can be.[45]

During December, when Jane was eight months pregnant, she heard from Felix that he intended to visit his sister in Italy, and she wrote to Ludwig that a meeting had at last been arranged. She had recently received a letter from a mutual friend which stated that all the barriers to marriage with her were in Felix's imagination. This forced her to conclude that Felix had never desired to marry her; 'if that is so, my pride must conquer my too long victorious passion.'[46] And if, she wrote, on meeting Felix she was able to say that passionate love no longer existed between them, she would probably marry Charles. She felt unable to be more precise, for despite everything Felix wrote regularly 'as though he still considered me his property. [And] I cannot be entirely free from all engagements towards him, particularly as much must be settled first with regard to his child.'[47]

On 27 January 1833 a healthy boy, Herberto, was born. There were no complications and as usual Jane recovered rapidly. The child was registered with the Austrian consul at Palermo, Signor Antonio de Laurin, simply as the son of 'LJD',[48] and placed in the care of foster parents. This arrangement had been made some months in advance and would last for three years, until Jane considered it safe to reveal the child's existence. As before, Jane liked the baby well enough but there was no fierce rush of joy, no maternal urge. She had not wished for this child any more than she had wished for the previous two; if anything, he was an embarrassment.

Her letters to Ludwig, written in reply to the King's frequent enquiries about her return, mention nothing of her confinement, though she took care to warn him that all his letters 'are received opened and fumigated!'[49] She advised him that she intended leaving Palermo in April but before returning to Italy she wished to tour Sicily, after which she expected to see Felix in Rome. This plan was changed when Felix wrote from Nice in March saying that he could no longer accommodate the appointment in his schedule; however, he would be grateful if Jane would instead join his sister Mathilde in Rome for the months of April and May. 'Is this not extraordinary?' Jane wrote in anguish:

> could he not have done more when we were on the best footing together, whereas now I am no longer his mistress, nor even engaged to him, he

volunteers to introduce me to his unmarried sister . . . [Still], the visit must have the good effect of justifying me as to the supposed cause of our rupture at Paris, as no one with common sense would believe after that, that he would seek my connection with his sister.

Something in the King's letter, which has not survived, prompted her to add a plea: 'one thing alone I beg, dearest Lewis, give [the Marchesa] no promises concerning me. The *first* place I yield, however reluctantly. The *second* – may it not be mine?'[50]

In the weeks between her confinement and her proposed visit to Italy, Jane settled down to enjoy the time she had left in Sicily. She threw off all care, and with the joy of a healthy young woman, her body no longer hampered by pregnancy, she pursued her ambition to tour the island. For the first time in years she felt truly happy.[51] In late April she arrived in Rome, where Charles and Jane parted after some eight months of constant companionship. Charles travelled on to his home near Baden and the duties he had abandoned to pursue Jane, while she went with renewed optimism to visit Princess Mathilde.

The visit lasted a month, and, when Jane left, the princess begged her to allow little Mathilde to remain with her until she returned to Austria. It may have been a deliberate attempt to sever Jane's last tie with her brother but in her letters Jane gives no hint that the visit had been unpleasant, nor that Felix's sister had been unfriendly towards her. She stated that she was making her way to a German spa town where the prince was shortly expected. Subsequently, Didi was taken to Princess Mathilde's home in Austria and grew up without any recollection of her mother, believing she was the adopted orphan of friends of the princess.[52]

From Rome, Jane travelled to the western borders of Germany, but she missed Felix and went to Paris, arriving there on 10 July 1833 with the primary intention of consulting a doctor, possibly regarding some complication arising from her recent confinement,[53] and also to meet her mother. Jane had no desire to prolong her stay in the French capital but it was restful to discuss her problems with someone on whom she could truly rely. She felt dispossessed, beginning to accept at last that the break with Felix was probably irrevocable and to realise that, despite having borne four children, the manner in which she had conducted her life had rendered her to all intents and purposes childless and rootless. Yet she still loved Felix; could she, *should* she marry Charles, feeling as she did? These questions haunted her, she told the King. Quite naturally her family strongly urged her to accept the baron and forget Felix. Steely, who had been told everything, also wrote unequivocally that she should take the opportunity of a fresh start. As to the prince, Steely wrote:

> Nothing will ever persuade me that he regrets the steps he took. Be assured that it is a matter of rejoicing with him that his fate was never linked with yours. *Self is his first idol.* You would have marred his ambition, had you even devoted your entire life to him, and such a conviction would have estranged his heart in no lengthened space of time.[54]

By the time Jane left Paris – which, she told Ludwig, she did gladly, for she now heartily disliked the city – she had made a decision to marry Charles, provided the appropriate dispensations to satisfy German law were forthcoming. Yet even then she insisted on giving Felix a further opportunity to return to her by advising him that she intended to marry Venningen *if he did not want her.* It seems inconceivable that she still was not convinced that Felix had written her off. But when she received no reply Jane found herself committed to marrying Charles simply because she liked him and was grateful to him.

She did not return to Munich from Paris but rented a house at Heilbronn, 'a stupid place', she wrote to Ludwig. She had chosen it for two reasons: it was close to where Charles was living at Schloss Grombach; and it was 'on the high road towards Felix, *if* I am ever to see him again'. Felix was now 'permanently at Berlin. His ambition seems at length on the eve of being gratified.' It was for this ambition, Felix had written Jane, that he had 'sacrificed' his relationship with her, though 'I doubt his being happy,' she noted miserably; 'at least his letters prove the contrary.'[55]

As the summer passed, Jane felt herself being sucked inexorably into a marriage of convenience with Charles. There was gentle pressure from her parents, who regarded the Venningen connection as a lifeline towards the restoration of Jane's social status, loving pressure from Charles, who wanted to make a home for her and his son, and now, apparently, royal pressure from Ludwig, who signified that though he longed to see her he thought it best that she should first 'positively settle and decide' about marriage to the baron.[56]

Jane's reservations about marriage without passionate love were many. However, she reasoned, she could never again expect to love as she loved Felix, and Felix seemed lost to her for ever. She had many correspondents in the courts of Europe and from them she knew that the prince had enjoyed several serious liaisons. The most serious, which dated from his time in Paris, was with Madame la Vaudeuil, whom he had installed as his mistress in Berlin where he had recently been appointed Imperial Ambassador.[57] While Jane was still agonising over him, Schwarzenberg visited London where a mutually advantageous interview with Lord Palmerston took place.[58] The prince's role as co-respondent in the sensational Ellenborough divorce, legally proven only two years earlier, was already forgotten. Henceforward he would always be a welcome visitor in top political circles in England. But Jane remained permanently *persona non grata*.[59]

At present, as she well knew, gossip linked Felix with another woman, a Countess Zappani, at the spa town where the prince was staying after his trip to England. Yet, despite knowledge of his latest affair, and everything that had happened during the past years, she found it impossible to give up her dream of marriage to him – even though she knew the baron's 'real worth', was confident in his love for her, and had a high regard for him. Indeed, she admitted to Ludwig that 'few women have before them a better *chance* of happiness in marriage than myself, if I can once summon the courage to take the great resolution.'[60] Nevertheless there was always at the back of her mind a hope that Felix would send for her. And at every stage on the road of her marriage to Charles she was always prepared to run to Felix had he given the slightest indication that he would welcome her back.

8

Ianthe's Secret
1833–1835

Because of Ludwig's personal intervention, the Grand Duke of Hesse-Darmstadt (Ludwig's cousin and overlord of the Venningens) agreed to overlook Jane's unusual marital status and allow her marriage to Charles to go forward without delay.[1] It is clear that Felix, with his own important connections, might have engineered a similar solution had he ever desired to do so.

For over two years the prince had written regularly to Jane, keeping her hopes alive with declarations of love and his casual acceptance that she was bound to him. It is worth recalling that his reason for abandoning Jane and their daughter in Paris was Jane's so-called unfaithfulness with Monsieur Labuteau. This story of Jane's infidelity had been assiduously spread about by members of Felix's family in Paris and Vienna, and several contemporary diarists, including Count Apponyi, reported it, apparently believing it to be true. Undoubtedly the very source of the rumour gave it credence.

But Jane had always maintained she was innocent of the charge and now, with every right to protect the honour of the woman to whom he was betrothed, Charles took action. He wrote to Felix challenging him to a duel unless he formally denied the stories. Some weeks earlier Jane had written to Felix informing him of her forthcoming marriage and hinting strongly that even at this eleventh hour she would drop all her plans for him. Felix's reply to Charles served as a reply to both letters. He completely denied ever having suspected Jane of unfaithfulness; they had parted, he said, merely because their 'tempers were incompatible'. He sent his good wishes for their marriage.[2]

This response might have infuriated Jane, but such anger as she felt was tinged with bitterness and misery, revealed in a note to Ludwig which commented: 'Felix Schwarzenberg seems to have succeeded in his mission; his ambition is now gratified and he is free from me! He has written a letter to the Baron at which I am surprised, but it only shows what conscience and injustice can force from a man at last.'[3] Her frequent letters to the King at this time plainly reveal her hesitancy and her unease with regard to marrying Charles, feeling that 'marriage is an awful engagement' without passionate commitment between two people. However, she could not ignore or deny Charles's steady devotion to her (nor, of course, the child they had created), and Ludwig assured her that it was possible to be contentedly married without the intense and delirious love that she (and apparently he) had experienced outside marriage. Furthermore, her family were pleased at the news. Her father (who despite his love for her had not really forgiven her for divorcing Ellenborough and causing the family so much obloquy) had come over from England for the ceremony, signalling his reconciliation, and bearing a document stating that her previous marriage had been annulled. This cleared the path for Jane's Catholic marriage to Charles.

Yet she could not rid herself of her qualms. She had been obsessed with Felix Schwarzenberg for five years, though they had lived together happily for only a year during that time. Now, against her better judgement, she was drifting into marriage with Charles. There was no doubting her good intention to 'make Charles a good wife', and when at last she made the final decision, as she wrote to the King, it cost her much pain: 'but I felt it was not honourable to trespass longer on the Baron's patience and affection.'[4]

Somewhat surprisingly, in view of his earlier antagonism towards her relationship with the baron, Ludwig now indicated his approval of the marriage by conferring upon the bridegroom the honorary office of chamberlain.[5] This thoughtful compliment ensured the couple's active participation in court life, ending at a stroke the social ostracism Jane had endured for several years.

The baron was gratified at the bestowal of the honour, for though, as he wrote, he brought with him 'the wealth of five seignorial and nobleman's [sic] rights in the Rhineland-Palatinate ... I really am in the greatest embarrassment over the numerous nuisances I have caused Your Majesty in the past.' In particular he was concerned about an unspecified incident involving Jane at Nymphenburg Palace which he believed had severely displeased the King.[6] In fact the King was puzzled as to what Charles referred to and asked Jane for clarification. In her uninformative reply Jane thanked Ludwig prettily for the honour which would be the means of her appearing at court, recalling that they had 'often spoken of this' in the past. 'One fear, however, remains in my mind,' she said, 'and that is how I shall be received by society. Not that I care for myself, but I dread the Baron's mortification if he finds I am looked down upon . . . which I suspect notwithstanding.'[7]

In a letter dated 3 November, written from The Hague, Jane received a final note from Felix. Expressing with cold formality his approval of Jane's engagement he stated that he was returning all her presents with the exception of a sketch of Didi, which he asked to be allowed to keep. He undertook to destroy all her letters to him, every one of which, he said, he had kept near him. Jane had kept his too; indeed, she still had all 200 of them in her possession when she died, almost fifty years later.[8]

Jane and Charles were married by the Bishop of Rothenburg, in the prescribed triple wedding ceremonies that satisfied civic and ecclesiastic conventions, on 16 November 1833 at Darmstadt in the Rhine Valley where the Venningen family owned several estates. Admiral Digby was a witness at the Protestant marriage service and at the civil ceremony later in the day. A Catholic service was held a few days later. His daughter was twenty-six years old, looked younger, and was even more ravishingly lovely than the virginal seventeen-year-old he had given away almost a decade earlier. He must have been only too aware that the bride was capable of changing her mind at the last minute and disappearing. It can only have been a great relief to Admiral Digby to know that Jane was safely married to a good man who clearly worshipped her and could provide her with a lifestyle not too dissimilar to that which she had so precipitately tossed aside. Conversely, Charles's widowed mother made no secret of the fact that she opposed the match, and withheld her approval.

On the eve of the first marriage ceremony Jane wrote to the King, telling him that, although she was reconciled to the marriage,

many, many subjects upon which I can speak with you *alone* are still in my heart. My best and *Dearest* Friend, what I am *now*, what my resolutions

now are, is *your work*. Without you I should have been inevitably lost . . .
Never shall I forget you, and let me, Dearest Lewis, once more say,
perhaps for the last time before I am chained to another, that your noble,
generous, conduct towards me on one occasion made a deeper, more
indelible impression on my heart than a thousand triumphs of vanity or
self love, and made you dearer than a thousand lovers. Would I could
prove my devotion in deeds not words.[9]

Jane and the King had not met since Munich a year and a half
earlier, and during that time the pair had written many letters to
each other. Now they could hardly wait to see each other. 'Your own
Ianthe is quite wild with impatience,' Jane wrote. If he would let her
know when he planned to call on her she would ensure that everyone
was sent away and she would be quite alone to receive him. 'You
cannot conceive the delight', she finished, 'with which I look forward
to the bliss of seeing you once more!'[10]

Three weeks after their marriage Charles and Jane left their castle
at Weinheim, about ten miles north-west of Heidelberg,[11] and after
a cold, slow journey arrived late on a December evening in Munich.
Attached to a posy of violets Jane found a note from the King, suggesting that he call on her later. Her response was warm and
immediate. 'Dearest, *dearest*, how happy I shall be to see you!'[12] Basily
and Ianthe picked up their relationship where they had left off, with
frequent meetings and notes and posies of violets. They wrote of whom
they had seen and of court gossip; they liaised with each other over
which play or opera performance or whose ball they would attend,
to be sure of seeing each other daily. When the Queen suddenly
consented to receive Jane at court, Jane begged the King to meet her
near the palace, 'at Tambosi's [coffee shop] . . . to which there is a
quiet entrance by the arches', to tell her what she should say and
do.[13]

An Englishman acquainted with the Coke family, who visited the
Bavarian court in February 1834, was intrigued to see the former
Lady Ellenborough in an elevated and respected position there and
he was in no doubt as to her present relationship with the King.

she has married a Bavarian Baron whose name I can neither remember
nor pronounce. She is received at court and everywhere. The ladies of
the Bavarian Almack's know all about her pranks and say the poor child
was sacrificed in marriage in London to an old, rich, ugly Lord. Her
liaison with the King is never denied.[14]

It soon became an assumption that Jane's marriage to the baron had been arranged for the convenience of King Ludwig; indeed, this quickly came to be the accepted view in England.[15]

Jane had lost her earlier unquestioning delight in the *haut ton*; no doubt it had been a lesson well learned. But she loved dancing and there were balls several times a week; she enjoyed meeting new people, especially anyone who travelled or painted, and she was a popular hostess who entertained elegantly. Apart from her daily rides upon her spirited thoroughbred, aptly named Mazeppa after a favourite poem by Byron,[16] and frequent meetings with the King, she enjoyed to the full all available social diversions such as the opera and theatre. her letters confirm that she was still painting: 'I send you this drawing and I am only sorry it is not better worthy of your acceptance,' she wrote to Ludwig. And there is a hint that their relationship had assumed, outwardly at least, a more discreet appearance: 'Take care not to increase your cold for if you are confined to the house, could I again come to see you as in former days? I fear you would answer, "No, Ianthe".'[17]

In April 1834 she sought his advice on how to handle the tricky matter of 'my sweet-tempered mother-in-law', who had invited Jane to her ancient castle at Grombach in order, she assumed, to seek a *rapprochement*. Jane had no desire to leave the delights of Munich. Furthermore, she had met the dowager on previous occasions and found her aloof and formidable. But she had little option other than to accept the invitation, and though Charles was to accompany her Jane was genuinely apprehensive. The meeting was as difficult as she feared; 'nothing could have been stiffer', Jane reported to Ludwig from Grombach. Both her mother-in-law and sister-in-law, Mimi Waldkirk, tried 'every possible means to estrange Charles and me'. In the same letter she also broke the news that she was again pregnant, but warned him to address his reply and future letters to 'the Baroness Venningen née Jane Digby' so that there could be no misunderstanding: 'I would not have either of those *cats* should have the pretence of opening them.'[18]

From her own home at Weinheim, a month later, she wrote that

unless any alteration occurs I intend to be confined at Weinheim. Tell me, dear friend, if I may name it after you. It would be a great honour ... to the Baron as to me if you would be Godfather, but if disagreeable to you for any other reason that may not occur to me at present, of course you will tell me with the frankness that has always reigned between us.[19]

The child Jane was bearing had been conceived in December 1833, shortly after her arrival in Munich. In asking to be allowed to name it after Ludwig, Jane was following in the footsteps of the Marchesa, whose son Ludovico, born in October 1821, was widely believed to be Ludwig's child. Ludwig generously agreed to Jane's request,[20] though he must have known that it would give rise to the belief that her child was a royal bastard. Jane too was surely aware of this, as is clear from underlined hints in several letters that she would forbear to call the child after him if it threatened to embarrass him. However, she wrote confidently, in August, 'as I shall be confined so far from Munich no gossip can arise on the subject . . . I shall hardly be confined before the beginning of September so there is plenty of time to let me know what you think.'[21]

Trapped once again by her own fertility, Jane found Weinheim picturesque, but dull. Local society was rather like Charles, likeable enough but lacking vitality. She longed for bright company and someone in whom to confide, she told Ludwig: 'Munich is the place of all others I love best but I can say with truth that you, my best and really true friend, are the charm that attaches me to it in so strong and peculiar a manner.'[22]

Jane was left alone for several weeks when Charles made a secret journey to Palermo to see their son, now referred to by his parents by the German version of his name, Heribert. He wrote to Jane of his discomfiture during the steamer journey from Naples, when he suddenly came face to face with his English cousin Lady Granville, and could think of no reason to give for his journey. However, little Heribert was well, Charles reported, and he was looking forward to the time when they might bring him home to Weinheim.

Jane's fifth child, a girl she called Bertha, was born in September 1834. It is impossible to know for sure who Bertha's father was but the childhood portrait in possession of the present-day Digby family bears no facial similarity to Charles Venningen, nor to the infant Heribert. Charles accepted the beautiful child as his, but the present-day Digbys suspect that the mental illness which descended upon Bertha in childhood, and which would confine her to an asylum before she was fully grown, was a Wittelsbach inheritance.[23] Surviving correspondence between Jane and Ludwig provides no answer, but as their channels of communication were not confidential this is perhaps not surprising. Throughout their relationship, messages of a truly delicate nature were communicated by the word of mouth of their most trusted servants. 'Do not fear, Emma will tell you more than I can write' was a typical note.[24]

Charles would have denied Jane little, but he steadfastly refused to allow her to go to Munich after Bertha's birth. Unfortunately this was the very thing that Jane wanted above anything; indeed, Charles's promises to her that she might have an establishment in Munich after their marriage had been one of the deciding factors in her decision to marry him.[25] The reason may have been simply that Charles could not spare the time to accompany Jane to Munich. During his eighteen months' courtship he had completely neglected his estates and given up what he described as 'a promising future' to follow her to Italy.[26] But it is more likely that he was jealous of her intimacy with the King, for, despite the fact that they were generally happy together, Jane and Charles bickered constantly on this subject. And without ever suggesting infidelity he accused her of behaving more like a giddy débutante than a married woman approaching middle age (she was twenty-seven) and mother of two young children.

Poor Charles must have been exceptionally short-sighted if he believed that his dear 'Jeane', as he called her, could be forced into the mould of *Hausfrau*. She was a creature of youth and gaiety, loving the banter, wit and intelligent discussion of salons, loving art, loving travel, loving people. It was these very qualities that had first drawn him to her. She found little fulfilment as chatelaine of Charles's great house, and exuberant rides around the surrounding countryside were the only outlet she found for the smothering boredom and restlessness she felt at Weinheim. Out of the gloomy mansion she created a charming home filled with laughter, but once she had finished decorating the house in her favourite French style of gilded pastels, replaced the old heavy German furniture with Chippendale and given instructions for English borders in the gardens, there was not enough to keep her occupied. She provided Charles with a happiness he had never known,[27] but Jane's *raison d'être*, the wish to live for a man with whom she was a twin soul, was frustrated. She wrote to the King of her wistful longing for Munich and himself, describing her affection for him as 'a feeling between exalted devotion and something more tender'.[28]

In the spring of 1835, after a long and quiet winter, Jane wrote to tell Ludwig of a visitor to Weinheim: 'During the absence of the Baron I made an interesting acquaintance in the person of M. de Balzac, the French author.'[29] Honoré de Balzac, already famous, was touring

Germany and Austria with Prince Alfred de Schönberg-Hartenstein, an old friend and admirer of Jane's. The prince was a junior diplomat when Jane first met him in Paris during 1830, and he had now risen to the rank of Envoy-Extraordinary to the Court of Württemberg. His younger brother married Felix Schwarzenberg's sister Aloyse, and it was through Prince Alfred (also a distant family connection of the Venningens) that Jane received much of her information about Felix. Balzac knew of Jane, or more accurately of her notoriety, for the family of Balzac's mistress, Evaline Hanska, lived in Vienna and were acquainted with the Schwarzenbergs. When offered the opportunity to meet Jane, Balzac accepted with alacrity.

For Jane the meeting relieved a tedious interlude while Charles was away. Her visitors stayed for a short time only, an afternoon spent mainly in the gardens – where the prince flirted outrageously with Jane, as he always did – followed by dinner; early next morning she rode with them as far as Heidelberg, and they continued on their journey. But Balzac, who once claimed that 'all fiction is symbolic biography', later admitted that 'Lady Ellenborough' provided the inspiration for one of his most colourful leading characters, lady Arabella Dudley, in *Le Lys dans la vallée*:

> this beautiful English lady, so slim, so fragile; this peaches and cream woman, so delicate, so gentle, with such a tender face crowned with shining, fawn coloured hair. This creature whose brilliancy seems phosphorescent and transient, has a constitution of iron.
>
> No horse, however fiery, can resist . . . her hand that appears so weak, and that nothing can tire. She has the foot of a roe, a small, hard, muscular foot of indescribable grace . . . no man can keep up with her on horseback . . . she shoots deer and stags without checking her horse.
>
> . . . her passion, too, is quite African; her desire speeds like a whirlwind in the desert, a desert whose burning space is portrayed in her eyes, a desert full of azure and love, with its unchanging sky, its cool starlit nights.[30]

Jane and Balzac met only on that one occasion. She subsequently wrote to him thanking him for the package he sent her, undoubtedly containing the manuscript (or part of it) of *Le Lys dans la vallée*, upon which he worked furiously after leaving Weinheim. The two never met again, and there is no foundation for the well-established belief that she was Balzac's mistress for a short period in Paris in 1831. The stories linking Jane romantically with Balzac and other colourful Parisian literary figures of the time have no substance – even though these accounts were previously accepted by most of Jane's biographers, and also by Balzac scholars who had not realised the existence of relevant material in the Wittelsbach archives. Jane's letters to the King and to Balzac, and Balzac's letters to his mistress, Madame Hanska, confirm that the limit of their acquaintance was confined to that one day in Weinheim.[31]

Balzac was a man over whom women frequently squabbled, though he was gross, unkempt, very often drunk and generally unfaithful. Perhaps his personality was as charismatic as his work, for he wrote like an angel. Clearly he spent his short time as Jane's guest in sharp observation. The result, his literary portrayal of Jane as Arabella, Lady Dudley, has been described as the most erotic female character in the whole of his *Comédie humaine*. Lady Arabella is introduced to the reader by Balzac's main character (coincidentally named Felix), who tells how he met her in a salon in the Elysée-Bourbon. She had an impeccable family background and was married to an English lord, far older than herself, 'one of the most eminent statesmen of England . . . stiff, cold, with the sneering air he wore in Parliament'.[32] The independently rich Arabella had borne two children but they had been left in England with their father. 'All these advantages were but accessories which enhanced the beauty of her person, her charms, her manners, her intelligence, an indescribable brilliancy which dazzled before fascinating. She was the idol of the day and reigned . . . over Parisian society.'

Balzac described her 'fatal notoriety', and 'she also possessed superiority of intellect; her satirical conversation embraced every subject.' She had a great rapport with all animals; her horses were thoroughbred Arabs and she never travelled in her barouche without her little dog. 'With horrible hypocrisy she kept up all the proprieties even while parading in the Bois' with her lover, Felix. Yet, 'when she loved, she loved with frenzy; no other woman of any country could compare with her, she was as good as an entire seraglio.'[33]

Lady Arabella resembled Jane in all but one respect. While Jane loved men as companions and friends, Arabella was – for all her physical charms – a hard and avaricious woman who used men ruthlessly and discarded them heartlessly. Balzac immortalised her as the vivid anti-heroine of his novel, the perfect foil for the gentle, virtuous heroine the 'lily of the valley' to whom Felix eventually returned.

Almost coinciding with the date of Balzac's visit to Weinheim another book was published in England by a former acquaintance of

Jane's, Marguerite, Countess of Blessington, under the title *The Two Friends*. It was transparently based on Jane's story, but the hero, Lord Arlington, closely resembled George Anson. Jane's family, who hoped when she married Charles that her past sins would be forgotten, were once again embarrassed by the publicity given the book's launch in the press.

In her letter to Balzac after his visit,[34] Jane revealed that her frequently expressed desire to return to Munich was about to be realised. However, the reason for it was 'most melancholy' as she later confided to the King. Her brother-in-law Philip Venningen was critically ill. Unfortunately, the court had already left Munich's summer heat for the Alps by the time Jane arrived there on 23 July, but she wrote to Ludwig immediately, saying that it would give her 'unspeakable pleasure' to see him again and asking when he planned to return. Meanwhile, though Munich was empty of virtually anybody of rank in the 'violent heat', she had toured the city, and told Ludwig: 'Since my last stay here Munich has greatly gained. The new buildings are quite magnificent.'[35]

It was early October 1835, before Ludwig returned officially to his capital, but before then, in late August, Basily had returned secretly on a brief visit to Ianthe. She had been afraid that her 'too long absence' might have chilled his regard for her, but he was as warmly affectionate as ever and the meeting made her 'unspeakably happy'. She referred to his visit several weeks later when she wrote to advise that they intended to stay for the Oktoberfest at least, and possibly remain for the winter, using the word 'love' in connection with her regard for the King. Conscious of his stern warnings about the security of their correspondence she wrote, 'A word has escaped my pen which ought to be retracted. I leave it because with you I have no need to disguise a feeling hardly to be defined. You know my well-founded reasons.'[36]

Years later long after their friendship had grown cold, Jane wrote in her diary of the King's sterling qualities, and in particular of his compassionate kindness. Whatever else he was, if Jane is to be believed, he was a good man. Meanwhile, in the autumn of 1835 they were still corresponding by long letter when they were apart, and by daily hand-delivered notes even when they were to see each other later in the day. 'Tomorrow I hope to have the happiness of seeing you in the tent, and probably tonight *at a distance* in the masked ball ... thanks for the violets,' Jane wrote during the Oktoberfest.[37] On one occasion she wrote to beg his assistance for the artist Heiss, who had completed a portrait of her during the summer months; it was sited badly at the Festival exhibition and 'I thought you could make it have a better place.'[38]

Within a month of such inconsequential chatter Jane had been whisked away from the diversions of Munich to the tedious isolation of their country estate. It was, as Jane used to say as a child, 'all most provocative and bothersome'. The reason was Jane's relationship with a dashing Greek count named Spiridon Theotoky, whom she had met at a masked ball in one of the Oktoberfest tents. He is first mentioned archly by her in a note to Ludwig regarding a ball to be held that night: 'I find the *dangerous* Ct. Theotoky is not invited, but that will not prevent me amusing myself as I did at the first carnival ... Many, many thanks for the violets.'[39] Charles found his wife's style of amusing herself singularly unfunny. Ludwig departed on a state visit to Greece and the Venningens left a few days afterwards. They were in Weinheim before the end of November.

Jane's immediate feeling was one of irritation at having been removed from all that was bright and charming, and not least from the proximity of the dangerous Count Theotoky. But as the days wore on she realised more and more that it was the latter she missed most of all.

9

A Duel for the Baroness
1836–1840

Count Spiridon Theotoky was all that Charles Venningen was not. He was tall, dashing, confident and talented – in fact, another Felix Schwarzenberg. Like Felix he had finely chiselled handsome features, liquid dark eyes and a charismatic charm. At twenty-four, Theotoky was four years younger than Jane and had not a care in the world, his entire life being given over to enjoying himself. He was the son of a noble Corfiote family, but he had no resources to speak of beyond some family property in Corfu. He appeared at Ludwig's court wearing his national costume at a carnival ball. Jane was a moth to his flame.

From all surviving evidence it appears that the attraction was not one-sided. Spiros (as Jane quickly came to call him) was used to women falling in love with him and was experienced, for all his youth. But he had never met anyone like Jane. He found the radiant young baroness, apparently a close friend of the King, the most desirable creature in a court of beautiful women. Around her gathered the brightest society, the most personable men, drawn by the same fascination as Theotoky experienced. What was more, she spoke Italian, French and even a little Greek, and was an intelligent conversationalist, especially on the subject of classical art and Greek mythology.

When Ludwig's second son Otto was proclaimed King of Greece in 1832, all the important positions of state and government in Greece were immediately filled by Bavarians. Subsequently there was an exchange of talented men between the two countries. Bavarians, particularly artists and builders who had found full occupation under Ludwig, as well as civil servants and military experts, were shipped to Greece to help Otto to achieve his (and probably his father's) hopelessly romantic dream of creating a city that would mirror the greatness of ancient Athens. Ludwig's court played host, meanwhile, to ambitious young Greeks with an eye to the future. They travelled to Bavaria to make contacts and to learn about the culture, military matters and German language, that were clearly going to be over-printed upon their own. Spiridon Theotoky was one such.

Although he was part of a mission, he appears to have had no formal brief that required his constant attendance at court, so that when the Venningens suddenly left Munich for Weinheim he too was able to depart. He took the same road and found himself lodgings in Heidelberg.

From the moment Jane and Spiros met, it seems, there was an intense attraction between them. Since her marriage Jane had lived a life of decorous pretence, but in his company she felt her own personality re-establish itself. The happy disorientation she describes would these days probably be termed a sexual *frisson*, but Jane believed she had rediscovered the passionate ideal of love that she had known with Felix and thought never to experience again.

She had promised herself that she would make Charles 'a good wife', and according to him she had more than fulfilled that vow, whether or not she had been Ludwig's lover. But, being the sort of woman she was, Jane could not help herself when she met Theotoky. She hungered for him. 'Being loved', she would tell the King, 'is to me as the air I breathe.' With hindsight, it is easy to see that Charles played his hand badly. He ought to have allowed Jane to indulge in a flirtation or even an affair with Theotoky at court, where Ludwig's influence (if not his immediate presence) might have ensured a degree of circumspection. Separating the two merely introduced an element which almost always fuels, rather than dampens, illicit romance.

Within days of the Venningens' return to Weinheim, Spiros Theotoky had also arrived in the neighbourhood. Jane flew to him or, rather, rode to him on her horse Mazeppa. She was no longer the raw adolescent setting out in a romantic haze to meet her princely lover in Harley Street. She was a mature woman, fully awakened to the joys of sexual communion.

For a few weeks they were able to conceal their affair from Charles.

Jane habitually rode out each day, and under cover of this routine exercise she was able to meet Spiros. Local legends grew up about the baroness's 'reckless rides' through the forest to meet her Greek lover. Their meetings during the day were insufficient; tales spread of how she slipped out of her house after her husband and children were asleep, saddled her horse and rode through the night to Spiros, returning home as dawn broke.

Less than a month after his return to Weinheim, however, Charles found out about Jane's affair. Until then, he wrote to Jane, he had been the happiest man alive, but 'after December 5th, 1835, all my happiness was destroyed'.[1] In a letter to Evaline Hanska, a month later in January 1836, Balzac wrote to say that he had seen the Princess Schönberg (Felix Schwarzenberg's sister) in Paris:

> I met her in the garden yesterday, and we talked about Vienna . . . She told me that Lady E[llenborough] has just run off with a Greek, and that Prince Alfred had prevented her going further than Stuttgart. Her husband came, fought the Greek and took his wife home again. What an extraordinary woman![2]

Stuttgart is over a hundred miles south-east of Weinheim, at a major junction on the high road; one fork leads to the south and Zurich, the other to the east and Munich. It seems inconceivable that Jane would have bolted with Spiros, leaving Charles and her children, after an affair that can have lasted a few weeks at the outside; and that in eloping she had the bad luck to run into Prince Alfred Schönberg in Stuttgart. Yet the incident quickly became the talk of court in Vienna, where Jane's old admirer, Count Apponyi, heard it from his Schwarzenberg and Schönberg contacts and wrote a more detailed report in his diary.

Prince Alfred, it seems, having met the lovers, delayed them while sending a warning message to his kinsman the baron. Apponyi writes that Charles overtook the lovers on the road, stopped them and pulled Theotoky from the coach, demanding satisfaction by duel to the death. For Charles it was the only honourable solution, according to the strict aristocratic code he had learned as a student at Heidelberg. He had been educated to believe that a wronged man could seek redress in such a manner, and he had undeniably been wronged.

Spiros Theotoky was disadvantaged here; no swordsman, and having no formal training in the art of duelling, he was understandably reluctant to oblige the baron. Nevertheless, a short time later, with the coachmen standing in as bewildered seconds, husband and lover faced each other along the barrels of Charles's duelling pistols. Apponyi adds a nice touch to the picture of Jane standing by in anguish, loving both men in different ways and knowing that if one were killed it would be all her fault.

Spiros nervously fired early and missed. How gallant he would have appeared to history had he deliberately fired wide. Unfortunately it seems he missed because he was a poor shot; Jane would have done far better. Charles fired immediately after and found his mark. Spiros fell to the ground, bleeding profusely from a wound just above his left breast, apparently mortally wounded. Jane was distraught, says Apponyi, and flung herself weeping upon the bloody victim. Charles, though filled with grim satisfaction, was pale with shock. It was not the first time he had offered to fight a duel on Jane's behalf, but it was the first time anyone had taken up his challenge. It was certainly the first time he had mortally wounded his man.

To his credit, Spiros, with what he and his companions believed to be his dying breaths, attempted to assuage the wrath that would almost certainly be Jane's lot after his demise.

> He then declared to the husband that he was innocent, and the victim of the most infamous calumny. He insisted that between him and the Baroness there had never been anything beyond a deep and sincere friendship. Then he clasped the hand of his friend, and with a deep sigh, shut his eyes.[3]

In his own words, Charles could not believe that a man could be 'capable of lies or deception . . . at a time like this . . . a dying man about to appear before the eternal judge who reads our hearts and who knows the innermost recesses of a human heart'[4] and began to think he had perhaps acted too hastily. Apponyi eloquently delineates Charles's dilemma. If Theotoky were telling the truth, the lovers were eloping at the start of an affair, not culminating a liaison. If, as it seemed, he had killed an innocent man, Charles, as a man of honour, could not continue to live. By the code he was bound to turn his pistol upon himself.

Fortunately he and Jane had their hands too full with the swooning and bleeding young man for him to take this point of nicety any further. Jane, frantic, called upon Charles and the coachmen to load Spiros into the coach. Apponyi tells us they took him a hundred miles back to Weinheim, where Jane nursed him. It was hardly a month since Theotoky had entered their lives.

Under Jane's dedicated nursing, the healthy young Greek rapidly recovered from his wound and on 26 February Count Apponyi, who was staying in Paris, recorded in his diary that 'I could hardly believe my eyes upon seeing Lady Ellenborough . . . in the Place Louis XV giving her arm to a very handsome young man.' He did not think the young man fitted the description of Charles Venningen, and so, having heard of the duel, concluded that Jane's companion was Spiros Theotoky. 'Here are the three of them, who, instead of returning to Munich, take the road to Paris under false names, but not disguised, which means that one has no trouble in identifying them in the street, or in a public square as happened to me.'[5]

It seems surprising that Charles, with his fierce jealousy of Jane, would willingly have travelled to Paris with Theotoky in his party, but he apparently did so. The very next day, 27 February 1836, Jane wrote to Ludwig from Paris, having received a letter from him full of descriptions of his travels in Greece and Turkey which delighted her. 'How I envy you . . . I am still living in hopes that one day it will be my turn!' Jane remarked. 'We are here on our way to fetch Heribert who must now be at Marseille and we shall probably return to Weinheim in the beginning of April. Father and mother intend spending this summer there with us.'[6] When Ludwig wrote, he had still not heard of Jane's affair with Theotoky; apart from the travelogue, his main subject was a plea to Jane that she should make him a new embroidered cap because the old one she had made him was worn out.

In the meantime the three players in the drama reached an agreement. Jane promised to remain with Charles and her children. Spiros agreed to return to Greece via Marseille. It was convenient that the Venningens were travelling there anyway to meet Heribert. For the time being, Spiros disappeared from Jane's life.

Ludwig wrote to Jane as he passed through Paris on his return from Greece to Munich in June. Undoubtedly he soon heard the story of Theotoky and the duel, for he did not answer several subsequent letters. From his silence throughout the summer and autumn Jane knew that she had hurt him and probably lost his friendship. So when in December Charles, in Munich on business, wrote saying that he had seen the King, who had mentioned her kindly, she immediately sent a letter to Ludwig:

Sire!

Your Majesty will no doubt be surprised if not displeased at receiving these lines. You will say, 'My silence ought to make her understand my wish that all correspondence should end' and I had thus interpreted it. [But] the Baron's last letter mentioned having seen you and that you had charged him with your remembrance to me, and that you regretted you could see me no more at Munich...

Much as the idea of never seeing your Majesty again pains me more deeply than I can ever express, still I would not for worlds [have]... you think that in Munich I regret aught else than that attachment I so highly prized, and which I have now lost...

There are some sentiments no time, no circumstances can efface, and such are those which must forever bind my heart in deepest attachment to Your Majesty, and make it impossible for me to be in a place where I should daily see you pass me by with indifference, if not aversion... Accept the warmest wishes for your happiness from her who has for years never ceased to *love* and revere you. Believe me... even should I never, never have the bliss of beholding you again,

Your Majesty's most devotedly attached
and truly affectionate
Ianthe[7]

There was no reply, and throughout that dreary winter and the following spring Jane attempted to come to terms with her changed life. Her heart was not in the struggle, of course. Her heart lay under the hot Greek skies described by the man who had reawakened her passion. As a result she and Charles quarrelled frequently. She was no longer the cheerful 'Jeane' she had always been prior to her meeting and Theotoky and, as couples in such a situation will, they said bitter things to each other. Jane was driven to remind her husband that she had told him many times before their marriage that she did not love him in the romantic sense. It had been he who insisted on marriage, not her. Charles later admitted that he too had 'said harsh things... I did not always behave well towards you.' But he justified himself: 'It was caused by the despair which invaded my soul and gnawed at my heart.'[8]

It was not until the following July that Jane heard again from the King. Chiding her for the 'cold respect' with which she had addressed him as 'Sire' in her December letter, he chatted about his busy life and asked her to let him know how she was. Jane's melancholia is obvious in the reply she made on 18 July 1837, when she reverted, at his request, to her usual form of address:

My Dearest Friend,

. . . The Baron and I go on what the world may call 'well' together; the difference that exists in our characters cannot be changed. His *really* noble qualities are justly appreciated and esteemed by me. I am attached to him from affection and habit, but between ourselves his want of *demonstration* and *warmth* of feeling stifles a passion I fain would feel, and which once felt and *returned* would prevent my wandering even in thought to other objects.

The misfortune of my nature is to consider 'Love' as *all in all*. Without this feeling, life is a dreary void. No earthly blessing can compensate its loss, and having at first setting out in life sacrificed *all*, without regret, to one great and absorbing passion the necessity of loving and *being loved* is to me as the air I breathe and the sole cause of all I have to reproach myself with.[9]

Her letter was written on the eve of her departure for England with the two children. Initially, Charles was to have accompanied her to spend the summer with her parents in what appears to have been a last-ditch attempt by this good and decent man to save his marriage, and to help Jane through a difficult patch. But his business affairs were difficult and he could not leave Germany. Jane was received pleasantly by her family in England, according to a letter she wrote to Ludwig, and by 'almost all my old friends' such as Lord Londonderry. Her brother Edward had recently married Theresa, daughter of Lord Ilchester, and Kenelm was Vicar of Tittleshall, the living of which was in the gift of his grandfather Coke, now created the Earl of Leicester by the new Queen. Jane did not visit her grandfather, indeed she never saw him nor even corresponded with him again.[10]

However, in Jane's letter to Ludwig, written before she departed for England, she mentioned her intention to call upon her former husband. 'I wish, if possible, to induce Lord Ellenborough to enter into another arrangement with me by which means I should possess a capital which I could employ in buying an estate in Bavaria instead of the pension he gives me. With his great fortune and no children it cannot to him make much difference.' Although no record exists of their meeting, Ellenborough clearly complied with Jane's request. At the time of his death in 1871 the only annuity he was providing for Jane was £360 a year. Jane's lavish lifestyle since her divorce from Ellenborough was not supported on £360, even taking into account the annual allowance her father made her and the small annuity from her grandfather. So the capital sum that must have been transferred by Ellenborough was never used to buy an estate in Bavaria but shrewdly invested by her father. Jane drew income from it for the remainder of her life. At one point her annual income from all sources was well over £3,000. This is an important factor for, according to the Bank of England, £1,000 in 1837 is the equivalent today of £34,450. Jane's future travels and adventures were therefore funded by an annual income of what today would be about £100,000 net.

Her meeting with Ellenborough may not have been an easy one, however. After her return to Germany Jane wrote that despite her kind reception by 'almost all' of her former friends she was glad to leave. 'England has too many painful associations for me to be sorry to quit it.'[11] Ellenborough would have known of Felix's abandonment of Jane and her subsequent marriage. He must have heard the rumours of her royal liaison which were rife in London. He and Jane were destined never to meet again, and on most occasions that Jane mentioned him in her diaries she hinted at his coldness.

The England that Jane saw in the summer of 1837 was not in mourning for William IV, who had died in June, but, rather, wild with enthusiasm for its new Queen. Jane had been twelve years old when Victoria was born and now this child had ascended the throne it seemed as though a breath of fresh air swept the country. Victoria was excluded by Salic law from dominion over Hanover, which passed to her uncle, the Duke of Cumberland, and her accession seemed to sweep from Great Britain the final traces of the Hanoverian era. Sweet, pretty and unspoiled, she was the antithesis of the gross and overindulgent sons of the old, 'mad' George III. A fresh start, a wave of revulsion for the sins of the flesh, rolled over the land. This would have been admirable were it not for the predictable piety and hyprocrisy that followed. Jane's sins were not forgotten, nor would they ever be forgiven.

Shortly after Jane returned from England in September 1837, the reason for her approach to Ellenborough became obvious. Charles sold the estate at Weinheim. During the years he had devoted to courting Jane he had neglected his inheritance, leaving it in the hands of agents who, he now discovered, had abused their position ever since. Creating for Jane the setting and lifestyle he thought would make her happy must have been a further heavy drain on his estate. When the true nature of his financial position was revealed, Charles was almost stupefied with anxiety. There was nothing for it but to sell off part of his property. Although the major proceeds of such a sale belonged to the entailed Venningen estate, an income would be generated for his family and save the expense of running the estate at Weinheim.

The couple subsequently moved to a family house in Mannheim, Charles steadfastly refusing to use Jane's money to assist him through his difficulties. It hurt him deeply to have to sell the estate he loved and where, before the appearance of Theotoky, he had known great happiness. The shame of his financial reverses was very great to him, but what caused him far greater distress was the fact that his marriage to Jane was inexorably coming to an end and he was powerless in the matter.[12]

When Jane wrote to Ludwig in January 1838 she mentioned nothing of her marital problems. Instead, she spoke of her dislike of Mannheim, whose inhabitants she found dull. She described some cheerful 'sledge parties', but the frozen winter landscape was bleak, and without riding there were few diversions. Mentioning that she and Charles might be passing through Munich in May *en route* to Austria on a matter of business, she reminded the King that it was two years since she had seen him and hoped it might be possible for them to meet.

It was the last letter she would write to Ludwig, and it reveals that Jane was still keeping to her resolution of trying to be a good wife to Charles and a good mother to their children, though the effort had depressed her spirit. But in the event there was no trip to Munich in May that year with Charles. Only a month after she wrote this letter Spiros Theotoky returned from Corfu and asked her to come away with him.

Jane could see before her an endless vista of domesticity, of cold dull winters, of growing old joylessly with the kind but stolid Charles, whose recent concern over finance had robbed him of any lightness of character he once possessed. The King appeared to have drawn away from her, and anyway Charles could not afford long periods spent in Munich with the court. Nor would his pride allow Jane to finance such diversions. But these were secondary considerations. Jane longed to be loved as she had loved Felix, as she now loved Spiros, and as he claimed he loved her.

Spiros's promises were irresistible. In them Jane glimpsed hot southern skies, white houses with cool stone floors and windows thrown wide to admit the summer breezes, the golden islands of Greece basking in turquoise seas; and was there a hint of nights scented with wild herbs, of loose robes, of wine, of lovers' murmurings? It was the call of passion that drove her to abandon her vows to Charles. But there was also the chance of freedom from the bonds of provincial German conventiality. Jane's spirit, likened by Balzac to a whirlwind in the desert, chose liberty.

Knowing that Charles would never willingly allow her to leave, she agreed to elope yet again. A ball was being held locally for visiting royalty and the event provided a suitable opportunity for their plans. Jane slipped away while Charles was engaged. Spiros was waiting close by with a carriage. They made directly for the French border thirty miles away, hoping to get across even though Jane's papers were not in order. Charles discovered their flight soon after they left and pursued their chaise, catching the errant pair at a post-house at the border town of Rastadt (now Rastatt).

This time there was no duel, but the verbal battle was more damaging. Charles would have done or said anything to keep Jane. He used every argument he could think of to change her mind, pointing out the inevitable permanent separation from the children, the further anguish and social embarrassment she would cause her family in England, Theotoky's lack of financial substance, Ludwig's reaction, her reputation. He might as well have saved his breath. In her mind, Jane had already accepted all these things and discounted them.

Her affection for Charles went deep, however. She agreed to his pleas that she should wait six months before taking the irrevocable step of leaving the country with Theotoky. But she refused to return home. Instead, in return for Charles's signature giving her permission to leave the country (under German law it was necessary for a wife to have her husband's permission to cross the border), Jane agreed to remain, living alone near the border.[13] Spiros was to return to live and work in Munich about a hundred miles away, and both men were to give her time and space for six months.

The three accordingly went their separate ways, Jane initially staying at Baden-Baden to recover from the traumatic events of the past days before moving to nearby Carlsburgh (now Karlsruhe). Charles wrote to her from Mannheim:

At the post-house in Rastadt I signed away all happiness in this world. There I rebelled for the last time against the harshness of my destiny.

What I suffered between 8 p.m. and 2 a.m. is beyond words. At present I am resigned, almost calm, or at least I hope to be soon. I have bowed my head and I shall no longer attempt to raise it.

At the moment my only preoccupation is with the planning of my children's future, of securing their fortune as far as possible. For the time being I cannot think beyond that. I will consider my own future later but I shall not trouble myself overmuch since I have no interest in anything, the shorter it is the better ... In spite of everything, it is your future, from which there is no escape, which causes me most pain ...

... farewell, dear ... Jeane. When the misfortunes which you are so blindly courting make your life difficult always come to me. The children are well and are always asking after their little mother ... Be happy![14]

Alas for Charles, when the agreed time elapsed Jane chose Spiros. She told Charles of her decision but remained at Carlsburgh until the following spring; occasionally Spiros stayed there but they were not living together. Charles visited her several times and their meetings 'though not conjugal were friendly'. As he told Jane's brother Edward, he sent Bertha to her, an 'amiable child ... as beautiful as an angel ... hoping that Jane would become attached to her'. But he overstepped the mark when, after some investigation, 'I revealed her lover to her in his true light. I told her that he had neither name, nor rank, nor fortune; nothing but a tarnished reputation.' And he lost her completely:

she has sent Bertha back to me and thrown herself headlong into the arms of this man without name without fortune and who has a very bad reputation. It was useless to try to stop her. She listened to nothing except her passion (but not her heart) and her hot-headedness ...

From her note [enclosed] you will see that I have returned everything to her, her diamonds, gold articles silver, etc. She is in possession of several thousand pounds sterling [worth nearly £70,000 in 1995]. When this is swallowed up she will be abandoned, I am sure of it, but it is humanly impossible to stop her. You can see from her letter that she has asked me to declare to you and her father that I renounce outright her fortune. That is what I am doing today. I renounce it entirely and I beg you to always remit her allowance directly to her without any deduction. I accept sole responsibility for the children's upbringing and education ...

You can see she is asking me to consent to a divorce so that she may remarry. I would willingly consent had she chosen better, but this is too much to ask. Even so, if you and your father wish it I promise to consent ... She has no ground for complaint against me, something she herself admits. Her only grievance is that I have exposed her lover, and that I do not admire him.[15]

Charles's attack on Spiros was all Jane needed to make the break. By March 1839 she and Theotoky were living together in Paris. Charles suggested to Edward that he go there to see the proof of what he had told him, 'with your own eyes'.[16] Had Edward done so he would have had to follow the lovers to Rouen, for by the time the letter reached him Jane and Spiros had taken a house there for the summer where, according to her sketchbook, Jane spent most of her afternoons painting on the river-bank. In spite of the bitter letter Charles wrote to Edward, however, he wrote to 'Jeane' asking her to forgive him for the harsh things he had said to her. It is a letter full of pain and love.

> For you I gave up a good life and a promising future, but I have no regrets. No price would have been too high for the happiness you gave me for four whole years ... If I have hurt you I ask you to forgive me ... if I wronged you I swear that I have sinned in error, my intentions were always good. I have *never* loved anyone, heart and soul, with my whole being, as I loved you. I *swear to you* now that no other woman will ever replace you, that no other will possess me as you so completely possessed me. I will have female friends, perhaps I will have a mistress, but I will never have another Jeane.

He told her what he had done with the jewels, among them Venningen heirlooms, which she had returned and which he refused to accept.

> I have spoken to Hecher about the jewel-case. He protested loudly, I knew he would. If you will entrust me with it I will deposit it in a safe place where you can reclaim it some day ... Do not sell Mazeppa. I would be distressed to meet your favourite pulling a cart or carrying some young rascal. I will ensure that the noble animal has a happy life in remembrance of you ... Farewell, my darling, farewell my life, farewell my Jeane.[17]

The news came as a blow to the Digby family; they had not known she was unhappy. Lady Andover, Margaret Steele and Kenelm set out immediately for Paris and there in June they met Spiros Theotoky for the first time. They found Jane wild with happiness and defensive of her situation. She was pregnant by her lover, and they must have seen from the first that it was a waste of energy to attempt to persuade her to leave Theotoky and return to Charles. Theotoky swore he wished to marry Jane as soon as she was free, and at their urging she wrote to Charles pleading for him to grant her a divorce to save further scandal for her family's sake.

Unfortunately for Charles, both Miss Steele and Lady Andover found they actually liked the man they had come to trounce. When Charles, hearing of their presence there, rushed to Paris to enlist their support to persuade Jane to return to him, he found they had adopted an inexplicably neutral stance.[18] He predicted that a marriage between Jane and Spiros would end in yet another divorce, and argued that the man was a fortune hunter. He begged them to dissuade her from any thought of marrying him. But Jane and Spiros had forewarned them of Charles's jealous rages; the two ladies and Jane's brother were placed in a situation for which nothing in their experience had prepared them. It says a great deal for Spiros's charm that he was able to win the support of Jane's family. Before he left Paris, Charles consented to the divorce.[19]

When her family returned home, Jane and Spiros went to Honfleur, the tiny Normandy fishing village, for the remainder of the summer. On 15 September they took up residence in Paris at 83 Place du Palais de Bourbon, using the names Monsieur et Madame Theotoky. It was there in the following spring that Jane's sixth child was born on 21 March 1840. It was a boy. This time the mother immediately fell in love with her baby.

She could hardly believe it. After so many years of dreariness, here she was with Spiros whom she adored, and here was this infant for whom, miraculously, the maternal love she had never felt for her previous five children gushed forth.[20] With the warmth Greek men always display for children, Spiros too seemed completely captivated by the child.

For the immediate purposes of registration the baby was named Jean Henry, Comte Theotoky. But Jane wanted something more memorable for her wonderful child. She dug into the epic stories of Greek history so beloved by Basily and decided to name him after the King of Sparta who, with only 300 men, had opposed Xerxes and the mighty Persian army at the narrow pass of Thermopylae. The Spartans fought a heroic battle to the last man, and their young king was among the last to fall. His name was Leonidas.

10

False Colours
1840–1846

Spiros went to London to meet Admiral Digby and to deliver in person news of the birth of Leonidas. He was welcomed into the family and his credentials were accepted by the admiral, who henceforward always referred to his daughter as the Countess Theotoky. While Spiros was away, Jane recovered from the birth and, having lost her personal maid, set about finding another. The replacement was Eugénie, a Frenchwoman whose history gained Jane's immediate sympathy. As the result of a love affair with a married man, identified by Jane only as Monsieur Benoît, Eugénie had given birth to a daughter. The child's father and his wife had agreed to foster the little girl, and Eugénie had given her week-old baby to them at her family's insistence. Eugénie would prove a rock for Jane for thirty years.

After his return from England, Spiros did not stay long in Paris but set out for Greece, where he planned to take Jane as soon as his duties enabled him to do so. It was considered too soon, anyway, to subject Leonidas to such an arduous journey. Jane planned to join her parents in England for the autumn and winter. Her father, now an Admiral of the Fleet, was to take over the Admiralty House at Sheerness in Kent.

Shortly after Spiros left for Greece, Charles Venningen arrived in Paris. It was to be the last meeting between Charles and Jane, though they would correspond until his death many years later. He had agreed to allow the divorce to go through, and she showed him the statement she had provided to her lawyers. He was shocked to see that in conceding entire responsibility for the breakdown of the marriage she had included many unnecessary facts which were inimical to herself. Charles, who was not a vindictive man, tried to persuade her to edit the document for the sake of her reputation, but she insisted, with the experience of her previous divorce, that she must be *sure* of a divorce being granted so that Leonidas could be made legitimate.

When he saw that she was so happy and heard her plans for the future, Charles relinquished all hope. In June 1840 he wrote to her, addressing the letter to 'Madame Theotoky'.

Chère amie,

When you receive these lines I shall be far away from Paris. But my last word for you must be to tell you once more what I have said so many times in person – that my friendship and my attachment to you will end only with my life . . .

May you find, in those faraway lands where you will live, the happiness I tried to give you, which . . . is now lost to me for ever. It is the only true happiness, the kind which lasts until the grave . . . Think then, under that beautiful sky of the Orient, that in sad cold Germany a warm and faithful heart is beating for you, a heart that will never forget the happiness and heavenly bliss you gave him during several years. If the Almighty should decide otherwise about our fate, remember me still – my house will always be a secure haven for an unhappy Jane.

Again, farewell my dear one. When I have seen the children to whom I shall give your love and your gifts I shall write again. Write to me soon and tell me your final plans.

Everything always to you.
Charles

Jane and Leonidas went to England in July 1840. On 4 August Jane was present when 'Sir Henry Digby hoisted his flag in HMS *How* 120 guns'. Later in the month she accompanied her mother to Minterne House in Dorset, which had become her parents' home, for a month in the peace and seclusion of the English countryside.[1] When the two women rejoined the admiral at Sheerness, Margaret Steele's sister came over from her home at Margate for a week 'thinking it would be a great pleasure and advantage to Jane for sketching'. Lady Andover and Jane with their maids accompanied Miss Steele back to Margate on the admiral's yacht and were caught in a vicious storm which prostrated crew and passengers, all except one.[2] 'Jane was the only person not sea-sick,' Lady Andover wrote in her diary; 'the maids nearly dead and myself very ill. I saw by the countenance of the stewards that it was very dangerous but distained to ask questions when I heard the alarms given during the night.' Jane, the seasoned traveller, actually enjoyed the experience.[3]

In November, Edward and Theresa arrived to collect their daughter after a European tour. 'It was a great happiness to Jane', wrote Lady Andover, 'to see her brother whom she thought much altered by the suffering he had endured for five years from *ici douloureuse* [*sic*]'. Lady Andover and Theresa tactfully went for a drive around the autumn lanes during which time 'Jane had a most interesting conversation with her brother in which many things were explained to their mutual satisfaction. The evening passed off very pleasantly.'[4] With Jane's planned departure for Greece, brother and sister thought it unlikely they would see each other again for many years and made the most of their time together.

Jane's one regret was that during her visit she did not see her brother Kenelm, to whom she would always be very close. But there was no intimacy between Jane and members of the wider family of Cokes, Ansons and Spencer-Stanhopes. Though her parents and brothers remained close to their relatives, there was never any discussion of Jane's progress. Her name was never mentioned to the children of the next generation. On one occasion Lady Andover's young half-brother Henry saw a portrait of a beautiful girl at Minterne and asked who she was. He was 'told to get on with breakfast' and not to refer to the matter again. When he next entered the room the picture had been removed. Some time later he found it hanging, face to the wall, in the housekeeper's room. It was only many years later that he realised who the girl was and why he had been made to feel he had committed a major crime by asking her identity.[5]

This may seem petty, but both sides of Jane's family were closely connected with Queen Victoria's court. The Queen had visited Holkham shortly before her accession; she was subsequently godmother to one of Edward's children; and the Ansons were often mentioned in court circulars. Jane was regarded by all as a fallen woman and her kinsmen had no wish to be tainted by association. She accepted that she had brought this upon her own head by yielding to her passionate instincts, and though she was inevitably hurt by the rejection of her wider family she knew that were she able to turn back the calendar she would do the same thing again. However, she deeply regretted the sorrow her choice had caused her parents and brothers and the pain she had caused Charles, for whom she retained a great deal of affection, and was sad that she had failed her Venningen children.

Jane left in February 1841 for Paris, where she had a joyful reunion with Spiros. A month was spent filling the lists of furniture, saddlery and household effects, and then the couple departed for Greece with Leonidas and the excellent Eugénie. Everything had fallen back into place, it was a new start, and Jane felt truly happy for the first time since her stay in Palermo eight years ago. She knew that she could never again make her home in England; nor, after her divorce, would she ever be allowed to live in Germany. But she was at peace with her family and was going into the future with her beloved Spiros and darling Leonidas. The parting from her parents had been hard, for she worshipped her father, her 'dearest Babou' who always forgave her transgressions, her 'sweet Madre' who never wavered in her love for her daughter, and Edward whose career and future had been blighted by Jane's scandals. All knew it would be a long time before they met again. Despite the pain she had caused the family, they loved Jane as though she was still their little Janet. There must have been great sweetness in her nature for her to have retained their affection throughout her tribulations.

The divorce from Charles was not granted until 1842, possibly because of the length of time it often took for legal documents requiring Jane's signature to reach her and be returned. In the meantime, as she wrote to her mother, she and Spiros were happy and had undergone a Greek marriage ceremony at Marseille for which Jane was first baptised into the Orthodox faith by immersion in a tin bath.[6]

Lady Andover's chatty letters kept Jane abreast of home news. Admiral Digby (now Admiral Sir Henry Digby) suffered a bad fall from his horse which left him concussed, but this did not prevent him from showing the twenty-year-old Queen Victoria around his flagship, nor from dancing at the Trafalgar Ball. Nor, on 9 November, when news was announced of the birth of a prince and heir to the throne, did his indisposition prevent him from ordering that the mainbrace be spliced, a gun salute fired and a dinner given for all officers in his command. Nearly twenty years later Jane would meet this prince in unusual circumstances. Christmas 1841 found the Digby family all suffering from heavy colds and, as Lady Andover wrote, 'too unwell to go to church'. By 20 January, Sir Henry's seventy-second birthday, the admiral was still unwell and had begun to complain of numbness, pains in his arms and nosebleeds. Nevertheless he accompanied Lady Andover and Lady Anson to Holkham.

Meanwhile Jane and Spiros had moved to the island of Tinos in the Aegean Sea. The island was part of the Cyclades archipelago and adjacent to Andros, Siros, Delos and Mykonos. Jane's arrival on Tinos was recorded by Alexandre Buchon, a French scholar of Greek medieval history, who was working in the islands. Buchon was aware of Jane's past:

> April 2nd 1841: We went to St Nicholas (the port of Tinos) to visit Comte Theotoky, the governor and father of Theotoky who has just married Lady Ellenborough. We saw in some of the rooms the furniture she had sent on to Tinos which was being unpacked, among which were her saddles. M. Theotoky told us that his son had sent on these things from Paris before coming to the island where he hoped to stay with his wife for six months at least, but more probably for a year . . .
>
> I do not know what stories Theotoky can have told Lady Ellenborough that could have decided her to settle in a country so utterly devoid of comfort, convenience, beautiful scenery and even decent conversation. That she should send her saddles where neither horse nor mule could hold its footing on the steep rocky slopes betrays absolute ignorance of the conditions under which she was going to live, and she will be bitterly disappointed when she sees Tinos as it is, one governor's house, one barracks, one naval station, one town and one country walk. It will be a bitter expiation of the follies of her youth.[7]

The governor knew nothing of Jane's past, but only a romantic version of her meeting with Spiros. He was under the impression that his son had won her from an English nobleman.

But that summer, even though she may not have been able to satisfy her urges to ride, was not a punishment for Jane, despite Monsieur Buchon's sour predictions. She loved the island, the people, learning about Spiros's family and their customs. Nor was the lack of luxury a penalty to her; the sparsely furnished rooms and the sand that blew in through the open shutters to whisper on the stone floors were the tokens of the life Spiros had promised. The simple freedom appealed greatly to her, and her child grew healthy and strong. She was content to spend her leisure time sketching, and frequently amused herself conducting her own semi-historical surveys of the island.

She learned that the columns in the tiny church in the village of Panagia had been taken from the temple of Apollo at Delos, and thus she began piecing together something of the island's history. With the classical history she had learned as a child, and encouraged by her relationship with Ludwig, she embarked upon what would become a lifelong interest that would take her far beyond the barren little Greek island.

Buchon writes in October of a ball given in honour of the governor's daughter-in-law, Madame Theotoky; of luncheon parties served by black servants in orange groves; lavish picnics taken by mule to beaches on the other side of the island where a whole lamb was roasted on hot stones and local wine flowed; painting expeditions, and village carnivals and fêtes, all participated in with obvious enjoyment by Jane. She began a new diary, writing neatly on the opening page: 'Ianthe. Tinos. October 10th 1841.' The second page is decorated with small pen-and-ink sketches of peasants, shepherds and goatherds in their traditional costume. She would keep this diary for thirteen years until the last page was filled up with her latest adventures in Syria on 31 December 1854.[8]

In the early spring of 1842, Jane and Spiros left Tinos for the family estates at Doukades on the island of Corfu. Here, generations of Theotokys had lived and held lands, and for Jane it was a place of enchantment, where lush vegetation flourished. She designed a beautiful garden of terraces and lawns, with roses and the English garden border plants she loved chiefly because they recalled her happy childhood. A cypress tree planted by her is the only surviving remnant of it now, but in Jane's time her garden was much admired.

During that spring and summer, she gutted the modest house and decorated it in her favourite classical style with pastel-washed walls, and carved and gilded woodwork reminiscent of that at Holkham. Exquisite watered-silk hangings formed a backdrop for huge mirrors, crystal chandeliers, silver, porcelain and the costly gilded furniture imported from Paris. For Spiros she built a magnificent library modelled on the one at Holkham. With marble pillars, a fireplace, comfortable sofas and Greek statuary it was Spiros's favourite room in the house.

The divorce from Charles had been formally granted, but it prohibited her from 'ever setting foot' in Germany or Bavaria. Baron Venningen spent the summer at Herrnsheim with his Granville cousins, who called him Baron von Pfeiningen and tried unsuccessfully to throw pretty girls in his way.[9] He was unfailingly courteous to them, but for Charles there would never be another woman in his life. He had temporarily lost touch with Jane but when he heard an ugly rumour about her he wrote immediately to the Bavarian consul in Athens for news. The consul replied with a full account of Jane's life on Tinos including her conversion to the Greek Orthodox faith, and also mentioned that Spiros, who had retired from the Greek army,

> came here [to Athens] last July to see how the land lay. But having ascertained that the Queen was little disposed to receive Madame Theotoky, and that several Athens society houses would perhaps remain closed to her, she seems to have preferred to remain in Tinos ... The young couple [are] well and comfortably established ... they had announced their intention of going to spend the winter in Corfu if Athens would not do ... As for the abduction of the lady by another young Greek, I have not been able to find any further information. If ... I should hear of it I should lose no time in writing to your Excellency.[10]

The rumour was one of many about Jane which would circulate over the years, as though her life were not exciting enough without any invention.

But Jane had put her German marriage out of mind; she was in love with Spiros and the manner in which they lived. For the first time she found real joy in motherhood. E. M. Oddie, who visited the Theotokys' house in the 1920s when many elderly residents still remembered them, wrote that Jane and Spiros

> kept open house and entertained lavishly. They both loved horses. They rode together round the island, exploring it. Sometimes they rode in a particularly ornate carriage, Spyro [sic], superb in his fustanello, attracting attention by sitting beside the coachman on the box, flag in hand. They lived indeed in the grand eighteenth-century manner ...
>
> There is still a marble-topped table with a bad crack in it which commemorates a gay party at which the guests so enjoyed themselves that they broke not only the glasses from which they drank their very numerous toasts, but smashed the entire dinner service. Had Jane known that the guests would prove so hilarious she might not have used her finest English dinner service for their open air meal. After the dinner, the Count, pleasantly satiated with good food and good drink and good company chose the table top as a couch on which to sleep off the effects.
>
> For all that it was marble and ... solid, it cracked beneath his weight. In England a table that had taken part in so undignified an episode would have been removed from sight but in Corfu they felt differently about things. The story of how the table got its crack was good fun in retrospect and the table still remains in the garden as a pleasant reminder that Uncle Spyro ... was once young and gay and human, and lacking the

wisdom that comes with years. The fragments of the dinner service are also in existence.[11]

In September 1842 a shadow fell across Jane's golden world when she received a letter from Lady Andover telling of her father's death three days after he had suffered a stroke. It was undoubtedly a long-term effect of his bad fall eighteen months earlier, for he had suffered headaches and nosebleeds ever since. Edward and the family were with Lady Andover when Sir Henry died. The unhappy widow wrote, 'he seemed to regain knowledge of those around him and got up in his dressing gown and stood at the window counting rabbits on the lawn.' After his death she had prayed 'alone by the body of a husband to whom I was deeply attached and giving a kiss to features that only appeared to be in a deep sleep'. Afterwards Edward and Kenelm had taken her to Theresa, who had cared for her until they all travelled back to Minterne for the funeral. His uncle, Lord Digby, 'was too unwell to be able to attend'. This was no surprise; Lord Digby had cut all social ties with Sir Henry's branch of the family after Jane's divorce from Ellenborough, and, though he could not choose to confer the barony elsewhere, he had otherwise cut Edward out of his will within a few months of the divorce case. The great estate of Sherborne (which was not entailed) and the old Digby fortune were left instead to Lord Digby's sister.

In a diary entry in September, Lady Andover describes receiving a 'most heart-broken letter from Jane from Corfu, enclosing a most affectionate one from the Count'. Jane was so upset at the loss of her father that she had made herself ill with weeping, Spiros wrote, and he therefore intended to take her away to Italy to 'change the scene'. Jane's grandfather had died six weeks before her father. Although she had had no contact with Thomas Coke for many years, the news of his death had seemed impossible to accept. Now with her dearest Babou, both her childhood gods had gone; it was the end of an era. Mixed with her grief at the loss of her father was guilt for the anguish she knew she had caused both men.

Ducades – Corfu
19th September, 1842

My dearest Kenelm,

I received but last night the stunning intelligence of our *dear, dear* Father's death. To me the blow came most unexpectedly, nor can I yet bring myself to believe that I am never, never to see him again!!!

For this at least you and Edward must be eternally grateful that you were both with him to the last, while *I*, to whom he was, ever, so kind, so generously forgiving, was thousands of miles away, and perhaps *even the very day he was expiring* was unconsciously engaged in some party of pleasure! This is such a dreadful thought . . .

I can hardly see to write more for head and heart feel as if they would burst. Still, wretched as I am that I did not, could not, see him, I am intensely grateful that the sad event did not occur on the visit to us which he had often talked over and planned. *Never* should I have fancied all had been done that *could* be done, in short it would have been a remorse more to add to the many others of my life. I *cannot* write more . . .

Your afflicted Sister
J. E. T.[12]

As expected, the admiral left Minterne House and the bulk of his fortune (which he had made, not inherited) to his son Edward. Kenelm received a capital sum of £10,000. To his daughter 'Elizabeth Jane, now the wife of the Count Theotoky', he left a capital sum of £10,000 and a cash legacy of £500 'as an undeniable provision for her sole and separate use, benefit and maintenance for her life, independent of the debts of her present or any future husbands . . . towards her support and that of her children . . . surviving their majorities . . . or reputed children of my daughter'.[13] From Lady Andover, Jane received soon after this a capital sum of £5,000 – £2,000 of which was added to her capital portfolio and the remainder sent to Baron Venningen for Heribert and Bertha. Jane's personal annual income from investments, rents and other sources appears at this point to have been well in excess of £4,000 sterling (today worth about £140,000). It was regarded as great wealth in Greece.

The late summer break in Italy with her husband and son helped to divert Jane from her grief but she did not recover her former high spirits until the end of the year. By then, despite apparent opposition from Queen Amalie, Spiros had been called to serve at King Otto's court in Athens as aide-de-camp to the King. Jane wrote to her mother that they were to leave Corfu the following morning to sail for Piraeus, from where they would ride to Athens.[14]

From the day of her arrival at court Jane was always known by the Greek version of her Christian name, Ianthe. And just as she had charmed King Ludwig, so she charmed his son. Things were not going too well for poor Otto. He was a likeable but inept young man who believed that his daydreams of a classical and philosophical Greek tradition were shared by everyone. One of his first acts as King was to declare Athens – or, rather, the site of ancient Athens – his capital. But Athens in 1837, when he first took the throne, was no more than a village:

> barely two streets were recognisable as streets and even they were still rough with rubble and heaps of stone. Few of the houses were finished. A roof was missing here; a wall there. Very few shops were in existence. There was a market-place [and] . . . two or three mediocre hotels. Under the shadow of the Acropolis which dwarfed the new Athens as King Otto's interest in the past dwarfed his interest in the . . . present, there was a bleak looking barracks.[15]

Had his father not sent an 'army of workmen from Bavaria' the King would not even had had a palace. Matters had improved a little, but the Theotokys knew what they were facing when they moved to Athens. There were no hotels suitable for residence, though the Hotel Europe served as a short-term *pied-à-terre*; nor were there any houses to rent.

As soon as they arrived, Jane purchased land, engaged the architect Kleanthes, who also designed the British embassy in Athens, and set about building a fine mansion in the Hodos Sokratans district which would become the most sought-after area in the city. With her money, drive and impatience, her house was ready for occupation in the autumn when the Theotokys returned from a summer in Italy. When Jane wanted something she threw herself into it in the 'head-long' manner described by both Steely and Charles Venningen. She worked with inexhaustible energy and when she was working and fulfilled she was devastating. Her house in Athens was among the most elegant in the city and it was generally agreed that Theotoky was a fortunate man to have as his wife the lovely and wealthy countess.

Each day she exercised her white Arabian horse on the outskirts of the city, jumping neatly over the ditches of building sites. In her superbly cut French riding habits and neat hats she was sometimes mistaken by urchins for the Queen and hailed as such. Such stories, when they reached the ear of Otto's wife, could hardly be expected to please. Queen Amalie, who prided herself on her skill as an equestrienne, had already marked Jane out with disapproval for overshadowing her in the ballroom. Prior to Jane's arrival the Queen had been regarded as the best rider and the most graceful dancer at court. Now she had a rival – not that there were many who would have told her to her face. But Amalie was no fool; she saw what she saw. She also knew that Jane had once been Ludwig's mistress. And when she observed how her husband admired Jane she instantly decided that if Jane had been mistress to one king there was little to stop her being mistress to another.

Jane fuelled the Queen's antagonism in many ways: by clothing her own more slender and youthful figure in the fashionable new crinoline styles lately imported from Paris even before the Queen had worn them; by her stable of fine horses including her favourite, the beautiful Arabian, Athos; by the manner in which she and Count Theotoky lived; by her well-stocked and well-managed garden (Amalie was also a keen gardener). Worst of all, knowing how much it annoyed the Queen, Jane wilfully encouraged the King's admiration of her. She meant nothing by it other than to tease, for she was still in love with Spiros.

The court at Athens was not a particularly happy place: the thirty-year-old King's ineptitude and the dour Queen's attitude to life in general, coupled with her childlessness, set the spirit of their court. It was not a spirit the Greeks admired, and a bloodless revolution in the summer of 1843 eventually forced Otto to sign a document dismissing from his service the hordes of foreigners – mainly Bavarians – who had swamped all the country's top positions. Spiros was made a colonel in the new army.

Despite its lack of the civilised amenities found in European cities, Jane nevertheless enjoyed Athens. It was a crossroads between Europe and what was known then as the Orient. In the salons of socialites, returning travellers told of ancient ruined cities in the desert, of nomad tribes whose manner of living had seen no change since biblical times. Outdoor cafés were crowded with men in Turkish baggy 'trowsers' smoking the aromatic narghiles and drinking tiny cups of thick Turkish coffee well into the night. Black-robed Muslim women who covered their faces, and colourfully costumed visitors from the Levant and Arabia, mingled in the few streets with Greeks in fustanellas and more soberly clad Europeans in frock-coats and crinolines. There were French and Italian sailors up from the ships in Piraeus harbour, sheep and goat herders, and the proud Palikares – the nomadic men from the mountains. All flocked to the regular Turkish market and jostled with the respectable citizens of Athens going about their daily tasks. Turkey was tantalisingly close and Jane found the lure strong. She meant to go there: to Constantinople; and to Arabia, where her cousin had met such a tragic end.

During the next two years of Jane's life, as confidante of the King, she was highly placed in Athenian society. Previous biographers, without access to Jane's papers and without quoting sources, have speculated that during this time she became Otto's mistress. Although the pages of the diary of that specific period were among those destroyed by a Digby niece after Jane's death, part of it survives. From Jane's subsequent few references to King Otto it appears unlikely that she ever regarded him as a lover. She offered him support and shared confidences; possibly she spoke of his father whom she still revered. But the absence of passion was no consolation to Amalie, whose dislike and distrust of Jane grew daily.

In 1846, although no evidence of the meeting exists, it seems that Jane met, or at least corresponded with, Prince Felix Schwarzenberg.[16] The prince spent two years as Austrian Ambassador at the court of the King of Naples between 1844 and 1846. The appointment was not generally approved, for though he was popular in his native land he had become imperious and arrogant; and the Italians did not see why they should accept such behaviour. When after two years the Austrian flag was torn down from the embassy building Felix departed hastily. Before that, however, there appears to have been some kind of contact between the former lovers.[17]

Certainly Jane and Spiros were in the habit of visiting Italy each summer and in Naples, a major port of steamships from Greece, they had many friends. The prince was 'with his family' in Naples, according to his biographers, the family consisting of his sister Mathilde and daughter Didi. Felix was no longer important to Jane and she regarded her relationship with him sadly, not from any sense of loss but because of the manner in which he had treated her youthful sacrifice. She always suffered guilt for the distress she had caused but, she once wrote, Felix had 'avenged most awfully' any wrong she had done by his cruel abandonment of her.[18] However, Jane almost certainly saw her daughter in 1846, when Didi was about the same age as Jane had been when she married Ellenborough.

Many years later Didi would recall an evening in Naples when she was sixteen or seventeen. Her father and aunt had gone out, and the servants admitted a lady who stayed chatting to Didi for a brief time without revealing her identity. It was not until shortly before his death that the prince admitted to Didi that he was her natural father; and that the woman who had called that evening in Naples was her mother, who had requested permission to see her daughter. Felix had allowed the visit, applying the condition of anonymity. Later that same year, according to family legend, Jane was allowed to see her daughter again while the girl was out walking. This time more stringent conditions were imposed: Jane was neither to speak nor even to approach the girl.[19] This was the last time Jane ever saw her daughter, and by that time Jane's world had fallen apart again.[20]

During the spring of 1846 Jane had suspected that Spiros was being unfaithful to her. Initially she could not bring herself to believe her suspicions, but investigation proved the matter and when she confronted Spiros he did not deny it. Worse, when Jane confided in Eugénie, the maid cautiously ventured the information that she had known all about the affair, and indeed that it was not the first occasion on which the count had strayed. Jane was hurt, humiliated and angry, and the scales fell from her eyes completely when she discovered that without her knowledge Spiros had made many incursions into her finances, for she had always been generous to him.

There was no agonising this time; Jane was her own woman now. She left Spiros with instructions to pack and move out of their home. Her behaviour suggests that their relationship had not been close for some time, since there was no attempt by either to repair the rift. Taking Leonidas and Eugénie, Jane left Athens for Corfu, and in July went on to Italy, where she was met by her mother and Steely.[21] As usual the two women had flown to Jane's aid as soon as they heard from her. She had taken a house for the summer at the Tuscan spa village of Bagni di Lucca in the foothills of the Apernnines where she had spent holidays in the past with Lady Andover. The large three-storey house is still standing, tall and square 'with a façade of egg-yolk stucco and dark green shutters'.[22] A typically Florentine-style villa of the period, it had a cool, lofty entrance hall and an impressive open stone stairway and polished banister which reached to the top floor some forty feet or so above the front door.

One of Jane's first actions on her arrival was to recruit a suitable person into whose care she could entrust Leonidas. He was an enchanting little boy, now aged six, and the remaining joy of Jane's life. He had outgrown nursemaids and she felt that his enquiring mind needed the stimulation of instruction. Mr Woodcock, a young English chaplain from the nearby town of Livorno, was happy to take on the role of tutor and companion to the boy for a few weeks that summer.

The exact date of the following incident is not known to the present-day family. Only the details of what happened to Jane on that awful day in 1846 survive.

Leonidas . . . had been taken upstairs, presumably to the nursery quarters at the top of the tall Italian house, while she remained talking to some friends in the large hall. Leonidas, wilful and adventurous as herself, knowing where she was, attempted by climbing the banisters at the top of the house to slide down to her. He overbalanced and was dashed to death on the marble floor at her feet.[23]

II

The Queen's Rival
1846–1852

It was some weeks after the funeral of Leonidas that Lady Andover and Steely left for England. Jane returned to Athens for a short time; presumably she felt she owed it to Spiros to tell him at first hand the details of the frightful accident that had befallen the child they both adored. Jane was said to be 'beside herself with grief',[1] and it is not difficult to believe this, given the frank admissions in her diary that Leonidas was the only one of her children for whom she felt real maternal love. For the two older women the shock was combined with the need to comfort Jane, and there had been a very tearful leavetaking at Pisa when Jane and her mother parted, uncertain of when they might meet again.

With the disintegration of six years of happy married life, Jane found no consolation as Spiros did. At thirty-three he was in the prime of his manhood and in love with a much younger woman. Though he had loved his son no less than Jane did, he already had a life beside the one he had formerly shared with Jane. The interview between husband and wife was painful; hardly less bitter than the previous one. They had both wept for Leonidas, but Spiros was now as ardent in his new love as he had once been for Jane. And when Jane recalled how he had pursued her to Heidelberg, and later returned from Greece to woo her afresh, she was well aware of the lengths to which he would go. There was no future for them as man and wife, and clearly they could not both remain in Athens. He must leave, she told him, in return for which she would continue the allowance she had always given him. As a result Spiros resigned his commission and took his mistress to Italy.[2]

The sudden loss of her husband and the death of her child left Jane rudderless. From being fulfilled and happy, she was reduced, at the age of almost forty, to a life with no direction. She knew that if she turned to Charles he would have taken her back, but that was no answer; she still recalled the utter boredom of her life in Mannheim. Nor would an appeal to the sixty-year-old Ludwig have been timely, for 'Basily' was ensconced in the arms of his greatest love, the beautiful raven-haired pseudo-Spanish dancer Lola Montez. Within two years, Ludwig's unquestioning championship of Lola's arrogant and tempes-tuous behaviour would cost him his throne, but in the meantime the man who had so often discussed with Jane the 'supreme joy' of 'being in love' was in thrall to the extent that nothing else mattered – not his kingdom, his family, nor even the city that had been his creation.[3]

What little information can be gleaned about Jane's life after Spiros left for Italy is contained in letters between her and Charles Ven-ningen in 1847. She had travelled to Italy from 'the East' where she had been touring, she wrote on 21 May 1847 from Livorno in Italy. She had just been to see Spiros, who was living in Pisa with his mistress, to try to get his agreement to a divorce. Spiros had countered that, though he hoped to obtain a consular position, he had at present no income, having given up his position at court on Jane's insistence. While he remained Jane's husband he still had a legal call on her income and properties; he insisted that in the event of divorce there would have to be some financial settlement.

Expecting no sympathy from Charles, she wrote to inform him that his instinctive distrust of the count had been completely vindicated. Venningen replied that he had already heard about the death of Leonidas and the situation regarding Jane's marriage from Edward Digby:

> Your letter . . . disclosed nothing new to me. I have known about it for a long time and could see that you would be forced to take the decision that you have. Your mother and Miss Steele will be able to tell you that in Paris I predicted everything that has just happened and begged them to dissuade you from taking the calamitous step of getting married. Unfor-tunately for you they thought it was my jealousy speaking . . . I was not listened to and now we have the result.
>
> You are mistaken . . . in thinking that your misfortune is my triumph. I never desired revenge; on the contrary I only ever wanted you to be

happy although I was certain that with a man such as he, no woman could be. But what is the use of vain words which cannot console you . . . it is your fault . . . You wanted and arrogantly demanded a legal judgement to separate from me. You had your way and it is beyond human power to efface the consequences.

Heribert was a page at court, Charles continued; he had been there for five years, in return receiving a first-class education. 'He is getting on very well there, they are pleased with him and he is happy. I have no worries on his account . . . he will have a brilliant future.' Bertha was causing him concern, for she could be difficult.

I was obliged to remove her from the institute in Munich for several reasons, the main one being my mother, who now lives in Munich. Bertha is now in a convent with a governess and a maid . . . in her own apartment. It is very expensive but at least I have the satisfaction of . . . knowing that since she has been there she is much better . . . If her character one day corresponds with her pretty face and her charming figure I will not be anxious about her future.[4]

Regarding financial matters, Charles had made provision for both children, and this, added to the sum of 20,000 florins 'that you have bequeathed' and a similar legacy from their grandmother Venningen, meant they would be respectably endowed. He ended by entreating her not to be foolish in her settlement with Theotoky. 'Do not', he begged, 'lose sight of your material interests in this sad event. In your case *generosity would be stupid*. It is a question of salvaging from this horrible shipwreck everything which you still have. At least salvage enough for a financially independent existence. The world is large and, with the exception of Germany, is open to you.'[5]

During the next year Jane travelled in Turkey, and from casual references years later we know that she also visited Egypt and sailed up the Nile.[6] Her diary entries for those lonely years have not survived, but subsequently she recalled that in Constantinople she had seen the whirling dervishes[7] and had visited a seraglio. Perhaps she noted from *Galliani*, a newspaper which she habitually read no matter where she travelled, that Felix Schwarzenberg had been made Prime Minister of Austria. But her life now was that of a wanderer, with no ties, no direction. She travelled from one city to another, observing in the detached manner of an artist the costumes and architecture, her only strong emotion being reserved for the lives of women in the East which she regarded as appalling.

Shortly after her return to Athens from a tour of Egypt in the winter of 1848–9 Jane, who had hardly known a day's illness in her life, contracted what she called 'brain fever', undoubtedly a severe case of malaria. For weeks she was dangerously ill, delirious and insensible, and if Eugénie had not nursed her so devotedly she might well have died. Even so, for the rest of her life she would suffer from nausea and headaches, sudden fevers and rigors that struck without warning. With the help of a quinine preparation she recovered, spending a long period convalescing; in the heat of the summer she went to stay in the cool mountains of Cyprus.

In the autumn of 1849 she took a house in Rome,[8] where, according to one biographer, she experienced some problems, being apparently involved with three suitors at one time.

At a ball given in Rome by the Princess Corci, Jane met an Italian artillery officer. She succumbed to his flattery, accepted his gift of a diamond necklace and was considering his proposal of marriage. Then another suitor, an Italian army captain, told her that her prospective groom was an impoverished scoundrel who had cheated a jeweller out of the necklace. This charge proved to be true.

The artillery officer went to jail, and the captain prepared to lead Jane to the altar. But by then she had turned to a young diplomat, the son of an Italian ambassador. Infuriated, the captain challenged the diplomat to a duel. Both assumed she would marry the survivor. The duel was fought with swords and the diplomat, though badly slashed about the face, ran the captain through. When the diplomat thereupon demanded Jane's hand and she refused him, he killed himself.[9]

It has not been possible to substantiate this story, and, whereas Jane subsequently occasionally mentioned in the diaries she kept until her death the names of Ellenborough, Anson, Schwarzenberg, Venningen and Theotoky, there was never any mention of this triumvirate of Italian suitors. However, since Jane had no ties and no responsibilities, there were undoubtedly casual love affairs about which no information survives.

By now she had passed her fortieth birthday. Yet many writers and diarists testified that she looked far younger than her age – no more than thirty, according to the writer, Edmond About, when he met her several years later. The illness following her long period of mourning had left her thin, but the only other obvious evidence of age was a number of white streaks in her golden hair, which added an attractive element of maturity and an appearance of fragility suggesting gentleness.

The winter of 1850 found Jane travelling again 'in the East', according to a family history. Later Edmond About would note she had travelled extensively in Turkey and spoke the language well.[10] Notes in her sketchbook recorded that she had returned to Athens by May 1851 before travelling via Corfu, Trieste, Venice and Milan to meet her mother in Switzerland.[11] Here she spent much of the time quietly painting, and produced a large portfolio of watercolours which were left to her brother Kenelm after her death. When she parted from her mother Jane went back to Athens via Rome and Naples.

Jane's lifelong habit of making lists of everything reveals what she wore, her taste in books, furniture, food and even flowers; what she packed to travel, what medications she took and the type of tack she carried around for her riding horses. There are lists of letters she needed to write, so we know who were her regular correspondents, while her detailed accounts reveal the manner in which she travelled. Thus on her journey to Switzerland we know that on the boat between Piraeus and Trieste she paid extra for a separate table and her own personal waiter. In Trieste she hired a carriage for herself and Eugénie, and a baggage car to follow them to Venice. There was the hire of a 'bateau' to take them into the city and, once settled in her hotel, she hired a gondola to go sightseeing and to make calls during her two-day stay. Each day she recorded her taking breakfast, tea and dinner, the cost of each meal and the gratuity. Seats were purchased on the *chemin de fer* to Milan, where she took a diligence to her hotel. Every item down to the smallest tip was written down and totalled.[12]

Her return to Athens, now as close to being her home as anywhere else, found her still footloose. The single constant in her life was Eugénie, to whom, after the break-up of her marriage, the death of Leonidas and her illness, Jane owed much.[13] In a period of some twenty-five years Jane had experienced three marriages and borne six children, yet she had nothing to show for it. She felt like a middle-aged nomad.

The house at Doukades was a Theotoky property, though she had ploughed large sums into its refurbishment. Spiros felt he had some claim on the Athens house, but following the baron's advice Jane sold it. Jane visited Corfu on several occasions during these years of wandering but never stayed there more than a few days at a time.

Eventually she agreed that Spiros was to take everything at Doukades, including all her silver and crystal, and a capital sum. It was the price demanded for her liberty, and she had reached a stage where she wanted to be free of the man for whom she had once cared enough to desert her home, but who had been unfaithful to her.

Despite her settlement on Spiros, Jane was still able to live lavishly. Her rented house was a rendezvous for the attractive young people of Athens and according to a friend she 'lived in the French manner', holding salons and regular dances.[14] It was a tolerable life, but it was empty of affection. Her return to the city was welcomed by King Otto, but Jane found the Queen still implacably opposed to her. Nevertheless she was a frequent guest at court in the winter season of 1851–2, usually in the company of her new friend, the bizarre Duchesse de Plaisance, in whose partly built palace she often stayed.

Athens had grown in the twelve years since Jane had known it, but it had many problems, chiefly overcrowding and the personal safety of its citizens. It was said that in 1852 Athens had 20,000 inhabitants but only 2,000 houses. Situated as it was amidst 'wild hills and mountains, it was Arcadia infested by brigands'.[15] When Athenians referred to brigands at that time, they often meant Palikares, the legendary Albanian mercenaries who had fought with such valour in the Greek War of Independence, or the Grizottis, who had banded together in something approximating an army. During the harsh winters these ruthless men were not above turning to highway robbery to support their families. Within an hour's ride of Athens travellers were frequently stripped of all their possessions and left to walk naked into the city for help.

In the winter of 1852 travelling conditions in northern Greece and Albania were so perilous that King Otto was forced by public indignation to take positive action. To curb the activities of the brigands was no easy task, and it was clear that anyone taking on such a task would need to know how these predators thought, where they hid, how they lived. Consequently Otto invited to Athens, as poacher turned gamekeeper, the man Palikares regarded almost as their king, Xristodolous Hadji-Petros. His brief was to restore and maintain safe passage on the highways and to quell skirmishes between the border factions. Hadji-Petros was appointed the King's General in the province of Lamia, and Governor of Albania.

When Hadji-Petros first came to court his wild romantic looks and dress, not to mention his reputation of being half soldier, half bandit, caused many hearts to flutter – even Queen Amalie's. Although he was past sixty he was still powerfully built, a tall, handsome man, full of humour, self-confidence and the joy of living.[16] Prior to his court appointment he had been chief of a former Moldavian colony settled for centuries in Albania, who made their living from tax collecting and acting as mountain guides and muleteers. 'He ruled in as princely fashion as he dressed. He wore Albanian costume, all crimson and gold embroideries, and he bristled with pistols and yataghans, which he did not hesitate to use. His horses were trapped out in gold and silver . . . he breathed fire and adventure.'[17]

At first Jane saw only the flamboyant chieftain of the mountain men. But when she was introduced to him and he confided something of his life in the mountains, and talked of his late wife and his love for his children, she began to see a man for whom she could care. It was five years since her marriage with Spiros had ended and Leonidas had been killed. Spiros was still living in Italy, separated from his first mistress and now talking of marrying the spoiled daughter of a rich Athenian family when he and Jane were divorced. There would be two more wives in quick succession before he died in Russia, where he was Greek consul.[18] Though the ties that had bound her to Spiros were not yet legally severed, Jane was responsible to no one. When Xristos, as she called him, began to court her she was ready for a romantic interlude.

Romance was exactly what she got. Xristos and his band of Palikares dressed, said Edmond About, in 'leggings fastened up to the knees, red slippers, fustanellas drawn tight around the waist in little folds, a sash and narrow garters of coloured silk . . . a red cap with blue tassel'; the ensemble was completed at court with scarlet silk jackets and gaiters embroidered with gold, and cloaks of white wool or less formally of sheepskin. When the Palikare troop left Lamia for the new governor's first tour of duty, Jane went with them. She was in love, and Xristos said he loved her. Perhaps it was not the great love she had shared with Felix and Spiros, but she felt secure in the relationship and for the first time in years was prepared to make a serious commitment.

The possibility of their marriage was under discussion; meanwhile she lived openly as his consort in caves, in open camps under a vast canopy of stars, in deserted castles or military forts. She rode alongside him across dusty plains or on mountain tracks, cooked for him over open fires and looked after his small daughter Eirini, who was then about eight and wrung Jane's heart with her dark curls, huge eyes and pathetically thin little body. Eirini filled a void left by Leonidas and came to mean a great deal to Jane. It was to Jane that the child went for comfort in the dark, and Jane who sang her to sleep with lullabies she had learned for Leonidas. And always there in the background was Eugénie, who kept Jane's clothes folded neatly, who washed and brushed her mistress's hair and found some way of organising a *toilette* even in the most difficult situations.

Jane had always been physically athletic; she was as good a rider and shot as any of Xristos's men; indeed, it was her proud boast that she could kill a partridge from the saddle at the gallop. Living rough was a challenge that she met happily and enjoyed. And after several years of wandering she felt there was, once again, a purpose in her life. In Xristos she found a tender and passionate lover, a man of stature who told her that she was a queen among women, that he was grateful for the love she gave his children, and that he was enslaved by her beauty.

In the province of Lamia, a Palikare stronghold that had once been the haunt of Mediterranean pirates, wrote Edmond About,

> Ianthe imagined she was born Palikar . . . and that she was a Queen reigning over Lamia. The entire town was at her feet and when she came out to go for a walk the drums were beating in the fields. This delicate woman lived with drunkards, galloped on horseback in the mountains, ate literally on the move, drank retsina, slept in the open beside a great fire.[19]

The 'delicate woman' had once been an elegant girl who sat on the gilded Chippendale chairs of Holkham Hall, singing Italian love-songs to a lovelorn scholar; and now she dressed in a simple cotton shift embroidered with coloured silks and adorned with a broad woollen sash.[20] This was freedom, this was life![21] Now she regretted selling the Athens mansion and decided that when they returned she would build another house there in which she and Xristos could live when he was not patrolling his territory. She planned that after her divorce from Spiros they would marry. Unfortunately, she reckoned without the woman she would subsequently describe in her diary as her 'rival'.[22]

When the Queen heard how Jane had left Athens, gaily riding beside Xristos Hadji-Petros at the head of the colourful troop of Palikares, she was filled with jealous anger. The daughter of a powerful

Grand Duke, she had come almost as a child to a kingdom that had seemed to everyone to have a golden future. But now she was an embittered woman, disappointed to find that her handsome bridegroom, hardly older than herself, was an inept ruler, his head filled with daydreams rather than plans, totally inadequate for the role history had allotted to him. Their Greek subjects had eventually rebelled at the Germanic culture the young couple imposed at court, and the consequences were that Otto and Amalie now had little real power other than as social leaders.

Amalie lived her life through the intrigues of the court and was renowned for her swift retribution against anyone who offended her. By 1852, when she was thirty-five, it was said that there was nothing easier than to displease the Queen and nothing harder than to win back her favour. It was also said that, while Otto reigned, Amalie ruled. She was as unhappy as she was unpopular.

She spent her considerable energy in gardening, hard riding and dancing, and it was not unusual for her to get up at 3 a.m. to go swimming in the sea at Phalerum. King Otto was as delicate as his queen was robust. Probably Amalie would have liked nothing better than to present her husband with a nursery of healthy heirs, but no children came.

However, the Queen was first a woman, and like many woman at court she had fancied herself half in love with the colourful General Hadji-Petros, who had obviously gone to some lengths to charm her. The writer Senior Nassau gave strong hints about the Queen's fascination for Hadji-Petros in his journal, saying that the general maintained his power at the court by virtue of 'a relationship that could not be openly avowed'. It is extremely unlikely that there was anything physical between Xristos and the Queen, but Amalie believed she owned his allegiance. Her court seemed dull in his absence, and, though she could not object when he left it to go about the work of keeping the King's peace, when she learned that Ianthe, her despised rival of many years, had apparently snatched the general from under her nose, she decided on revenge. In the meantime she obtained petty satisfaction by bringing to the attention of Athenian society the most recent disgraceful episode in Ianthe's shameful life. It was surely scandalous, she averred, that such a woman should be openly living with the King's general; and furthermore it was an insult to the high office granted to the chief of the Palikares. Obviously Ianthe was using her personal wealth to hold the general in thrall. The constant drip of acid, allied to the necessity of retaining the Queen's favour, took effect. People who had once admired Jane now recognised that she was not acceptable.

At last the Queen saw a way to revenge herself for all the imagined slights. When the King left Athens on a three-month trip for health reasons, Amalie was appointed Regent. One of her first actions was to send a messenger to Lamia, where General Hadji-Petros was quartered with his troops. The general was to be relieved of his command and the governorship with immediate effect, Amalie ordered.

Of course, there was nothing to be done except strike camp and return to Athens. But this was not something that could be done in a few hours, and to placate the Queen Xristos scribbled a hasty private message and sent it via her messenger:

> Your Majesty has dismissed me, doubtless because I am living with the Countess Theotoky, but whatever my enemies have told you I can assure you on my word of honour as a soldier, that though I am this woman's lover it is not for love's sake, but purely for self-interest!
>
> She is rich. And I am poor. I have a position to maintain and children to educate.[23]

Amalie was not to be placated so easily; she had copies of the letter prominently posted throughout the city for all to read. When Xristos and Jane reached Athens, Jane found herself the target of ridicule and pity.

Jane would have been justified had she been angry at Hadji-Petros's public betrayal of her love. It appears that she was not, however, or that any anger she felt was swiftly dispelled when he swore that his letter had been a lie to placate the Queen. Jane chose to believe and forgive him. Xristos and little Eirini were her life now and, as usual when she fell in love, nothing else mattered. But she recognised that if she and Xristos were to make a life for themselves they would have to follow, publicly at least, the rules set up by society. She therefore rented two neighbouring houses with gardens that adjoined, on the outskirts of the city, one for herself and her personal staff, one for Hadji-Petros, his daughter and his retinue of followers.

Her new accommodation compared poorly with the handsome Kleanthes mansion which was now an embassy. Her friends said that 'to see Ianthe in such a setting was like seeing a portrait by Lawrence hanging in a kitchen',[24] but she was too busy for self-pity. She set about building a house for herself and Hadji-Petros that was the equal of her former home, with a receiving room fit for a tribal chief to hold his own court, with stables for the Arab horses she intended to buy, and with accommodation and stabling for his Pali-kare followers. She instructed her legal advisers to obtain an annul-ment of her marriage with Spiros, on the technical grounds that her Greek Orthodox marriage to him in Marseille in 1841 had been effected before her divorce from the baron had been granted.

Jane still had a few friends, though she was now ostracised at court under pain of the Queen's displeasure.[25] She met the King privately to beg his intercession but it appears he could do little for her. Amalie's petty vindictiveness held sway, and those who hoped to retain the Queen's favour took pains not to be too closely associated with the lovely Ianthe. Of important Athenians only Sophie de Barbe-Marbois, Duchesse de Plaisance, could afford to disregard this edict.

The Duchesse de Plaisance was a legendary figure in Athens. She was French, the daughter of the Marquis de Barbe-Marbois. As a young woman she married one of Napoleon's greatest generals, Lebrun, who for his successes was made Duc de Plaisance; his bride was appointed lady-in-waiting to the Empress Marie-Louise. Jane had first met her in Paris in 1831 when her own relationship with Felix was failing and the duchess's marriage was in much the same state, for she was extremely eccentric and eventually her husband refused to tolerate her whims. Taking her daughter Louise, who – her mother insisted – would marry a prince or no one, she lived a peripatetic existence in various capital cities until she came to Athens, where her daughter died young without fulfilling the regal destiny her mother had predicted for her.

Living alone with a pack of dogs in a massive mansion on the Kephissa road,[26] the old lady suffered many delusions of a mild schizo-phrenic nature, believing she had been chosen to build a temple on the summit of Mount Pentelicon which would give the world a new faith, an alternative to the Christian religion, with herself as the chief priestess. She also believed, having been told so by a fortune-teller, that she would die within a year of completing the building of a house. Consequently, though she had begun many houses, none was ever completed and thus she expected to live a long time. Despite such whimsical notions she was a harmless creature, and Jane enjoyed her company, for she was an intelligent conversationalist. She is important to Jane's story because through her we know the chain of circum-stances as they next occurred.

Although immensely wealthy, the duchess was astonishingly mean to all except her dogs, upon whom she doted and lavished every comfort. When she went out in her carriage she was invariably accompanied by half a dozen wolfhounds. 'Any man who wears gloves' could introduce himself at her house and be sure of admittance, even if only briefly, but as a rule the duchess did not like women. For some reason, however, she took a great fancy to Jane, who she said was the only woman she could bear to have around her. Jane was staying with the duchess when the French writer Edmond About paid the old lady a visit in February 1852.

For two years About had been working on a book about contemporary Greece, and wished to talk to the duchess about a recent incident in which she had been held up by the infamous highwayman Bibichi. This gentleman, who turned highwayman when his wife ran off with a lover, was currently operating right up to the outskirts of Athens. He had demanded a ransom of 200,000 drachmas for the old lady's freedom. She haggled with him, eventually signing an order for 15,000 drachmas which her servant was sent to collect from the city. The servant naturally returned with help and Bibichi was forced to flee without the ransom, but with a present of ten francs which his captive gave him out of pity for his naïvety.

About found the old lady unwilling to discuss her own adventure, but happy to divert him with an amusing story about Jane, who, while painting a view of the city from a vantage-point on Mount Lycabettus,[27] had been robbed of a gold chain from around her neck by a handsome young Greek. 'She told the story all over Athens . . . "But why", someone asked, "did you let him come so near?" "But how could I guess", she answered playfully, "that he was only interested in my chain?" '[28]

About was completely disarmed by Ianthe, who was friendly and amusing and had a voice of peculiar sweetness. She was quite different from the hard woman he had been led to expect, and he found the idea of this beautiful and gently bred aristocrat living as a queen of the banditti irresistible.[29] Occasionally they met and spoke of her travels in Turkey, and when he wrote his book About devoted more pages to Jane than to the Queen, about whom he was not complimentary. He referred to Jane always by the name Ianthe, and stated that she was by far the most interesting woman in Athens. At the age of forty-five, About said, she was 'the incarnation of vitality and health'.

She is tall and slim, without being too thin; if she were a little longer in the waist it would be impossible to find a woman with better proportions. Her feet and hands are those of a thoroughbred, the lines of her face are of incredible purity.

She has great blue eyes, as deep as the sea, beautiful chestnut hair, highlighted with gold. As for her teeth, she belongs to that elite of the English nation who have pearls in their mouths instead of piano keys. Her complexion has kept that milky whiteness that seems to flourish only in English fogs, but she flushes at the slightest emotion. It is as though this fine transparent skin is only a screen for the passions enclosed within her, which can still be seen stirring beneath the surface, all trembling and rosy.[30]

About writes little about Jane's relationship with Hadji-Petros except a remark that the general was growing old and a curious statement that he 'sometimes beat her and was capable of killing her one fine day . . . not out of love', said About wryly, mimicking the general's letter to the Queen, 'but self-interest'. This suggestion of violence sounds an odd note, for it is the only time it was ever mentioned; Jane's diary entries over the next years, where she discusses the general on many occasions with the greatest affection, make no mention of it.

It was just at this point that Jane heard of the death of Felix Schwarzenberg. He had suffered a stroke while dressing to dine with the latest in a long procession of mistresses. He had never married and was just fifty-one when he died with the Austrian Emperor Franz Josef at his bedside. It had been twenty years since Jane had parted from him in Paris. Many years later she spoke of him to a friend, and it is recorded that her eyes filled with tears.[31] She always kept a miniature of Schwarzenberg with her.

When About next visited Athens the following spring the talk of the town was that Ianthe had at last regained her freedom after a tribunal had met to annul her marriage to Theotoky. Her new house was completed and ready for furnishing, and she had given notice on the two rented cottages, devoting her energies to decorating the house ready for occupation. It was said that the bedroom she was decorating for Xristos resembled a throne-room, that there was a garrison for the followers of her affianced lover, complete with a gatehouse for an armed guard, and a uniformed captain, 'a genuine one', to serve as gatekeeper.[32]

The stables were almost complete, and it was Jane's intention to return to Syria to purchase one of the rare and costly Arab horses that she had seen and coveted there. She had carefully drawn up lists of items needed to equip the stables: bridles, bits, snaffles and curb chains, Turkish saddles and silk halters, blue horse blankets embroidered in gold, snaffle bridle and saddle for groom, pantaloons for herself. The list had been sent to a French saddler on 17 September 1852,[33] and the items arrived as winter gave way to spring. All that was needed now was horses.

She discussed her forthcoming journey with Edmond About, telling him she would be sailing in early April 1853 from Piraeus to Smyrna in Turkey, where she would take a steamer to Syria. It was the best time of the year to travel in the Lebanon and Syria, when the spring sun was hot but without the oppressive heat of the high summer months. About was himself going to Turkey and would be in Smyrna during the first week of April. They arranged to meet briefly during her stay there.[34]

Jane was forty-six on 3 April 1853, and the celebration was marred only by a disagreement with the duchess over the sum settled by Jane on Spiros Theotoky, which the old lady thought stupidly extravagant, and Jane's equally lavish expenditure on the quarters she was providing for Hadji-Petros in her new house. When the two women parted Jane was full of happy plans for the future, her heart – as her older friend shrewdly perceived – ruling her head. But three days later when, together with Eugénie, she embarked on a ship bound from Piraeus for Beirut, the maid was tearful and Jane was grim-faced. In those few days between her birthday and her departure from Athens Jane had learned that her trusted and much-loved maid Eugénie was having an affair with Xristos.

Jane had somehow discovered the relationship and Eugéne had confessed, revealing, during one of the many typical stormy exchanges between mistress and maid during their years together, that Xristos had sworn that it was Eugénie he loved, not her mistress. Jane could have forgiven Xristos much, as witnessed by her acceptance of his letter to Amalie, but she would not accept infidelity. She believed Eugénie, for not only had the maid never lied to her, but it seemed to confirm what others had said at the time of his letter to the Queen – that the general was only interested in Jane's wealth and was not truly in love with her.

What would any woman do faced with such a dilemma? On the one hand was a faithless lover, on the other an indispensable servant regarded almost as a friend who, though she had acted shamefully in this instance, had supported Jane through joys and great sadnesses, had nursed her through sickness and had always made her life tolerable no matter what the difficulties. Who can blame Jane for concluding that, while men were relatively easy to come by, a good maid was beyond price? With her trip to Syria already organised and her luggage packed, Jane departed, leaving only a curt note for Xristos and, accompanied by an unusually truculent Eugénie, embarked on the steamer to Beirut.

Edmund About missed meeting Jane at Smyrna. He had arranged an onward journey to Constantinople and had to leave the day before Jane arrived. For months afterwards he made inquiries about her, but a year elapsed before he discovered, on his next visit to the Duchesse de Plaisance in Athens, what had happened.

Jane's chief emotion at this time was anger. From her diary we know that she continually asked herself how Xristos could have betrayed her so disgracefully. But her anger was directed at herself rather than at her lover; it was annoyance that she had allowed herself to be talked into almost marrying him. And now, approaching fifty, she was yet again 'alone, quite alone'. It was time, she reflected, to be done with men and the problems they had caused her throughout her life.[35]

She decided to extend the planned trip. It had been her ambition for many years to visit Jerusalem and Damascus, and especially Palmyra, where the ruins of Queen Zenobia's fabled city lay in the heart of the desert. This was as good a time as any to visit some of those 'sites of antiquity', as she called them. Her return to Athens could be delayed indefinitely, until she had decided what to do. Though she did not yet know it, she was about to begin the most interesting years of her life.

12

The Road to Damascus
1853

It is unfortunate that Jane and Edmund About did not keep their appointment at Smyrna.[1] Had they met there a detailed version of what Eugénie told Jane, and Jane's reaction, would surely exist. As it was, she was in Smyrna alone for a week before she could obtain passage on a ship bound for Jaffa (now part of Tel Aviv) calling at half a dozen other ports, including Beirut.

On her previous visit to 'Beyrout' she had apparently gone little further than the port, probably because of the rigid quarantine precautions that prevailed throughout the eastern Mediterranean. Visitors of all ranks were taken from the ships by lighter and herded with long poles into a prison-like building for up to five days. During this time travellers could order meals from a nearby hotel and though the food was good, according to the accounts of diners, the prices were extortionate. There was no alternative; payment was made by dropping coins into a bucket of salt water for cleansing purposes. This time Jane opted for the port of Jaffa, where quarantine was more relaxed and with the aid of well-placed baksheesh might last no more than twenty-four hours.

As the ship anchored off Beirut she sketched the port from the deck, intending to see more of it on her return, when quarantine would not apply. According to a contemporary writer's account:

> The world must be very rich in beauty if there exist half-a-dozen places more beautiful than Beyrout . . . the amphitheatre of mountains, clothed in every hue . . . the snowy summits towering up behind them; the rugged headland of rocks over which the sea dashes ceaseless wreathes of foam;

the city rising from the water's edge, climbing up the slopes of hills, adorned with gardens, minarets, domes and mosques, castles and palaces, the scattered palm trees and bright colours dotting every street and quay make a *tout ensemble* which . . . rests in the mind in an everlasting memory of loveliness.[2]

At each port of call, loading and unloading could take twenty-four hours or more, but Jane had no reason to hurry and as a seasoned traveller was happy to be diverted by new sights, sounds and scents. From Jaffa, she intended to visit Jerusalem and other biblical and archaeological sites before making her way to Damascus.

During the journey she spent most of her time reading the new books she had acquired about Syria, and sketching.[3] More importantly, by the end of the sea journey she had already resolved that there would be no reconciliation with Hadji-Petros. Though she felt great affection for him, she had no desire to be financier for a man who could deceive her with her own maid. This still hurt. 'Why was he so infamous with Eugénie?' she wrote agitatedly in her diary. 'Eugénie! who he could never love. While I? . . .' She did not finish the entry.[4] There were to be many similar entries over a period of eighteen months, as if she could not bring herself to believe that the two people closest to her could be guilty of such betrayal, but she never wavered in her resolve to cut him out of her life. Yet for a long time she worried about the 'fate' of the general and his daughter Eirini.

At Jaffa, where the ships of the King of Tyre had once brought the materials to build the Temple of Solomon, and the whale had cast up Jonah upon the beach, her depression lifted. The perfidy of Xristos and Eugénie diminished and she became 'elate[d] and happy as usual on commencing a journey, especially one in search of *l'inconnu*'.[5] Her first task was to engage a dragoman – a useful combination of guide, secretary and interpreter whose duty was to organise the route and see to all the necessary details regarding the comfort and feeding of travellers and animals and pitching and striking camp. More importantly, he would steer the party clear of any difficulties and danger. The Druses were apparently in revolt in Djebel Hauran and parts of the Anti-Lebanon, and several roads were notorious for violent robberies, especially of rich 'Franks' (as Europeans were known), so a strong escort of guards was essential.

The dragoman was Sheikh Selaine, a well-built man of about forty, who spoke several European languages as well as Turkish. When all was ready they set off for Jerusalem, across the great plain of Sharon with its orchards of orange trees and fabled roses. After two days of climbing they reached the last ridge, almost 2,000 feet above the Mediterranean, and saw the walls, fortresses and domes of the City of David.[6]

Jane had already stated her intention to visit Damascus and Palmyra, and with Selaine's help a tour was arranged which wound north in reasonable safety to the Syrian border. The British consul in Jerusalem advised her that Selaine would not be of any use to her in Syria; she would need another dragoman or a bedouin guide, especially for her journey through the desert, assuming she could get anyone to act for an unaccompanied European woman. A message was sent to the consul in Damascus, who duly organised a suitable escort. They were to rendezvous north of Lake Galilee.

Afterwards Jane always regarded her visit to Jerusalem as the start of her new life – though at the time she was not aware of its significance. She did what all European visitors did: she toured the main features of the city, sat and sketched the town from the Mount of Olives, and walked or rode around the walls. Being in any new place, especially one so full of interest, always brought her to life. When at last Jane and her party left Jerusalem and rode on towards the Jordan they were stopped on the road by a sheikh and made to pay a small 'toll' as his payment for keeping the road free of robbers. She was amused to learn that prior to his toll-keeping duties he had been the robber.

There were few occasions when she could rely on an inn or hotel and Jane always preferred camping out to staying in a dirty hovel. In her diaries Jane hardly mentions the problems that must have arisen regarding the frequent baths which Jane always took in her portable canvas tub, or the days when menstruation must have brought inevitable difficulties for both women. The only reason she ever broke her journeys was because of the intermittent malarial fevers when she was incapable of even standing upright.

Though her surviving notes of this stage of her journey do not detail what she wore, we know from the journal of a fellow traveller that she rode side-saddle, while Edward Lear, who spent many years in the Levant on sketching tours, recorded in his diary that he met 'Lady Ellenborough in a crimson velvet Pelisse and a green satin riding habit going up . . . to Jerusalem'.[7] We know from Jane's packing list that at this point she was still one of those intrepid Victorian women who added to the rigours of any journey in a hot climate by wearing her stays and a full complement of European clothes, and that her luggage contained some of her favourite items of jewellery such as 'the King's bracelet' as well as painting supplies. But Jane could also dress and ride like a Palikare tribesman when she wished to do so.

From Jerusalem, she headed for Jericho, each day bringing new experiences. She enjoyed the company of the laughing young men, the 'handsome Jordan set' as she called her escort, who jostled with each other to ride alongside her white horse and talk to her in Turkish. These men had possibly never seen a European woman before and certainly would never have spoken to one. They were uncomplicated and unsophisticated, and so unashamedly admiring of her person and her riding ability that Jane could not help being amused by them. She had taken along side-saddles and English tack for her and Eugénie, for she preferred this to riding 'Turkish' fashion for long distances. But she noted the skilful manner in which these Arabs rode their small, strong, and agile horses, holding them on a single rein attached to a bitless headstall. By 4 May the small group had welded into a friendly party. That morning they rode down from Jericho into the Jordan Valley at Ein-es-Sultan where they encamped. Here they met a group of bedouin Arabs who were travelling in the same direction.

Heading the group was a man whose name was Saleh, a ruddy, handsome man whose frank visual examination amused rather than embarrassed Jane. He courteously invited Jane's party to join them for dinner, and after a rudimentary toilet they went to his tent. The diners sat on rugs on the ground, around a dish containing a freshly killed lamb, rice, raisins and herbs; all present helped themselves with their hands. Jane did not then realise how unusual it was for these men to invite a woman to join them. Afterwards Saleh served thick aromatic coffee, and the group sat around the coffee hearth chatting.

Shortly before the sun set, Saleh rose and mounted his horse. The scene that followed lodged in Jane's memory for many years, and indeed was partly responsible for her long-term enchantment with Arabia. It was for her that Saleh performed the mock combat, a *jerid*, cantering past his audience with his lance couched. Some hundred yards away he turned and, screaming his battle-cry, kicked the mare into her fastest gallop while he wielded his bamboo lance above his head making it quiver until it almost bent double. His horse galloped at them as though intending to ride them down, stopping abruptly a few feet from them, snorting and pounding the earth with a delicate hoof.

Saleh had many tricks – galloping his horse while clinging to its side so that from one perspective the horse might have been riderless, then suddenly wheeling without warning and sitting upright as though to confront an attacker. He held his twelve-foot lance, tipped with metal and decorated with a knot of black ostrich feathers, poised for a strike. As he pulled his horse up sharply, again within feet of the seated audience, he plunged it into the sand at Jane's feet.

Some of the younger men could not resist joining in and the knots of riders swooped along the plain, lances poised, robes flying, dust rising, to the sound of the shrill warbling shrieks of the riders and the encouragement of some of their audience. The raw excitement of the scene, horses and riders amid the swirling dust lit by the red ball of the setting sun, thrilled Jane and made her all the more determined to acquire one of the sure-footed horses capable of such fleetness of foot and dexterity of movement. No mean rider herself, she was fully appreciative of the horsemanship involved in the pageant she had just witnessed.

They rode north with Saleh's caravan, the concatenated group ensuring extra protection for both parties. In the lush Jordan Valley they halted for Jane to visit interesting sites. Selaine was a knowledge-able guide, and Jane found herself more and more enjoying the jour-ney. Each day brought some new diversion: a name from the Bible, a story recalled. Hours spent crossing the barren scree hills called 'the wilderness' where Christ fasted, under cloudless skies, ended abruptly when they emerged into a valley flecked with brilliant pop-pies, fragrant with camomile and lavender, a fringe of pink-flowered oleander bushes bordering a sparkling stream. Oh, she was enchanted with this blessed land.

She gave only passing thought to Hadji-Petros: 'Poor Xristos, how is he now?' she wrote in her journal. 'Yet why should I say "poor"; was it not all *his* fault!'[8] Hadji-Petros, as it turns out, was not doing too badly. Though much of his current notoriety rested a great deal upon his relationship with Jane, according to Nassau Senior's contem-porary journal,

the reclaimed robber . . . is kept in reserve for the next invasion of Turkey. The court have learned nothing from experience, or rather [the Palikare] have learned from experience that they can violate audaciously every principle of public and private morality, and whenever their attempts fail be rewarded with popularity.[9]

Had she known, would she have cared? By the time Jane's party reached Nazareth, after nearly two weeks' rambling, she was infatuated with Saleh, and appeared to think he returned her affection. At an encampment at a small village called Rihah, said by the inhabitants to date from the time of Herod, she was sure that Saleh felt as she did. 'Rihah, Rihah!' she would write in her diary some months later. 'Oh that name! What memories does it call up . . . It was at Rihah that I fondly dreamed that [Saleh] loved me . . . loved as I did!'

At Nazareth, Jane went to a hotel so that she could bathe. Her party camped outside the town. But the visit was memorable to Jane not for visiting the 'house of Joseph the carpenter' nor 'the house of the virgin', where she was shown what was purported to be the angel's footprint in the floor. At some point during her visit to the hillside town, she went to Salah's bed. He made love efficiently but distantly, and she was confused and hurt by his coldness. They had been eyeing each other for some days in what she had construed as a meaningful manner. Still, Jane being Jane, the encounter heightened her interest rather than warned her off. Obviously, her love for Hadji-Petros had not had the lasting quality of her feelings for Felix or for Spiros, because it was only a matter of weeks since she had turned her back on him and on Athens.

From Nazareth the group dropped down to the town of Tiberias on the shores of Lake Galilee, the middle sea that feeds the Jordan. Jane had no strong religious leanings; it was many years since she had taken Communion. In the meantime she had attended church when social obligation required it, but her upbringing had instilled in her a thorough knowledge of the Bible and she experienced an unexpected reverence towards the places where Christ was known to have walked and preached.

By 20 May the group had travelled well north of the inland sea to the point where Saleh and his group were to part from them. Notwithstanding his apparent reticence at Nazareth, Jane felt she had reason to believe that Saleh returned her affection. When they parted he took with him Jane's promise that though she had to return to Greece in July she would return to the Lebanon in the winter and visit him at his winter camp near Hebron. Saleh must have made her believe that he would welcome this, for the thought of it coloured her plans through many long months.

At a nearby well, fed from an underground cistern, they came across some low black bedouin tents – the camp of her new escort. Here Jane met Sheikh Medjuel el Mezrab, who was to conduct her through Syria to Palmyra. Dressed in the flowing robes of a bedouin sheikh, a scarlet cloak with the gold insignia of a desert prince, Medjuel presented a striking figure. He was an intelligent young man in his late twenties, roughly the age that – had he lived – Jane's first son Arthur would have been. He spoke several languages, including Turkish and a little Italian, the lingua franca of the eastern Mediterranean, and unusually for a bedouin could read and write Arabic, having been taught at his father's insistence. He was softly spoken and extremely cultured, according to other travellers who met him.

Jane liked him immediately, but with visions of Saleh still filling her mind she did not recognise Medjuel as an important figure in her life. Selaine and his Jordan Arabs departed, having arranged to meet again on her return journey, to conduct her to Beirut. She made several sketches of Selaine in her notebook, sorry to part with her handsome escort, and went on with Medjuel.

There are two great tribes of bedouin in Arabia, the Anazeh and the Shemmar. They are deadly enemies. The Mezrabs were a small but noble branch of the Sebbah, a sub-tribe of the Anazeh. They earned a living by virtue of the fact that they controlled the desert around Palmyra, an important oasis, and protected the town from the raids of other tribes, receiving from the Palmyrans an annual tribute of 150 camels. The caravan trade routes from the East, in particular between Baghdad and Damascus, pre-dated the Roman Empire, and invariably called at Palmyra, where a toll was levied on travellers entering the walled enclosure and access to the springs. In addition to the trader caravans, any travellers wishing to use the desert routes to Palmyra needed an escort from the Mezrab tribe, for only they knew the position of the wells.

Medjuel was not the head of his tribe. That position was held by his elder brother Sheikh Mohammed; however, the bedouin laws of succession are based not on primogeniture but on ability. It was well known that Medjuel, Mohammed's favourite brother, would be the next leader, and meanwhile he bore the title of sheikh as his birthright. Mohammed lived with the tribe, while Medjuel escorted travellers and maintained the Mezrabs' ancient rights to do so by repelling repeated attacks by marauders.

This escort duty was a vital source of income for the small tribe, enabling them to buy supplies which they could not otherwise produce such as rice or material for clothes. Recently a few intrepid European travellers had begun to arrive in Damascus wishing to visit Palmyra. A handful had been granted that rare privilege, and in the year prior to Jane's arrival half a dozen European men had preceded her there. The 'Franks' paid well, but even so Medjuel did not accept all comers.

Like all bedouin Arabs of pure stock, Sheikh Medjuel was short in height – about 5 feet 6 inches – but he was slim and well proportioned and moved gracefully. He was a magnificent rider and Jane quickly noted the respect paid to him by the bedouins he had brought with him. They always hailed him with the deferential 'O, Sheikh', and in his tents a strict etiquette was observed:

> When the Sheikh enters every person rises, and stands till he bades [*sic*] them be seated, and they do not permit him when encamped to do any menial work; but out in the plain a Sheikh would be greatly despised who made any difference between himself and his people, or who did not attend to his own camel and eat the same food as the others.[10]

Initially, it was Medjuel's horse that caught her eye, for it was just such a horse that Jane wanted for herself. When she raised the matter with him he told her that few mares were sold outside the tribes, for they were a precious commodity and guarded jealously to ensure the purity of lineage. The history of every thoroughbred mare and stallion was known among the tribes and, although occasionally a horse might be exported at a huge price, he thought it unlikely she would get a really good one. Jane told him she would pay almost any price for such a horse. It was perhaps not a sensible thing to say to an Arab she had just met.

During their journey Medjuel and Jane spoke of many things and fell into an easy comradeship. He told her of Damascus, called the 'Pearl in the Desert', which had been open to Europeans and Christians only twenty years earlier; of Tadmor, which Jane learned was the Arabic name for the 3rd Century AD ruins near the present Arab town of Palmyra, to which only the Mezrab tribe had passage rights; of the bedouin way of life; of his two wives; of his small son Schebibb. Jane told him of her attraction to Sheikh Saleh; of the things she had seen on her tour and her journey across the Mediterranean. She was surprised to learn that Medjuel had never seen the sea, and also to learn in one long conversation that Muslims held Christ in high esteem. As a contemporary writer put it, 'They accept the history of

Christ, except his crucifixion, believing that he passed to heaven without death . . . they call him *Roh-Allah*, meaning Spirit of God, and
consider him, after Mahomet, as the holiest of prophets.'[11]

Medjuel had deliberately ensured that Jane's first view of Damascus
was the best possible one – from the camomile-covered slopes of Salhiyeh.[12] No one looked down upon that view in the soft cool air of
sunrise without a catch at the heart, and the Prophet Mohammed is
said to have turned away at this point, declining to go further, saying
that as man could only enter one paradise he preferred to wait for
Allah's. Damascus was called Esh-Sham (or simply Sham) by the
bedouins, Medjuel told her, and had been founded by Uz, son of
Aram, son of Shem, son of Noah. It already existed at the time of
Abraham and was the oldest inhabited city in the world.

It was bewitching with its fragile white minarets tapering into the
blue sky. Its swelling domes and gilded palaces, set among thirty
square miles of lush orchards and gardens, seemed opalescent in the
morning light. The wide River Barada flowed through the city past
flat verdant banks where travellers set up tents and refreshed themselves and their animals. Every house in the city had its own direct
water supply, and myriads of waterways, siphoned off the river,
gurgled and flashed in the sun as the water plashed from pool to pool
along stone culverts.[13] To the west was Mount Hermon, ice-capped
even in June; a long way to the south were the mauve-tinted mountains of the Hauran, while to the east – where Medjuel pointed out
the route to Palmyra – were the sands of the Syrian desert, 'as if
nature had drawn a line between green and yellow'.

After the barren mountains the massive oasis was stunning. The
silence hitherto broken only by birdsong and sheepbells was suddenly
filled by the haunting call to the first prayer of the day as the muezzin's
voice echoing from the minaret of the Great Mosque of the Umayyeds
and bouncing off the hillside behind them, was taken up from minarets
all over the city: 'God is great. There is no God but Allah, and
Mohammed is his prophet! Let us kneel before him, and to him alone
be the glory! Come to prayer, there is no God but Allah . . . God is
great . . .'

A messenger was sent ahead to warn of their arrival, and the party
rode eagerly towards the city. From Salhiyeh to Damascus was a ride
of half an hour or so through cool gardens and orchards. Roses and
pomegranate bushes, with flowers like handfuls of crumpled scarlet
silk, were all around them. Despite the early hour, when they reached

the outskirts of the city people turned out to welcome Medjuel, who was obviously a well-known personage, and to see the unusual sight of two 'Frank' ladies who were neither missionaries nor yet accompanied by husbands. A fresh horse was brought out to meet the sheikh and he dashed about on it, showing off the horse and generally performing with his tribesmen. A *darabouka* (drum) was produced by one of the bedouin outriders and provided a throbbing background as they processed through the fabled gardens to the city wall. For Jane such exuberance was a tonic and she was happy and elated. Within the ancient walls, the city of Damascus did not always live up to the exquisite view from the hills. But Jane was not in a mood to be critical on this occasion, and Damascus would always be to her that first sight from Salhiyeh.

They crossed the River Barada by the old wooden bridge leading to the north-eastern gate, Bab Tuma (Thomas's Gate). Unlike other visiting Europeans, Jane did not notice the dirt, being fascinated by the soaring architecture of the Great Mosque, and the brightly painted cafés and bath-houses. She saw quaint gilded lattices on windows projecting over the narrow crooked streets, and occasionally caught a glimpse through an open carved door of a cool marble courtyard; she heard the music of fountains behind high walls, and the cry of the milk-seller '*Leben, Lebe-e-e-en!*'; inhaled the scent of spices from the souk, and drank in the exotic and picturesque forms of dress and people – Persians, Kurds, Circassians, Anatolians, African slaves and Turks.

There was only one hotel in the city, owned by a Greek, Demetri, who was 'civil, obliging and attentive . . . though he can afford to be a little independent in his manner because he has no opposition and if you object to his hotel you must wend your way, as a pilgrim, to the khan'. With her knowledge of Greek and her obvious importance Jane was welcomed with particular warmth. Demetri's was for many years the headquarters of any European visitor who found their way to Damascus.

The hotel . . . [was] in the Frank quarter. It had once been the house of some rich merchant. The court into which we were ushered is paved with marble, with a great stone fountain and basin with goldfish, surrounded with vases of flowering plants in the centre. Two large lemon trees shade the entrance, and a vine climbing to the top of the house, makes a leafy arbor over the flat roof . . . The *liwan* is a vaulted apartment twenty foot high entirely open to the court.

In front a pavement of marble leads to the chambers. Beyond this is a raised floor covered in carpet and at the far end a divan piled with cushions and carpets. Leaning back, cross legged against the cushions . . . the view of the court, the water basin, the flowers and lemon trees, the servants and dragomen going back and forth or smoking their narghilehs in the shade, all framed in the beautiful arched entrance, is perfectly Oriental.[14]

There was no baths in the hotel, but the women's *hammam*, the public bath-house, was close by. In the late afternoon Jane retired to the bath and then returned to eat and sit in the *liwan* lit with brilliantly coloured lamps hung in the oleander and lemon trees. Afterwards she slept. The soporific music of the fountain through the open lattice windows of her room, and the feeling of satisfaction, even permeated her dreams. She was in Damascus at last.

The next days were spent visiting the famous sights of the city with its 'Street called Straight' mentioned in the Bible, the house of Ananias where Paul lodged after his divine revelation struck him blind, and the window in the city walls from which he was lowered in a basket to escape his pursuers.[15] Jane and Eugénie explored the souks with delight. Here one could (and still can) buy anything from spices to gold, and silver filigree, from Damascene inlaid furniture to sweetmeats or the fabled Aleppo silk. Travellers wrote of how one could shop in succession through 'the Mercer's, Tailor's, Spice, Tobacco, Shoe, Silversmith's, Book, Saddler's, Seed, Clothes, and the Silk Bazaars'.[16]

Jane went shopping for the clothes Medjuel told her were essential for the journey to Palmyra. Her European clothes – which drew the attention of small crowds as she sat cross-legged on cushions opposite a turbaned merchant in the souk, gravely discussing the price of a purchase over a cup of coffee or a lemon ice – would have to be left behind, for not only were they impractical but they would create unnecessary danger. Having already noted the lightness, grace and freedom of the Arab dress, Jane had no qualms on this score.

While Jane explored, Medjuel was organising the small caravan that would take her to Palmyra. This trip was to be the apogee of her tour; probably less than a score of Europeans had ever been there. Lady Hester Stanhope, the great eccentric of Lady Andover's generation, had made the trip thirty years earlier. Her bedouin escort (from Medjuel's tribe) had crowned her arrival with floral wreaths, which she took to mean that they had proclaimed her their 'queen'.

Since that time no European woman had visited Palmyra; it remained a dangerous and arduous journey.

Possibly it was Hester Stanhope's story that had provoked Jane's interest, but equally likely was the older story of Queen Zenobia and her fight against the Romans in the third century AD. At the head of 70,000 Arabs, Zenobia drove the Romans out of Syria before marching into Egypt to destroy the Roman garrisons there, thus gaining control of all Syria and the neighbouring provinces. For some years she ruled the entire desert from her magnificent palace at Palmyra, where she made her capital on the ancient biblical site of Soloman's Tadmor. The warrior Queen was eventually defeated, and carted off to Rome, where she was displayed decked out in jewels, and fettered in gold chains, in the Romans' triumphal homecoming procession. The city of Palmyra was sacked and razed in retribution.

But Jane's plan to visit Palmyra was not straightforward. The British consul, Richard Wood, was determined to put a stop to such a foolhardy notion. He invited her to the consulate a few days after her arrival and strongly advised her against making the journey. His concern was undoubtedly that Jane could cause a potential 'incident' on his patch, for despite her battered reputation as Lady Ellenborough, as he insisted on calling her, she was the granddaughter of the Earl of Leicester and had important connections in England. The mere thought of an Englishwoman travelling alone (apart from her maid) in the desert with a group of Arabs was distressing to him.

Though he frequently travelled on the road between Damascus, Homs and Aleppo in the north of the country, the consul told her, he had never dared to make the journey across the trackless desert to Palmyra. Six months earlier Lord Dalkeith and a few other English gentlemen had made the journey and had been obliged to travel 'almost wholly by night, running the gauntlet of a dozen Arab encampments' and allowed only a day's stay at Palmyra. On the return journey they had been captured and imprisoned for four days, escaping only by the merest good fortune, and had returned ill and exhausted. Indeed, said Wood, the best one could hope for if attacked was that the warriors were merciful and would not kill and bury one – that is, if one considered it merciful to be stripped naked and turned loose without food or water in the desert.

Jane knew that Medjuel had not been escort to the Dalkeith expedition but that it was his tribe who were suspected of having captured the travellers in retaliation for the poaching of their rights of way. So she thanked Mr Wood but declined his advice. She was aware that the journey would not be easy and that there was potentially great danger; probably it was part of the attraction. And she knew that even when they reached Palmyra there would be little respite. For many years the Palmyrans (inhabitants of the nearby town) had allowed no one to spend more than twenty-four hours at the ruins of Zenobia's city.

> You must be almost *inhumanly* strong if you can make the long journey there and back, fifty hours of camel riding and not spend those twenty hours in sleep or rest.
>   ... The ruins are three miles in extent and no one could take more than a glance at the principal objects, even if ten hours were spent in traversing them; and as the fear of Bedouin *ghazzous* and the want of water necessitate riding that part of the journey *nearest* to Palmyra at a stretch of twenty-four hours without stop or stay, both going and returning, few persons like to undertake it. Then the fee given to the tribe for allowing visitors to go there, with safe-conduct, is usually £30 each.[17]

Medjuel had told Jane that most Ferengi (European or 'Frankish') travellers who wished to make the journey were turned down because he considered they would not stand up physically to the rigours of the journey, or sometimes simply because he did not like them. He was *bedu*, he told her proudly, implying that anything else was inferior.

In early June 1853 Jane set out on what she would ever after call the 'greatest adventure, probably, of all my journeys'.[18] Wearing a cloak, called an *abba*, over a simple cotton shift, a square white keffiyeh folded into a triangle and fixed on her head with an *agal* (headband) of coloured silks, and soft kid ankle-high boots with pointed toes, dyed lemon yellow, Jane emerged from Demetri's accompanied by Eugénie in a similar outfit.

Outside the hotel she found a scene of confusion, a team of dromedaries on their knees, groaning, roaring and growling, 'as if they were about to be killed, after the manner of dromedaries the moment they are requested to kneel and the whole time they are kneeling'.[19] Camel drivers ran around shouting at each other and in the midst of the commotion stood Sheikh Medjuel, calmly waiting. He wore his usual clothes – scarlet cloak over striped shift, a bright silk keffiyeh on his head. Around his waist he had wound and knotted several coloured scarves and into this wide sash had thrust a number of knives and pistols. Around his neck was a silken cord upon which hung a sword, and on his feet were red leather boots with upturned toes. On his wrist he carried a hooded hawk. This final touch was not showmanship: the bird would be used to catch small birds and game as fresh food on the journey, as would his salukis – the elegant hunting dogs of the desert – which always travelled with him. His long black hair, the sidelocks of which had formerly hung in ringlets around his ears, was neatly plaited.

Medjuel instructed the *argeels* (camel drivers) to keep their animals lying down by standing on the forelegs of the beasts while the women scrambled awkwardly into the seats. Jane's camel immediately jumped up, raising its hind legs and throwing her almost over its head, then raising its forelegs and throwing her backwards against the wooden frame of the saddle. She would quickly learn the art of mounting as the bedouin women did, by stepping lightly on to the camel's neck and springing into position as the beast lifted its head, but this required practice, and her first experience was awkward. The small amount of baggage she had been allowed to bring – some changes of linen, a few toilet items, sketchbook, pencils and paints, and a book – was handed over by Eugénie and safely stowed in her saddle-bags.

At last they were on their way, Jane sitting easily in the middle of the rug-covered saddle with her legs crossed around the front pommel. On either side of the saddle, or *schedad*, were large saddle-bags made of woven camel hair into which had been sewn rows of coloured silk tassels, bunches of ostrich feathers and tiny turquoise beads to 'ward off the evil eye'. Long cords ending in dyed woollen tassels hung down almost to the ground and swayed as the camel walked. Soon the party cleared the city, the drums ceased beating, the camel drivers ceased singing, the last goodbye faded in the distance. As they passed out upon the great plain beyond the village of Doumah they met the postman galloping in after his nine-day ride from Baghdad.[20]

The first night they camped at a khan, a desert enclosure on the outskirts of a small village where they could buy limited foods such as camel's milk and *leben* (a yoghurt-like substance made from the milk of sheep, goat or camel), and fresh oranges and *dibs* (honeyed raisins). Jane was happy to sleep in the open on a mound of rugs under blankets, gazing up at the moon hanging low in the sky. There is nowhere in the world where the moon hangs so close and so bright as in the desert. And there is such silence that the very sound of it seems to enter the soul.

The women were woken at daybreak with hot coffee, and set off into the desert with four days of hard riding ahead of them. Medjuel had been explicit about the dangers that threatened and he had not lightly undertaken to shepherd the two women on a journey fraught with possible dangers. He warned Jane of the bedouin *ghazous* (raids), when fierce groups of tribesmen would swoop down on encampments, club the travellers senseless and loot the camp. With infidels they were not bound by the rules that made it unlawful to kill another bedouin, thus creating a blood feud that could last generations.

Jane's diary was full of the beauty of the desert and the mountain range that they were to follow almost all the way to Palmyra. She had anticipated miles of arid sand, but there were frequent patches of aromatic bushes, splashes of bright scarlet poppies and tufts of herbs for over half the journey – all material for her sketchbook. At times Medjuel stopped to allow the camels to graze this foliage which, he told her, assuaged their thirst. They saw gerboas, desert rats and hares. Occasionally a gazelle bounded stiff-legged across their path. Hoopoes and brilliantly coloured rollers flashed against the dark mountains, and in the sky above them eagles wheeled. The colours, the never-ending changes of tints in the sands and the mountain backdrop made her itch to paint. Endless streaks of pinks, lilacs, mauves, reds and deep purple-browns changed as the sun dropped to hazy blues and deep smoky-grey.

Several times great blue lakes appeared at the foot of the mountains, and initially Jane could hardly credit it when Medjuel told her that there was no water, but only a mirage on the great salt pan. The lakes faded away after several hours as the light changed. In the desert the view was limitless and perspective distorted, so that an item seen clearly in the early morning might take ten hours to reach, never seeming to come closer until almost under the camel's feet.

The next day they pitched camp in the open desert. Within fifteen minutes the low black tents had been erected, a fire was blazing brightly, the camels had been strung in lines and the saddles set at the open side of the sheikh's tent, covered with carpets to act as seat backs. The women had their own accommodation, rugs to lie upon and saddle-bags as pillows. Jane loved the bedouin tents, the sight of which, she said, made her heart beat with pleasure: 'Lovely to my eye are these . . . low, black tents.'[21] A friend of Jane's would describe them as long and narrow, closed at the back but partially open in front. When walking in the camp one must pass at the back of the tent and not peep into any at the front – any more than we should think of peeping into a gentleman's window. To look into an arab's tent, even to pass too near the front of it, would give the deepest offence.[22]

In camp the men prayed regularly, spreading out their prayer mats and performing the washing ritual with sand, in the absence of water, before bowing to Mecca. Since it was Ramadan, they had all fasted between sunrise and sunset, so the meal – which consisted of broth made from a desert partridge caught that day by Medjuel's hawk, which had dropped on the creature from the sky and held it on the sands until the unleashed salukis seized and killed it – was welcome. The women had taken sips of water during the day but the men, she noted, took nothing; though a traveller was permitted to drink during Ramadan, additional grace could be earned by abstinence.

Afterwards the sun dropped suddenly and the wonderful desert night skies filled with bright pinpricks of light until the moon rose, turning the sand into molten silver. Behind the tents they could hear jackals howling, a lonely, eerie sound that set the camels groaning, and the hunting dogs crept closer to the fire. Jane was told to try to sleep for a few hours, for they were to rise and ride through the night. Jane 'more than ever enjoyed the night, the camels kept together better than in the day, and the *argeels* indulged in a number of wild songs . . . some of the tunes wild and sad'. The songs that the *argeels* sang to their camels, which Medjuel translated for her, Jane found particularly amusing:

> Oh, Camel, my love, my beauty, go on quickly and the prettiest girls of the village shall come out to meet you. Go on, and when you kneel, the maidens will feed you with fresh sugar-canes and stroke you with their soft hands.[23]

She found it a delicious experience to trot along under the moon; without the burning heat of the day, the smooth trot of the camel was more exhilarating than the long striding walk.

On the next evening, as they made camp, they were attacked. Medjuel had never relaxed his guard from the moment they left Damascus. Whenever they stopped he posted lookouts; when they were on the move he himself constantly circled the group, peering into the distance. Scouts were sent ahead and some made to lag behind to warn of any strangers who approached. Jane did not underestimate his concern. Once or twice they had seen riders in the distance, but it was not until the dreadful cry of '*Ghazou, ghazou*' went up from all sides and riders poured into the camp brandishing lances and uttering a blood-curdling war-cry that she felt any apprehension.

Medjuel's one thought was to protect his client and he sprang in front of her tent with a pistol in one hand and a sabre in the other. Jane, taken by surprise, could do little but watch as he parried the attack, calling out orders to his men. They had few items of value and were carrying only what was necessary for the journey. All jewellery had, at the sheikh's instruction, been left behind with the consul in Damascus. The money she had brought for expenses on the journey had been given into his safe-keeping. But there were some good riding camels and much equipment of value to bedouins. No shots were fired, but there was some hand-to-hand fighting until Medjuel's energetic defence drove the raiders back into the desert.

Jane believed that she owed her life to Medjuel on that occasion, and even twenty-five years later, when she described the incident to a visitor, she recalled the breathtaking excitement of the moment and her debt to him.[24] It also gave her a great respect for the ways of the desert, for she had learned that these raids were a way of life for the bedouin, as sudden as they were vicious.

Jane's niece, the writer A. M. Stirling, who produced a condensed career of Jane for a family history, wrote that it was quite usual for travellers to pay their 6,000 francs for a visit to Palmyra and later to find themselves held up by members of the same tribe for a similar sum of 'ransom' money. E. M. Oddie believed that the raiders were from one of the branches of the Anazeh tribe, to which the Mezrabs belonged, and, having identified Medjuel as one of their own sheikhs, had no intention of harming anyone. Had they made off with any booty, she thought, they would have shared it with Medjuel later, and Medjuel's actions were thus an act for his client's benefit.[25]

This theory does not accord with bedouin tribal custom. It would have been the height of impropriety to continue to attack the caravan after having identified a friend. The marauders would have been forced to apologise immediately they realised such a mistake, and Medjuel would have been obliged to invite them to join in their meal.[26] That the raiders were Anazeh is more than likely, for the Anazeh frequented that part of the desert. But the Anazeh had many branches and there was great internecine rivalry between them. It was not considered especially unfriendly to attack another Anazeh tribe by *ghazou*; raiding for plunder was a way of life, and the answer was a counter-raid. The main danger lay in the fact that as in any society there were unscrupulous elements, and that a *ghazou* of so-called bedouins might in reality have been one of the many itinerant gangs of ruthless men who were not pure-blood bedouins and therefore lacked their code of honour.

For the next two days the party did not make camp but took short breaks during the day to feed and rest. After four days' toiling under a desert sun even the most ardent conversationalist grows quiet. The eyes ache from the reflected glare of the sun, sand dries the nostrils, and the burning air hurts the nasal membranes with each intake of breath. Medjuel showed Jane how to cover her face with the keffiyeh, and even how to sleep by twisting and lying down curled around the pommel. The long, even stride of the camel, unlike the short, quick step of a horse, made this feasible, and she found that to ease the tedium of the hours she could read, or even write in her diary, as they rode.

A general listlessness settled on the party, except for the ever alert Medjuel, but at last they reached the pass that led to the ruined city, always thereafter called by Jane by its old Arab name of Tadmor rather than the classical Palmyra. According to the Bible,[27] the ancient oasis city of 'Tadmor in the wilderness' was built by King Solomon (*tedmur* being ancient Hebrew for palm). After the defeat of Queen Zenobia the Romans called the ruins Adrianopolis, but the Arabs have never called it by anything other than its ancient Arabic name.

Apathy dropped away, and the party quickened their pace and craned eagerly for the first glimpse of their goal, the 12th century Saracen citadel built on the hill overlooking the ruined city. First they had to ride through the Valley of the Dead with its unique tower tombs, 150 of them, bearing names such as the Bride's Tomb, Maiden's Tomb or King's Tomb, not because of the status of the inhabitants but because the style of building suggested such a name.

At last they crested a hill and the ruined city lay spread out before them. If Jane had been struck by Damascus, how much more moved was she now by this massive uninhabited city with its magnificent temples, triumphal arches and colonnaded streets. More than three miles in length, Tadmor gleamed with the dazzling purity of ivory. At dawn the stone would flush pink, and in the rays of the setting sun turn to rose-gold.

News of their arrival had preceded them. Horsemen galloped out to meet them from the nearby village, welcoming them noisily as they relayed an invitation from Sheikh Mohammed (no relation to Medjuel) to his home. First, however, Medjuel led his party to a large walled garden shaded by trees. A small pool, fed by a hot sulphur spring, gave off an unpleasant smell, but the waters were crystalline.

The first necessity was to bathe, and Medjuel showed the women where they could wash in private in a warm stream. The men meanwhile erected the tents and formed the camp that would be their base for the duration of their stay. The great floppy water-bags made of goatskins were refilled from the stream and hung in the branches of a tree. Within hours the smell of sulphur had disappeared and the water was cool and sweet to drink.

By the time they had eaten it was dark, and Jane's first, unforgettable experience of the ancient city was by moonlight as she wandered about with Medjuel through the Great Arch and along the main street, its paving still bearing ruts made by the wheels of chariots. The colonnade and buildings were now bathed in delicate light, and the desert air was warm and soft.

Next morning she was up at dawn and spent part of the day going over the massive temple of Bel, the sun-god, and the other major buildings. Medjuel accompanied her and sat watching as she sketched, keeping at bay the inquisitive townspeople who had wandered over to see the Christian woman. Apart from architectural detail her notebook is dotted with small pencilled working sketches of cloaked figures hunched round a fire, tents and ropes forming a background, with camels grazing, and picturesque bunches of bedouin lances, their metal tips stuck into the sand, but always ready as weapons.

In the evening they visited the Sheikh of Palmyra, a privilege Jane did not enjoy. As they rode into the town the people swarmed out in a mob and hung on to Medjuel's legs, kissing his hands and knees, shrieking a noisy welcome. Jane feared they would pull him off his camel. She and Eugénie were objects of considerable curiosity and were pulled this way and that by the women who also wished to hug and kiss them. She was not impressed by the townspeople, who she decided were

unmitigated barbarians; they are *fellaheen* of the lowest order, permitted by the Bedouins to live within the town, on condition of their acting as purveyors to the tribes. The caravans from Aleppo, Damascus and Bagdad all touch there . . . They are a rough, rude set and have all the vices of the Bedouin without any of his virtues.[28]

Wherever she went the women tried to examine her person, her hair and her clothes. She found them ignorant, verminous and revolting, and her impression of the men was not much better. The only mitigation she admitted was in the display of horsemanship and obvious love of the Sheikh of Palmyra for his beautiful Arab mare, which Medjuel valued at £1,800, stressing that even so she would only be sold in the event of some great misfortune which obliged her owner to part with her.[29]

Too soon, it was time to leave. Jane was already planning a return visit the following year. Medjuel may have smiled at this. The few European travellers he had escorted all said the same thing but none had ever returned. So unique was the experience that almost everyone who made the trip wrote about it, and so unusual that most accounts were published. By now Medjuel was fairly bewitched by Jane, but strangely, perhaps because of his age, she appears to have been unaware of it. Her journal speaks of Saleh and Selaine, her 'handsome, tall Jordan friends', and she was looking forward to seeing them again. The return to Damascus was as full of interest for Jane as the journey out, but it was free of incident.

During one of their conversations Medjuel told her that this was the year he was to make his hadj to Mecca. It is a measure of his regard for Jane that he suggested she accompany him, and a little surprising that she did not accept the offer.[30] That *would* have been an adventure. The only infidel ever to visit the holy city and live to tell the story was the adventurer and explorer Richard Burton. Burton spoke fluent Arabic and with his swarthy skin and black hair had disguised himself effectively enough to get away with it, all the time knowing that had he been discovered, by the merest slip in the Muslim ritual, it would have meant instant death. The hadj was filled with dangers of all sorts, not only from the arduous journey itself but from the risks of cholera and plague that every year broke out and killed thousands of pilgrims.

At last the travellers came in sight of Damascus and its trees, orchards and gardens. After days in the arid wastes the desert travellers could smell the water,

> like a thirsty horse, [and] hear its gurgling long before [reaching] the rills and fountains . . . scent, and then see, the fruit, the limes, figs, citron and

water-melon . . . feel a madness to jump into the water, to eat a fill of fruit, to go to sleep under the delicious shade . . . forget the bitter wind, the scorching sun, the blistering sand.

You dream away the last two or three hours of the journey, wondering if it is true, or [whether] your brain is hurt by the sun, or your blinded eyes see a mirage. But your tired, drooping horse tells you it is true. He pricks up his ears, knows he is near home, would like to break out into a mild trot if he could, stops to drink at every rill and with a low whinny of joy gathers a mouthful of grass as he passes every crop.[31]

The sensual joys of a bath are truly known only to those who have journeyed long in the desert. Bathed and rested, Jane spent some time looking at horses recommended by Medjuel. She decided to wait in Damascus to watch him depart on the hadj. It was a spectacle not to be missed and one, though she did not yet know it, she would witness many times in the future.

For weeks, since the start of Ramadan, pilgrims from all over central Asia had converged on Damascus. Here they sold their horses and purchased camels for the desert march. The departure of the pilgrims occurred after several days of feasting, celebrations and processions, all accompanied by military bands, during which excited crowds of citizens, from shopkeepers to the pampered inhabitants of harems, went *en fête* in the streets.

Every balcony and window overlooking the route was packed with sightseers, and with the assistance of the British consul Jane obtained a good view. All around them was the sound of bands playing 'wild and wailing music', and street vendors, the sweetmeat-sellers, carpet-sellers, water-carriers, all vying with each other to advertise their wares. As the procession approached, a deathly silence fell as thousands of pilgrims, from the opulent court of the emir, wali and mushir in their golden palanquins, to the military escort and bedouins who would protect and police the massive caravan, down to the poorest pilgrim, filed through the gates of the city. Many were riding the hadj donkeys but among them sheikhs on their priceless desert horses that were 'only seen on such days. A blood horse seldom costs here less than 200 or 300 Napoleons, but a mare has no price, she is too precious. She might be £40,000 in shares, if one of the three real old races, and her pedigree beyond dispute.' Finally the hundreds of baggage camels, bearing chests of luggage and merchandise, marked the end of the procession.

Jane stayed on in Damascus for a few days before leaving with a small escort organised by Medjuel for the return journey. She met Selaine as arranged, and when she parted from him at Beirut repeated her intention of returning again in three months. She was already thinking of buying a house in Syria, perhaps as a *pied-à-tere* for expeditions.

She arrived in Greece in July, but there was no sensation of home-coming. She spent her entire time there, some six weeks, placing her affairs in order so that she could return to Syria in the autumn. Hadji-Petros was not in Athens, which was probably a good thing; but Jane was annoyed to find that her jewellery casket, which she had left behind, had vanished. She hoped that the general had taken it for safe-keeping and could only be grateful that the more important pieces she had either placed in a vault or taken with her.

Somehow, the story of the adventurous trip to Syria had reached the ears of the Duchesse de Plaisance, though the two women did not see each other during those weeks. Jane's trip to Palmyra, her attrac-tion to Saleh, her search for a horse and her imminent return to Syria gave birth to the extraordinary tales that would spread about Athens after her departure, adding to the 'Ianthe' legend.

Among the correspondence that Jane found awaiting her was news from her mother that her first love, George Anson, had achieved the rank of major-general, and had been appointed to command a division in India. How long ago that life seemed to her now.

When Jane had left Athens a few months earlier she had been full of anger. Indignation had sustained her in the initial stages of her journey and caused her conclusion that men had brought her nothing but problems. But when the anger subsided uncertainty had taken over. She was nearly fifty, with no direction to her life. What was she to do, where go? In Athens she was unwelcome in top society because of her rivalry with the Queen; and she had quarrelled with the duch-ess, removing her only real mainstay (later, Jane would regret not calling on her old friend to make peace).[32] Secure in her relation-ship with Hadji-Petros these things had seemed unimportant. Recent events had changed that perspective and Jane knew that, were it to become gossip that her high-profile relationship with Hadji-Petros had ended because he had preferred her maid, her enemies would ensure she became a laughing stock as well as a social pariah. But her journey to Jordan and Syria had opened new vistas. She went about her business decisively, buoyed by the excit-ing prospect of a new home in an exotic location, new friends and a fresh purpose. By the beginning of October Jane had put the newly completed house in Athens up for sale and was on her way back to Beirut.[33]

13

Arabian Nights
1853–1854

9 October 1853. Off Beyrout.
Here I am at last. My ardent wish is almost gratified, to see Saleh again
... before long I shall know if I am to remain. Syria, Palestine. With
how many sweet and fraught remembrances are you known to me.[1]

The above extract was written in code, not in Jane's diary but in a
page of one of the small leather-bound pocket sketchbooks she always
carried with her. As with her diary, anything Jane considered to be
especially sensitive was written in this code. She knew her brother
Edward would remember it, and in letters to him she included phrases
written in it.[2] In her diaries it was probably done to ensure that her
most private thoughts were not read by Eugénie.

Jane rode from Beirut to Jerusalem, then south to Hebron (present-
day Al Khalil), where she expected to meet Saleh. But he was away
when she arrived and it was close to the end of the month when she
wrote, 'He came at last!' A few days later, on 2 November, she was
jotting down hints of disillusionment. 'Hebron. The charm is dissolv-
ing. Night at Hebron a disappointment. Grasping disposition. Gave
£20 to Selaine; £3 to Saleh; £2 to Abou. Not so poor as they look,
live well in their way.' Then she made a list of what look to be the
disadvantages of Saleh:

His fanaticism
Coldness in love.
Can he obtain Selaine's position?
Sabba![3]

It was the last disadvantage, however, that tipped the balance. Saleh had with him a young, dark-eyed girl of the Moseineh tribe. Confident in her youth and 'insolent in her beauty', her name was Sabba. It was 'Sabba ... who kept Saleh's heart from me,' Jane wrote; and she had no intention of playing second fiddle to a girl half her age. Apart from this, though not actually stated, there are sufficient hints throughout her diary that there were frequent calls upon her purse from both Selaine and Saleh. Jane returned to Beirut, and there on 26 November she wrote in her notebook, 'Second departure from Beyrout and parting from Saleh.'[4]

The note 'departure from Beyrout' is intriguing, for it sounds as though she sailed from the port. Yet three weeks later she was in Damascus, having talked her way into another 'adventure', even more fraught with danger than the trip to Palmyra. The journey from Beirut to Piraeus could hardly be done in under twelve days and she could not have travelled to and from Greece in three weeks. The probability is that even when the promised relationship with Saleh failed to materialise she could not bring herself to return to Greece. Arabia still promised much.

At Damascus she met Medjuel and told him that she wished to make another desert journey. He was unable to escort her, since he was obliged to go with his tribe to their winter grazing. She explained what had happened at Hebron, which she said had ended any possibility of her making her home there. Instead she was now considering building a house in Damascus.

To her surprise Medjuel then asked her if she was willing to marry a bedouin. Himself. She had known he was attracted to her, but, since 'no word of love had ever passed his lips', she was, unusually for Jane, taken aback by the question. She told him that if she loved him she would certainly be prepared to consider his proposition were he not already married, but it was against her religion for a man to take more than one wife. The word 'divorce' hung over the discussion.

Afterwards Jane hardly knew what to think, and her questions and reasoning on the matter run like a theme through her diary. Was it a serious proposal? Medjuel was twenty years younger than she. She was not in love with him, at least not in the way she had always defined love. Was their genuine liking for each other a sufficient starsight by which to set her compass? Could he grow to love her? Could she grow to love him? What part in the marriage of a bedouin did love, as opposed to sex, play? She had been told that the bedouin never married outside their culture; indeed, their own blood-lines were as pure as those of their prized mares. Would she be accepted by his people? And, supposing Medjuel divorced his wife to marry Jane, what would her family in England think of her marrying an Arab? 'What an abyss into which I have plunged,' she wrote.

Soon afterwards Jane arranged to join a desert caravan under the direction of Sheikh el Barak, a bedouin well known to Medjuel. Barak was not the cultured man that Medjuel was, but it would be some time before Jane discovered this flaw. Meanwhile he was another striking and confident man of the desert who flattered her with attention; furthermore, for an undisclosed sum he was prepared to take Jane along on his four-month trip across the desert to Baghdad to buy camels and other commodities. Medjuel appears to have made no attempt to dissuade her from going. When they parted he had still spoken no word of love, nor had he even kissed her, and Jane was unsure whether or not to take seriously their earlier conversation regarding marriage.

She had learned that Medjuel now had only one wife, Mascha. She was the mother of his two sons, one of whom, Afet (meaning 'gift), had been born to Mascha since Jane's trip to Palmyra. A second and younger wife, Minouah, who had been very beautiful, had been divorced for some reason that Medjuel seemed reluctant to discuss, but that Jane later learned was because (as Jane wrote in code) 'of her bad smell'. Would he really be prepared to divorce the mother of his two sons, Jane wondered. And could she, Jane, live with the knowledge that he had cast off a wife for her? And, supposing Jane was to become Medjuel's wife, could she live as a bedouin? She had enjoyed the desert journeys more than any experience in her life, but was honest enough to recognise that discomfort had been tempered by novelty and the knowledge that she would return shortly to a normal life. The considerations seemed endless and were still troubling her when she left Damascus with Eugénie. A measure of her intentions can be divined by her determination to make the journey to Baghdad not as a Frankish tourist but as a working member of the caravan, to see how she might adapt to the life of a bedouin.

Just as on the previous trip, the women agreed to wear Arab clothes, but they felt less self-conscious this time, recognising their advantages. On Monday 19 December Jane left Demetri's hotel at Damascus, 'dressed as a Bedouin Sheikh in holiday clothes, to join my camp. Thus I begin my assay into Bedouin life'.[5] Eugénie, ever faithful, shadowed Jane. Because so little is known of Eugénie, it would be easy to think of her as a faithful but insipid servant. Certainly she was faithful (apart from her lapse with Hadji-Petros) but as the next few weeks would reveal she was far from insipid.

When she kept her face covered, Jane's stature usually fooled people, for she was as tall as a bedouin man; 'the women crowded around and took me for a man, but they were not intrusive,' she wrote.[6] It was to occur several times. But it was agreed that, should there be no alternative but to admit her gender, it would be best if she pretended to be Barak's wife. The party consisted of Barak, Jane and Eugénie, twenty-five *aghaylats* (guards), some camel drivers and sundry others. The journey began well. 'Lovely was Damascus last night,' Jane wrote, 'and lovely too in the morning as I mounted my donkey, elate in spirits. But as I passed the well-known road which branched off to Tadmor thoughts and regrets of Medjuel intruded themselves and made me look upon my present journey with distaste.'[7]

Barak had made it clear from the beginning that it was not going to be a pleasure trip – the winter months in the desert are often bitterly cold and wet – and the first week was as miserable as he had forecast. Jane made light of the hardships, but a man who was to become her friend, the great and fearless traveller, Richard Burton, who made the same trip at the same time of year a decade later, said of it:

> Our hardships were considerable; the country was under water and the rushing torrents and deep ditches caused long detours. We had heavy and continuous rain, furious blasts, snow and sleet like Norway. One of the followers sickened and died, and we were all frostbitten . . . Throughout Syria, when the basaltic soil runs to any depth the earth is loose and treacherous, fatiguing to traverse in summer and impassable in winter.[8]

Each day was the same: they got out of their beds more or less fully dressed, and a *toilette* usually consisted of shaking the sand or mud out of one's clothes and hair. Those responsible for the animals went to see to them, some coaxed the embers of the fire into life and heated coffee, or fetched bowls of warm, frothy camel's milk. Others started to strike the tents to pack and load them, or fill the leather water-bags for refreshment while they travelled. Jane would travel this route many times in the future and her experience would stand her in good stead. Christmas came and went, marked only by the fact that a camel was lost or stolen during the night. 'It is astonishing to see the rising frustration with every misfortune,' Jane wrote. 'But our fires at night are delightful. I fetch food for the sheikh's tent, and [for] my dromedary to which one becomes quite attached when one appreciates their instincts.'

She was slightly bored with the cold, wet trek, but the men were happy about the rain, for it presaged a 'green spring' and therefore good forage for camels. And Jane consoled herself with the thought that she was on her way to Baghdad, the city of a thousand Arabian nights. Soon, boredom gave way to excitement. The caravan paused for the night, and with the cessation of rain it grew warmer. Jane took a bath in a deep pool of rainwater in the sand, and had just finished dressing when she heard the familiar and dreaded cry go up that a raid was in progress.

Barak rushed into her tent demanding that she hide her sheikh's scarlet mantle, but it was already too late. Jane heard the cries of the attackers and reached for a gun but, as she turned, an Arab on a chestnut horse, the sharpened point of his lance held before him, rode into the open tent and 'made us fairly his prisoners'.[9] A large group of 'ruffians' herded them off to the conquerors' tents.

Not surprisingly Eugénie was extremely frightened, insisting hysterically, 'Oh, we shall be sold as slaves.' Not so Jane. The raiders, she learned, were members of the M'wayaja tribe. She scribbled hurried notes in her small brown notebook, dismissing her captors as *canaille*. 'Not one prepossessing face amongst them!' she wrote. 'How different from the handsome Jordan set.' She was unafraid and, though she felt sorry for Eugénie's distress, had to admit that 'in my heart I have enjoyed the experience so far, and was glad of witnessing it'.[10]

The following day, after much consultation, Barak paid the ransom demanded for the release of persons, camels and tents, but they had to stand by while many of their personal belongings were openly taken off them. When this was done Jane assumed they would be released, but they were still guarded by a fierce Arab woman wielding a large club and ruffian-looking guards who insisted they were not to move until their sheikh, Faris ebn Hedeb, returned. It seemed that Sheikh Faris had had second thoughts and now wished to press for more ransom money. As night fell, the men gathered around the coffee hearth to negotiate terms. Fascinated, Jane placed her bed-roll outside the tent so that she could watch and listen.

1 Jane's mother Lady Andover, described by George IV as the handsomest woman in London. 2 Jane's father Admiral Sir Henry Digby, a Trafalgar hero. 3 Holkham Hall where Jane spent much of her childhood. 4 Jane's grandfather, Thomas Coke, farsighted landowner and agriculturist. 5 Jane and her two brothers Edward and Kenelm.

6

7

8

6 Elm Grove, the Ellenboroughs' country
house at Roehampton.
7 Engraving of Jane as a society beauty in a
popular series of engravings sold in print
shops c.1828.
8 Edward, Lord Ellenborough c.1831.
9 Lord Ellenborough between Wellington and
Peel; his thick dark curls were a magnet for
contemporary satirists.

"A WILD ELEPHANT led BETWEEN TWO TAME ONES"

9

11 Colonel George Anson, Jane's cousin. Their affair was conducted discreetly, but she believed him to be the father of her child.

10 Frederick Madden (later Sir Frederick). The talented classical scholar was bewitched by Jane's singing and became her lover.

12 The Ellenboroughs' divorce case scandalised society and was the subject of sensational media coverage providing rich pickings for cartoonists.

13 For HRH Prince Felix Schwarzenberg it was love at first sight when he met Jane at an embassy ball.

14 King Ludwig I of Bavaria; Jane's 'dearest and best friend'.

15 The portrait of Jane painted by Stieler for the King's *Gallery of Beauty*. The artist stated in his diary that she was one of the two most beautiful women he ever painted.

16 'Lady Ellenborough' by the court sculptor Josef Bandel; one of several images of Jane commissioned by the King.

17

18

19

17 Baron Carl 'Charles' Venningen. Totally
devoted to Jane, he even forgave her
abandonment of him and their children and
wrote affectionately to her until his death.
18 Marble bust of Jane, believed carved at the
time of her marriage to the Baron. The
classical profile is almost identical to the Carl
Haag portrait (see plate 36). 19 Schloss
Weinheim, the Venningens' home near
Heidelberg where Balzac was a guest. It is
now the town hall. 20 Jane's children,
Heribert and Bertha Venningen. Bertha who
became hopelessly insane was almost certainly
the child of King Ludwig. Painted before Jane
eloped in 1836 this miniature was still in her
possession on her death in 1881.

20

21 The handsome 'dangerous' Count Spiros Theotoky. He duelled with the Baron for Jane and finally eloped with her.

22 Leonidas Theotoky. The only one of Jane's children for whom she felt real love. This portrait believed to have been painted after his tragic death at the age of 6.

23 The Athens mansion built by Jane for her and Spiros, at the time considered the finest house in the city.

24 'Ianthe'; the Queen's rival for the affections of Colonel Hadji-Petros, charismatic leader of the Palikare mountain people of north Greece.
25 Queen Amalie of Greece; jealous of Jane, she took a public revenge.
26 Xristodolous Hadji-Petros, the King's governor in northern Greece and Albania.
27 While Jane was making this sketch of Mount Lycabettus her gold chain was stolen.

28

29

30

28 Damascus, the oriental 'pearl of the desert'. Jane's
first sight of it took her breath away.
29 A typical picture from Jane's sketchbook.

30–31 Two of the many paintings of Baghdad by Jane.

31

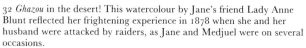

32 *Ghazou* in the desert! This watercolour by Jane's friend Lady Anne Blunt reflected her frightening experience in 1878 when she and her husband were attacked by raiders, as Jane and Medjuel were on several occasions.

33 The Blunts at the tents of Sheikh el Dhuki on their way to visit Jane in Damascus where they bought the neighbouring property. Jane's own entourage would have looked similar to the one in this very early photo.

34

34 The fabled desert ruins at Palmyra where Jane spent her honeymoon
and some of the happiest times of her life – an early photograph by Frith.
35 One of Jane's watercolours of Palmyra which she called by the old Arab
name, Tadmor.

36–37 The magnificent portrait of Jane (and detail above) painted by Carl Haag in 1859 is the last known image of her, and the only one in her desert clothes.

38–39 Sheikh Medjuel el Mezrab, Palmyra, December 1859, by Carl Haag (and detail above). This is the only known formal image of him.

40–41 Jane's Damascus house. A rare early photograph of the *liwan* and courtyard taken during Edward Prince of Wales's visit to her in 1862, and Jane's sketch.

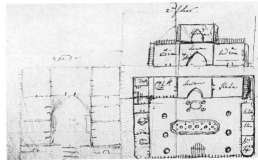

42 Photograph taken recently inside the old hall of Jane's former house. The original wallpaper and gilded woodcarvings, designed by Jane, still survive amidst the clutter of modern day builders' tools. Over 30 families now live on the site of Jane's property.

43

44

45

43 Isabel Burton. Jane liked her and
enjoyed her 'lively company' but was
hurt by Isabel's exaggerated public
account of their friendship.
44 Richard Burton; explorer,
adventurer, writer and British
Consul at Damascus. Much of the
'secret' information on life in the
harem used in his famous sex
manuals (such as the *Kama Sutra*) he
obtained from Jane.
45 The Burtons' house at Damascus
by Sir Frederick Leighton RA.
46 The roof garden of the Burtons'
house. After dinner the Burtons, Jane
and Abd el Kader 'would go to the
roof . . . and talk far into the night'.

46

47 OPPOSITE ABOVE The Street called
Straight (mentioned in the Bible) in
the Christian Quarter, before the
massacre.
49 OPPOSITE BELOW The Street called
Straight photographed during the
Prince of Wales's visit to Damascus
in 1862, showing the devastation still
prevailing 2 years after the massacre.

48 The Emir Abd el Kader.
Legendary former leader of the
Algerians against the French. A
devout Muslim, his heroism during
the 1860 massacre saved many
Christian lives.

50 The friend of Jane's last years, Lady Anne Blunt, wearing desert costume and riding an Arab mare. Jane would have dressed in a similar fashion though she always rode astride in the desert.

51 Wilfred Scawen Blunt, Lady Anne's husband 'with desert hawk and gazelle hound'. The Blunts' marriage was a disaster and both marvelled at and envied Jane and Medjuel's obvious contentment.

52 Jane's grave in Damascus today. The lighter block across the foot is pink limestone brought from Palmyra by Medjuel. He personally carved her name on it in Arabic characters.

Another day dawned and there was still no certainty of release. At that time Jane knew only a few phrases in Arabic, so she spoke Turkish and assumed the role of a Circassian to pass off her fair colouring. Fortunately, as the supposed wife of Sheikh el Barak, she received from the women a limited respect and was not roughly treated, but all knew that things could go badly if it was discovered that Jane and Eugénie were Europeans. Christians, and especially 'Franks', were not covered by the bedouin code of honour, and Eugénie's fears of slavery were not without foundation.

Eventually, after plundering Barak's camp and exchanging their best camels for some poor ones of his own, Sheikh Faris gave the order that the prisoners might go free. Jane watched the ransack, reminding herself that this was her introduction to the bedouin life but that not all bedouins were like these people: 'Their faces were demonical, I shall never forget the expressions on their faces . . . but I am not disgusted with Bedouins and Bedouin life.'[11] When the robbers finally let them go, they quickly packed and were on their way before the sheikh suffered another change of mind. They rode until nearly midnight, then camped and tried to get some sleep.

Next day one of the men caught a hare by pulling it out of a burrow. They cooked it whole, pieces being allocated by lot. The frugal meal was supplemented by bowls of camel's milk. As they rode along afterwards Jane noticed small cairns of rocks in a remote valley and was told they were bedouin graves: 'what a tale of sorrow it brings to one's mind, of illness without help, without sympathy perhaps, and the cold, desolate grave covered with a few stones . . . In ten days, *Inshallah*, we shall be at Bagdad. Bagdad! Wonderful!'

On 4 January, writing her diary, she recalled that it was Christmas in Greece for 'poor Xristos'. But she reserved any emotion for recording how they had seen yet another party of bedouins, fortunately not hostile; 'I am always excited by them,' she wrote. They had arrived at the village of Kosbe, 'and stayed in the garden of friends of Barak's . . . the Sheikh's wife has heard of Medjuel and spoke affectionately!' Jane made a note of all the ritual, such as the hostess washing the hands of guests before dinner by pouring water from a tall copper vessel with a long spout. 'When I returned to our camp the scene was semi-savage, semi-oriental by the light of the fires, amid palm trees, the camels gravely looking on behind. Oh! It was striking.'[12]

On the following day they caught the first sight of the Euphrates, and the famous bitumen springs which provide the pitch for the giant coracles used as ferries on the Tigris. It was

> a desolate and burning country. Saw a Bedouin on a fine horse. I walked with the Sheikh to our dinner and paid a visit to his wives. What an environment those women have. In what darkness they live. Everyone screaming, pushing, talking at once and I gravely seated in the midst. Oh! Could la Madre have seen me, clapping my hands with the harem and joining the chorus, *Tahire ha.!*[13]

The ensuing days were miserable. Their way lay over desolate stony country; mile after mile of dreary black basalt stones which, polished by the winds, gleamed under the sun, wearying the eyes. There was nothing for the camels to eat, and the few wells had sour brackish water that humans drank mixed with camel's milk to make it palatable. The camels would not touch it; indeed, to Jane's distress, they started to collapse and die. The men too were distressed, for they cared greatly for their beasts; they spent as much time talking about camels and looking at them as a contemporary Englishman would a good horse. They could not comprehend a land without camels.

It was on Sunday evening of that week as they drew near to their proposed camping ground that things took a surprising and not entirely welcome turn. As they stopped, Barak 'said something I hardly like, in helping me down from my camel, and slightly fussed and rather alarmed me . . . After dinner he proposed sleeping in my tent! [saying] "Sacso sacso, etc."' The word 'sacso', which Jane does not explain but obviously understood, is not an Arabic word. A modern-day interpreter suggests that it was a corruption of the word 'sex' which Barak had possibly learned from a European visitor. Not surprisingly, she was very uneasy as she accepted Barak's pressing invitations to join him after dinner. 'I went to his fire after dinner on his pressing me . . . Oh the night, and the times. Nine [unreadable] a Bedouin!'[14]

This frank, though irritatingly incomplete, coded entry might, even so, be ambiguous were it not that a year later in her diary she referred to the occasion as the anniversary of the night when 'I gave myself to Barak'.[15] The act itself gave her no cause for guilt, then or later. She was not at that time confident of her feelings for Medjuel, nor did she owe sexual loyalty to any other man. It is interesting to the biographer, though, as an illustration of her attitude towards casual sexual encounters, in direct contravention of the mores of an English-

woman of her generation. Barak was not a man to whom she would
have turned willingly for sex, but in a difficult situation she was not
prepared to make a big issue of it. So she recorded the incident briefly,
more concerned to note the chorus at night of prowling wolves, jackals
and lynxes.

They reached Baghdad on 12 February, after a journey of eight
weeks. The Tigris–Euphrates valley has long been assumed to be
the site of the Garden of Eden; and Baghdad, the magnificent city
built by the mighty caliphs, was its metropolis, famed for its beautiful
buildings, a mixture of Saracenic and Byzantine architecture.
Fatigued and dirty, Jane was disappointed at first, but after a bath
and a rest she felt better. The *hammam* itself, however, she described
as frightful, with the harem women behaving stupidly at the colour
of her hair. That night she again slept with Barak but the day was
memorable for another reason: at the bath-house she had discovered
that her hair was turning 'quite grey'. Next day she went shopping
for henna. She found two types of dye: the black, made of powdered
indigo leaf, which was only made near Baghdad; and the red or
'Mecca' variety of henna. She favoured the black dye which she
thought might make her disguise more effective.

She had half hoped that Medjuel might turn up in Baghdad during
the three weeks Barak planned to spend there, and when he did not
she wrote him a letter in case he should arrive after her departure.
She toured the city from one end to the other, saw everything there
was to see and met everyone worth meeting from the emir and his
harem to Sir Henry Rawlinson, the British consul, with whom she
dined.[16] At Rawlinson's suggestion, she decided to go to Mosul, 160
miles to the north on the Tigris River, from where she hoped to visit
some interesting ruins. Barak refused to go with her; he had business
to transact in Baghdad, he said. Eugénie sulked and said she needed
to rest before the arduous return journey. So Jane went with only a
small party of guards to protect her. At Mosul she met Sheikh Ferhan
of the Shemmar tribe (the ancient enemy of the Anazeh) and charmed
him into sending some of his people with her to Nineveh and El
Haddr.[17] She sketched quickly all she saw before returning to Baghdad, knowing that she would have to set out again almost immediately
for the journey back to Damascus.

The decision about what to do on her arrival there troubled her
greatly. 'Where is the joy anticipated on returning to Damascus, as
[there was] at Jerusalem? Sorrow in many shapes waits for me at

Damascus,' she wrote. In Baghdad she found Eugénie defensive and prickly. She suspected that in her absence Eugénie had taken her place in Barak's bed. The fact itself was of no great moment – Jane's feelings for Barak were objective – but the implied disloyalty, a repetition of Eugénie's behaviour at Lamia with Hadji-Petros, rankled.

The journey from Baghdad to Damascus was free from attack but had its share of discomforts. There were fleas that kept her from sleeping, a violent storm that blew away their tents in the night, and days of trekking without any nourishing food, 'the camels, poor things, vicious from their hunger'. On the other hand, there was the unexpected sight of a wonderful hill town; the site of ancient Babylon; a Saracen castle with beautiful carvings that she paused to sketch in blissful solitude on a hillside while her companions set up camp out of her sight; and the simple joy of a long smooth canter on the camels as they stretched their necks towards an oasis. The weather too, with the approach of spring warmth, was pleasant.

They were travelling now as camel herders, with the string of beasts stretching far behind them. Each camel wore a bell. Barak explained to her that each bell had a different note, and that a good camel master, with his ear finely tuned, could tell immediately if a single camel halted or stumbled. Once they had to pitch camp a long way from other travellers because some of the camels had developed mange. But the bedouins, whose ingrained hospitality towards other travellers is unlimited, courteously invited them to join them. 'I went with El Barak to pay several visits and was struck by a grave [gathering] of about 55 sheikhs and higher Bedouins sitting in a formal circle,' Jane wrote, having sketched the impressive scene.[18] Their host, Sheikh Jerhan, she thought, was

> not handsome or particularly prepossessing, he has three wives, [all] are kind in manner. [European] people are so much out in supposing that they are giving the Bedouins pleasure or doing them *honour* in condescending to visit them. They don't care a straw for it, but as the visit invariably brings them presents . . . something in it appeals to them.
>
> He sent in the evening an abundance of excellent warm sheep-leben and hot camel's milk. All is on a grand scale of friendly hospitality . . . In the evening Jerhan came to see me attended by as numerous and noble a suite as Basily. I afterwards sent a present.
>
> *Thursday 6th April, 1854.* This day year I left Athens on my ill-fated journey to Syria which seems to have changed all the current course of my life.

Friday 7th. . . . A dreadful night of wind and rain . . . I was struck by Barak's selfishness about letting people come into my tent for shelter! A vision passed before my eyes, of a small house and garden at Athens.[19]

As they plodded along day after day, uncertainty about her future tormented Jane. Sometimes she would look back at Eugénie faithfully trailing in her wake, Eugénie who always managed to make her tent welcoming and comfortable for her, though not always uncomplainingly, it must be said. Eugénie had told Jane unequivocally that she would not stay with her if she made her home in Syria. 'What is before me if I lose Eugénie, one of the very few who is really attached to me?' Jane asked herself; and in the next entry: 'Slept in the mountains where the thunder rolled awfully and I was annoyed at the sheikh's taking Eugénie on his shoulders to cross some water.'

Jane thought that during this incident Eugénie looked at her with a challenge in her eyes, and she could not help recalling, once again, the maid's appalling behaviour with Hadji-Petros. On this occasion, however, Jane decided, 'I could not *affect* jealousy where none is felt.' Later in the trip the two women would quarrel again. 'I had a dreadful falling out with Eugénie on the sheikh's account. She told me I was *jealous* of her! I was furious at the imputation.'[20]

Sheikh Barak, too, she alternately liked and disliked.

Barak displayed a temper and violence, and stinginess over a little flour I wanted for a stray camel we picked up who came with touching confidence into the tent. He shocked, offended and disgusted me and I foresee the end of his reign. He was cross, too, to poor Eugénie.[21]

On many occasions, though, Barak's sun rode high in her sky, as when the stopped at the towns along the way and

Barak good-naturedly took me on a walk all round the town where I saw several things worth sketching; a fine mosque where I saw the Pasha going to Mardin . . . In the evening raiders passed and took three [camels] by force – poor things. The Sheikh went after them and returned late without money. He is certainly a man of energy and courage![22]

For the most part, Jane revelled in the experience of travelling as a bedouin: 'What a journey this would be with someone I really loved with enthusiasm and who understood me, and returned my attachment . . . there are moments in which if I had no mirror and no memory to remind me I would think I was still fifteen years old.'

On 6 May they reached Aleppo. Jane had been ill with malaria, which held them up for several days, but she recovered quickly and was eager to visit the city which in her youth had seemed to her so remote, another world. After accompanying Barak to buy oats for the camels and ensuring that they were properly fed, she went to meet the German consul. The consul 'knew poor Henry Anson, who died in a field of the plague 27 years ago, and today, he comes with me to see the place of Henry's long-forgotten grave.'[23]

She made many acquaintances in a very short time in Aleppo. There was a far larger European presence than in Damascus, of Greeks, Hungarians, French and a few English missionaries. To her great surprise she met Mr Kissini, a former acquaintance from Greece, who spoke of Hadji-Petros and other friends, and dredged up 'strange, uncertain and sad remembrances'. Kissini took her to visit 'Suleyman Pasha . . . he was very pleasant and polite. Walked afterwards around the castle, its mound curious and said to have been built by Solomon.' But even more interesting was news Mr Kissini had just received from Greece – that Otto had been relieved of power. While sad for the King, Jane could not resist a feeling of satisfaction that Amelie, who had made Ianthe's life so difficult, had also been toppled: 'So my wish is granted! My rival the Queen is annihilated! But what of Greece . . . my friends? Xristodoulos. Can I be indifferent to *his* fate?'[24]

At Hamah, in the wide, fertile Orontes Valley, there was a pretty menzil (camping place) with bathing in a waterfall. Afterwards Jane toured the labyrinthine streets of the old town and went to see the famous and massive medieval *norias*, waterwheels which took water from the river and fed the orchards and gardens high above the town, creaking sonorously like tormented souls as they turned ceaselessly in the rushing waters. Later she went to the souk, where 'I fancied I saw Medjuel in every Bedouin in a white abba'.[25]

But Medjuel was not at Hamah; nor was he at Homs, where he told her his tribe always camped in the spring months. Jane began to fear a repeat of her experience with Saleh. As the caravan wound its way south towards Damascus they thought nothing of spending fourteen hours at a stretch in the saddle as they neared their destination, but though she suffered from saddle-soreness, as they all did, Jane was extremely fit and strong. Indeed, she could hardly remember a time when she had felt better.

"*Friday 19th May*. Stopped at Khan el Arrouss. A lovely sparkling stream and I have heard that Medjuel is at Scham.' She could not avoid suspecting that she was behaving foolishly. She constantly reminded herself that he was young enough to be her son, yet the more she thought of him the more she longed to see him. If he asked her again to marry him and was prepared to divorce Mascha, she was tempted to accept. But in any case she intended to build a house in Damascus. Having decided this all her doubts returned. 'Oh what folly! Not to say worse . . . The day after tomorrow the journey is at an end, and the next phase of my life begins *without Eugénie* whom I delight to badger. I know not why.'

Next day the party rose before dawn and set off on the final stage of their journey. After an hour a lone figure leading a riderless horse rode towards them. It was Medjuel bringing a horse for Jane. Thrilled at the compliment, Jane transferred to the fresh dancing Arabian and completed her adventure by riding dashingly into Damascus *en cavalier* (riding astride) like a desert princess approaching her kingdom. As they rode she told Medjuel of the highlights of her journey. He listened with interest and 'his eyes spoke immense pleasure. Can *he* too be false?' Her first thoughts were for a bath, and after she had rested Medjuel called again and proposed that they should ride together the following day. He still mentioned 'not a word of love,' she wrote in her diary, 'although his eyes spoke it!'[26]

It was while they were riding together that Medjuel first said the words Jane had been waiting to hear. He told her he loved her, and that he was prepared to divorce Mascha if Jane would agree to marry him. The following day while she was dressing in 'fantasia' to attend a celebration party at Barak's house, Medjuel kissed her for the first time. She recorded it in code, 'Received 1st kiss',[27] with far more emotion than she had noted the nights shared with Barak.

Later, at Barak's house, Barak caught her eye several times and she wondered again if she was doing the right thing. She had shared Barak's life for five months and he was close to her own age. He had told her that he would marry her if she was willing. Yet she did not love Barak. And Medjuel: did she love him? She thought she did. Or was she being foolish yet again?

During the night she reached a decision. She would travel at once to Athens to finalise her affairs there, and transfer her assets to Syria. In the changes that had taken place since she left Athens it was inevitable that her belongings would have suffered, but she would sell everything that remained and leave Eugénie settled comfortably. Then she would return to Syria, build a house in Damascus and, perhaps, become Medjuel's wife. Her departure was arranged for the following day.

'How unlooked for!!' she reflected. 'Medjuel, and Barak, both risked! But I go – *allons. Du courage!*' Medjuel begged her to leave most of her luggage as a token that she would return and was clearly distressed that she might never come back. Jane knew she would miss him, but her doubts regarding his feelings later returned to worry her. 'Does he love me?' she anguished, writing in code, 'or is money his desire?' She had learned, the hard way, to be cautious about believing what men told her.

Five days after returning from her epic journey to Baghdad she left Damascus for Beirut. Medjuel did not accompany her beyond the city, but Barak did and embraced her, saying he regretted losing her. He gave her, as a parting gift and memento of the Baghdad journey, a sabre of Damascus steel with silver and gold wire filigree, said to have once belonged to a Saracen warrior. 'I left the sabre with him, and tears rose in my eyes at the wrenched link and my untimely journey.' Three days later she arrived at Beirut and suffered the first inevitable consequence of her proposal to adopt another culture. The English consul made it obvious that he strongly disapproved of her behaviour, while her escort, Sheikh Sabt, was 'kind and pleasant to all but me'. He obviously felt that Medjuel was making a mistake.[28]

But the spirit that Jane had once described as 'a rebel heart' would not be crushed by disapproval. Within twenty-four hours she sailed for Greece, invigorated by her intention to sever her old life for good.

14

Honeymoon in Palmyra
1854–1855

Once again Edmond About narrowly missed seeing 'Ianthe' when he called to see his friend the Duchesse de Plaisance in the spring of 1854 while he put the finishing touches to his book *La Grèce contemporaine*. It was now a year since Jane had left Athens after the quarrel with Hadji-Petros, and though About had asked after her continuously during that time he heard no news of her. He was thrilled to hear from the duchess the latest chapter in the life of his lovely friend, which was all Jane left behind her in Athens.

In a desert encampment Ianthe had seen a thoroughbred Arabian horse which exactly matched her requirements, the duchess said. It belonged to a handsome young sheikh who, when Jane offered to buy the magnificent creature, told her that it was unridable. 'If the horse were able to be broken to ride,' the sheikh told Ianthe, 'it would be beyond price.' But even as she stood, the sheikh said, he valued the animal above his three beautiful wives. Jane replied that, though a fine horse was to be treasured, three beautiful wives should not be disdained. She suggested that he sent the horse to her to see if she could ride it. Agreeing that 'sometimes a woman succeeds where a man fails because she knows when to yield', the sheikh had two of his Arabs lead the horse to Jane.

She had been breaking and riding thoroughbred horses all her life, and, knowing her skill as an equestrienne, the duchess and About found no difficulty in believing that within a short period their friend had managed to persuade the horse to take a saddle and was able to ride her.

When he saw her galloping the 'unbreakable' horse, the sheikh found Ianthe more exciting than his three wives put together. He said to her, 'This animal is now priceless but since you were able to dominate her, but if you still want her it is not with your money that you will have to pay for her.'

Ianthe, who had been admiring the sheikh, replied: 'I will pay what you wish for the horse, I have not come such a great distance to haggle. But the women of my country are too proud to share a man's heart; they only enter a tent on condition that they reign alone, and I will pay you for your horse only on condition that you dismiss your harem.'

The sheikh said heatedly, 'Men of my country take as many wives as they can afford to keep; if I dismiss my harem to live with one woman alone I will appear like a 1,200 franc clerk. Besides I must follow my religion, set an example to my people and respect the old ways.'

. . . They discussed the matter for a long time before they reached an agreement, and at the present time Ianthe is the sole wife of the sheikh. She has a three year contract and when this expires the sheikh, if he so wishes, may take back his harem. The contract is renewable, but will it be renewed? I doubt it. Woman is a fruit that ripens quickly under the Syrian sun.

The Duchesse soon got over Ianthe's departure, having taken the precaution of quarrelling with her prior to her departure so as not to miss her.[1]

The duchess died while the book was in the press and never saw the published result of her gossipy chats with the writer. Undoubtedly she had heard the story from someone who knew both her and Jane, for though it is highly coloured some elements of the story are too close to fact to be mere coincidence. We know she did not hear it from Jane herself. A diary entry makes it clear they never met after Jane left Athens in the spring of 1853, for the old lady died in the spring of 1854, and Jane wrote of her, 'How I regret not seeing her when I returned from Syria in 1853, and no longer having the portrait she gave me.'[2]

Jane's visit to Athens in June 1854 lasted three weeks while she 'ran about town' sorting out her financial affairs and leaving instructions for the shipment of her chattels. She did not see Hadji-Petros, for he was in the north with his Palikares. She was able to recover her jewellery, the most important piece being 'the King's bracelet' with a miniature of King Ludwig painted on ivory set in a gold frame. Some items, such as the duchess's portrait, were gone for ever, but Jane was never too concerned with material goods. At the end of June she sailed for Smyrna. With the exception of one short visit a few years later, Jane kicked the dust of Athens from her shoes and hardly looked back.

Edmond About never saw Jane again. In a footnote to his book he wrote that she had announced her return for the winter of 1856. Meanwhile, he said, 'Hadj-Petros has returned to Athens and is swaggering along the Palissia Road, younger and more adored than ever.'[3]

It cannot be said that Jane's new determination carried her through all the inevitable problems that arose. She had qualms about whether she was doing the right thing in casting herself adrift, yet further from her family. But her conclusion was that she had nothing to lose by starting a new life in Syria, and if the venture failed she would be in no worse a position than at present. Three concerns were uppermost in her mind: her worry that she might never again see her mother alive, the difficulties of making a new life without Eugénie's help, and – primarily – Medjuel's youth and his true feeling for her.

She arrived in Damascus to find that the sheikh was still in the desert with his tribe. She sent a message to him and set about buying a site for a house. When Medjuel arrived a few weeks later it was to find Jane deeply involved in directing builders for the house which she had designed. Those who saw it described it as a small palace. Jane called it a villa, often admitting it was far too large, but it is true that apart from the emir's and pasha's palaces this first house of Jane's was widely considered to be the most important in Damascus. Medjuel was exhausted and ill after his time in the desert, a situation which was to repeat itself in the future, but he was young and strong and Jane nursed him to health. As soon as he could ride he set off again to find his brother Mohammed, to ask permission to divorce Mascha so that he could marry Jane on her terms.

In October Jane moved into her house, or at least the part that was habitable. At her urgent entreaty Eugénie agreed to come out in December to assist in getting the house in order, and this relieved her mind a great deal. But as weeks passed she heard nothing from Medjuel, and by mid-November Jane was in a state of constant anxiety that he might have been killed, or alternatively that he had realised he did not love her and had simply decided to stay away.

Barak questioned travellers coming in from the desert and told Jane she must not look for Medjuel to return until mid-December. This satisfied her, and she set about making a home as comfortable as any she ever created. As usual no detail was too small for Jane's attention;

every piece of carved 'festooning' in wood or stone was designed by herself. She spent hours compiling lists of furniture and other fittings which were commissioned from Paris and London. Among these were gifts for Medjuel, to be purchased by her mother and sent out care of the consul.

Each day she rode on the pretty Arab mare given her by Medjuel to visit friends. One day she might call on 'Madame Barak', who despite not being a Christian was morally 'far superior' to herself, Jane wrote candidly (recalling her sexual encounters with the lady's husband). On another day she would ride to Salhiyeh, where she had had her wonderful first sight of Damascus, and where her new friends the Reis Pasha and his wives lived. Jane was very friendly with the pasha's oldest wife, who had 'a kind and ladylike manner' and who told her many things about the role of a Muslim wife.[4]

> *Wednesday November 22nd*: Dear kind Barak brought me the news that Sheikh Medjuel has not forgotten me. That he rides around the desert like a *Medjnoun* [madman], and only thinks of how he can get to Scham and me!!! But that his brother Mohammed insists on coming and seeing me first, before he gives his consent to our marriage ... And poor Barak, shall I not miss his society, my expeditions with him to Bagdad?
>
> *Persia, Egypt, Paris*? Are not these, and my liberty, in *fact*, more necessary to me in the long run than marriage and home?
>
> My house is getting on, and my garden. I am only afraid of becoming too taken up with it. Without *children* to enjoy it why should I spend money in aggrandising it ... at my time of life, 47?[5]

Despite her anxiety she went on throwing her considerable energies into the house and garden. The garden would become a showpiece in Damascus because she cleverly combined all that was best of a cool eastern courtyard and an English country garden. She was able to buy roses locally and often went off on her horse with her Spanish gardener, Francisco, on 'plant hunting' expeditions. Small palms and flowering shrubs that had self-seeded on the roadsides outside the city, and clumps of wild flowers – all were carefully lifted and transplanted to her huge garden. She wrote to Messrs Carters Fine Seeds in England ordering seeds and plants, the latter with meticulous packing instructions, but these would not arrive until the spring. Meanwhile the post brought news from Eugénie: 'The cholera [at Beirut] prevents her coming, and she is in a bad humour.'[6]

Jane wrote to her mother, but on her own admission 'had not the courage to write to Steely' and tell her of her contemplated marriage to a bedouin. The weeks dragged on. Barak had gone at Jane's request to find Medjuel but she had heard nothing yet. The builders, the garden, riding and visiting helped to take her mind off her increasing concern. Her chimney caught fire and deprived her of the one really comfortable room in the house and she began to feel nostalgic for the time a year earlier when she had been on her exciting journey to Baghdad. Had she not been in Damascus overseeing the building project, she grumbled to her diary, she might have been travelling, seeing new places.

Each night she hoped that the next day Medjuel would arrive. But even as she wrote of her dreams she agonised at the potential folly of marrying a man so much younger: 'Oh, if I were but seventeen years younger. It is *madness* . . . he can be no more than thirty!'[7]

Thursday 8th February. My evening passed more than usually sad . . . I went to bed but not to rest. At about one in the morning came a loud knocking at the door. A horse, and Barak's well-known voice. Oh, these are moments in a life, worth a life in themselves!

I started to my feet; Barak came in and in hurried accents greeted me with 'He comes! He comes here like a mad one. He became so weak that Mohammed was pleased [to allow it].'

In a few hours he arrived. Neither of us spoke much, as he was evidently suffering from fatigue and latent fever.

Medjuel's few words and his tender attitude towards her told her all she needed to know. From that moment, she wrote, all of her days were 'of gold, and filled with joy'. She recalled that on the return journey from Palmyra when she had fancied herself in love with the cold-blooded Saleh she had made a wish 'to be once sincerely and ardently loved by a Bedouin'. And now, it seemed, her wish was about to be realised. With the single exception of Medjuel's age, he was everything she wished for, and, though they had so far not enjoyed any physical relationship, she believed him to be truthful in his declarations of love. His brother was opposed to their marriage; it was unheard of for a bedouin sheikh to marry a Christian – and a Ferengi woman at that – who wished to impose the terms of monogamy. But her faith in Medjuel was justified when he declared that he intended to marry her no matter what his brother said. At last, a man who was prepared to defy convention and family disapproval for her! The major problem was Mascha. He could not in honour divorce her without Mohammed's approval, though it was what he, Medjuel, desired for Jane's sake.

Jane began to make inquiries about a marriage ceremony and ran immediately into problems. The consul, Richard Wood, put every obstacle he could think of in Jane's way in the hope that she would recognise the impossibility of such a marriage, suggesting that British protection might be invalid if she married Medjuel. With her background she would never be able to merge into the role of a bedouin wife, he pointed out, even the wife of an important sheikh. And if the marriage failed? Divorce in the East was for a man only, he said; a woman could be thrown aside like a chattel.[8]

But the consul had no more success on this occasion than when he attempted to dissuade Jane from going to Palmyra. For every argument she had a counter-argument. It was not her intention, she said, to *live* always as a bedouin wife; she would live in her own house in Damascus most of the year. However, she would naturally expect to accompany her husband for part of the year when he travelled with his tribe. She had already proved to her own satisfaction that she could live in such a manner for up to five months at a time. When he saw that his words had no effect on her, Wood played his trump card. He went to see the pasha, whose permission was essential to Medjuel. If Medjuel disobeyed, the pasha's retribution would fall on the entire tribe. 'Difficulty on difficulty succeed each other . . . a letter from the Consul communicating the course the Pasha has taken on the subject . . . I felt ill and uncomfortable. Dear Medjuel consoles me with his love, and bears it all with the patience of an angel.'

Saturday 24th March. Again difficulties arise which seemed to have been cleared away . . . the last real obstacle is Medjuel's wife and he today offered [publicly] that if that was the *real* difficulty he would divorce her from hence. He said that if one must die and he must decide which, he would condemn her. Can I doubt his love? But can I accept such proof of it? Vengeance would surely follow such atrocious injustice.

Though Medjuel declared that if necessary, in order to obtain the permission of the consul and the pasha, he would divorce Mascha immediately in her absence, Jane had already agreed to the marriage without an immediate divorce. There was no question of a marriage in the Christian Church; Jane did not even consider approaching a clergyman. On a former occasion she had embraced a different branch of the Christian faith in order to marry, but there was no requirement this time for her to undergo a change of professed faith. Because Jane was genuinely concerned about Mascha's fate, believing that the position of a woman cast off in the tribe was an invidious one, she had reluctantly agreed to become a member of Medjuel's harem, provided Mascha remained a wife in name only.

Each day the couple met new problems, but Jane was bolstered throughout by Medjuel, 'during our long *tête-à-têtes* . . . his charming, simple and truthful character shows itself more and more to his advantage.'[9]

> *Tuesday March 27th*. Today, at last, Barak came and announced [the marriage] for this evening . . . I put on my blue and white embroidered dress, and passed a dreadful day at Barak's, melancholy with a thousand reminiscences. Ghosts of past and vanished loves arose before my memory and seem to mock my present vision of anticipated happiness.
>
> At length evening came and brought three *Ullemas* who married us according to the Moslem ceremony. Poor faithful Eugénie was present and in a short time I was his, and I gave him my hand in token of Love, Faith and Service.
>
> We walked home, those two [Eugénie and Barak] before; we following. About an hour after I was *alone* with him . . . and his! His, I trust, for ever.

A wonderful night of love-making followed their marriage. Medjuel was an ardent man and their physical union was 'more like a real wedding night than any since Lord Ellenborough', Jane wrote. Medjuel had been thrilled to discover his bride was as youthful 'as a girl'. Jane was happy in the belief that 'neither he nor I had anything to reproach ourselves with', and she delighted in Medjuel's lovemaking, so different 'from Saleh's coldness, and lack of interest in love'.[10]

> *Wednesday 28th, Thursday 29th, Friday April 1st, Saturday 2nd, Sunday 3rd, Monday 4th, Tuesday 5th*: All days *d'or and de joie*, passed in delightful intercourse with this simple, upright and affectionate character. May I not be deceived (as usual)! . . .
>
> *Thursday April 14th*. Today . . . my dream has begun its accomplishment. I leave Damascus for the loved desert with my adored, and adoring, Medjuel. His *slave*. Oh that I had 20 years less to excuse this last folly.

The majority of these honeymoon entries were written in code and the only cloud on her ecstatic horizon was the thought of Mascha. Jane's conscience pricked her, for whatever else she might have been guilty of in the past she had never deliberately taken another woman's husband. She offered to provide Mascha's dowry which was repayable on divorce, but Medjuel would not allow it. Her only consolation was

Medjuel's insistence that divorce entailed no disgrace to the bedouins, indeed he had already divorced one wife. If only Mascha were really as reconciled to the divorce as Medjuel claimed, Jane felt she could be completely happy.

Barak escorted them from the city as far as Doumah, a small settlement two hours' ride from Damascus. Eugénie agreed to remain in Damascus to keep house during their honeymoon. Jane took with her as personal maid one of the house servants, an old woman called Munni Abdallah 'who is *inefficiency* itself!' Jane wrote (not unkindly). Barak slept in a curtained section of their tent at Douma before setting off for Damascus at dawn; during the night Jane heard him turning over. 'I sighed and wandered back in thought to our Bagdad journey that I so much enjoyed,' she wrote, but she had no regrets.[11]

They travelled slowly, calling on friends of Medjuel's to introduce Jane. As a visitor to Damascus, Emily Beaufort, explained:

> When a woman is newly married, she is, a few days after, dressed in her best attire, with all her richest ornaments and taken round by her husband to visit every tent in the tribe . . . in turn. She has to drink coffee with everyone, in token of their friendliness and acceptance of her as wife among them.
>
> Nor is the choice of wife . . . a simple affair . . . The Anazeh are exceedingly proud, and particular to an extreme degree about descent and pedigree. The rank of husband and wife must be equal. If marriage with a stranger is in question enquiry is made about the age of the family and pureness of her descent as in the case of any Spanish grandee. If every step in the pedigree is not satisfactory . . . the engagement is broken off.[12]

At one house Jane missed some money from her luggage and Medjuel, 'stung at the idea of what would be said at Scham if I was supposed to be robbed hardly outside its gates!', nearly came to blows with his host's servant. But it was smoothed over and Jane was obliged to 'lug out my things and dress up as an *Arrouss* [bride], and here again I felt the need of Eugénie to "do me up" . . . I saw a nice black slave, that I think would just suit me as femme de chambre.' For the remainder of her life Jane always had a small girl 'slave' among her retinue (when they reached maturity they were released by her with a dowry), to run errands and plump cushions. Emily Beaufort commented on the bedouin attitude to slaves:

> All Bedouin sheikhs have their black slaves, for they are the only servants they can have; no Bedouin of any tribe will hire himself or herself as

servant to anyone ... But these slaves are always kindly treated, and generally are much attached ... to their owners; we used to see Sheikh Miguel [*sic*] giving his little black boy his food with much care ... the interpreter told us that if his master was to forget ... he would neither ask for food nor complain, until he starved. They are valuable servants and sometimes cost huge sums of money.[13]

Emily Beaufort also noted that on a cold night in the desert Medjuel took off his own fur-lined cloak to wrap it around the child.

The honeymoon journey in the spring of 1855 was the happiest period in Jane's life. She was travelling in the desert, not as an outsider but as the beloved wife of a desert prince. In that simple fact lay the fulfilment of all the adventure and romance she had ever craved; and in Medjuel's attitude towards her all the tenderness she had ever longed for in a relationship.

They arrived at Tadmor at sunset and camped 'in a nice place out of the town amongst gardens with a tepid spring under a cluster of palm trees, of which I profited at night to bathe by a splendid moon-light'.[14] It was a sensual pleasure to wash the sand from her hair and body, and she was inordinately proud that she had kept her youthful figure and agility as Medjuel sat and watched her while she bathed. Later, when she thanked him for the happiness he had brought her as he promised, 'he replied in the kindest and simplest manner, "*Badein* [Later], you shall see if I do not keep my word in *all* things".' He had his own bedouin name for her, 'Frangya'; it was merely an affectionate corruption of the bedouin word for western Europeans, Ferengi (or Franks), but Jane liked it, for it sounded fragrant and flower-like.[15]

For the next few days she was bothered by the wives of the fellahin, or town Arabs, from modern Palmyra who were eager to meet *el Arrouss Medjuel* (Medjuel's bride). She found their vulgar obtrusiveness irritating, 'so different from the ways of the Bedouin, and their children rude, dirty and unmannered'. They asked innumerable questions. Did she know God, they asked her. Did Christians pray and fast as they did? Was it true that Christian men were uncircumcised and took a woman when they wished? When they married, did they pay a bride-price? Was it true there were no camels in her country? What was the name of her tribe? Finally the couple decided to move further away from the town and the prying women.

We removed the tents into a little garden of palms and olives. And ever, ever, shall I remember the happy fortnight I passed there. It may have been more for in the all engrossing happiness of the honeymoon I have forgotten time and date!

. . . at length it was decided that we set off to meet Sheikh Mohammed and the rest, and not least for my curiosity, Mascha, of whom I am, and am not, jealous![16]

The journey took some days. As they rode across the featureless plain the only moving things Jane could see were tall columns of whirling dust and sand racing across the desert. When they were caught in a sandstorm, Medjuel showed her how to couch the camels and shelter in their lee, pulling her *abba* over her head to form a tent. Afterwards she found that nothing in her luggage, not even a tightly closed 'jar of cold-cream', was free of sand. At night their lullaby was the chorus of jackals, and at dawn she was wakened by Medjuel offering hot coffee. The days took on a dreamlike quality, and she wanted the time never to end, but she was about to meet Sheikh Mohammed:

at last we heard they were near us so we halted in a low glen and sent a messenger. He returned early in the morning and said 'the Sheikh is coming.'

I dressed in my *best*, put on every item of gold I had, and waited, no longer sure (as formerly) of the impression I might make . . . my heart beat rather as they came in sight, for in fact they are now my relations, and nearest to me in this far-off portion of the world.

It was pretty to see Sheikh Mohammed, the dark and renowned Bedouin Sheikh winding up the glen with his [tribesmen] behind him on horseback with their long spears. He alighted, embraced his brother and received me cordially.

An hour afterwards came the women. Mascha foremost in her *Dhalleh* [palanquin]. I was breathless as I took in her whole person at a glance . . . and felt vexed that she was not so ugly as people said.

We embraced *cordially* (false on both sides), and the day passed in mutual recognitions. Shortly after, while I was sitting in the men's tent, a conversation took place between Medjuel and Sheikh Mohammed I would have given worlds to understand, on the subject of Mascha's separation.

She herself came in afterwards and seemed to me to be in a mighty hurry to grasp at the money, as she grasped at the clothes . . . A true peasant and a fit companion for Saleh of old!

The next morning we all set off together making a pretty picturesque sight, I riding Sheikh Mohammed's Seglawi mare with a halter — the *takht*, on the adorning of which the women spend much of their thoughts and time, and a new *takht* appearing with some fresh fantasia makes as much sensation as would some new fashioned carriage in London.

There seemed so much to learn, chiefly the customs of the tribe, Jane wrote, but she was always interested to note 'a strange bird, a new plant'. She became inured to 'the utter astonishment of other bedouins at this European wife'. It was unheard of for a bedouin to marry outside the tribal system. Was she a Circassian, the daughter of a bondwoman, they wondered. Perhaps the whiteness of her skin was due to leprosy? The softness of her feet was remarked by 'soft glucking noises of pity', and necessitated her wearing kid slippers when all other women went barefoot.

Jane was only too well aware of the need to conduct herself with great care; her family background meant nothing to the bedouin. They did not regard her as being *asil* (of noble blood) as Medjuel was, for all her trappings, for they believed only the *bedu* to be of pure blood. Honed by harsh living over centuries, only the finest of their race survived to breed. They were a lean, hard, proud people who were not prepared to take an outsider at face value, despite her bride gifts of a flock of sheep and herd of camels. She had Medjuel's protection, but to win their respect and approval would take time.

One day Medjuel came to her and explained that he had either to give Mascha a settlement of money and leave her, or to sleep with her. He said he wished therefore to make the settlement arrangements before they left for Damascus. The manner in which he told her pleased her. 'He and Basily are my ideals of men as their character, and their humour are too civilised, too sensitive to dwell on certain points.' However, she insisted on making a contribution towards Mascha's divorce settlement as her own 'gift to Mascha' which he could not refuse. In fact the divorce was not effected during their honeymoon.

As his marriage gift to Jane, Medjuel bought her another horse, a mare called Midjioumah, which gave her great kudos in the tribe. No woman had ever been known to ride a horse unless mounted behind her husband; to own one and to ride with such skill set her apart from them almost more than the cultural differences. Women rode camels, and the wives of sheikhs travelled in ornate curtained *dhallas* on the backs of camels. Though they appeared content, Jane considered the lives of bedouin women desperately hard, their lot one of unequal concubinage and weary servitude.

It was not easy for her in those early days of her marriage. Often she felt isolated, especially among the women. She was exasperated by their constantly asking for things until she came to accept that to ask for a gift is not shameful to the bedouin. Nor was there any need to thank the giver, for the act of giving was in itself greatly admired. They could pay a man no greater compliment than to say enviously, '*Wullah* [By God!], he is a generous man!'

Unless she and Medjuel retired to their sleeping tent there was no privacy; therefore she had to get used to being constantly interrupted. She learned how to milk a camel and carry the bowl of frothy liquid to Medjuel; any in excess of their immediate needs was poured into a 'sour-milk skin', to be rocked back and forth on her knees until it turned into *leben*. The woman who throughout her life had been served by hundreds of retainers (even in Damascus her staff were numbered in dozens) had to learn how to keep the fire alight with faggots and roots gathered in the desert, or with dried camel droppings. She revelled in her new knowledge, performing her tasks with increasing expertise as an offering to Medjuel.

Her most immediate problem was to learn the cheerful gossiping patois of the bedouin, and their habit of frequent cursing – 'God curse thy beard; thy house fall upon thee' – or the simple courtesy of greeting a guest, meant to be taken literally, 'Oh guest, you are lord of this house . . . everything I have is yours.' The poorest family would happily kill their only sheep to provide a complete stranger with a feast: such was the code. Before long, Jane recognised that for the bedouin raiding was a way of life, a means of increasing the wealth of the tribe. Though she would never find it acceptable, she saw that the custom was hedged about with its own code of honour regarding the safety of women and children. The tribe were always ready for attack, but did not allow it to affect celebrations.

A strange people I have adopted as my own. By early morning we were all ready to meet the expected enemy in chain armour. This evening all given up to fantasia and gaiety for the *misuma* [circumcision] of Schebibb [Medjuel's elder son].

The wild dance of the *Binnaat* [maidens] is . . . to show off their hair which at other times is kept hidden, they throw it about, as well as their bodies, in all directions. The men . . . throw their *agals* over the Binnaat as a crown, and stick an ostrich feather in her hair as the award of beauty . . . Yet their dances have none of the indecency of the town arabs.

The feasting lasted some days, presided over by Medjuel and Mascha, but Medjuel was careful to involve Jane in the festivities and make her status plain.

> The sword dance, where men and women joined, I thought graceful, and pleased me as more characteristic of their manners . . . we joined in . . . to the *delight* of the Bedouins and though I felt a sort of shyness steal over me in the presence of so many, I knew that if I chose I could surpass them all in fire and agility.

Her interest in archaeology was unabated, and Medjuel, who knew all the ancient desert sites, often organised an excursion for her as the tribe moved around the desert in search of fresh grazing for the camel herds. His knowledge was inherited through the strong oral-history tradition of the bedouins. One day he took her to Sclamya.

> there are some remains of black stone columns of unusual architecture, neither Corinthian nor Doric; and a more modern Frank fortress of the middle ages commanded by a Turkish Emir (nominally to protect the villagers from the Bedouins), who espying us from the top of the wall, insisted upon our going up . . .
>
> Next day we rode across the desert to the water 'el Moy' and here is to be the ending of the *Misuma* for Schebibb. A viper 'dabb' started and slightly stung my dromedary today, and . . . a poor camel was slaughtered in honour of the ceremony. The whole tribe partook of the hospitality.
>
> Today, there came into my tent a . . . handsome young man who has been to Greece. Greece! Always connected in my mind with painful and tender recollections of Hadji-Petros. Why do I still start and my eyes grow dim as I write that name? But for *him* I had not been here . . . the wife of a Bedouin Sheikh, a marauding Chief whose only domain is the desert, whose will is sovereign – and my only – law. And what was he and his Palikari? And with far less moral virtues than our wild Bedouins. Away with these thoughts.
>
> This evening was the fete, the fantasia (*Traad*) and splendid horseman-ship. Medjuel rode the two year old without saddle or bridle. The horse slipped on the grass and fell, and he defended himself with the sabre. [It was] good riding, but none – I thought – had the ardour of Saleh on the plain of Jericho! I was dressed *à la Bédouine* and pronounced by these simple people to be still *el a Kwoyss*! Why did I not come here and marry Medjuel 10 years back? I should like to have a Bedouin child. What would it be like I wonder? Syrra, Sheikh Mohammed's son, arrived and poor Joffell [Mohammed's wife and Jane's best friend] after working all day like a slave – as the women are in most respects – was beaten on account of some crotchet of Mohammed's . . .

... Our departure is final and I am not sorry for the women are becoming tiresome ... and I am most anxious for a good *hammam*. Medjuel bought me a handsome black horse, *Soultan*, two years old for 4,000 piastres ... We departed with many feigned, and perhaps two or three real, regrets and wishes of our returning.

The homeward journey took two weeks. Often they were 'burning hot, tired and sunburnt'. As it was Ramadan, there was no possibility of getting food during the day, even when they came near a town or khan, and Jane was not sorry when they reached the mountains. They spent their last night in a field, and next morning Barak came to meet them and give them news, 'while we were talking ... who should come up but the Consul who caught me bare-footed and *unveiled*! But his manner struck me as kind and cordial to Medjuel which I was glad to observe.' The consul was clearly a diplomat. On the previous occasions that he had seen Jane she dressed as any Englishwoman of distinction would. To meet 'Lady Ellenborough', as he called her in his reports, barefooted and wearing nothing but a bedouin shift, would have been far more alarming to him than the fact that she was unveiled.

When it became a little cooler, I mounted and we arrived in due time at home where I was warmly welcomed in my *nice* house by my affectionate and faithful Eugénie. I was delighted with the appearance of the house, and gardens. She always contrives to give an appearance of *fête* to everything whenever I return from a journey.[17]

To Jane's delight Medjuel grew in her estimation each day. The petty trivialities of life in Damascus such as servant problems that once would have vexed her unreasonably she laughed away. Some matters were of concern, however. They discovered that Barak had behaved badly in their absence, keeping back some of the money he had collected from Medjuel's clients for escort to Palmyra, and that he had also accepted a generous commission on the items ordered by Jane as gifts to the tribe. She found herself quarrelling with Barak each time he came to the house, but no matter how rude she was to him he always returned. 'I suspect his whole aim is to gain money,' she wrote, 'and to set me and the Sheikh at variance by insinuations ... and by trying to persuade [Medjuel] to do things he knows I do not like him to do.' The situation became a long-term nuisance, for he told lies about her to Medjuel, made worse by the fact that some lies contained a grain of truth such as when he told Medjuel that Jane had 'had fourteen husbands'.

It is quite possible that Jane had had fourteen lovers, for, including her husbands, eleven lovers were admitted in her diaries: Lord Ellenborough, Frederick Madden, George Anson, Felix Schwarzenberg, Charles Venningen, King Ludwig, Spiros Theotoky, Hadji-Petros, Saleh (and possibly Selaine), Barak himself and Medjuel. In addition there were rumoured affairs for which no evidence is available, with King Otto, and the two duellists during her time in Italy after her separation from the count. Probably she had confided this to Barak; it was certainly in her nature to do so, but from her annoyance on this occasion it is clear that she had not confessed them all to Medjuel.

But worse news was to come. Eugénie, 'ill and tired . . . worn out, I fear chiefly in my service', decided she must return to Athens. In August, Jane escorted her part of the way and sent her on with an escort of two guards. As she watched the riders depart out of sight down the road towards Jerusalem, all her longing to travel surged up. 'I turned my eyes towards Djebel Scheikh [Mount Hermon] and longed to [travel] . . . please God, next winter.'

> I returned home and found the Sheikh all kindness, trying to make up for Eugénie's going in any way. Oh! He is so very kind, a second Basily in his way, and I am very fond of him and reproach myself for ever snubbing him as I sometimes do when his childish simplicity sometimes irritates my hasty temper.[18]

Among the letters awaiting her was one from Steely, who had now learned of Jane's latest 'act of folly' and wrote to deprecate her latest marriage – assuming, as Steely appeared to doubt, that it really was 'a marriage'. Jane was furious, feeling that she did not need her old governess to castigate her. 'I *know* what I am. I *know* and would give worlds to recall and live over again with other ties, thoughts and feelings, the last 15 years, aye 20 years of my misspent life. Still I would choose Medjuel as my *husband*. Where could I find a better?'[19]

The differences in their ages continued to nag at her, and in spite of Medjuel's ardent love-making she worried about the future. When Medjuel reached her present age, she would be almost seventy, and she could not bear to think of a time when he might be revolted by her body. She felt she was already

> hastening downhill in every way! . . . how I regret the atrocious folly of having dyed my hair when a little henna would have sufficed, and saved me worlds of trouble and vexation. How I would *now* enjoy and rejoice

in a child, and yet it is perhaps better that this blessing be withheld. How could I bring it up? [Yet] should Mascha marry [again], I should like to have Afet as my own![20]

Medjuel was to leave on 10 September to go to Tadmor with his brother Sheikh Mohammed 'on account of a mare'. Although the impending separation was disagreeable to her she did not attempt to dissuade him, for she felt it would be unfair to deprive Mohammed of 'his lawful income'. Although it irked her to miss an opportunity to travel in the desert, she decided to remain in Damascus alone. Each day she compiled seemingly interminable lists for her mother or Steely of commissions to be fulfilled – a piece of furniture, a pair of pistols for Medjuel, books on gardening – and sent out to her.

At this point she came to the end of the journal she had begun as 'Ianthe' fourteen years earlier on the island of Tinos. She browsed through it one evening, regretting many of the things she had done and wondering at the extraordinary course her life had taken. Before she slept she wrote that if only her marriage to Medjuel was lawful, and Mascha's future settled, she wanted for nothing else.

Jane began a new journal immediately and this chronicle survives intact, unlike the previous one which was 'censored' by having pages removed by protective family members after Jane's death. Consequently from 9 September 1855 until her death in 1881 we have an authentic memoir of Jane's activities, thoughts, fears and hopes in her own words. Together with a large tranche of letters to various members of her family and friends, her drawing books, account books and pocket notebooks, it provides a remarkable record of the unique life of the woman who now called herself Jane Digby el Mezrab.

A honeymoon sketch of Medjuel by Jane dated April 1855.

15

Wife to the Sheikh
1855–1856

In September 1855, a month after their return to Damascus, Medjuel set off for Palmyra as planned, and also escorting two rich Englishmen there. Left alone, Jane began her life as a Damascene gentlewoman and a pattern emerged that would be repeated for the remainder of her life. Missing Medjuel she was irritable with the many callers, such as the emir's son and a harem who called to welcome her home 'bringing unwanted gifts'. She showed them over the grounds of her house with ill-disguised impatience and was afterwards shocked at her inhospitable behaviour, realising that she had not even invited the ladies to sit. This, she felt, was inexcusable when she had been given so much both in personal happiness and in worldly goods. But two letters received that day had not improved her humour. Eugénie wrote to say she was still unwell and could not return to Syria, and Jane's English banker Mr Drummond advised that news had reached London that 'Lady Ellenborough had married her camel-driver'.

'Why is the world so constantly spiteful and ill-natured towards me?' she scribbled furiously. She tried to assuage her irritability in hard work in the garden, and in schooling some young horses that Medjuel had brought in before his departure. But in Medjuel's absence nothing pleased her. 'A very pretty ride through tree-covered lanes,' she wrote gloomily, 'but these unbroken horses give no amusement.'

Medjuel returned after ten days and the sun came out again for her. She went shopping and bought a violet-and-gold fantasia cloak to add to her desert wardrobe. To please Medjuel she dressed *à l'arabe* as she worked around the house and garden. Her light skin and blue eyes were accentuated now by her black-dyed hair, which she wore in a plait. On her slight figure the simple blue shift of the bedouin, with its pointed sleeves that trailed to the ground unless they were tied back out of the way for work, looked elegant and youthful; indeed, at first glance she could still pass for a woman of thirty, as Edmond About had said.

Medjuel's open admiration of her always thrilled her, and in deference to his tribe's custom she began to wear a fine gauze veil over the lower part of her face when any male callers came to the house. As a gift to Medjuel during their honeymoon she had commissioned a new tent to be made and the great lengths of woven black goat-hair now duly arrived, followed by a gaggle of women from the tribe to make it up in the garden. It was a significant occasion, for a sheikh's tent is an important accoutrement reflecting his wealth and status, and like any nobleman's dwelling in the West the bedouin tent is a principal heirloom passed down in the family. Sheikh Mohammed lived in their father's tent, while Medjuel had formerly lived in a small inconspicuous tent and shared his brother's divan.

But Medjuel's 'new house', as Jane called it, was a massive affair some thirty yards long and twelve yards wide, able to accommodate fifty or sixty people for a celebration or a conference.[1] The sleeping quarters, with Jane's own separate room, were arranged to one side of the massive divan, which was a central feature of the tent and in front of which the central hearth would be built in camp. Working offices such as kitchen, servants' quarters, and storage space for corn, rice and rock salt were arranged on the other side. The entire structure was so made that a small section could be hastily erected as shelter for short halts, and it was impervious to sun, wind and rain. All the walls could be raised and lowered to welcome or exclude weather from any direction. Medjuel was delighted.

So was Jane, not only because it had given such great pleasure to Medjuel but because it was important to her that his people came to accept that Medjuel had chosen his wife wisely. In return for Jane's gift Medjuel bought her the prettiest riding camel he could find, a gentle, good-natured creature which Jane loved on sight and called 'Oudiada'. On the day after Oudiada's arrival the British consul visited and was surprised to find Jane in the garden dressed *à l'arabe*, making a cake of flour and milk to feed the camel. She would ride this cream dromedary for many years and develop a close relationship with her; often at night in the desert Jane would be awakened by the camel gently nuzzling her feet.

Medjuel gave Jane another present at the same time which meant a great deal to her. It was the custom after a bedouin marriage, as soon as the husband regarded the marriage as successful, for him to provide a traditional bridal gift of silver bracelets. This symbolic jewellery, the equivalent of a wedding ring, became absolutely the property of the wife, her wealth, and often to poorer women their only security against the risk of widowhood or divorce. 'Dear Medjuel,' Jane wrote in November 1855. 'How I value this proof of his affection, far more than the costly gifts I used to receive from Lord Ellenborough.'[2] Medjuel also gave her a tiny pair of silver pincers to be worn on a silver chain around her neck for removing thorns from feet.

Her growing contentment was marred only by the guilt she felt over Mascha. 'The more time I spend with the man I am happy with, Medjuel (whose equal I met but once in Basily), the more my conscience reproves me for my conduct towards Mascha . . . and yet were I to renounce him whom I adore, would he return to her? No! He is no Spiros, no *General*, he knows not deceit and treachery.'[3]

When Medjuel suggested that they join the tribe during their winter trek into the desert Jane agreed readily, anxious to please him. She would match any bedouin woman in wifely attributes. She had spent long enough in Medjuel's tent to note those items that were lacking in his establishment, and one of the first things she did was to purchase her own kitchen, a complete range of pots, pans and utensils for the desert. She wrote that because of the negotiation rituals it took two days to make a purchase in Damascus that would take only half an hour in London. Her list included a homely touch: mounds of coloured beads to give to the children of the tribe to make bracelets and necklaces.

The Damascus house was nearing completion as Jane prepared to leave. According to descriptions of visitors it stood in a great garden outside the city wall, and was built on three sides around a large central court. The main room of the house, facing north, was used for receiving important visitors and consisted of a huge octagonal atrium which opened on to a *liwan* strewn with carpets and cushions. The atrium had an octagonal domed ceiling set into the flat roof, and was decorated in typically Arabic fashion with heavy carvings, rare Persian rugs and porcelain. The shape of this room had been

suggested by the priceless gift to the newly wed couple of a lamp
which had originally hung in the Great Mosque at Mecca, on one of
the eight side panes of which 'in token of special consideration' the
Sultan had scratched his seal.[4] Both Jane and Medjuel regarded the
item as a great treasure.

On the ground floor of the other three sides of the house were the
kitchens, housekeeper's room and staff quarters, stores, stables and
gatehouse. On the upper floor Medjuel and Jane each had a suite,
Jane's boudoir giving on to an English drawing-room. Straw-coloured
silk drapes hung at the windows and complemented the ornate mirrors
and European furnishings. Her massive, carved bed was overhung
with gauze-like drapes falling from a large coronet. There were several
guest apartments, and all the rooms led on to the flat roof, where the
household sat on summer nights.

But the garden was her chief pride. In the courtyard was a large
oblong pool fed by water from the river, with raised sides upon which
one could sit to trail a hand and watch the fish hiding under lily pads.
Four fountains bubbled gently to provide the soft sounds of trickling
rather than splashing water. Doves fluttered from a dovecote, and
she had planted trees – citrus, flowering hibiscus, pomegranate, mul-
berry and, to remind her of England, a pear tree, unheard of in
Damascus. There were also old-established trees which gave welcome
shade and to these she added a horse chestnut. She laid paths which
wound informally through English herbaceous borders, and rose-beds
which vied with native plants and palm trees. Climbing roses and
jasmine scrambled in profusion up arches, along walls and over the
little *kiosque* she had built, where she could sit and read.[5]

She had quickly collected a large number of small animals, which
she called her menagerie: stray cats, a large collection of poultry, both
domestic and decorative, and dogs, all of which lived in the garden.
Never, throughout her life, was Jane without a dog, and she was
particularly fond of the good-natured Bijon Frise breed, which she
referred to as 'Angora Dogs' for their long white silky hair. All her
pets lived happily alongside Medjuel's elegant salukis and the watch-
dogs. The salukis must have been extremely well trained, for sometimes Jane had tame gazelles living in her garden, brought to her as
abandoned kids by the bedouins, and the gazelles seemed to dwell
happily with the salukis which had been bred to hunt them.

There was adequate grazing near the stables (built on the lines of
the stableyard at Holkham[6]) for their town horses and camels.

Members of the tribe and bedouin guests were welcome to set up camp in the garden when they passed through Damascus. To one side of the property was a large uninhabited plot of land which Jane coveted as extra quarters for visitors. She asked Mr Hannah Misk, dragoman to the British consul, to try to find out who owned the land and negotiate its purchase, but old Sheikh Seyd who owned it refused to part with it. It was not a wasted effort, however, for Seyd was an artist of some ability; he and Jane subsequently spent many happy hours together painting and exchanging information.

It is hardly surprising that Jane's ménage came to be regarded as one of the most remarkable houses in Damascus, and an essential port of call for any important foreign visitor. Jane loved it as she had loved no other home, though her childhood memories of Holkham and Minterne meant much to her. Her other homes had, each in its way, been spoiled for her by shattered relationships. Here at last she believed she had found and created her spiritual home.

It was January 1856 before Jane and Medjuel could leave Damascus. Myriad details claimed her attention and delayed her departure, from Eugénie's arrival with all the latest Athens gossip to the heavy-handedness of a new gardener. Amidst this, in November she had received a censorious letter from Steely addressed – insultingly, Jane thought – to 'the Countess Theotoky'; for Steely would not accept Jane's marriage to 'a heathen'. Jane was furious. 'Oh, that hated name,' she wrote in her diary, 'cause of much, much evil to me . . . [I am] annoyed and vexed beyond measure.'[7]

However, a letter from her Beirut banker, advising her that she had overdrawn her annual income by the recent heavy expenditure on her house, created not concern but delight, for on sharing the information with Medjuel she was told she must never worry about money. He would always provide for her; her welfare was his responsibility. This simple declaration thrilled and touched her. 'How different from the Count, from the General, from *all*,' she marvelled. 'Oh, that I had felt and thought at 18 as I *now* feel and think, what a load of misery I might have spared myself and others.'[8]

At last they were ready to leave and Eugénie helped to pack Jane's personal baggage, including two long black plaits to attach to her own hair, extending it to hem length. She planned to bind them with silver or gold ribbon on gala occasions. She had begun to apply kohl to the rims of her eyelids, as the bedouins did. The chief purpose of this was to prevent sunburn of the eyelid rims which could eventually cause painful scarring; but Jane was not wholly unappreciative of the added emphasis it gave to her huge blue eyes.

As they travelled the beloved road to Palmyra for the third time together Jane was touched by Medjuel's care for her. It was bitterly cold and he was always concerned for her comfort. In the mornings he woke her with a bowl of delicious warm camel's milk or hot coffee. In the evenings, he sometimes rode ahead in order to have a fire ready for her arrival at the stopping place. They were escorting a caravan of 150 donkeys, and on one occasion when Medjuel had ridden to the front of the caravan to check the leaders Jane got down off her camel to stretch her numbed leg; she tripped and lost the halter and got left behind. 'I had a long and stumbling walk for it,' she noted, but eventually Medjuel came back to find her.

At Palmyra it was too cold to stay in the tents so they were accommodated with Sheikh Fares of Tadmor while they waited for news of the tribe. Jane disliked the town Arabs' houses at Palmyra, finding them dirty and noisy, but on this occasion she was too tired and cold to protest. After a few days they changed to 'another house, more airy and spacious, where I get to my bedroom across the sawn trunk of a palm tree!' she wrote with amusement. 'Who would have thought that the ridiculously *exclusive* and *fine* (as it was then called) Lady Ellenborough of thirty years ago would bear to sit down, even in near neighbourhood with the dirty and rude fellah of Palmyra. Time, age and circumstances change almost one's very nature.'[9]

She spent the next week drawing the wonderful ruins of Tadmor for a series of major works,[10] and wandering around the ruins trying to place each building into context. Medjuel had told her a great deal about the city and showed her the old baths, cisterns and stables. Many buildings such as the temple needed no explanations but there were others which puzzled her for Medjuel did not know, and she could not imagine, their purpose. Her extensive knowledge of the city was absorbed in a leisured manner denied other Europeans and, given her interest in architecture, gave her great satisfaction.

The only drawback to visiting Palmyra was the constant attention of the townswomen wishing to hug her and examine her hair and person. One day when she tried to avoid them they took offence and were rude to her. They were immediately 'set down' by their menfolk but she realised that she would have to be more tolerant for Medjuel's sake. That night they were invited to dine with Sheikh Fares:

I put on all my arab fantasia for the good of the public, and went to the Sheikh's, and . . . threw away three medjidis [Turkish silver dollars] upon a wandering Schai'ir, an old crazed singer, for his high flown compliments. I felt, to my confusion and annoyance, as young and vain as I was 30 years ago, at seeing how my finery attracted the wild eyes of the large circle of Arabs assembled around us.[11]

After two weeks they had received no news of the Mezrab tribe's whereabouts, but, happy simply to be with Medjuel, Jane was not as anxious as he to rush to the tents. She knew that Joffell, a wife of Mohammed's whom Jane had especially liked and made her confidante during her last visit, had been divorced and gone off to marry in another tribe. 'Furthermore,' she wrote, 'Mascha's return promises me no very delightful stay.' She suspected that life with the tribe might not be unmitigated pleasure for her.

One night they were awoken by a *ghazou* during which thirty cows were carried off. To Jane's dismay, Medjuel decided it was his duty to go alone to recapture them. She stood at his mare's head, handed him his lance, wished him victory, knowing that for the sake of the onlookers she must behave properly.

Trying not to think that Medjuel might be defeated and lie injured in the desert, she spent the day nursing a sick man. She gave the patient quinine from her extensive medicine box and bathed him with cold sheets to reduce his fever, but he died. Within two hours of his death he was in his grave, and the earth closed over him as though he had never been. 'Of what avail are beauty, riches, *love*,' Jane wrote, depressed both by the death and Medjuel's absence. 'In a few short years shall I, the unworthy object of Madre's idolatry and early care, be destined for a Bedouin's unmarked, unheeded tomb in some far-off desert . . . ?'

But when Medjuel returned victorious with the cows her pride was unbounded. It was yet another of his feats that would be spun into Palmyran folklore and repeated to travellers.[12] A few days later Jane accompanied him to the tents of the Amoureh tribe, from whom he had retaken the cows, to look at some camels they had for sale. She had yet to accept that war between these tribesmen, though bearing all the noise and hallmarks of war, only rarely involved fatalities and bred little ill-feeling. The whole purpose of the *ghazou* was to capture camels, tents and other riches. On the few occasions when a man was killed by a stray lance-stroke, blood money was payable to the victim's family, so killing an enemy did not pay. Consequently Jane was surprised at the friendly manner in which she and Medjuel were received by those whom a few days earlier she had considered their enemies. She travelled there and back as a bedouin wife. 'I rode behind him on the dromedary, full trot all the way and as pleased with myself as a girl of 15!' she wrote that night.

At their first stop, they received some mail sent by messenger from Damascus and Jane was mortified to hear from Steely that she had again featured in a newspaper report identified as Lady Ellenborough. On this occasion Lady Ellenborough was reported as having been murdered by the jealous harem of the Arab sheikh she had recently married. Jane wrote hurriedly to her mother and Steely to set their minds at rest, and to Eugénie, who had been ill again in Damascus. Forgetting earlier qualms about Eugénie's betrayals, Jane wrote, 'If I should lose that good devoted creature what remains to me, whose attachment was ever like hers? . . . Yet Basily and Medjuel are images that float above the rest.'

Medjuel was always able to right her world. Seeing her glum expression the following morning, 'Medjuel, kind and good beyond all measure of expectations, said on serving me my beautiful breakfast amidst hurricanes of wind and sleet, "Could I but give you El Ferdouss [Paradise] I would do it. Do you not do everything for me at Sham [Damascus]?" Such words said in his simple and unaffected way to go to my heart and rest there for ever!'[13]

After trekking across the desert for a week in April they caught up with the Mezrab tribe, and Medjuel sent back to Palmyra for their tent and heavy luggage. Jane was welcomed by the tribe with such warmth that she felt herself drawn into a family.

> Were it not for Eugénie's loneliness and failing health, I would willingly remain some time here. My heart warms towards these wild arabs. They have many qualities we want in *civilized* life, unbounded hospitality, respect for strangers or guests (*Diouff*), good faith and simplicity of dealing amongst themselves, and a certain high bred politeness and unobtrusiveness; quite unlike the vulgar *fellah*.[14]

After a few days Medjuel's favourite brother, 'dear good Manah', arrived with Medjuel's children, 'all jacked up on a *Hedgin*'. His two sons, Schebibb and Afet, and his daughter Aafteh, were accompanied by several cousins. Jane's enjoyment of the children was interrupted when their mother arrived a few days afterwards:

Mascha is quite changed from last year, and *prettier* and *all alive*, no longer the lazy apathetic creature she was. What can be the reason? . . . Schaiba told me Mohammed intended marrying Mascha as soon as divorced! Can this be so?

Days have passed on and as usual I have lost track of the day and even month. We are arrived at the waters and I am come to an open *nouille* with Mascha . . . Medjuel behaves like an angel for the Bedouin are not used to bursts of temper and jealousy in their wives. But I must not try him *too* far.

. . . For four or five days I neither spoke nor looked at Mascha but at length my conscience reproached me and when I met her at Feyda's tent we spoke. She suffered horribly with the toothache so I made her a cataplasm of camomile. When I think of her extraordinary position my only consolation regarding my own conscience is that certainly her conduct is not praiseworthy, nor ever was, towards Medjuel.

Jane's attempt to live in peace with Mascha was soon rewarded by an unexpected incident.

Afet was ill and to crown all fell into the *bir* [well] while trying to drink water. Medjuel fell into a rage and without telling me his intentions, went, took Kalaori as witness and without further ceremony divorced Mascha, and insisted on her leaving his brother's tent! Next day she removed her bedroll to her uncle's tent next door.

Medjuel was now hers alone. Though she had shared him in name only her relief was enormous and she hugged to herself her new status as Medjuel's only wife, feeling absolved of the guilt she had been carrying with her since her marriage.

During the weeks she spent with the tribe she began to appreciate the position of a sheikh. He must act as the 'father of his people'. As his wife Jane found herself increasingly called upon to play a leadership role among the wives, to mediate in disputes, administer medicine to sick children, and to provide the poorer wives with gifts of clothing or kitchen utensils. Later she would look back on this period as her apprenticeship, a time of learning and of forging relationships.

I have chosen Endaya, Manah's wife, and my sister-in-law in fact . . . as my particular friend. She, Bettli and Hassanah are all pregnant and I feel that my present sterility (how unlike former days) is almost a reproach in the eyes of the Arabs who long to see another child of Medjuel's.

At length one fine morning I mounted Oudiada and we took a final departure for Sham, leaving the children with Jassin's wife. We slept at the Meidan, an encampment of Ebn Merschid's. They are evidently richer than our tribe with their slaves, and their tents are better appointed than ours. We met his wife in full dress going *mardoufa* [in state] to her parents, and I actually am *fool* enough to throw time and thoughts away upon various vanities relating to my *next* appearance among them! When and how – an old lady of 50!

Within two weeks they were back in Damascus, Jane delighted with the house and Eugénie's management, and amused by praises received from those who had visited her 'show house' (as she heard it called). By now it was June, and a backlog of mail had built up in her absence, including, to her great pleasure, letters from both her brothers and her mother. To her brother Kenelm and his wife Caroline she replied at once:

It is indeed a long time since we have written to each other but I was not a little delighted on returning after five months wandering in the desert to receive your letter with several others ... How I rejoice that that ill natured, and utterly unfounded report of my assassination by the 'Sheikh's *Harem*' did not reach our poor dear Madre's ears!

First I must assure you, my dearest brother, however much as a Protestant clergyman you may be averse to the idea of my husband being a Mohametan, his principles of honour and morality of conduct, are such as would do honour to many a Christian. Secondly, he *has no other* wife but me but 3 children by a former one, and is so good and kind that I only regret I did not know him *long* and *long* before. It might have spared me, and all, much misery. You will smile, and say 'a Bedouin's morality'. But believe me the Arabs are governed amongst themselves by as strict a code of laws as any other, and many a curious fact I know which would throw light on this most *ancient and peculiar* race.

As to the rest, for which I know *you* care but little, he is a great and renowned Chief of a tribe, the Anazeh Bedouins, which have always refused to enter into a pact with the [Turkish] government, but make their own terms and dictate their own conditions. An intermarriage with a European, it is true, is a new thing under the sun to them. But I am very popular amongst them and when amongst them adopt their customs, dress, manners etc. I hold my open *divan* for the women and do what little good I can in the way of medicine, clothing, settling differences etc. But they fancy I know something of *magic*, and many are the consultations that you would laugh to hear.

My riding and my real fondness for animals has made me a great favourite with them, and I can now ride the swiftest Meccan Dromedary across the desert with the best! We hawk with beautiful falcons and Persian greyhounds, hunt the 'b'tiddin' (wild goat), antelope, grey crane, etc., *and I have shot D'jerboa* (a sort of kangaroo), to their amazement. Their women, only riding on camels, are timid when out of the precincts of their tents.

The moment when my heart fails me is when I am obliged – as is the custom – to give the Sheikh his lance, or other arms, when he mounts his magnificent mare to go off with his tribe against some rival one that approaches to seize our camels and tents. And smile and encourage him with hopes of a speedy and victorious return etc., when I feel 'who knows if I will ever see him again'. But enough of this.

I am now in my cool, shady garden kiosk at Damascus with water and turtle doves bubbling and cooing in every direction, and here I hope to remain until the next campaign. Many and many are the English and other foreigners who come and see the house and garden while I am away and express themselves enchanted. How I wish you or Ed could be hit by a longing for the east and come over. Your account of your *nine* children is most interesting . . . what a troop![15]

A similar letter went to Edward's wife Theresa, expressing Jane's sympathy on hearing that old Lord Digby had died leaving a will disinheriting Edward. Although Edward became Lord Digby, the late Lord Digby's personal fortune and Sherbourne Castle had been left to his sister Charlotte.[16] The will had been made shortly after Jane's divorce and, despite Admiral Digby's attempts to persuade his uncle not to visit his distaste for Jane's behaviour on her family, the will remained as written. Edward and Theresa lived at Minterne but without his uncle's fortune could not match the lifestyle of his forebears. Jane sympathised at the couple's disappointment, not realising that she may have been a contributory factor: 'But I have often had misgivings, for when I asked Madre how he was with [Edward and Kenelm], and heard her answer, I set him down in my mind as a nasty old crab!'[17] She added a few words for her long-estranged brother Edward, reminding him that she was still his loving 'Jenny', and begged him to restore their relationship, 'Let me write to you or Theresa sometimes for you shall *never again have reason* to break it off!'

In her diary in September she noted that Hadji-Petros had written to say that Eirini, about whom Jane had enquired, had been seriously ill but now seemed a little better.

his letter touched me with its tones of affection, sincerity and confusion of my former affection (alas, how sincere) for himself. The ways of providence are inscrutable! A widower in Athens would have been far more *suitable* than a Bedouin Sheikh and the Desert. But oh, the truth of one, and his morality (though classed as an infidel), against the laxity of the other![18]

The letters from home increased her longing to see her family, and she mooted the possibility of a trip to England, probably the last time she would see her mother. Medjuel quashed any thoughts that he might accompany her and she put off the idea until, as the autumn set in, Medjuel began thinking of again joining the tribe for the winter months. It was finally decided that Jane should go to England, and Medjuel to the tribe.

Jane left Damascus with Eugénie in early November armed with daunting shopping lists of furniture, saddlery, guns and ammunition. Medjuel accompanied her as far as Doumah, where he set off for the desert. As he turned and rode away she almost abandoned her plan and galloped after him. Thoroughly dejected at the thought of six months without her husband, she wept as her ship sailed from Beirut, fearing that something might occur to prevent her return. She would never be parted from Medjuel again, she wrote, except by death.

> *Monday 24th.* Arrived at Piraeus and was most happy to find there was no quarantine . . . I sent a message afterwards to the General [Hadji-Petros] who soon arrived. What I felt, I cannot express. Emotion at seeing once more that once-loved face, suffocated me. He remained an hour or more and then left. I went and saw the Palace gardens.
> *Tuesday 25th.* I went early to see poor Eirini . . . Nothing short of a miracle can save her. She is evidently dying. Poor, poor Eirini, so young . . . her father is very low and unhappy.

She spent a week visiting old friends and in the company of the general, often at the bedside of Eirini. Hadji-Petros was bluff and outspoken as usual, and fiercely loyal to the new king, George, to whom he was senior military adviser. Later he was to be dismissed by the Prime Minister, who thought the general's close relationship to the new king a danger to the constitution,[19] but now his stock was high.

Eugénie, who owned several tenanted properties in Athens, had business to conduct and took care never to be around when the general called on Jane. Hadji-Petros spent the entire time trying to persuade Jane to return to him, saying that Eugénie's reports had been a misunderstanding, that she had entirely mistaken his intentions. He might have saved his breath. Jane felt great affection for him, but her heart belonged now in a low black tent in the desert and, had it not been for her eighty-year-old mother, she would have hastened back there with all possible speed.

She rode one day to the abandoned villa of her friend the Duchesse de Plaisance, its pink marble walls partly hidden behind a jungle of overgrown shrubs and brambles. In its bright garden she used to sit and look out over the distant Aegean but there was nothing here for her now and nothing to regret leaving behind.

Suspecting she would never see the child alive again, she 'took leave of Eirini with a low foreboding and an aching heart'. She doubted that she would ever return to Athens and when Hadji-Petros said goodbye to her at the docks of Piraeus they were both in tears. Jane's were for him rather than herself: 'I felt very, very low to leave him to whom I was once so attached. Poor man.'[20]

As the ship set sail into a tempestuous gale which confined Eugénie to her bunk, Jane spent her time on deck, annoyed that a letter from Medjuel, handed to her as she boarded the ship, had been forwarded without translation by Monsieur Le Roy of Damascus. It was written in Arabic script and Jane had no means of knowing what it said. She vowed that as soon as she returned to Syria she would improve her Arabic speech and learn to read and write it as well. '*Tuesday* [December] *9th 1856*. We arrived at Marseilles after wonderfully good passage for the season. I spent the rest of the day in running over the shops which seem beautiful.'

They set off next day for Paris on one of the first major railways in France, a novel experience marred only by the attentions of a young officer, Major Campbell, who had made a nuisance of himself on the ship. Finding Jane on the train to Paris he took the same compartment. Fortunately, his behaviour stopped at flirting, but she resented his attentions.

In Paris she stayed at a small and gloomy hotel and spent a few days shopping. Eugénie went to meet her former lover, the father of her daughter, who was recently widowed. Eugénie was now a middle-aged woman of some substance, for she had saved and invested well, and clearly hoped for marriage. Torn between her own needs and Eugénie's wildest hopes, Jane wrote, 'I think she may . . . attain the summit of her ambitions. Poor thing! . . . she has waited long and patiently enough.' But the longed-for meeting was unsuccessful and Eugénie returned downcast.

Friday 19th. We left Boulogne at 12 o'clock and embarked for England. England! *I* in England in about three hours. A good passage. I was landed at Folkestone and *warmly*, how warmly greeted by my excellent and never failing friend, Miss Jane. My long and wearisome journey is over . . . I passed a most pleasant and cheerful evening by a blazing fire and felt a foretaste of the pleasures that await me when I join dear Madre. This day 3 years ago I set off for Bagdad.

In a way this visit to Europe was to be a test of her true commitment to her life in the East. A period of living with her loving family, in the manner to which she had been raised, would make it difficult to contemplate returning to life as a desert nomad unless her heart was in it. The comfortable life of a modern Victorian house equipped with cooking ranges, gas lighting, bathrooms and running water, and staffed by attentive and efficient servants, might make Damascus appear undesirable for all its exotic appeal. And there was always the possibility, as she went about discreetly with her family, that among people of her own kind she might meet a man who could offer a more congenial life.

Equally important, Medjuel's love for Jane was on test during the long separation. He was a young and virile man in the prime of manhood. In all probability he would be subjected to more temptation than she. There would be young, dusky and beautiful *binaat* around him in the desert, only too eager to shake their long silken hair at the handsome young sheikh during the dance of the maidens: women of his own race and creed, who would willingly accept the status of a second wife, and who could give him sons. Would he think of his 'Frangya' then, she wondered.[21] She put these fears out of her mind, and only at her lowest ebb did she allow them to creep out to haunt her.

Jane's design sketch for the impressive bed in her *boudoir*.

16

Return to England
1856–1858

That Christmas in England, her last visit there, was happier than she had dared hope. On her arrival at Ernstein Villa, Tunbridge Wells ('a nice cheerful house'), where Lady Andover now lived with the two Steele sisters, Jane was relieved to find her mother 'little changed'. Lady Andover and the Steele sisters were no doubt equally relieved to see Jane wearing the latest in fashionable gowns from Paris; there were no visible traces, outwardly at least, of her exotic life.

Christmas Day with its traditions brought echoes of her childhood, including the walk to church before breakfast across a frost-covered Rustall Common.[1] 'Oh, how ever far one may wander,' she wrote, 'there is a spell in one's native country that speaks to one's heart and calls to memory long forgotten and early ties.'[2] On the last day of the year, however, it was to her ties in Syria that Jane's thoughts turned and when she went to church with Miss Jane it was for Medjuel she prayed. Already she had begun to long for her return, realising that no matter how strong the pull of her roots England was no place for her now.

Her brother Edward and his wife Theresa came to visit for several days. Estranged from Jane since she left Charles Venningen, Edward had hardened his attitude when the Theotoky marriage failed and he believed his sister incapable of constancy. But recent letters from Jane to his wife Theresa had healed the breach and he greeted her affectionately. Jane's stories of her more amusing or exciting experiences were listened to with interest but she noticed that whenever she mentioned Medjuel the subject was changed, as though her family

215

were pretending he did not exist. Then she learned that they believed her disgrace to be the reason behind Edward's being disinherited, and she was mortified at 'the grief I have brought upon others, upon my dear kind parent, by my fatal misconduct'.[3]

On 22 January 1857 she received word from the general that Eirini had died the day after Jane left Athens. This depressed her and recalled the death of 'my own Leonidas'. By coincidence she received on the following day a disturbing letter from her daughter Bertha. She was deeply unhappy with her father, Bertha wrote; she begged her mother to allow her to come and live with her in Damascus. The ranting tone seemed reminiscent of Jane's hated former mother-in-law's 'strange and wrong ideas' and Jane had known for some time that Bertha was mentally unstable. Occasional letters from the Baron revealed that the beautiful girl was becoming increasingly difficult to handle and he blamed his mother's influence, until he eventually accepted that Bertha's behaviour was more than mere adolescent rebellion. Jane replied to her daughter that she had remarried, and that the East was no place for her. She sent Bertha's letter to Charles, suggesting he bring the girl to England to stay with her family and consult specialists in mental illness. She wrote that she would gladly help with the arrangements and cost.

Eugénie became ill with a fever, and when she recovered she told Jane she must resign her service, for she could not face a further spell in Syria. As if this were not enough, there was no letter from Medjuel when the monthly 'Indian Mail' arrived in January. A letter from Monsieur Le Roy came from Damascus in February, passing on local gossip, but it did not ease her mind, for he told her that Medjuel had gone 'to join his brothers in the midst of malady and war. A sort of cholera has broken out among them.'

It was not until 10 March that she heard from Medjuel. His letter informing her he was well and looking forward to her return was enclosed and translated by Monsieur Le Roy. A covering note told her in glowing terms of Medjuel's part in the fighting which was 'the talk of Damascus', but all Jane cared for was that her 'dear, *dear* Medjuel' was safe and well. She attempted to share her news but Steely cut her off, and left Jane in no uncertainty about her continuing disapproval of her marriage. Jane heard the reproof in silence, wanting to defend her husband but unwilling to cause wounds that she knew would remain unhealed long after her departure.

Kenelm came from Norfolk to see her and asked her about her

husband. He did not condemn her marriage, perhaps recognising that for his three-times-divorced sister the 'heathen' ceremony she had undergone meant far more than a conventional marriage service in a cathedral. It is obvious from his letters to Jane over the next quarter of a century that Kenelm found his *métier* when he became a clergyman. His caring nature made him ideal in the role, for he was always the healer, always the comforter, yet despite his deep and patient faith he was never piously 'holy'. He enjoyed his life and was amusing and bright; his faith was a happy thing and he must have been literally a godsend to his congregation. It was said by his family, generally known for their good looks, that he was a physically ugly man, and this together with his lack of expectations may account, in part, for the extraordinary beauty of his nature.

He offered to meet Jane in town and take her to the Crystal Palace exhibition. In London Jane stayed at the old house in Harley Street, but she only hinted at bygone memories in her diary, dwelling instead on her father's rooms, 'his old stuffed birds and many things reminding me of him'.[4]

She went shopping in Baker Street bazaar for fabrics, and on a special errand to purchase guns and ammunition for the tribe. Except in America, where a small new industry was just developing, firearms in those days were not mass-produced but hand-made. The notes on her shopping list, written first in Arabic by Medjuel and then in English by Jane, were specific: 'Adam's registered Wadded bullets for revolvers, rifles, Carbines etc. 50 conical, 54 bore. Ely Brothers Manufacturers, London.'

Another errand was a visit with Kenelm to the College of Arms. As children of a baron, Kenelm and Jane were entitled to the prefix 'the Honorable', but as this was not effected prior to their father's death they needed to establish their claim for approval by the Queen. More important, Jane needed a family tree to send to Charles Venningen. Heribert's cousins had told the baron that unless Heribert could prove his parentage they would contest his inheritance in the event of his father's death; and the records of his birth, as Jane was only too aware, were obscure.

Brother and sister visited the fabulous Crystal Palace, originally built in Hyde Park to house Prince Albert's Great Exhibition of 1851. Designed to marry art with engineering skill, the astonishing building was 95 per cent glass, the remainder being thin iron frames. Two years before Jane's visit the breathtaking structure had been dismantled and re-erected in South London to provide half as much space again. Inside were '100,000 objects of beauty, interest and craft', reflecting the wealth and diversity of Queen Victoria's vast empire, but also demonstrating the skills and cultures of other nations. 'Wonderful, beautiful, beyond description,' Jane wrote in her diary and, perhaps predictably, 'but I overdid it and returned home dead tired.'

Despite the 'retired life' she was leading, the house in Harley Street was busy with callers. Her cousin and friend from the Holkham schoolroom, 'dear, kind' Fanny Anson, now Mrs Isted, dropped by to pass on 'a perfect avalanche of news'. Friends from Jane's 'palmy days' at Almack's, such as Lord Londonderry and Lady Roseby, mingled with others whom she had come to know since. One day 'unexpectedly walked in Sir Henry Rawlinson [lately HBM Consul in Baghdad] and I spent a pleasant hour with him talking over old friends in the East. He told me that the Governor of Buschin's wife was in town, a Bagdad grande-dame, and a great friend of mine.' Next day Jane set out to visit her friend, delighted to be able to speak in Arabic and talk of Medjuel to someone who appreciated his fine qualities.

Rawlinson, with whom Jane had been corresponding on the subject of ancient desert ruins, called again and advised on the legality of her marriage, instructing her to register the Muslim ceremony formally with the British consul in Damascus, and to obtain two copies of the certificate from the consul and send them home to her family.

Jane returned to Tunbridge Wells for the last days of her visit. She dreaded the final parting from her mother and the Steele sisters, but ached to return to Medjuel, on whom her thoughts constantly centred. On 3 April 1857 she wrote in her diary: 'My Birthday! Fifty! . . . all the romance and poetry of life ought to be long since past and over, and here I am still with a beating and burning heart.' Three days later Jane left England. The parting from her mother was as sad as she anticipated, both knowing that they would probably never see each other again.

In Paris, Jane 'ran about like a wild thing' in search of furniture, mirrors, crystal, books. Her leather-bound pocketbook was filled with lists of things she needed in Damascus: fine table- and bedlinen (she was particularly eager to purchase supplies of yellow table-linen that would complement her porcelain dinner service); towels and toiletries such as perfumed soap and cold-cream; supplies of eye ointment and drops, quinine, iodine, various oils for rheumatism, cough linctus and toothache tincture, in such quantities that it is clear she intended to treat the entire tribe; parasols; sketching materials; shoes; and undergarments.

She called at a gunsmith to collect a matched pair of silver-chased pistols she had commissioned for Medjuel three months earlier. And she bought a piano, having desired one since she left Athens. She had no great confidence that it would arrive in Damascus intact but believed it worth the effort, for when Medjuel was away she would find it soothing to have an instrument to play upon, and she thought that Medjuel would find her playing and singing an enjoyable novelty.

The frantic shopping continued in Marseille, she and Eugénie 'worn to death' after almost a week of ceaseless spending on items that they could not easily buy outside Europe. At Marseille, Jane had hoped to recruit several French servants; but she was disappointed in the applicants, and Eugénie loyally agreed to accompany her to Beirut.

On 16 April the two set off for Alexandria on an old steamer, *La Tamise*. It was a miserable trip, the ship rolled badly and Eugénie hardly moved from her bunk. At Malta all the shops were closed and there was little to see. Alexandria too was a disappointment. Jane took a carriage to see Pompey's Pillar and Cleopatra's Needle, ordered some plants to be sent on to her and interviewed a maid, whom she had almost engaged when she found her '*fighting* with the Arab porters on the shore!'

Eugénie was still ill when they arrived at Beirut. There was the usual period of quarantine to endure, but Jane managed to fill it by checking on her packing-cases and arranging for their transport with her agent with whom she communicated through an open window. A message from Medjuel that all was well had been waiting for her, and she telegraphed confirmation of her safe arrival through the British consul. She could hardly contain her anxiety to get to him and when released from quarantine on 1 May she did not waste an hour before setting off for Damascus. Eugénie remained at the coast to recover in the cool air, still undecided whether to rejoin Jane's household or to return to Greece.

With a single guard and spare horses, Jane set off for Damascus in oppressive heat; her luggage would follow on behind her. She travelled impatiently, stopping only twice to snatch a nap of several hours. The next day she 'slept at Mejdel for 4 hours and rode all night.' Early on 3 May she passed through Doumah, expecting at every step to see Medjuel or one of her servants coming to greet her, never considering the possibility that they might not expect her for at least another day. When she arrived at the house, Medjuel was not there, nor did the surprised servants know when he might return. Jane was utterly exhausted, having accomplished a three-day journey in two. She sank on to her bed wondering how she could get a message to Medjuel when there was a tap at the door. It was Medjuel, as tender and loving as in the first days of their marriage, 'and in the happiness of that moment I forgot all else'.

> *Monday 4th.* We passed the day in talking over our affairs. Great have been his losses . . . but he does not seem to have acted wrongly in all this winter of war and troubles, and has but defended his rights.

One of Medjuel's problems appeared to be that others now believed they too should be allowed to provide escort for European travellers to Palmyra. In Jane's wake had come the more adventurous – not many, but in a steady trickle of twos and threes. Without exception they clamoured to be taken to the fabled ruins at Palmyra. If Medjuel refused them, there was virtually no price they would not offer to an alternative guide. Others coveted this lucrative new business.

The weeks that followed Jane's return to Syria were pleasantly domesticated. Barrels of plants arrived and Jane threw herself with renewed enthusiasm into work on her garden. 'I sowed many of Carters fine seeds in hot beds and elsewhere . . . one of the apricot trees fell down because of too much water . . . the turkey hen began sitting upon the Cochin China and Persian eggs, I also have a sitting canary.' And, despite their great love, she and Medjuel, like any married couple, had occasional disagreements.

> *June. Monday 8th.* My bad temper and bad humour got the better of me and I picked a quarrel with dear Medjuel who was really hurt, and offended by my unreasonableness. A sweet reconciliation afterwards took place between us, but I must not trifle thus with his character.

Two days later, Medjuel went off to the desert to join his brothers for two weeks. Jane tried to fill her time as she had done before he went away, gardening and exercising the horses, but whereas her daily rides with Medjuel had been so pleasurable now they were a bore and 'the young horses are odious . . . house, garden, all lose their charm when the heart is lonely.' One evening she re-read her diaries from start to finish. From the security of her loving relationship with Medjuel she could hardly credit what she read. '[I had] a strong inclination to put them on the fire.'

To her delight, Medjuel returned a day early. '[He] brought me
the account of the two Frenchmen being arrested by Manah. How I
wish this affair of the road to Palmyra was arranged properly in favour
of Medjuel without all these disagreeable altercations every moment!'

She commissioned masons to build new stables and an extension
to her boudoir, 'the whole to be finished in 30 days for 9,000 piastres
without boiserie'. Meanwhile packing-cases began to arrive with the
results of her shopping trips. The piano arrived mercifully intact but
badly in need of tuning. And a French couple appeared as housekeeper and gardener. In July she wrote to Kenelm in good spirits:

Since my return, my time has been engrossed in putting this straggling
house in order . . . everything having been put away in odd corners . . .
then come tiresome visits of congratulation as if I had come from an
unknown land, and now I have workmen in the house repairing and building. I hope tho' this year to finish all there is to do inside the garden wall,
for these same arab workmen steal my fruit, and break the young trees
etc. which ruffles my temper not a little. Eugénie too is returning to
Athens, and as yet I have no replacement, which is a terrible bore to me
as I must turn housekeeper *myself*, which is not my line.

The Sheikh was delighted with the sporting prints [you sent him]; but
the fox not being [included in the picture] he has decided that such
leaps and scamperings must be after *human* enemies and not for 'Kayf'
[enjoyment] only. The prints of our Queen receiving the troops at Alder-
shot, which I thought rather a good [illustration of] the *prerogatives of
women in the West*, is thought here rather an *effrontée* thing . . . presenting
herself unveiled before so many men!!!!

All the other fruits of our indefatigable shopping have been duly
admired and appreciated – glasses, toothbrushes etc. I am now studying
hard, Arabic, as well as reading and writing it, and am getting on [well]

[Tell Edward] his Cochins are splendid and I have a brood of 29!!
What with Persians and Cochin *pur-sang* . . . they make a sort of 'happy
family' . . . of desert partridges, gazelles, turkies, ducks, etc. I would fain
add an ostrich and young lion from 'our estates' near Bagdad, but I like
to see beasts walking about . . . not cooped up. I treasure my print of the
Crystal Palace in remembrance of one of the pleasantest and most wonderful days I ever spent. Poor Eugénie has not yet recovered from it; a sort
of fairyland she thought.

In about three months, I believe, we are going to the desert. I fear this
winter will not be very pleasant as a great expedition is meditated against
the Shemmaar Arabs who are always 'taking what is not his'n'. And so
several Anazeh Sheikhs have settled to drive them out of Mesopotamia.
If this takes place I shall most likely be able to make other sketches of

Babel and other places in 'Shina'. The Sheikh admired the Bible and begs to send his best 'Sal'aams, and peace to your house'. The Turkish government is trying to get him to take the town of Hammah (near Aleppo) under his protection for a consideration of a good sum of tribute money, and forage for so many horses. He goes on this business tomorrow which is not very amusing as he must stay away about 20 days. And now, my dearest Kenny, I have told you all my news.[5]

A letter from home brought sad news about George Anson. Jane had heard much of his successful career. After his marriage he settled down, worked hard and had been a major-general for some years when in 1856 he was appointed Commander-in-Chief of the British forces in India. He was holding this important post when the mutiny of the Bengal army broke out and he immediately marched against Delhi, where he contracted cholera. He died on 27 May, only a month after Fanny Isted had proudly detailed her brother's progress when she called on Jane at Harley Street. Jane was 'sadder than sad' until, 'Oh day of days! Medjuel arrived and kinder, more *tender* than ever!'[6]

Now her daily rides were a joy. One wonders if she was riding the same horses, since one day they were 'odious and boring', yet in Medjuel's presence they all appear to be Pegasus reincarnated. 'I had a delightful ride with Medjuel towards Djoba, which reminded me of my younger days.'

She was invited by the pasha's harem to attend the pre-nuptial celebrations of a favourite daughter. As an important personage in the city Jane was often invited to attend such celebrations; she enjoyed the spectacle and the opportunity to wear one of her Parisian crinoline dresses which always pleased her hostesses by their novelty. As she returned home after midnight she was touched to find Medjuel waiting outside the gate of their house, watching for her return. On the following day he was unwell and she fussed over him, blaming his long wait for her in the cold night air. 'Where is the European who would thus love me day in and day out?' she asked.

Medjuel's next absence accidentally provided a watershed for Jane. Three English travellers, Messrs Pennant, Ralley and Radcliffe arrived in Damascus with the express wish of visiting Palmyra; the British consul brought them to Jane and asked if a trip might be arranged. Jane explained that Medjuel was already in the desert, but when she saw the men's disappointment a daring solution presented itself to her. The words were out of her mouth before she could recall them. If they agreed, she suggested, she would escort them herself. She knew the route now as well as anyone. She had access to some fast, strong dromedaries, and there were several members of the Mezrab tribe encamped near the house whom she could press into duty as guards.

The Englishmen accepted. What a tale they would have to tell on their return! They would have travelled with the personal escort of the beautiful former Lady Ellenborough.

Jane immediately sent a messenger ahead to advise Medjuel that she would meet him in five days at Tadmor, and within hours had arranged everything. Her impulsiveness was worthy of the young Jane Digby and lacked the wisdom she had shown of late; were the party to be attacked by bedouins friendly to Medjuel, her status as his wife would have protected them. But they would have fared ill had they been attacked by enemy tribesmen who had cast envious eyes on Medjuel's money-spinning tourist trade. Without Medjuel's famous valour as a warrior to call upon she could not guarantee her clients' safety and she could not have been unaware of this. Yet dressed in her sheikh's robes, riding as a man, carrying a lance, Jane rode out on her Arab mare ahead of the small train of fast camels, circling as Medjuel did to look ahead and behind them. Later when they reached the desert she changed her favourite dromedary Oudiada, and led the mare. Perhaps she hoped that from a distance she would pass for Medjuel.

Once her diaries had contained descriptions of the tints and colours in the sands and the mountains at dawn and sunset. Now her observations were more prosaic (though she continued to press within the pages, wild flowers) and she noted herbage that had sprung up after rain, providing grazing for camels. She was responsible on this journey for the tourists, for rationing the water, nursing the camels along, deciding the pace and stopping places, and her diary entries were the terse comments of a commanding officer:

Tuesday 27th October. We set off. I riding the Saklowyeh, and we slept at Ataiff in the khan.
Wednesday 28th. Lunch at Djirrouda, and on to Karyetein.
Thursday 29th. Arrived at Karyetein and rested, and on through the night.
Friday 30th. At about 2 o'clock set off on the last long stage for Palmyra. Travelled all night with a half hour rest and arrived in sight of Tadmor.
Saturday 31st. Medjuel came to meet us with fantasia, which pleased the English much as a romantic novelty.

These words mark Jane's final transition from a Westerner playing at living among the bedouins, to full acceptance of her position as wife to the sheikh. Only a few years earlier it was she who was pleased with the romantic novelty of the *jerid*. Now she watched the exuberant spectacle with the complacent insouciance of the provider of the entertainment. These were *her* people now. This was *her* culture; while the visitors, 'the English', were mere tourists enjoying an experience novel to them.

They stayed three days, more than the time usually allotted, for Jane's exploit was the talk of Palmyra, and the inhabitants were inclined to be generous to her countrymen. Such a deed was the stuff of legends to add to the tales told by the storyteller around the fire. The bedouins loved to hear stories, the favourite one of unrequited love between Antar and Abbla being an Arab version of Romeo and Juliet. Sometimes the storyteller told of Medjuel's bravery, and now he could add that the Ferengi Sitt who had married the Sheikh of the Mezrabs had proved to be a woman worthy of him, even though such independence was an unusual asset in an Arab wife. In such a manner desert news spread across vast distances in a remarkably short time.[7]

It was soon after this that Jane was seen by an English friend of the Cokes, who was travelling in the East and procured an invitation to meet Jane:

> She met her swathed in a veil and Arab garments, and riding at the head of a cavalcade of wild Arabs – a veritable Queen of the Banditti – in surroundings which rendered her gracious, courteous manners, her air of *grande dame* and her sweet low voice more singularly impressive, even though her beauty – all but her glorious eyes – was scrupulously concealed from view. And still her thoughts turned to the life from which she was severed; all her questions were of Holkham Hall and Cannon Hall, of the relations whom she was fated never to see again.[8]

Yet despite the exotic splendour and adventure of her life Jane also had domestic harassments with which to contend. There was a heavy fall of 'wet snow' over Christmas, the weight of which demolished her stables, her pretty garden *kiosque* and her greenhouses, and tore branches from her fruit trees. Without Eugénie, she had to oversee everything personally – the mopping up, the clearing, the repairs, and so on. 'All my attachment for this place is gone. I am ready to sell it,' she wrote in irritation at the end of several trying days; and, to crown it all, 'Soultan sickened with the strangles'. Soultan was the great black horse that Medjuel had given her as a two-year-old during their honeymoon. In February 1858 she wrote to Kenelm of her household,

> sitting like so many despondent cocks and hens under the dripping ceilings and streaming walls. Our oriental, romantic and picturesque houses are fit emblems of 'luxury and misery'; mud without, and ditto (with marble fountains, and gilded cornices inlaid with mirrors) within!
>
> I fancied I would show [the builders] a little better building in baking my bricks longer in the sun, but here we are; the garden wall flat on the ground in three places, the pretty rooms filled with dishes of all sorts to catch the muddy water; the front of my grand stable (on an English plan) fallen, and our beautiful arab horses are camped, one in the old Mosque – our present dining room – the other in the dromedary's box who eats up all her food. A whole brood of cochins just hatched are with their stately mother in a large basket in my bedroom, amongst damask hangings and other items and relics of former splendour!
>
> To say nothing of the garden. It looks like chaos and my new French gardener who is a man of projects was interrupted in his transplantations, making [paths] etc.; so that now the Sheikh says, 'it looks as tho' all the wild boars had been working there' . . .
>
> I am contemplating an excursion to the Hauran [desert] . . . the ancient *Bashan* where there exist still the habitations of the 'giants' with their massive stone doors and shutters, beautifully sculptured. How interesting!! I trust your 'depression of spirit without visible cause' has worn off? Why don't you try Camphor Julip? According to the French doctor, Raspail, camphor is good for everything, externally and internally, and cures every disorder but *death.*
>
> The desert is very unquiet and we are waiting with impatience to set off on our spring excursion. When you write give me some Holkham news . . . the Sheikh always sends his salaams and should you ever want any Eastern articles, begs you will tell him. He manages Trant's revolver beautifully and has got a Minié [rifle] which carries 1,000 metres.[9]

As a result of the unrest throughout the desert (the Shemmar were plotting to avenge their defeat the previous year), Medjuel could not make up his mind whether to lead the tribe east to Mesopotamia or south towards Mecca that winter and waited anxiously for word from his brother, which never arrived. Eventually he set off alone to find the tribe.

He would be gone for a month, he said. Some weeks later Jane wrote, in code, of a fear that had been eating at her like a worm in an apple. 'The fourth week is passed and Medjuel is not returned . . . but his speech on the day before he went accusing me of no longer loving him as I once did, on account of our disagreeable discussions about money, cuts to the heart in his absence.' Would he turn to another woman in the desert, one who was not so quick-tempered as she, she wondered. She had merely snapped at him over some trifle after receiving a statement from her banker showing her expenditure to be over budget. After his departure she discovered errors in the statement in her favour.

Her relationship with Medjuel was unique; few bedouin men could have tolerated Jane's independence, yet he accepted it with grace and patience, showing his displeasure when she overstepped the mark only by a tight, hurt expression around his eyes. It was this look he had worn when he left Damascus and Jane was anxious to set matters right between them. Her irritation had been caused because of his impending journey without her. However, she reasoned, 'I must not be unjust or unreasonable. A great part of his desert fortune is at stake, and nor can he leave this affair at sixes and sevens' – any more than she could leave her house in the hands of inefficient servants.

But when a further week went by without his return she could no longer bear to wait in Damascus. She set the house to rights as far as possible, and with Moussa, one of Medjuel's best men, and a Mr Walter Cave who wished to see Palmyra, she set off to find Medjuel. The novelty of her first lone escort duty was absent; now her wish was to reach Medjuel and the tribe. He did not come riding towards her on this occasion and was clearly still annoyed with her. The road between Damascus and Palmyra was 'not safe' and her precipitate dash with the English traveller was foolish. Medjuel dispatched the Englishman back to Damascus with Manah as soon as was decent.

Jane soon overcame Medjuel's mood of wounded pride, and rapidly became absorbed into the politics of the tribe. One week her diary was full of the domestic problems of her Damascus mansion, the next of a sister-in-law's unhappiness because her husband, the childless Sheikh Mohammed, planned to take another, younger wife. When Mohammed returned from his bridal sortie he brought with him Medjuel's son Schebibb, whom Jane 'was really glad to see. [He is] a nice, clever and well-behaved boy.'[10]

In a letter to Kenelm, Jane described her desert clothing as a dark-blue shift – no different from, 'but cleaner' than, those of the other women 'of my tribe' – and her dark gauze veil was larger than those of the other women. Dangling about her head she wore 'handsome gold coins' and on her cloak the gold insignia of a sheikh, to indicate her high rank in the desert. She was bare-legged, but yellow kid boots still protected her feet, for they refused to harden sufficiently to allow her to go barefoot. 'But', she said with pride, 'I attend to the Sheikh's mares and camels, and the arrangement of our tent, better than *anyone*' . . . and I doctor as far as I am able, man and beast.'[11]

She writes of a mare taking all day to deliver a foal which was badly presented, which meant her remaining with the animal and its owner while the tribe moved on. Her knowledge of horses and their care was above all things a reason why the men of the tribe, in addition to the women, accepted her with respect.

She was touched at Medjuel's moving their tent and heavy luggage at considerable trouble to a place where she might get more shade and be less troubled by the heat. But as the summer heat increased she became unwell and was not sorry when he suggested he would take her to Damascus and return alone for a month with the tribe. Her 'nice, cool, comfortable house at Damascus' was a relief after the heat of the desert, even though the temperature was over 100 degrees Fahrenheit in Damascus.

Eugénie's replacement, Madame Buffet, had produced a baby but the child sickened in the heat and died, to the great distress of the entire household. Jane was soberly reflective in her diary entry that night: 'I have deprived myself of all such pains, and pleasures by my unnatural conduct in former days.'[12] She seldom referred in her diary to the children she had left behind with their respective fathers, probably because she felt uncomfortable at her abandonment of them. At the time it had seemed better for Didi, Heribert and Bertha to be left in a stable domestic environment rather than be dragged around with Jane to share her unconventional lifestyle and the disgrace that clung to her name in Europe. It had always been her intention to send for them at some convenient time, but the time when she could offer them a suitable home had never materialised. Only very occasionally did she pull out this particular private shame to admit regretfully that her behaviour had been 'unnatural'.

Medjuel went back to the desert and Jane rode with him as far as Doumah. On her return to the house she 'could not get cool again'. Next day she was ill with a recurrence of her fever, shivering and hot with a severe headache. With no Eugénie and no Medjuel to care for her, the illness brought home the vulnerability of her position. The only European doctor in Damascus, the aged Dr Nicorat, was summoned and put on leeches, but the intense migraines and severe fevers did not abate for two weeks.

> *July 29th 1858.* My convalescence slowly progressing, but I am very weak and still annoyed by a strange pain in the bones of my head. The days are past when I recovered as quickly as I was down, but I have great reason for thankfulness that I was spared the awful brain fever that threatened.

As soon as word reached him, Medjuel rushed back from the desert, the important negotiations forgotten in his anxiety for her. A note to Eugénie brought her rushing out to Syria also, though she was hardly in a fitter state than Jane and quite unable to deal with the uproar in the household when the indoor and outdoor servants quarrelled violently between themselves. Jane wrote that she longed to accompany Medjuel to the comparative peace of the desert, and when he left she made plans to join him as soon as she felt well enough. But things did not go as planned.

In November she received a long letter from Charles Venningen, the first since her visit to England. He too had been ill but was recovering. Bertha had become hopelessly insane. His main concern, though, was for Heribert and the lack of paperwork concerning his birth.

> [Heribert] often used to ask about you but [recently] he has not spoken your name. This leads me to suppose that he has . . . learned about what happened twenty years ago. I tried several times to speak to him about you but he listened without saying a word. This distresses me deeply as . . . I think . . . that as soon as I die his enemies [i.e. his cousins] will raise their heads on all sides and if by that time all the English documents are not in order he will very probably go under.

Charles hoped she would somehow find a way of seeing her 'only son' and forecast earnestly that she might some day be glad of his service. His letter reveals everything one needs to know about Charles: his kindness, his conservatism, his utter worthiness. It also makes it manifestly obvious why Jane could never have remained happily married to him.

> Lady Andover is very old, and when she is gone you can hardly return to England. With her gone your family will be dead to you. One day you will inevitably tire of your present way of life and will not be able to continue. Old age will come with all its accompaniments, from which no mortal escapes, and you will be glad to settle in a civilised country and

to find a soul who will take your side. Believe me, I know something about what it is like to always be alone, to have no one to whom one can turn to open one's heart, and yet I am a man who has been cruelly tried from a young age . . . I wish you a long life and perfect health. If this letter seems rather long . . . reflect that it may be my last, for my days are numbered.[13]

Jane did not react to this depressing letter in her diary except to note that she had written to Steely on Heribert's behalf. She was certainly not yet ready to roll over and die, nor prepare for old age. She knew that there would be fierce fighting between the tribes that winter and was anxious to be at Medjuel's side. She wrote home:

On the eve of my winter flitting I am this moment sitting surrounded by iron pots and pans, saddle bags, water skins and other gipsy-like preparations. My old black woman, Munni [Abdallah], is pounding a supply of various spices as her kitchen ingredients . . . We bend our steps first to Palmyra and then towards the Euphrates, Bagdad and Bassorah country where all is at sixes and sevens with a renegade Pasha who has been beaten by the Bedouins over and over again, and is now recalled.[14]

In this letter she sounded confident about her immediate plans, but her diary on the previous evening records a dilemma.

Saturday, November 6th 1858. The last fortnight has been occupied by preparations of various kinds for my expected, and long wished-for journey when Nehabi called and brought me a letter from Medjuel, but not such as I wish to receive. He positively forbids, and adjures me not to move from Scham until a second letter arrives . . .

I [am] convinced that he has *scherraked* [gone with the tribe into the desert for the winter] without me!!! I feel utterly low and cast down and know not what to do. Whether to obey – as is my duty – or risk all and go?

She hesitated for several days, while Damascus reverberated with news of the fighting on twin fronts when Sheikh Faris el Meziad of the Hessienne tribe and Sheikh Mohammed ebn Dukhi of the Wuld Ali tribe, one of the most powerful in the desert and said to number 5,000 tents and command a thousand lances, respectively began attacking other tribes. Then she decided that anything, even Medjuel's possible anger, was better than spending the winter in constant anxiety about him. If there was danger to be faced, she wanted to be at his side.

Leaving Munni Abdallah behind to await further orders, and taking

Moussa and Hamwoya as guards, she set off for Palmyra, deciding that if they came across any bedouin encampments they would beg shelter rather than risk being set upon as a small party.

The journey was not without incident. On the second night the trio came across the tents of the Hessienne. They were well received and offered food and shelter. The following night they came across a small and disreputable encampment at the foot of the mountains. Upon requesting somewhere to sleep she found to her astonishment that her hosts were the very group of M'wayaja who had captured her on her trip to Baghdad five years earlier.

It is not surprising that they did not recognise her, though the fact that she was veiled must have helped. Previously she had masqueraded as the Turkish-speaking wife of Sheikh el Barak, a man of no particular position. This time, as the wife of the renowned Sheikh Medjuel el Mezrab, she was a person of mark. She came riding into their camp dressed as an *asil* bedouin mounted on a fine camel, assertive and confident, a known European but speaking their own language, accompanied by – but very much in charge of – two of Medjuel's most trusted young *ayghals*.

The M'wayajas had heard much of this Ferengi Sitt. Her very presence in their tents conveyed distinction upon them. They killed a sheep in her honour.

17

Alone in Palmyra
1858–1859

Jane arrived at Tadmor on 1 December 1858 to find, as she suspected, that the tribe had gone off towards Baghdad some weeks earlier. This was useless information, for Jane knew only too well that the tribe did not move in any predetermined direction but went wherever their scouts discovered grazing for the animals. She decided to try to send a message to Medjuel that she wished to join him and to wait in Palmyra until he sent for her.

Meanwhile she had no desire to live in the town of Palmyra among the fellahin, and she had no tent with her, having travelled fast and light through the desert. Among the ruins of the old city some 'hovels' had been thrown up against the great wall of the Temple of Bel. Itinerant bedouins lived in these dwellings which, being a mile or so from the modern town, were reasonably vermin-free. Jane rented one from its owner and moved in.

To her annoyance, the 'hot-headed' Hamwoya, believing he had discharged his duty, set off to find the tribe before Jane had an opportunity to give him a letter to take to Medjuel. Possibly he had not wanted to risk Jane demanding to accompany him in a search of the desert that could take weeks. She knew that if he found the tribe Hamwoya would tell Medjuel that she was at Palmyra, but not necessarily in the way she might have wished to break the news. She decided she would have to find a reliable messenger of her own and sent Moussa back to Damascus with some travellers to look after their horses there. Munni Abdallah was to bring Jane's desert luggage to her with the next trade caravan. Meanwhile she

231

employed a young man called Sedran to care for her horse and act as factotum.

Jane found a messenger who she thought was reasonably trustworthy, offering him a substantial reward for bringing her written word from Medjuel. The letter she sent to Medjuel was the first she had ever written in Arabic, which she had been studying ever since her return from England. She practised the opening phrases in Arabic script in her pocket notebook, 'Salaam to you every day and night, my darling. It is now more than a month since I heard . . .'[1] Would he receive it safely, and if he did, she wondered, would he be able to read it?

Had she known how long her lone sojourn in the desert would last she might have gone back to Damascus with Moussa. But various bedouins who passed through Tadmor told her, with typical desire to give her good news, that Medjuel would probably return within three weeks, and so she settled down to wait.

She spent her days sketching and painting among the ruins, and tending to the illnesses of the townspeople who sought remedies for every ailment from ophthalmia to piles. Eye infections were most common, due to grit, sunburn scarring and flies. She sometimes thought that there was not a pair of sound eyes in the entire place, and some of her patients looked so diseased 'you could catch it just by looking at them!' Meanwhile she wrote long letters to her family and to Eugénie to let them know that she was safe despite widespread reports of warfare in the desert.

On 20 December 'a ghazou of 500 from Sheikh Feydan' attacked the town and the little houses scattered among the ruins. Jane was more angry than frightened, knowing that it was the responsibility of the Mezrabs to protect Palmyra; it was why the townspeople paid them annual tribute money. She sat with a pistol at the ready, waiting for the invaders to break in. To her surprise, though they 'forced themselves upon my neighbour', Jane was studiously left alone. Next day she learned the reason for the *ghazou*. It was apparently known throughout the desert that Medjuel had gone 'to Schedada' in preparation for the predicted war between the Mezrab tribe and its allies, against Mohammed ebn Dhuki, one of the most evil men in the desert. This meant he could not possibly return in under twenty-one days.

It was probably her most unusual Christmas, spent 'among the great and lovely ruins of a long past generation. The day was clear, frosty, and lovely . . . I went and sketched a new drawing of a new mass of ruins.' On New Year's Day she was predictably depressed, having already spent a month waiting in vain for word from Medjuel,

> far away from husband, family, friends, country. Alone. A stranger in a dark land ... My womanly vanity as well as my affection is deeply wounded by this prolonged absence and seeming neglect ... Sedran alone gives me some little consolation by his kind vows and promises to take another letter to Medjuel ... I went and coloured the amphitheatre, but even this talent seems to have deserted me for I can do nothing to my satisfaction.[2]

One evening she went to the sheikh's house 'to pass the time', and after a while a traveller came in from the desert. After he was refreshed he was asked for his 'news'. It was news Jane did not wish to hear. He said that Medjuel had returned to Mascha and married her. Heads nodded; before the Mezrab tribe left Palmyra Mascha had been here in the sheikh's house with Medjuel. Jane left quickly, deeply upset at the conversation.

> *Wednesday 5th [January].* Many men came in the morning with kind intentions to console me for last evening's conversation, and Sedran swore it was not, *could not* be true. Yet why did Mascha go to the Sheikh's house? ... and Medjuel was there with Mascha ... This month must pass before he comes.

All her peace of mind was gone, and it was typical of Jane that she insisted on pouring salt into the wound: 'Today I walked to the arch and thought mournfully on those days when Medjuel walked there with me, and watched me while I bathed, and again I glanced at the gate of the garden where we spent our honeymoon; so happy.'[3] From angry frustration more than anything else she joined in an activity she would later regret.

> *Tuesday February 17th.* I went with an old Hadji to the tombs to dig for Mummien among the dead of long gone by ages, and threw out their dried bones and tore open their scarlet and green winding sheets without compunction. Their costly tombs still remain, fresh and new as though built yesterday ... oh the *horror* I have of death and of being shut up in a dark narrow tomb!![4]

Matters improved somewhat when Munni Abdallah joined her with her desert luggage. Each day Jane rode her mare in the desert, but it was a dreary and anxious time for her. Letters from home brought no relief from her misery. On 20 February, she wrote, 'I learned of poor Isabella's awful death by poison, and the family's melancholy and touching letter. Oh my past life!'[5]

Isabella, the widow of George Anson, had died as the result of a frightful accident. She had been staying with Fanny Isted and had taken a large measure of laudanum in mistake for a tonic.[6] Normally laudanum was measured out in drops, and the amount Isabella took was lethal many times over. Realising almost immediately what she had done, she ran down to the drawing-room 'still *en déshabille* with her lovely hair in disarray' to tell the Isteds what she had done. They sent for the doctor, gave her an emetic and walked her up and down the drawing-room to try to keep her conscious, but unfortunately she died before the doctor arrived.[7] The only interpretation one can place on Jane's exclamation, 'Oh, my past life!', is remorse over her affair with George Anson, but it was irrelevant. George and Isabella had many years of happy marriage together after each had enjoyed youthful spells of wildness in varying degrees.

Though she wrote disconsolately from time to time of returning to Damascus without Medjuel, by March Jane seemed determined to wait for him no matter how long it took. After all, she was in a place that she loved. The winter was ended and the desert around the oasis was covered in spring flowers and foliage. But she longed for Medjuel, and there lurked always the fear that he no longer loved her. The rumours of his return to Mascha had now been discounted, but she worried that Medjuel might be attracted by a younger woman, a fear almost inevitable in a relationship when the woman is so much older and the man so eligible and in his physical prime.

> *Sunday March 5th.* What a Sunday. People came and told me that Medjuel was only two hours off, looking after a mare . . . this turned out to be only Medjuel's sheep, whilst I, who *gave* the sheep, am here in a furnace of grief and desolation . . . trying to fathom the reason for his non-appearance.
>
> *Monday 6th.* Unspeakable, untold happiness! I awoke in despair . . . breakfasted and then went with Sheikh Ali *much against my will* to the school picnic where I . . . sat under the trees watching the children. Sheikh Fares and others came [and sat with me] when . . . Mahmoud came and said an arab was coming with a letter from *Medjuel* . . . that he was coming in a few hours.

Jane wrote that she nearly fainted with relief. Having ascertained that the stories were true, she sent for her Seglawi mare, which was stabled in the sheikh's house in the town, and rode out to the Ras el

Ain. Here, a mile outside the ruined city, beside a cleft in the foothills, was a small cave from which a stream bubbled out. Medjuel had to pass this way on his road into Palmyra.

After a short wait she saw him riding fast ahead of a group of 'cavaliers' towards her. All her anxieties were forgotten in an instant. 'What a moment of joy was our meeting . . . and that night one of ardent happiness.' In the morning they walked to Ras el Ain and bathed together. Medjuel was full of love. He told her of the fighting, but of greater concern was the inability to find adequate grazing, as a consequence of which the tribe had lost many camels from starvation. He had not been able to leave the tribe and come to her, he explained, for it was his duty to stay with them and help. These simple and logical explanations soothed her jealous fears and doubts. He *had* seen Mascha but only in connection with their children. And he promised that he would never go off without her again, at least not without discussing it.

The days that followed almost equalled those of their honeymoon. Sometimes at his request she dressed in 'stupid fantasia', for he loved to see her in her most beautiful clothes and jewellery, and was proud to show her off. Nothing could spoil her mood of happiness and her pride in him, which even escalated when he left one afternoon to go after a *ghazou* 'and *alone* brought back 100 sheep and goats'.[8] Only the sudden death from a stroke of her old servant Munni Abdallah clouded her joy.

It was the end of May, six months after her departure from Damascus, before Medjuel judged the desert calm enough for him to leave and return with Jane to the city. The house, running smoothly under Eugénie's care, was cool and welcoming in the relentless heat of summer. Jane took a fever but shook it off after a week or so and then she wrote home, pleased at the news that she and Kenelm had been granted permission by the Queen to use the title 'Honourable', and that the College of Arms had produced a family tree:

> Heribert's tree has blossomed at last . . . From the Baron's great stress upon it it seemed to have been the branch upon which hung all his earthly prospects of rank and fortune. Poor boy I fear his regiment, the Archduke Charles, is in the very thick of this horrid war [the French–Austrian war of 1859].

Though it was the hottest summer for many years, life was pleasant in Damascus. Knowing that she would be in the desert during the coming winter, Jane settled to domestic tasks, such as making quince jelly and garlic paste, and enjoyed it, even when Medjuel went off on business.

Meanwhile, riding Soultan or Nourah, a white mare, she made calls upon local friends, often travelling considerable distances to outlying towns to visit dignitaries who could be helpful to Medjuel. By far the most interesting of her acquaintances, someone she would come to know far better at a later date, was His Highness the Emir Abd el Khader, an Algerian nobleman. Born in the same year as Jane, el Khader was a hero in his own country, having been elected emir by the combined tribes of Oran to lead the struggle against the French. This made him virtually the absolute sovereign of two-thirds of Algeria. He was known in England for his fifteen-year fight against the French and for several major victories, but in the end he surrendered and was imprisoned. Eventually, in 1852, Louis-Napoleon released him and exiled him to Broussa with an annual pension of £4,000 on condition that he never returned to Algeria and stayed out of politics. He arrived in Damascus in 1855 and lived there in great state with five wives and a personal army of 500 devoted Algerians.[9]

From Charles Venningen she heard that Heribert was safe and his regiment ordered to return to Hungary upon the declaration of peace. Bertha's condition was unchanged. Charles still urged her to consider her position in the future:

> old age is approaching, and with it infirmities, and one day or another your present way of life will weigh heavily upon you and will perhaps seem odious to you. Look at how devastating it is to lose your trusted housekeeper. What would it be like if you were ailing, or feeling the effects of age . . . meanwhile I hope you will enjoy perfect health for many years to come.[10]

Jane was more concerned by Eugénie's impending departure, but then they quarrelled again.

> *Monday August 15th 1859.* I had a terrible fall-out with Eugénie. She is in reality an invaluable servant, but her temper is so irritable, susceptible and suspicious that she torments herself and everyone around her.
>
> I privately have a painful remembrance of her concealing what she positively knew of the Count's errors, and then saying she had been the object of the General's pursuit, which can never be pleasing to me. Never! Having now made her fortune, she is neither servant nor mistress; an undefined position which she sometimes forgets! But what I shall do *without* her as to my *ménage* affairs I know not!!

In September some interesting travellers from England arrived in Damascus and the consul brought them to meet Jane. Travelling in separate parties they were Mr Carl Haag with his travelling companion Mr Roden Noel, and two young ladies in their early twenties, the Misses Beaufort. They were shown Jane's portfolio of drawings and paintings of Palmyra and were so overcome with the magnificence of the ruins that they were 'seized with an intense desire to see them. However the more we asked . . . the more impossible it seemed . . . the fatigue and expense combined made it out of the question,' Emily Beaufort wrote. Carl Haag was made of sterner stuff. 'If I am a ruined man all my life, or if I walk there in Bedouin sandals, I *must* go to Palmyra!' he said. So the following day they went to see Medjuel to plead with him. Medjuel agreed, for the tribe were encamped at Palmyra, and he had been torn between remaining with Jane and a desire to see his brothers and sons before they went off into the desert.

he engaged to let us stay five whole days . . . if all the party in the hotel joined together at the price of £15 a head, and good dromedaries [at] £2 each extra. It was a golden opportunity of seeing a real, true Bedouin tribe in the desert, and we were promised to live among them as the Sheikh's guests, and live upon camel's milk and flesh.[11]

The party set off on 7 November and after an uneventful journey arrived safely on the 11th. Jane's description is laconic, but the starry-eyed Emily Beaufort described each hour, each view, each discomfort and novelty vividly in her diary. It is her character portraits that are most interesting – for example, the following account of Medjuel:

our friend Sheikh Miguel (pronounced Midgewell) is, like all *true* Bedouins, a small man . . . slightly made, but erect, very graceful in all his movements and with a light easy step. His face is really beautiful – of a perfect oval – a long aquiline nose, delicately formed mouth, small regular teeth of dazzling whiteness, and large black eyes that could be soft and sweet as any woman's, or flash with a fierce, wild, eagle glance that really made one start. He wore a short black beard, and long crisp ringlets under his *kefiyeh* which was of the finest and brightest Damascus silk . . .

As to his manners the 'best bred' polished Englishman is not more polished than he . . . From the time we left Damascus and became his 'charge' until we re-entered the city his kindness and thoughtfulness never ceased – morning, noon and night, travelling or stationary, whatever we might be doing, alone or surrounded by Arabs, he had an eye and an ear always ready for any want of ours.[12]

Jane's diary reveals the disappointment that greeted them in Palmyra: 'Alas, Mohammed and Manah went three days before. Poor Medjuel was disappointed not to see them and so was I ... We encamped in a garden with a pleasant running stream for a bath.' Since Jane had made the trip upwards of a dozen times and spent many months at Palmyra, her diary contained no long descriptions. Miss Beaufort fleshes out the skeleton considerably as the party came, at long last, in sight of Tadmor:

> Suddenly there dashed up ... towards us some seven or eight men, armed to the teeth, brandishing their long lances, shrieking and yelling and shouting to welcome our good Sheikh Miguel ... we dismounted to rest ... in the shade ... while the Sheikh heard all the news ... It was very bad news indeed for him and a grievous disappointment for us all: the famine was so great in the land in consequence of the drought, that the [tribe] knowing nothing of their beloved Sheikh's approach had broken up their encampment and departed only three days before ...
>
> So there was goodbye to all our promised plans, and our hopes of living among the Bedouins ... feasting on camel's meat and milk, seeing all sorts of Bedouin mares and sports; and our Sheikh's new tent, too, which he had promised for our special use had been carried off to be 'seasoned' ...
>
> So we went on ... till ... we reached a small terrace, secluded and quiet, from whence a very low, ancient stone door, still turning on its original stone hinges admitted us into a delicious garden of olives, plums and pomegranates ... Here we had the graceful branches of a palm tree waving above us and we slept well, night after night, in the warm, soft, delicious air.

Around the fire at night the two sisters listened, as entranced as the Arabs, to the storyteller's tales:

> Some hostile Arabs came down one night last winter and stole all the cattle of the Tudmor townspeople. Sheikh Miguel was staying there at the time, *en passant* ... but of course the affair was no concern of his, nor do the Bedouin like interfering in each other's quarrels. So he sat in his tent smoking, not thinking to be mixed up in it, when Sheikh Fares and some of the townspeople came and petitioned his help.
>
> He could not resist the appeal for he is a most generous and kind-hearted man, and in a few moments he rose and mounted his mare. Then turning round quietly to the Sheikh of Tudmor [Fares] ... a great blusterer and little doer ... he said 'You can stay in the valley; I will go up the mountain and bring back the cattle.' He galloped off and before long caught sight of the cattle collected together and guarded by seven

or eight men. Though alone he rode straight up to them and demanded in a loud voice, 'How dare you take these cattle when I am here!' and fired off his revolver among them. In a moment the whole set of men ran off, and the Sheikh quietly drove back all the cattle himself.[13]

Emily Beaufort's minutely detailed observations not only corroborate Jane's diaries but enhance her often spare narrative. During their time in Tadmor, Carl Haag, a brilliant watercolour artist, painted several views of the ruins which are arguably the finest archaeological representations in existence. He also painted two full-length portraits: one of Jane wearing one of her bedouin 'fantasia' outfits, the other of Medjuel. This was the only image of Jane after she moved to Syria and, with the exception of a watercolour sketch by Emily Beaufort which obscures his features and a few working sketches by Jane, the only known portrait of Medjuel. Jane never actually saw them, but she obtained a photograph of Haag's portrait of Medjuel and this was displayed at the house in Damascus for many years until she reluctantly gave it to a royal visitor as a parting gift.

Haag was a Bavarian, born in 1820 at Erlangen (where Charles Venningen had a home). He had studied in Munich and indeed had spent the previous winter there, so he and Jane undoubtedly had much to talk about on their desert trek. He moved to England in 1848 to study at the Royal Academy and was already a naturalised subject before Queen Victoria commissioned him for a series of portraits of herself, the Prince Consort and their children. The Queen also commissioned several landscapes of the highlands of Scotland by Haag, and with his reputation well established he decided to travel to the Levant to find exotic subjects.

The result of his two trips to Egypt and Palestine were to bring him to the pinnacle of his fame, especially his paintings of Palmyra and the desert encampments during the journey there and back. He added colour to his exhibition by describing his acquaintance with the beautiful former Lady Ellenborough and her princely sheikh.[14]

Jane enjoyed the company of the two intelligent Beaufort sisters. Their mother had died when they were children, and they had been raised by their father, an admiral, a point not lost on Jane. When he died suddenly in 1859 the two girls mourned him deeply and decided, as a distraction, to tour the Holy Land. A year later Jane would receive a copy of Emily's two-volume book about the trip, *Egyptian Sepulchres and Syrian Shrines*. She especially appreciated the author's 'delicacy of feeling', for, though Medjuel and the other travellers on the Palmyra journey were all included, Jane was never mentioned by name. The Misses Beaufort left Damascus to be in Jerusalem by Christmas.

As the year drew to an end Jane found her household constantly split by disagreements, including quarrels with Eugénie, who was still acting as housekeeper despite almost daily threats of leaving. Jane wrote to Kenelm regarding 'the impending loss of Eugénie after 18 years service . . . I have some thoughts of taking the English Consul's wife's maid, a Mrs Tappenden, whom I call turpentine for she looks rather peppery.'[15] The dreary winter was enlivened when Colonel Charles Churchill and his wife came to live in Damascus for a while. The colonel had lived in Syria on and off since 1842, initially as a staff officer with the British expedition to Syria. An acknowledged expert on the uneasy struggle between the Druses and Maronite Christians and their Ottoman rulers, he had produced two books on the subject. He called on Jane in December 1859 to persuade her to introduce him to her friend, the Emir Abd el Khader, and Jane readily obliged. While the two men talked, she and Mrs Churchill called upon the emir's harem.

The lives led by these women was ever a subject of morbid fascination to Jane. She was alternately sad for their ignorance and shocked at the uselessness of 'their pretty, painted' lives. The senior wife, el Khader's first and eldest spouse, was the wife of his youth, a native of Algeria. Massively fat and physically ugly, she impressed with her stately dignity as she presided calmly over the harem. El Khader valued her opinion highly and never made a move without consulting her. It was said el Khader took a new wife each year, mostly Circassian girls no older than fifteen to sixteen. However, Jane talked of the emir's five wives, so unless he divorced a few the rumour seems exaggerated.

Abd el Khader is a man of middle height and of muscular frame. A broad brow with marked straight eyebrows, large dark brown eyes, bright and piercing but full of softness and intelligence, . . . and a lively warm brown . . . complexion, combine to make a handsome face. He has a Grecian nose, a delicately carved but firm mouth, a broad chin . . . his hands and his whole personal appearance show blood, and his dignified bearing and cool self-possession are characteristic of his life.

He dresses purely in white and is enveloped in the usual snowy [Algerian] burnous . . . if you see him on horseback without knowing him to be Abd el Khader you would single him out from a million and ask who that distinguished looking chief might be. He has the seat of a gentle-man and a soldier. His mind is as beautiful as his face; he is every inch a Sultan.[16]

Within the year Jane's name would be linked for ever with the Emir Abd el Khader, in a way that neither could have anticipated.

18

The Massacre
1860–1861

The year 1860 began ordinarily enough. Jane obtained from the consul, not without a great deal of effort, a certificate recording her marriage, which she sent at once to Steely to be lodged with a copy of her will. This gave her peace of mind, for she had sometimes wondered if the marriage was legal.

Eugénie had relapsed into poor health, and developed a form of paranoia that everyone hated her, provoking almost continuous disharmony in the household. Finally, a week of bickering culminated in a scene. Eugénie had stormed into Jane's boudoir after listening at the door while one of the other servants was being interviewed by Jane. She had been drinking heavily, 'and she was so abusive and violent in her language that I was obliged to positively turn her out of the room and decline her further services. And so ends the maid who has been with me through thick and thin for 18 years!!!' Jane wrote:

> *Monday 20th.* Mrs Tappenden came as Femme de Chambre and now all is over between Eugénie and me. She is no longer belonging to me. She had a dreadful attack, the longest and the worst.
> *Friday March 9th.* Today we set off for Beyrout with Eugénie, I and the Sheikh and D'jebran.

When Eugénie sailed from Beirut for Athens, it marked the end of an eighteen-year partnership, but Jane 'could not regret her as she is now, her temper is grown so bad ... may she be happy in her new life.' It was Medjuel's first visit to Beirut; he was fascinated with the seventy-mile stretch of tarmacadam road leading to the city, and even more so with the sea, which he had never seen. Before they left, Jane sold Soultan; he had never suited her. She received a good price but she was sad to part with him, for Medjuel had given him to her during their honeymoon.

In May, Jane travelled as an emissary of the tribe to the desert fortress of Sheikh Feisal at Mezarib in the Hauran, sixty miles south of Damascus, where there was a huge assembly of bedouin sheikhs. These assemblies were held periodically for the purpose of agreeing arrangements such as the amount of tribute money payable between the sheikhs and the village chiefs, who 'troop in from all directions'.[1]

Medjuel rode with her and her entourage to the outskirts of Damascus. It was Mrs Tappenden's first desert trip, a test of her suitability, for Jane always appreciated the touches of civilisation that a good maid brought to the wildest environment. Originally Jane was to have accompanied Medjuel, but his eyes were 'very bad with ophthalmia' and he was suffering from bad headaches, so she went to represent him. Jane had made friends with Feisal some time earlier and was received as an honoured guest, although it seems unlikely that she would have been allowed to join the sheikhs in council on the twin counts of being a woman and a Christian. Jane's diary is irritatingly silent on the content of the mission and instead deplores the intense heat and her annoyance at being bothered by 'the multitudes'. Medjuel's Ferengi wife was a desert legend and everyone, it seemed, wanted to see her, touch her and speak to her.

A pencil sketch, hardly more than working notes for a composition, shows a huge encampment of thousands of black tents on a plain beside a lake. Above the encampment on a hill towers the bastioned fortress constructed of black basalt by the Ottoman conqueror of Suria, Sultan Salim, in 1518. Jane had long wished to see the massive doors, said by the Arabs to have been made by giants, carved from a single piece of dressed stone with a pintle at top and bottom that fitted into carved sockets in floor and lintel. Though they weighed several tons, the doors were so beautifully made and balanced that they could be swung to and fro with ease.[2]

At the gathering of sheikhs were two of the most formidable men in the desert, Sheikh Faris el Meziad of the Hessienne and Sheikh Mohammed ebn Dukhi of the Wuld Ali. Bloodthirsty and avaricious, they had turned the entire desert into a field of war several years earlier. Ebn Dukhi received an annual sum of 200,000 piastres from the Turkish government, nominally to supply 650 camels and men to carry the barley for the hadj, but in reality to allow the hadj to pass through the Hauran in peace. Citizens of Damascus called this 'Sultan's blackmail'.[3]

Jane had met ebn Dukhi and Meziad previously. They did not improve with greater familiarity and were 'odious in every way', she wrote in her journal, 'perfectly ignorant brutes'. But there were other sheikhs whom Medjuel knew and trusted and in this mixed company Jane spent six days. When the conference ended the tents were packed and the massed tribes departed.

Sheikh Feisal, whom she considered her 'ideal of a Bedouin Sheikh', impressed Jane greatly, 'so noble, reserved and dignified in his demeanour, so truly the *grand seigneur* in his manner and address. I wish dear Medjuel had a little more of his hauteur – at least in manner, and a little more height to command respect.'[4] This is the only time that Jane voiced even a breath of criticism of Medjuel, and the entry was written in code. On 19 May, she recorded, 'At last we set off today on our return, I happy in the thought of seeing dear Medjuel. We left Sheikh Feisal and ebn Dukhi on the point of coming to blows.'

On her arrival in Damascus, Jane found to her disappointment that Medjuel had taken some French princes to Tadmor and would be away for ten days. The next day Schebibb, who was staying at the Damascus house, came to tell Jane that his mother, Mascha, had died. 'Her death', Jane wrote with mixed feelings of guilt and relief, 'does not mitigate my sin in having been the prime cause of Medjuel putting away the wife of his youth. Plain accusing words.' But almost at once news came that took her mind off personal considerations.

Monday June 5th. . . . poor Sheikh Feisal has been killed, and his son! The Druses and [the] Christians are fighting dreadfully and the whole country is said to be in a state of excitement . . . the fights [threaten] to break out in Damascus.

The Druse, an ancient Muslim sect, normally lived in the mountainous area of the Hauran. Recently they had spread into traditional bedouin territory. The road along the hadj route had become notoriously dangerous for travellers and there were frequent reports of murder and robbery. But the latest fighting was more than a simple eruption between the bedouin and Druse people over territorial rights. A deep-seated resentment of the spread of Christianity in the Islamic countries had led to isolated incidents where a Christian had been beaten or killed, and shortly afterwards a Druse was killed in retaliation. In the spring of 1859 the balance had tipped between limited, though bitter, attrition and open conflict.

Fighting and killing erupted like a flash fire throughout the country. The Christians were outnumbered three to one, and it became genocide. The harvest had failed and the spectre of a possible famine added fuel to the fire. Initially the Turkish government turned a blind eye to the fighting, having a great deal to gain by adopting a *laissez-faire* attitude. This policy allowed the sparks of intolerance, fear and hatred to fan into conflagration.

The fighting raced towards Damascus; reports ran ahead of the deaths of hundreds of Christians, whole families and villages wiped out. Jane was greatly relieved when Medjuel came racing back early from the desert after hearing of the troubles. He sent his royal clients to the safety of Aleppo and they gave him a gold pocket-watch as a parting gift, which he presented to Jane.

Medjuel at once began to make siege preparations in Damascus, where there was a large community of Christians. Jane was not overtly religious; however, since the Christian missionaries in the city formed the major part of the small European community, they were all known to Jane. For this reason, as well as a promise to Kenelm during her visit to England, she had taken to occasionally attending church. Medjuel had never interfered with Jane's observance of Christianity, just as she had never interfered with his faithful adherence to Islam. But he was painfully aware that Jane was a potential target.

He considered the house safer than the open road for the time being, but he instructed Jane to pack and be prepared to flee to the desert at a moment's notice.[5] Despite the danger, Jane felt she owed a show of allegiance to the alarmed English and French missionaries. Medjuel and his men loyally escorted her to the convent to see if there was anything that might be done to make the inhabitants safer. A large party, including Jane's friends, Dr Robson and his wife, left the city for Beirut, which Medjuel thought foolish, for they were vulnerable on the roads. One of the party, the missionary Mr Graham, had been ready to leave, but changed his mind at the last moment and stayed to help those left in the city, especially the nuns of the Little Sisters of Charity.

It was on Monday 9 July 1860 that the massacre began. Christians had been reviled, menaced and insulted in the bazaars for some days previously, and went in fear as reports came in of the slaughter of entire Christian communities elsewhere. An appeal to the governor, Achmed Pasha, to assume control of the situation was a wasted effort. He claimed he was unaware of any crisis, and that he had insufficient resources to declare martial law in the city. A similar reaction occurred when the Christian citizens of other cities – Homs, Beirut and Hamah – complained to their governors. Yet it was known that the Turkish government were supplying the Druses with weapons and ammunition; indeed, the cannons of the fort in Damascus were pointed at the Christian quarter.[6]

The merest spark was needed to set off the tinderbox. On the morning of 9 July the cry (probably incorrect) went up that a Muslim had been killed by a Christian near the mosque and that the victim's blood had been used to etch a cross on the wall nearby. Jane's friend, Colonel Charles Churchill, described how

> the awful cry was caught up from mouth to mouth, a terrific commotion spread about like lightning from street to street. All business was abandoned, the shops were closed; and in less than a quarter of an hour an infuriated mob brandishing weapons, guns, swords, axes and every description of weapon was in full career to the Christian quarter.
>
> From all directions was seen and was heard the rush of men armed to the teeth; and from unarmed women and boys, shouts, imprecations on the infidels, the *giaours*, and cries of 'Kill them! Butcher them! Plunder! Burn! Leave not one alive, not a house, anything!!!'[7]

A cannon was discharged from the fortress by the Turkish guard; it was loaded only with powder, but flaming wadding landed on the matting stretched over the bazaar to provide shade. The tinder-dry matting caught fire and, aided by arsonists, the flames rapidly spread to consume a large area. Gangs of men ran into Christian houses, plundering everything they could carry away before setting fire to what remained. People from the suburbs poured into the city before the gates were shut, to help in the destruction.

On the previous day, Abd el Khader had sent his son to Jane, inviting her to come to his palace and remain there while the trouble lasted, for no Muslim would dare to invade his home. Jane sent her thanks to her friend, saying she believed she incurred no risk by remaining in her husband's house, he being a Muslim, but that in any case she had Christian servants in the house and whatever danger they had to endure she would share with them.[8] However, at

Medjuel's insistence, she had not left their property for several days. After feeding her animals as usual, she had gone into the house while the sheikh went into the city to see what he could discover.

I was sitting quietly, drawing, when D'jebran rushed in and announced that the Turks were risen. Shortly after the Sheikh returned and confirmed the fearful news. The insurrection was begun, the Druses and Kurds began to slaughter every Christian man they met.[9]

Our house is outside the city walls, in the Moslem quarter, so we had the satisfaction and comfort of seeing the city gate shut against us, had we wanted to enter. But knowing a great variety of people, 'every sort of bird' (as the Arabs say), Druzes, Kurds and villagers in passing to their work of destruction stopped here and offered their services to help in guarding our house.

The Sheikh thought it wise to accept none and arming himself, and a few very determined spirits of our tribe, took his long *chibougue* [pipe], shut our gates behind him and sat with them outside, awaiting events.

I was all the time . . . on the roof from whence I could see all around and command the road filled with goers and comers, all armed for *action*; reap hooks, axes, clubs studded with nails, daggers, etc. . . . Many Christians were attacked and killed in their shops before they knew what the uproar was about, and in less than an hour . . . all was a scene of murder, and plunder which we saw being carried to and fro; the Kurdish women inciting and helping the men. It was *awful* to behold.[10]

Supplies of water were cut off and by sunset the entire Christian quarter was ablaze, in a sea of fire. In the midst of the smoke Jane was appalled to see crowds of women, some carrying infants, shrieking and rushing along flat roofs, jumping from house to house. Some fell and perished in the fire. Others were captured and sexually violated in the streets before jeering crowds. Some, especially young girls, were carried off; some were made pregnant and set free; some never returned; others were sold into the harems of Turks. Nor did the men escape. Young boys and old men were forced to apostatise and were derisorily circumcised before being put to death. At one point Jane took out her sketchbook and in a few pencil strokes drew in the outline of the city with its pall of smoke. Working notes read: 'very red', 'dark', 'flames', 'smoke'.

As the violence mounted, despite his promise to the French to retire into private life, Abd el Khader felt unable to stand by and watch murder and rapine. He had his own army of 500 devoted Algerian followers, well salted in conflict, and he sent these tough men into the Christian quarter in his name, to rescue as many of the Christians as they could. Some families refused to come out of their houses, fearing a trick, but many hundreds were safely collected and escorted to safety. A mob subsequently converged on the gates of el Khader's palace demanding that the Christians be handed over. After several hours the emir decided that ignoring them was not enough. He had the gates opened and rode out alone to confront the howling crowd. It was a measure of the respect in which he was held that they did not attack him, especially when he shouted to them, 'Not a Christian will I give you. Stand back or I will give the order to fire.'

Around the walls of his palace stood Algerians with rifles. They were outnumbered, but their reputation did much to even the score against a crowd armed with crude clubs and pickaxes. The mob dispersed, but the building was under siege for several days by growling knots of Muslims. The emir made a point of sleeping on a mattress by the gate of his palace in case any Christians should come knocking at the door at night and be turned away by his Algerians, who were Muslims and therefore might turn a deaf ear. A similar mob converged on the British consulate where numbers of Christians had been given shelter; the consul and his party escaped and made their way, disguised in Arab clothing, to the emir's palace.

The bedouins headed by Medjuel and stationed around the outside their house were armed 'to the teeth', but Medjuel wisely instructed them to adopt the casual attitude of watchkeepers rather than aggressive protectors. The noise of the burning city and the screams of victims went on through the night. Next day, Jane saw that there was no abatement of the horror: 'Still worse! Murder, fire and plunder were the order of the day. Poor Mr Graham was killed [on his way from the church to the English consulate], and the convent and other churches were burnt down.'[11] The school went too, and one of our schoolmasters saved his life only by becoming a Moslem.'[12]

The nuns of the Sisters of Charity were rescued and taken to safety by el Khader's men, but their convent was burned to the ground and several monks in a nearby monastery were butchered. By the third day Jane thought that the murders had almost ceased, though the rape, arson and looting continued. Like el Khader, Jane and Medjuel gave sanctuary to Christians who ran to their gates. Medjuel warned that there was a real danger of the mob rising during the night and returning to storm the emir's palace, and any other houses sheltering Christians.[13] Still, for Jane's sake he would not turn anyone away.

After several days the city became calmer and a deathly quiet fell over the carnage. Thanks to Medjuel and his grim, armed bedouin sentries, Jane was at last able to write that she and all her household

> have been wonderfully and mercifully preserved during the days that the storm raged around us, and murder, fire and plunder were the order of the day! . . . [But] in all the many wanderings of my adventurous and *adventureful* life I never was in such a *mess* as this and the distress of those around is heart rending.[14]

When the fighting ceased, she dressed in enveloping robes and veil and walked alone through the Christian quarter to the consulate, where families were still hiding in fear of their lives. From there she went to Abd el Khader's palace, where she found the British and French consuls, and Monsieur Le Roy, who had been her Arabic interpreter and sometime teacher. The courtyard was packed with people and in a garden beside the walls, guarded by his men, thousands more were fed on rations of 'bread and cucumber'. El Khader received her with calm nobility, and she saw why the emir valued so highly his placid aged wife, for she greeted Jane as though she were calling for a tea party.

The following day Jane went out to another part of the Christian quarter, having heard that there were people in need of help. In her bedouin clothes she would not be taken for a Christian. The sight of mutilated bodies and the stench of putrefaction and smouldering rubble were stomach-turning, 'sixteen corpses in one spot, still unburied [after a week], half devoured by the dogs, filling the air with all the elements of plague and cholera. Awful to behold.'[15] She called on a number of Christian friends to ascertain their well-being. Jane could have remained within the safety of her home; Medjuel would probably have preferred that she did. But each day she went out, dispensing flat unleavened bread to those too afraid to leave their homes, or simple medicines to those in greatest need. She made no mention of this in her diary, nor did she write home about it, but eventually word of it reached Charles Venningen via the German consul and he wrote to tell her that he had 'learned about your brave acts during the massacre . . . by chance. Knowing you as I know you I was not at all surprised.'[16]

It was not until the end of July that the city returned to a reasonably stable state, but the plight of many thousands of homeless Christians living on the roadsides and existing on public charity was pitiable.

Up to 14,000 deaths occurred in Syria during the massacre, some 2,000 – many of them men who had been breadwinners and heads of families – in Damascus alone. The hardships of the families left without support was almost as appalling to Jane as the massacre itself.

The incident was too serious to be contained nationally, and when strong international representations were made Constantinople had no alternative but to move strongly against the perpetrators of the atrocities. The governor, Achmed Pasha, was deposed and jailed pending trial. The city returned to normal except for the trials of those accused of murder, and formal executions by the hundred went on for weeks. El Khader was decorated by the French for his part in saving many hundreds of lives. Monsieur Le Roy left Damascus for Beirut but died of a heart attack shortly after reaching the coast, said to have been brought on by grief at what he had seen during the massacre. Mrs Tappenden had been 'useless' during the entire episode, and Jane decided that 'with all her faults' Eugénie was worth ten of her replacement, who was 'too concerned' with the safety of her person. Unintentionally, this reveals a great deal about Eugénie, who had accompanied Jane through many adventures over a number of years.

Tuesday August 20th. Today Mustafa Talou, my former porter and 205 others were hung and shot. I rode on Nourah in the evening with the Sheikh, and Sheikh Fares, to the empty burying ground to see the havoc made there [Christian bodies had been exhumed and defiled]. That quiet little nook, destined in all probability to be also *my* last resting place if I am to die in this far off land. We then returned all round the formerly joyous road and gay gardens, now quite silent and deserted, the mourning and sorrowing city like a heap of desolation.

Yet there were bright spots in the bleakness. To her astonishment and delight, Sheikh Feisal, whom she had declared to be her 'ideal of a Bedouin Sheikh' and whom she believed dead, suddenly appeared at their house. He brought 'many of his Arabs with him', and the house was full of people for a few days; when he left, Medjuel went with him for the first part of his journey.

Within hours of their departure a message came from Medjuel's brother Manah to say that the Shemmar had made a large *ghazou* and taken all the Mesrabi tents in retaliation for his attack on them with a small number of *khayals* (warriors). Jane sent for Medjuel, who came racing back, furious at the losses and Manah's foolishness at bating a much larger and more powerful force. Fortunately his own tent was still at Tadmor but the raid was a significant loss for the tribe and caused great hardship, which Medjuel would have to mitigate.

Meanwhile Achmed Pasha, the former governor, was executed along with twenty-four other high-ranking government officials. Jane helped to set up a committee at the British consulate with the wife of the consul and Lord Dufferin, to see what might be done to rescue the girls captured and carried off by the Kurds, and to discuss the problems that would undoubtedly occur when the raped women and girls gave birth.

The city that had once captivated her now seemed a dreadful place, shamed and despoiled. However, confident that Jane was in no further danger, Medjuel left for Homs to recover the valuable tents taken in the Shemmar raid, expecting to be gone at least a month. Jane accompanied him to Doumah, where they had an affectionate parting. They had agreed that while he was in Homs Medjuel should look at property there, for both were 'sickened' by Damascus.

When Medjuel wrote to say that he had seen a smallholding at Homs that he thought he might buy with his own money, Jane wrote that she was in favour of the purchase: 'it is not a bad way I think of investing his money; houses and ground are more stable than camels . . . !'

While Medjuel was away she decided to show her support for the Christians who had so bravely defended their faith. Christian worship in Damascus was always conducted in Arabic and although Jane now spoke fluently, and read and wrote Arabic reasonably well, she could not follow the services because, as she later told Kenelm, 'the scriptural language is so different to the language in common use that I do not understand it.'[17] From this date onwards Jane became a regular churchgoer. She felt she owed some recognition to the faith of those who died for their belief, and this was coupled with deep anger towards the Muslim perpetrators of the acts of brutality she had witnessed, particularly against Christian women.

Her first venture into church after the massacre was to the small room which some new missionaries had taken after their church had been destroyed. Dr Robson, whom she had known for some years, had gone to Beirut and the service was being taken by a Dr Meschaka, whom she had not met. Robed and veiled as a bedouin she slipped unobtrusively into the room and took her place at the back, sitting on her heels. With her startling blue eyes, upright carriage and presence she was not a figure to pass unnoticed and the minister and his team were curious about the stranger, for a bedouin woman seemed a most unlikely convert. After the service they waited to speak to her and welcome her to the mission.

> They were astounded when she replied in English, flabbergasted to learn that she was the Honourable Mrs Digby [and that] she was interested in their work, and in the progress they were making towards repairing the damage of [the massacre]. She implied that she was always at home to them, and from this meeting which resulted in her entertaining them hospitably, new acquaintances were made from whose number [in her later years] she drew some of her closest friends.[18]

Jane's friend, Dr Robson, returned to the city, and after a great deal of deliberation Jane took Communion from him 'for the first time in 36 years'. Since her marriage to Lord Ellenborough she had regarded attendance at church as a social rather than spiritual obligation. Even now she was doubtful about her real feelings but felt she ought to support Robson, that 'dear, good man, [so] willing to "spend and be spent" in doing service to others while I, blessed with health and strength and an abundance of earthly comforts, what do I do?'[19]

In November, Jane and Medjuel set off for Homs, prior to joining the tribe for the winter trek. Jane was to look at the house and land that Medjuel wished to purchase. Mrs Tappenden, having failed the test of travelling maid, was left in charge of the house at Damascus. Jane took Fidayah, a young girl from the house, instead.

> *Saturday 1st December 1860.* Up very early and rode to Nöbk, stopping at Geustall for some of its famous dibs. We arrived early at Nöbk and I was pleased and thankful to find that Fidayah turns out to be an excellent desert servant. I much enjoyed my luncheon today with dear Medjuel. We rode on alone, and climbed the horses to the brow of a hill before turning them loose to graze. We sat down, *en vrais bédouins*, to breathe the fresh mountain air! Such scenes as this engrave themselves on my memory for always . . .
>
> *Sunday 2nd.* I was sorry to be obliged to go on to Gharrah when we stopped and I dined with the Aga's wife and a very pretty Circassian, Emmie. What a very melancholy sight to me are these harems, and the [poor wives] black or white. What a total waste is their mind. Every thought concerned on dress or the means of pleasing – not a husband, or even a lover – but a cold, selfish master at most![20]

Homs seemed pleasant and relaxed after Damascus and Jane was eager for them to buy a house there. 'The cheapness of the old stone houses on the ramparts' was tempting, and she accepted Medjuel's wish to live 'in the place he now prefers to desolate Damascus'.[21] They stayed in a rented house while they waited for their large tent to arrive from the desert. After a few weeks Medjuel decided that the tribe would probably not return from the desert until June, and that he should go and fetch the tent himself to ensure its safety. Jane decided to slip back to Damascus while he was away, to ensure that all was well there. The thought of her lovely home, left for six months in the worst weather under the direction of Mrs Tappenden, made her uneasy.

Medjuel accompanied her halfway to Hessia and she went on with Fidayah and a single guard, planning to ride fast and sleep at the houses of village notables. On the first night, she was stung to fury when the wife of the emir (sister to the objectionable Faris el Meziad) asked her offhandedly what sum she had given Medjuel to bribe him not to take other wives.[22]

Apparently without her noticing it Christmas slipped by while she was on the road, for she never mentioned it in her diary; but she was happy to find the house at Damascus 'in order and very comfortable, and the servants *agreeing*' when she arrived there on 27 December. Even in her absence she had arranged the annual Christmas party for her household, with a turkey from her small flock and small presents for everyone, and 'with snap dragons [flambéed raisins] and so on. The little black children were delighted.'[23]

One domestic problem after another conspired to prevent Jane rejoining Medjuel. She fretted when she did not hear from him but there seemed so much to do. A heavy fall of snow had broken many plants and she wished to oversee the work. In the evenings she took up her Arabic studies again, under instruction from a young Arab who had renounced his Christian belief during the massacre. She also finished some paintings and received a parcel of useful and warm dresses from her mother. Almost before she knew it, it was spring. On 21 March 1861 she wrote to Kenelm:

> There is not much news here beyond what you learn from the papers. Syria is in an awful state of misrule, and if stronger, *prudent* measures are not soon taken to put things on a better footing, the pent up volcano may soon break out again. Fuad Pacha, from weakness, or Turkish policy, had not touched the Kurds, who were by far the worst at Damascus, whatever the Druses may have been in the mountains. These Kurds carried off the women, burned, killed and plundered, and now they are untouched and

enrolled by the government into an irregular corps. They are ruining the villages wherever they go and it is hardly safe, even, to ride out . . .

[I have written to Miss Jane for] a list of common, easy growing, showy flowers and bulbs for my garden. I have no gardener but myself and books, nothing but a native man, who – when I attempt a rockery, or rootery, and have toiled all day scratching my hands to pieces – goes and throws it all down calling it rubbish! . . . We intend shortly, returning to the desert for a couple of months although the weather now is getting very warm.[24]

There is no mention in this letter of the fears she was beginning to hint at in her diary that started with a chance remark of Mrs Tappenden's when Jane wondered aloud why she had not heard from her husband in some weeks. The servant had merely been repeating gossip among the European community that Medjuel had been 'cheating her in love'. Jane was 'sad and low' as she wrote her diary, feeling the 'cold thrill of jealousy . . . at the thought that he might be unfaithful, as well as anxiety that he might be ill or hurt and therefore not able to communicate'.

Medjuel was, in fact, busy trying to extract compensation from Sheikh Beteyen ebn Merschid of the Hessienne tribe. Some months earlier he had purchased from the sheikh a large flock of sheep on the understanding that Merschid would over-winter them with his own flocks in the desert. When Medjuel attempted to collect his flock he was told that they had perished during the severe winter. He wrote to Jane to explain this but it took a month for his letter to reach Damascus. Meanwhile, a visitor called on Jane, an aide of Sheikh Fares of Tadmor. Jane was obliged to offer him hospitality though she did not enjoy the company of men of his ilk. She was an easy target for mischief and was predictably upset when he told her that it was common knowledge in the desert that Medjuel no longer loved her and was indifferent to her. However, said her informant, she need not worry, for Sheikh Fares had long wished to marry her.

Most of the sheikhs in the desert would have married Jane like a shot, even had she not been a still lovely woman with a reputation in her own right. Her wealth alone, which had brought prestige to the Mezrabs in terms of herds of animals, slaves, weapons and ammunition, was sufficient to attract the attention of men who believed that any woman would be flattered by their attentions. But this woman, who owned and rode the fleetest horse and who could doctor and deliver a mare, who could spend days travelling and living as did the men of the tribe – she was something to be prized. Jane was appalled; the very thought of the dirty ruffian fellah sheikh made her cringe.[25]

She decided to return at once to Homs and if necessary travel into the desert to find Medjuel and put an end to her anxiety. Two Arabs told her they had heard that Medjuel had married another wife, but next day others told her that her informants were Hessienne, and their gossip petty spite. It is surprising that over the years Jane did not realise how often the 'news' she was given by fellow travellers and callers was incorrect.

At Homs she had word that Medjuel was safe and well, and within a day he had ridden into town. Her delight in their loving reunion was tempered by tidings that he was obliged to spend the summer months with the tribe and attempt to recover the sheep from the Hessienne. Jane could accompany him or return to Damascus to wait for him. She chose to go with her husband.

It was that summer that the tribe accepted her as one of themselves, and bestowed upon her the name 'Umm el Laban' – literally 'Mother of milk', which has hitherto been accepted as a reference to her milky complexion; however, a contemporary who wrote to Edward Digby after his sister's death explained that it actually meant 'our gracious lady'.[26]

The Mezrab tribe in the Midian Desert. Watercoloured pencil sketch from Jane's notebook.

19

Visitors from England
1862–1863

At first Jane's acceptance by the tribe as first lady stemmed out of respect for Medjuel, and Jane's wealth. Her generosity became the talk of the desert,[1] enhancing Medjuel's reputation as an active and fair-minded heir to the leadership of the tribe.

In an environment where guns were still the exception rather than the rule, the Mezrabs became armed with the latest weapons from Europe and so could increasingly protect themselves against attack. Their flocks of sheep and strings of camels were among the best in the desert. The mares that Medjuel and Jane rode had the most sought-after breeding-lines. This policy of improved stocks by selective breeding Jane learned at her grandfather Coke's knee, and she needed no urging to bestow good beasts upon Medjuel and his family.

By 1862 the tribe had freely adopted Jane as a sort of matriarch, and she found herself increasingly called upon to adjudicate in squabbles, counsel the sick and bereaved, and comfort divorced wives. Members of the tribe would even ride to Damascus to ask her opinion, and she was highly regarded as both doctor and vet. To all these roles she brought a grace and leadership that came not only from her upbringing, but from her natural intelligence. People sought her help, knowing that she was trustworthy; women who had a grievance against their husbands went to her knowing that she would listen with sympathy, and that if she believed them she would place the matter directly before Mohammed, which they would not dare to do. She was generous to the poorer members of the tribe, but they accepted her now for herself and not just her riches. She milked the camels and goat-like sheep, cared for her husband's mares, washed his hair, bathed his feet and anointed his sores as any caring wife did.[2] She often walked behind the caravan with the other women collecting dried camel droppings for use as fuel.

Yet she ignored the custom that decreed she should wait in her tent for her husband's return after a fight. A returning warrior would customarily be greeted by everyone in the camp before he went to the privacy of his tent and the company of his wife. The *Sitt* (the Lady) not only disregarded this custom but had even been known to mount one of Medjuel's mares and ride out to meet him. *Wullah!* It was unheard of. But for all that she was a good wife to the sheikh and brought honour to the Mezrab tribe.[3]

In addition, she had many contacts outside normal bedouin connections – with the British consul, for example, and the Emir el Khader; and she was on calling terms with the governor-general and his harem and anyone of rank in Damascus, for she was arguably the most important European citizen in Syria.[4] She needed all these contacts, for in the early 1860s every kind of trouble visited Jane and Medjuel, and 1862 in particular brought many irritations.

In his attempts to recover some of his lost and stolen property through the traditional methods of *divan* and, ultimately, *ghazou*, Medjuel fell foul of the authorities. The warlike Faris el Meziad managed to persuade the Governor of Homs that Medjuel was causing trouble in the desert, and in January 1862 Medjuel was captured and thrown into prison. After strong representations of the new British consul, Richard Rogers, he was released on a bond pending trial. Jane's ability to obtain powerful assistance further enhanced her reputation in the desert. In March she recorded that 'After much hesitation and indecision, and with the prospect of a long Turkish imprisonment before him, [Medjuel] left at half an hour's notice for the desert on Nourah, to insist upon (what ought to have been done last year) Ebn Merschid's settling and *finishing* this dreadful Hessienne affair.'[5] But Jane's troubles were not limited to Medjuel. A caravan she had personally commissioned was long overdue arriving in Damascus from Baghdad; it had been attacked by the notorious Sheikh ebn Dukhi.[6]

During these turbulent months, her time was divided between the desert and Damascus; letters from home seemed almost to hail from another age. When Jane heard that Kenelm's daughter Emmie was to be married to Edward Buxton and that their honeymoon was to be spent in Egypt and possibly the Lebanon, she wrote at once:

I rejoice most sincerely in her happy prospects and I smiled within myself as I pictured the happy Wedding gathering at quiet Tittleshall. I have written her a line 'Post Restante Cairo' . . . whether there be any hopes of their coming to Damascus and *when*? Even were I in the desert . . . an express would soon bring me striding back on my swift dromedary.

By this post also goes a letter to my friend Admiral Drummond on the subject of your son, Henry. I have not heard from him since I was last in England in '57, still, I think he would be ready to oblige me if possible, and as soon as I hear from him, I will be sure to let you know the result. I envy Henry his travels amongst the Chinese and Pacific people. What variety he must see, and still so young.

I intend writing soon to Edward and Theresa. I hear they have been enlarging dear old Minterne of my early days, but how *could* he cut down that fine old cedar on the drawing room lawn, that it takes years and years to replace!!? Holkham too, with its new and magnificent flower gardens and coloured spar paved walks. How unknown all this is to us Easterns who in our gardens in winter move about on high *kabkabs* [strap-on platforms in iron or wood] to be out of the greasy slippery clay.

Damascus since the insurrection is duller than dull, and we have had the misfortune to lose Fuad Pacha, a thorough gentleman and really patriotic; in short a *rara avis* here. Lord Dufferin's proposal of making Syria a hereditary vice-royalty with him for viceroy *might* have been the salvation of Syria, but he is gone and we are falling back into the old system of bribing etc, the road insecure . . .

The Beyrout French road too, does not promise, as the winters in Mount Lebanon are so severe they break down the constructions; but we have a wire telegraph which is little used. I was shocked at the unexpected news of poor Prince Albert's death. What a break up of the Queen's private happiness for they were, it seemed, a model *ménage* . . . I hear the Prince of Wales is still to go up the Nile and come here for April, perhaps he may go to Tadmor if there is time.[7]

Possibly it never occurred to Jane that her descriptions of the conditions of the roads and the dangers might give her brother and sister-in-law qualms at the thought of their newly married daughter visiting there. Deep in problems of her own, such dangers probably seemed insignificant. When she wrote, Medjuel was still in serious trouble with the Governor of Homs, due, Jane suspected, to bribes given by his enemies.

Jane began a campaign to obtain British protection for Medjuel, to which she claimed he was entitled on account of his marriage to an Englishwoman. She also lobbied the pasha and the Turkish government representatives, using every contact she could, including

Cabouly Effendi, whom she had met through the Duchesse de Plaisance in Athens, and who came to visit the pasha in April 1862. Jane wrung from the pasha, with Cabouly's help, a promise that he would ensure Medjuel came to no harm.[8]

From Tittleshall, Kenelm's wife Caroline wrote that Emmie and her husband fully intended to visit Damascus; indeed, she had heard that day from the couple in Cairo. Caroline told Jane, 'She can hardly believe it is in the same world as Tittleshall, everything so different, so new, so strange. She is horrified at the *dirt* of the Arabs . . . she says it is so hot she can only bear the lightest apparel. She delights in the donkeys, what will she say to your camels and dromedaries?'[9] In April the newly weds arrived in Damascus. Their visit coincided with that of Edward, Prince of Wales, upon whose birth in 1841 Jane's father had ordered a naval salute and the mainbrace spliced. Prince Edward, whose trip to Palestine and the Near East had been planned by Prince Albert before his death as a means of completing his son's education, was twenty years old. The royal party had come to Damascus and pitched their tents, Arab-fashion, on a large piece of land next to Jane's house.

Emmie was unwell when she arrived, and Jane put her to bed for a day in her own cool high boudoir with windows on three sides to catch every breeze. Jane liked her niece on sight, and the two women passed the first day together quietly and pleasantly. Emmie was 'unaffected and a *perfect* lady in manner and mind', Jane wrote in her diary.

On the afternoon of 29 April the Prince of Wales visited Jane, informally and 'with no great show'. Jane could not think why he called on her. 'Mere curiosity I suppose,' she concluded in her diary. Without fuss, she showed the prince and his entourage over the house – one of the sights of Damascus for any British visitor of rank – and obliged them by exhibiting her paintings of Palmyra. The menagerie of animals and birds was 'much appreciated' by the royal party. Afterwards they looked at the horses, especially her latest and favourite mare, Hadibah. In her diary Jane wrote that the prince admired all he was shown and was gracious and polite, thanking her and apologising for the intrusion as he said goodbye. In his own diary the prince noted that Jane 'was once very handsome, & is still very good looking tho' more than 50. Her house is charmingly arranged in true oriental style, as is her garden, which is full of roses.'[10]

When Emmie and her husband left, Jane wrote in her diary, 'I rode with them to the top of the mountain at Salhiyeh.' She was anxious that they should see Damascus as she had first seen it, and how – despite the damage caused during the massacre – it could still look from a distance. The dazzling white minarets still tapered into the flawless blue of the sky, the gold and white domes of palaces still shimmered under the sun; it was still the Pearl of the Desert. 'Sixteen worlds full of gardens rolled out flat,' wrote the painter Edward Lear at the time, 'with a river and a glittering city in the middle.'[11]

Emmie sketched Damascus from the vantage point, as Jane had done several times, and the party enjoyed a picnic lunch before it was, at last, time for the travellers to go. 'I felt inexpressibly sad as I gazed at her, and after them,' Jane wrote in her diary on 1st May 1862; reflecting that once, long ago, she too had been an innocent and trusting young bride, before her passionate obsession for Felix Schwarzenberg had turned her life upside down and 'cast a poisonous shade' upon the lives of her family.

When she wrote to Emmie's parents on the 10th May to tell them about 'the *very* pleasant but too short visit' of the newly married couple, there was a veiled hint to Emmie's mother of an interesting condition that would later prove to be accurate:

the sight of them has indeed been a treat to me. We were acquainted in a moment, and seeing her sweet, youthful, happy countenance I felt myself wafted back to her age, and it seemed as though all sad experiences and troubles were blown away in her society . . . she charmed everyone who saw her, native or European, Christian or Moslem, and they seem to be setting out in life with as fair a hope of happiness as any I ever saw . . .

. . . Of course I saw that the fatigue of Palmyra was at this moment out of the question, and only showed her my drawings, without much comment not to tantalise . . . She was very well in health. The day of, and day after, her arrival a little tired and *sick*, but one day's perfect rest set her all right again, and I hope she enjoyed her three days rambling in the bazaars etc.

On the Tuesday, the Prince of Wales . . . told Mr Buxton he would like to call here, which he did, and was very affable and pleasant. I heard afterwards from the Consul that he (the Prince) had asked many questions about my Sheikh and what part he took in the insurrection, and seemed very pleased with what he heard. His visit may perhaps be . . . conducive to Medjuel's obtaining English Protection later . . .

They [the Buxtons] are on their way home via Constantinople and my great regret is that they have not seen the Sheikh, nor he them. I think he is the sort of man Mr Buxton would like, making of course due allowance for differences of custom and race.

Jane left the next day for Homs, where she expected to meet Medjuel, who was still evading arrest, having technically jumped bail so to speak. Her diary reveals that she was anxious for Medjuel's safety, and concerned about her finances. During the previous winter she had commissioned at a cost of some £3,000 – virtually a year's income – a caravan to Baghdad. She had personally selected the forty *ayghals* and camel drivers who made up the heavily armed party. Their mission was to buy good camels, a stock of the warm and light cashmere *abbas* manufactured only in Baghdad, and other goods that had been in short supply in Damascus since the massacre. The few caravans that had ventured through the shortest desert route via Palmyra had been preyed upon by Sheikh Mohammed ebn Dukhi. Jane detested him as a person but had forced herself to be polite to him for Medjuel's sake; he had even been a guest in her home. In February, as Jane's caravan was returning to Damascus, it was attacked viciously by ebn Dukhi's men. Jane immediately complained formally to the British consul, who reported to the Foreign Office in London 'the pillage of a caravan of 250 camels while crossing the desert between Bagdad and Damascus'.

This caravan was attended by 40 armed men, inclusive of camel drivers, and were within two days journey of this city when it was set upon by a large body of Anazeh Arabs who succeeded in capturing about half of the camels. Several men were killed and others wounded. Goods to the value of £2,000 were stolen . . . This is only one raid of many, but it is likely to be the death blow of trade between Bagdad and Damascus worth £160,000 per annum.[12]

Jane was also worried about her household, for Mrs Tappenden was proving more nuisance than she was worth. Just as Jane set out for Homs, she received a letter from Eugénie asking if she might return to Damascus. But Jane recalled the episodes of paranoia and did not wish Eugénie to return. Furthermore, Jane had been suffering for some months from severe pain which she self-diagnosed in code in her diary as 'piles', but which she half suspected might be something more sinister.

Thursday May 15th 1862. . . . arrived at Homs early but I was dead tired with the heat and the road. On arrival found that Medjuel had been twice for me but was now in the mountains for the camels to eat *zhuti*, and I must now wait until he can fetch me . . .

Monday 26th. I rode Hadibah, Yadeh taking her colt. She was very disagreeable and needs a *groom*, for taking care of her is very fatiguing to me in this dreadful heat.

Tuesday 27th. I have, with joy, seen Medjuel again! . . . I rode out with them, and then went to Der Albee to pass the night with him.

Thursday 29th. I drew for Medjuel £216 for another batch of camels. Sheikh Mohammed [el Mezrab] and some Khayal . . . arrived to escort me to the Meidan [desert] five hours off. We arrived before sunset after some tremendous galloping. We left Moussa and the baggage camels behind and they arrived one and a half hours later. The desert is still green and our camp is a nice grassy place with water and a fresh spring . . . Zoyah, Boughah and Howdjah are all dead since last year; all young girls . . . [I heard] that Mohammed Dukhi was in Damascus and escaped without my camels being recovered.

Thursday 12th. We set off by night suddenly, it having been reported that soldiers were coming to attack us, and arrived at Firsgleh at daybreak.

Sunday 22nd. Reports all day that the Pashas of Homs and Hamah were coming out against us with soldiers and cannon. The Sheikh did not believe it but on a repeated message from Solyman ebn Merschid we set off at midnight, by a beautiful moonlight to Firgloss. I, for one, enjoyed the ride excessively. We arrived at sunrise and encamped there about seven days. Not very pleasant, nothing for the horses [to eat] and scorpions in plenty, from which however our tent was mercifully free. I got a few bathes. The Sulymiat from the Medjid came with beautiful camels.

Monday 30th. . . . . our affair with ebn Merschid makes no progress towards a favourable settlement.

The tribe spent several months evading government troops and Jane became accustomed to the life of a fugitive. She revelled in the wild rides to hidden encampments in the mountains to evade government troops. Whenever they rejoined the tribe she sat with the men where there was constant talk of waging a war on various groups whom Sheikh Mohammed el Mezrab blamed for their problems. Eventually a three-sided solution was decided upon. Mohammed would go with the tribe to Tadmor where there was relative safety from the Turkish troops. Medjuel and his brother Manah would go to ebn Merschid to try to bring their dispute to a satisfactory conclusion. And Jane was to go alone to Damascus as an official envoy of the tribe to obtain a pardon for Medjuel from the governor, but if she did not succeed she was to join the tribe at Tadmor for the winter trek.[13]

She set off with Fidayah and Moussa, nursing in her lap her latest little 'Angora Dog' Bijou, which was ill because of the intense heat. Jane had had a succession of these little dogs with long white silken hair, ever since King Ludwig had given her one as a puppy; she had called that first one 'Tuilly'.

In Damascus she was distressed because the consul, Richard Rogers, appeared to be avoiding her, but she eventually tracked him down and extracted his promise to stand as guarantor for Medjuel's good behaviour when Jane was granted an audience with the governor. Monsieur Heuguard, the French chargé d'affaires, seconded Roger's guarantee and also offered French protection to Medjuel. Jane became friendly with Monsieur and Madame Heuguard, and travelled with them in a *calèche*, 'a novelty to travel in a carriage in Damascus', along the hadj road to Abd el Khader's summer palace, where as always she was greeted warmly. 'Bad news from Aleppo; roads intercepted by the Ansari and Mowah Arabs. Ditto from the Hauran from Arabs and Druses; Ditto from Mount Lebanon from Christians,' Jane recorded in her diary on 10 September 1862. It was not safe to travel anywhere.

As a result of her meetings with the pasha she believed she had obtained a measure of safety for Medjuel, at least in Damascus, but her pleasure in achieving this vanished when she discovered several young camels in the city with her own brand on their hides. She was simmering about this when she wrote to England, explaining her long delay in answering Kenelm's enquiry about the sheikh's affairs:

In the desert, even were there a regular post, one is so overcome with the scorching summer heat, so bothered by a continual squatting position, and all sorts of things, and animals running over one (I mean sometimes a gazelle kid, sometimes a greyhound etc. etc.) and the outside noises to boot, that correspondence, reading and all quite sedentary employment is uphill work.

. . . The *two* Consuls have so far befriended [Medjuel] that a 'bouy-ourdi', a safe conduct, has been obtained which protects him. Official French protection has been offered him, but we are hesitating until all hope of English protection is lost. I heard through Steely that Edward had kindly called on Lord Russell to speak upon the subject . . . I know that it is difficult even to get a shadow of protection for a foreign subject but this case has become notorious here, and the Turkish government is so corrupt and treacherous that they have got a notion that by attacking and persecuting the Sheikh when in Damascus they can, through him, get at English gold!! . . . It is said that they have offered the Denge Chief a price for Mohammed Dukhi's head, and vice versa to Mohammed Dukhi for Ismael el Euttrasch (of the Druses); so each will be on their guard and they will get *neither*. But what a government!!

I am now claiming from the government indemnity or restitution of a set of my own private camels which were taken by an Agent of the Government [Dukhi] who afterwards rebelled and fought the Sultan's troops. The camels were seized by the latter, brought into town and *actually sold* by order of the Government without giving notice to the British consulate to apprise me that I might go and claim my own! I was in the desert at the time or I should certainly have gone and laid hands on them, and the little ones, all marked with my own mark 'MI' . . .

I wish that Syria was not separated from England by the long and expensive sea trip. The fatigue of travel I count as nothing but a visit to England must take five months or it is not worth while. I much enjoyed my last trip, just 6 years ago, but I fear dear Madre [now eighty-five] must be altered and aged . . . and I should dread to see it.[14]

In December 1862, with the assistance of Mr Hannah Misk, senior dragoman to the British consul, Jane again petitioned Rogers regarding her '250 Camels – white, black, and brown, large and small; plundered by Sheikh Mohammed Dukhi of the Wuld Ali Tribe of Bedouin Arabs to the value of 250,000 piastres in the neighbourhood of Sakhay near Palmyra'.[15] She asked Rogers to approach the Turkish authorities to insist that the allowance payable to ebn Dukhi be sequestered and she be repaid from the money. 'Also,' she said logically, 'some of the stolen camels have been recovered by the Turkish government. Why can I not have them back?' Mohammed ebn Dukhi had received money for the camels from the government when he leased them to the hadj. The Emir Pasha had already agreed to her plaint, she argued, and had ordered that ebn Dukhi restore the camels or their value. Hannah Misk had attended the meeting on her behalf when she had been in the desert. The Grand Council had decided that 'it is customary for the Bedouins to plunder each other' and ruled that ebn Dukhi should restore to Medjuel el Mezrab the camels or their value. 'But,' Jane explained, 'the 250 camels are *mine*! The sheikh had nothing to do with them. *I* am the plaintive.'[16]

Rogers reported the case to the Foreign Office. But it was not a straightforward matter, as Jane appeared to believe; for Mohammed ebn Dukhi had fled the area, undoubtedly warned.

Re: Mrs Digby's claim for the recovery of camels from Mohammed Dukhi, on which subject a Vizirial Order was obtained and presented. This case was fully reported in my no 48 of December 31st, 1862 . . . Sheikh Mohammed [ebn Dukhi] had been recognised as the guardian of the district, but had become obnoxious to the authorities who strengthened his old rival Sheikh Feisal and supported [Feisal] in attacking the former.

In the encounter that ensued Mohammed Dukhi's party lost about 40,000 (forty thousand) camels. This is a very large number but I have been assured by a good authority that it is not exaggerated. Thus Mohammed Dukhi was reduced to comparative poverty, and when he attacked Feisal, the authorities deserted the latter, who lost a large number of men. This quarrel is one of very long-standing – indeed the blood-feud is an inheritance on both sides, and nothing definite having been settled it is most probable that hostilities will be recommenced next spring.[17]

As the year moved to an end, Monsieur Heuguard, hearing that Jane was thinking of selling her lovely house, offered to buy it. 'My love of change and occupation will easily induce me to sell if I could get my price . . . [I have] a longing to sell this house, the fruits of 8 years labour and expense, and buy part of Assad and Hadji Nounych's [neighbours] garden and build a pleasant, more compact house, there.'[18]

The Heuguards told Jane that King Otto and Queen Amalie of Greece had recently fled to Germany. Madame Heuguard was ill and Jane spent the day sitting with her. The close, quiet atmosphere of the sick-room and talk of King Otto led Jane into exchanging confidences. She could not stop herself as the story of her relationships with Felix Schwarzenberg, with King Ludwig, Baron Venningen, Count Theotoky, and King Otto, tumbled out. Afterwards she wrote in her diary that she was 'vexed with myself for speaking to them of . . . bye-gone days. *Why?* I neither did the noble-minded Baron justice, nor the love I bear to the dear Sheikh.'[19]

Christmas came and went with only Jane's party for her servants to mark its passing. But at least for once she had Medjuel with her, for as the year ended Jane obtained 'an order from Mohammed Pasha to Abdou Aga, liberating the Sheikh from his dreadful *kefab*'. In the first days of 1863 her mare Hadibah gave birth to a beautiful little filly foal. Except for her loss of £3,000, all was well.

20

The Sitt el Mezrab
1863–1867

The middle years of the 1860s were filled with colourful incident and domestic contentment. As there were frequent fights between the tribes, Medjuel was often away for months at a time. They made Medjuel's house at Homs their base, since his representations on behalf of the tribe had to be made to the governor there. Jane did not care for Homs, a small hot rural town with none of the diversions of Damascus.

In June 1863 Lady Andover died. Although eighty-six years of age she had been in good health and died suddenly and quietly while sitting with Miss Jane Steele in her drawing-room at Tunbridge Wells, according to letters from England. 'I understand perfectly how deeply this sad event must have affected you,' wrote Charles Venningen, 'for she was certainly the very best of mothers; at least I never met another to compare with her.'[1] Jane's sadness was intensified by a resurgence of guilt at the distress her career had caused both her parents, whom she had loved deeply. But it was characteristic of her – since she observed scrupulously the niceties of both cultures – that she agonised over the fact that she could get no black-edged paper, nor even a black waxed crayon to edge her paper, when she wrote to her brother about their mother's death.

> Poor dear Madre! It always seemed strange to me, that with all her nervousness she never appeared to be afraid of death . . . which I think a most natural shrinking, however brave you may be. And in the East another terror is added to the rest, that of being *buried alive* which constantly happens . . . I am very glad to hear that you and Edward have

settled an annuity on the Steelys [and] have begged him to add my quota
so that they cannot refuse to accept . . .

Edward told me in his letter that Lord Russell had told him the author-
isation had been sent either to Damascus or Stamboul, he is not sure
which, but Mr Rogers has received nothing yet from the Foreign Office
. . . I have come to the conclusion by experience that there is no living
in the towns for the Sheikh without a European protection.[2]

Medjuel, still unpopular with the Turkish government, was busy
buying up more property in Homs, having sold a flock of sheep and
several very valuable horses, since he wished to be the owner of their
new home at Homs which, though small, Jane made as pleasant as
the one in Damascus.

The weather in 1863 began with a hot and 'hollow sirocco' that
gave Jane headaches. The heavy, sultry heat made her feel listless
and ill, so that she began to worry about cholera. However, it was
Medjuel who became ill. A fever, which Jane treated with cold com-
presses and analgesics, appeared to abate, and Medjuel said he felt
a little better. He was anxious to clear up several matters that had
been worrying him, and they rode together to the tents of the tribe,
a few hours from Homs. But soon it became obvious that he was in
distress; despite Jane's careful nursing, he collapsed into a delirious
coma.

Tuesday, 14th July 1863. Dear Medjuel's illness is decidedly either typhus
or something very dangerous, and here we are in the desert with no
human aid! His fever is raging and he is delirious; day and night there is
no change . . . I am at my wits' end not daring to think of the dreaded
possibility of his death.
Wednesday 15th. The worst day and night! His eyes wide with a dreadful
glazed expression in them, the fever raging more and more. I prayed
earnestly.

When they saw that her nursing had no effect, the bedouins gathered at the entrance to the tent begged her to let them treat him with
the traditional cures. They knew this illness; they told her they could
help him. Jane had seen some of the rough bedouin medicine – a
child with a terrible skin disease anointed with ointment made of
pounded camel dung and ashes; a dying man placed in the midday
sun to 'burn out' the evil spirit. Much of the nursing involved magic
spells and the chasing away of evil spirits by the use of turquoise stones
and amulets of various kinds, and the 'burning-out' or cauterization of
afflictions with hot irons. Yet Jane's own methods had had no effect,

and it was clear that unless something was done, and soon, Medjuel would almost certainly die. The treatment was even worse than she imagined.

> without hope, but in despair I committed him to the curing of the Bedouins who burned four *miṣamar* in his head with a hot iron which hissed as it touched him!
>
> What I *felt* I cannot express ... but shortly after he broke out into a profuse perspiration, which I trust has spared him.[3]

From that day Medjuel began to recover. It was a slow process during which Jane never left his side, but as he gained in strength she relaxed.

> *Friday 24th.* I rode into Homs with Nehabi for my letters, called upon the Aga about the odious kefab, which notwithstanding all we have done, *still* seems far from being finished. I rode back in the evening and galloped Midjioumah up to the tent as if I was bringing her up to a winning post! A reminiscence of long gone by days when I used to run races with my brothers.[4]

As soon as Medjuel was sufficiently recovered to ride a horse they returned to Homs with his children. Often, during the intensely hot July and August of that year they spent the day beside the River Asy as a family, lolling under the trees, splashing about in a shallow inlet. A small donkey carried the picnic. In one quickly executed cartoon Jane places the children, now adolescents, up a tree over the heads of herself and Medjuel. Sometimes Jane and Medjuel went alone and Jane swam naked in the wide, deep and fast river with a rope around her waist – the other end held by an anxious Medjuel. In the cool of the evenings they exercised the horses, and sometimes they rode to the vineyards 'to eat grapes, and then all round the town after a nice gallop'.

Medjuel was still as loving as in the early days of their marriage. 'How he tries to please me in everything,' Jane wrote when he gave her Aidaah, a splendid dromedary, in gratitude for her nursing.[5] They held mock races, and Jane – confident that she was as good a rider as Medjuel and could beat him if she really tried – sometimes held back. Her beautiful horse Midjioumah (which she had bred and broken) was one of the fleetest in the desert and gave Jane enormous pleasure: 'Midjioumah would have beat Nourah had I let her.'[6]

From Charles Venningen came news that Heribert had married the granddaughter of Lord Erskine, her grandfather's old friend, who had been kind to her when she first arrived in Munich in 1831. The 'pretty' bride, Countess Gabrielle de Paumgarten, was, like Heribert, half English:

> she is very blonde with a pink complexion and skin so fine one can see the blood circulating in her veins. She is a little shorter than you. I fear her health is delicate, in contrast to that of her husband who is built like a Hercules. They do not match physically, but . . . they have married purely for love, and there is nothing to be said against that.[7]

In Damascus Mrs Tappenden was proving to be a wasteful and gossiping servant, and Jane learned she had been indiscreet with several of the male servants. Eventually Jane felt obliged to go alone to Damascus. By coincidence Eugénie now appeared back in Syria and, as she seemed more her old self Jane re-employed her with relief. In addition to her other defects, Mrs Tappenden was a poor needlewoman, whereas Eugénie was a first-class dressmaker. In Eugénie's absence Jane had relied on her two sisters-in-law to send her up-to-date fashions from England in the crates which still arrived three or four times a year.

> the riding jacket and muslin dress are capitally chosen. I have a small grey French strap riding hat for visits, but for real country riding and cantering yours is just the thing! In your next letter please to send me the bill for I carefully opened all the papers and did not find any list or the bill.
>
> I long to be into my new books but I am still busy resettling the house. After a long absence Eugénie is returned I am happy to say, but did not bring any *aide de camp* with her, which I am sorry for as the chief plague of Syria is the want of servants.[8]

In the spring of 1864 Jane once again personally escorted a party of five English travellers to Palmyra when Medjuel had to remain at Homs. The extreme heat was enervating, but she had a longing to see Tadmor again. She set off with Mr and Mrs Amherst and their daughter, Sir Patrick Murray and Mr Noeys, and sixty-five men as escort. Jane rode Oudiada, given by Medjuel as a bride-gift and still Jane's favourite camel. She was delighted to be away from the towns and in the desert with only the sound of birdsong.

> *Friday June 10th, 1864.* . . . near Bella Tiass we [stopped] and I slept the sleep I delight in, under the broad and brilliant canopy of heaven, with all sorts of aromatic herbs all round, Bedouin fires, and the dear, useful dromedaries chewing the cud . . .
>
> *Saturday 11th.* We rose for our last stage through the Dhow . . . after

luncheon caught sight of the well-known (to me) pyramidical hills that descend upon Tadmor, still far, far off in the slight blue distance. We went the whole day without stopping, mostly trotting in order to get in before sunset, and at last attained the last hill and the ever glorious panorama of Tadmor and its long-departed glories lay stretched before us. Alas, half an hour too late, for the sun no longer brightly illuminated the colonnade; the columns were white instead of golden as I wished them to be. Still, the party were *astounded* and our entry to Tadmor was like a triumph, all the villagers turning out to shout a welcome.

Sunday 12th. I bathed in a garden . . . and afterwards walked through the ruins. I delighted to do the honour of the place, dear to me by a thousand memories of love and tenderness.

After several days the party set out for home but Jane, to her surprise, became affected with ophthalmia. She had often treated members of the tribe, including Medjuel, for eye infections but assumed that because of her own scrupulous hygiene she was immune.

Thursday 16th. I rose with one of my eyes painfully inflamed; 'gummed in' as the Bedouins would say, and before we reached the long stage to the water at Bella Tiass in the evening I was affected in both eyes, though not at all tired. I envied Miss Amherst being able to sketch the deep, dark tints and the glorious sunset looking up the narrow gully with the Bedouin figures, and reflections in the water. She sketches rapidly and well with deep colours *at once*, using the brush, but I do not like her prodigality of Indian yellow on her buildings . . .

Friday 17th. A most painful day to me with both eyes completely closed with inflammation and pain. The blazing sun full on my face I was obliged to be led by another Bedouin, the dromedary trotting as it liked, and the saddle quite broken. We arrived at length at the tents [of the Mezrab], I in a pitiable state doctored by Arglyeh.

Saturday 18th. The worst day of all! . . . When we arrived at Ayfir I could not possibly open either eye. After luncheon we went on, I suffering inexpressible shooting pains and on nearing Homs to my inexpressible vexation I heard them exclaim "Here's the Sheikh . . . on his beautiful chestnut mare etc. etc." . . . It was impossible for me to open my eyes or see him, or greet him as I wished. What must *real* blindness be like?

Jane fretted more about the incapacity it brought than the condition itself, recalling that on a previous return when Medjuel had come to greet her they had raced towards each other. 'Oh how I *love* such excitement,' she had written joyously, proud of her fitness and still-youthful agility. But her illness only seemed to make Medjuel more caring. 'What an *angel's* temper, and patience he has proved on so many occasions', she marvelled.[9]

Eugénie wrote saying she had to go to France in the hope of being allowed to see her daughter whom, twenty years earlier, she had given up to a foster family. Ever since, she had made attempts to see the girl and she believed it might at last be possible. This meant Jane had to return to Damascus again, but Medjuel was able to accompany her. They were both invited to the levee held by the British consul in honour of Queen Victoria's birthday, as 'protégés of Her Majesty'. Jane was thrilled by the invitation because she believed it indicated that Medjuel was about to be given British protection; but her campaign was doomed to failure, as a letter from Rogers, still in the Foreign Office files, reveals:

Damascus, March 16th

Sir Henry Bulwer,
F.O. London

Sir,
I have the honour to acknowledge your Excellency's despatch dated March 2nd in relation to Mrs Digby's claim for the reinstatement of camels plundered by Sheikh Mohammed Dukhi, instructing me that the lady is not entitled to British protection – to do what I can officiously in her behalf, but not to get into an official quarrel on the matter.

I have hitherto afforded official protection to Mrs Digby by virtue of her F.O. Passport granted her in the year 1857 by the Earl of Clarendon, which states her to be a British Subject, and I consequently defended her interests to the best of my ability, but if I have overstepped the bounds of prudence I hope your Excellency will excuse it,

Mr Consul E. J. Rogers[10]

This was answered by an instruction to 'continue to assist Mrs Digby, but avoid quarrelling with the authorities on her behalf'.[11] It was several years before Jane discovered that she had lost her British nationality: Rogers let it be assumed that Medjuel, like Jane, was under his protection.

All around Homs *ghazous* threatened the encampment of bedouins. 'A ghazou of 150 khayal' one day; another day 'a ghazou of 50 attacked Yousef Redouan near Seukarah'; yet another 'killed six persons and carried off all the cattle'.[12] And when Medjuel wished to set out for Palmyra via Homs, with a party of travellers, Faris el Meziad made it clear that the group would not be allowed to pass in safety unless he received a share of the travellers' fee. After a *divan* Medjuel felt he had no alternative but to consider first the safety of his travellers. 'Faris pocketed 15 Napoleons that he had no right to,' Jane wrote in annoyance.[13]

Shortly after Medjuel left Damascus in the spring of 1865 Jane had a visitor. 'To my great disgust Sheikh Faris el Meziad arrived with 10 khayal to remain here a day or two.' By the bedouin code Jane could not in honour turn him away, but she found it difficult to carry out the prescribed show of welcome and hospitality that a host must offer to his guests for three and one-third days. Faris el Meziad reported to her that war had been declared between the Wuld Ali tribe and the Sebbah, to whom Medjuel and the Mezrabs owed allegiance. This would mean Medjuel could not return for some weeks. Jane decided that if she heard nothing within ten days she would go to him at Homs. In April she wrote to England:

> I . . . intend leaving for the desert next week, although the garden is just now in high beauty. Roses, bulbs, tubers and climbers succeed better than annuals generally, and my new French man although not a professional gardener is a great amateur and works very hard. Towards autumn he urges me to write to Carter for some of the wonderful roots etc., of which his *Vade Mecum* speaks, but really one should be bewildered in the choice among so many lovely and new things.
>
> Here, notwithstanding the climate and quantities of water and shade . . . there are lovely wild flowers, quite worthy of any garden. What I find most difficult, and indeed have not yet succeeded in raising are verbenas, of which I am very fond but have none but the older brilliant scarlet.
>
> . . . I have now heard that Heribert has gone honeymooning in Italy; maybe he will return by Paris. His father has given him Riegarding near Linz and I suppose will live himself at Munich.[14]

Jane sent all the jewels given to her by the baron during her marriage to her daughter-in-law; she had left the Venningen heirloom pieces and other expensive items with the baron on their divorce.[15]

She rejoined Medjuel at Homs and every evening they had 'delicious' competitive rides together. 'I rode with the Sheikh to see Ismael Pasha's camels and galloped Midjioumah, almost catching the Sheikh on [the splendid mare] Hadibah.' And she measured her riding ability not only against Medjuel but against other sheikhs, who would not have welcomed the prospect of being outridden by a woman. 'I raced with Feisal and I think Midjioumah would have beaten him had he continued, but he drew up, not to be beaten before the Arabs who were all in sight.'[16]

In August Medjuel left for the tents with Manah and Schebibb to organise his flocks of sheep during the coming winter. Jane elected to stay in Homs because of the heat. To her dismay, a few days later she heard from Eugénie that cholera had broken out in Damascus, having been brought back by the pilgrims of the hadj. Richard Rogers's wife and Catherine Payen, assistant housekeeper to Eugénie in Jane's own house in Damascus, died within days, and Eugénie was 'terror-struck at being in the middle of it'. Equally terror-struck, Jane wrote to Medjuel and asked if he would come and take her to the desert, away from the threat of the disease being carried to Homs by northbound pilgrims.

Unfortunately, it was two months before Medjuel received her letter, and in the meantime Jane met with a nasty accident. Hearing a knock at her door and thinking it might be a messenger from Medjuel, she ran to open it, tripped and fell, spraining her back and arm badly.[17] While she was recovering, the cholera epidemic reached Homs, and death became commonplace. 'Mr Lucas came in and said that 25 had died of cholera this day,' Jane wrote.[18] With no word from Medjuel, and without knowing that he had not received her letter, she was stung by his apparent indifference to her appeal. There was no mail from Damascus and each day she feared hearing that Eugénie had succumbed. Although she always displayed great physical courage, Jane was frightened of illness and death. This probably stemmed from her fear (begun by the Duchesse de Plaisance) of being buried alive. Because of the heat, people were customarily buried on the day of their death. Many were the spine-chilling stories of 'corpses' recovering consciousness in a tomb.

As soon as she was able, she rode into the desert to get news of Medjuel from a large encampment of Sebbah about a day and a half's journey away. There an old man told her he had seen Medjuel several weeks earlier, and in praising him told her that 'the mark of the Mecca hadj was upon his forehead'. It was one of Jane's worst fears that Medjuel would make another hadj, and be away for half a year with all the dangers of plague and cholera that seemed to accompany such a journey. Indeed, it was one of the reasons she had not made another journey to England, for she feared he would go to Mecca in her absence. She rode back to Homs in deep depression.

But within a short time of her return to Homs this worry seemed insignificant. During a visit to the missionary, Mr Lucas, to whom Medjuel had rented a small house outside the walls of the town, Jane heard a rumour that the reason Medjuel spent so much time away from her was that he had another wife, a bedouin wife, in the desert. Jane vehemently denied it and wrote furiously in her journal that night of her anger that they could imagine that she would ever tolerate such an arrangement. She wrote several letters to her family during this time, heading her letters 'Homs (ancient Emesa)'. Yet, though her diary mirrors her personal anguish, her letters did not even hint of a problem; indeed, quite the reverse.

You ask for details of my Arab life; as far as health and pleasure goes I prefer the wide and boundless desert to the cooped up town life. There is always some excitement or other going on, and constant horse or Dromedary exercise, as well as the good bowls of pure camel's milk which suit me.

The Sheikh, *my* Sheikh, never leads, joins or abets a plundering party because he thinks it wrong to seize other people's property, but if *we* are attacked, or even our allies when he is there, or if there is a regular war, he is first and foremost to defend or pursue. This, I cannot think any more wrong than our more civilised, and murderous warfare for I do not know of any command to allow of 'the goods being spoiled' ... He is not fanatic, although he is strict as to his fasts, *namaz* (prayers), and in morals acts in all things to his light. [He] disapproves of polygamy, and doubts it being right, although allowed by the Muslim creed, and as to slaves black or white used in the Harem in the Turkish and Syrian sense, this is refuted by *all* Bedouin Sheikhs who, when they have black slave boys, bring them up as their own children and when of age, say 16 or 18, give them their liberty and marry them to some black girl equally liberated.

As to the Bedouin women, they are – almost all of them – [ignorant] ... and often more savage than the men. I asked a cleverish one one day about the [marital] conduct of the women in the desert. 'Oh!' she replied, 'it [adultery] is almost unheard of, for we always have a sabre hanging over our heads for that, as we have also if we have *too long tongues* without being able to *prove* what we say.' But the idea of [adultery] being a crime didn't seem to occur in the desert.

I do a little doctoring ... [try] to teach them their letters, and preach by example ... a strict regard for truth, honesty in little, as in great, affairs such as domestic harmony.[19]

By December 1865 Medjuel had been away five months and the only word Jane had received was by messenger. He was unable to return because war had broken out between the major tribes and the desert was in turmoil. She knew it was no time for a sheikh to desert his people and, despite her desperation, Jane appreciated that his duty came first.

Having given up expecting him during the worst of the winter and after receiving complaints of loneliness from Eugénie, Jane decided to go quickly to Damascus and arrived there on the anniversary of her mother's birthday, 'once so joyously kept when we were all children at Holkham, and now only a reminiscence of innocent joys'. Next day brought a heavy snowfall which remained over Christmas, and the mail from England carried news of Miss Jane Steele's death. As Jane mourned the severance of another link with her childhood, her melancholy grew. The poison of Lucas's gossip about Medjuel took effect: 'I passed the most wretched evening. Is he ill? Is he dead? Is he *married*? Oh what shall I do? What think?'[20]

Sunday 14th January 1866. Rain in torrents all day . . . and night. So again the roads are closed, and the mystery of Medjuel's prolonged stay is explained by the news of a great ghazou having left the Sebbah for the Wuld Ali tents. Medjuel alone disobliged, to remain in command of the tents! Norah [Jane's maid] came in having been to an Egyptian Cheikh and bought a charm (without my knowledge or consent) which is 'to bring Medjuel home on the wings of the wind!!!'

After a few weeks she returned to Homs, travelling with the harem of a Turk for safety, and they broke the journey, staying in Hessia as the guests of a pasha. To her distress the entire talk of the harem was of a Circassian wife, owned by one of the 'young Agas', who had been discovered in an illicit liaison. The penalty for infidelity by a wife was final; she was beheaded.

Jane's depressed spirit rose again when in February Medjuel came back to her. He denied Lucas's gossip. 'Sweet are the moments when one forgets all the sorrows and endless anxieties of the past months in the great bliss of meeting again,' she wrote. The normal patterns of life resumed. Her fifty-ninth birthday came and went. Schebibb, now a grown man, was often in and out of Jane's home, and she was fond of him; he had asked permission to marry his cousin, the daughter of one of Medjuel's brothers, feeling that it was time he married. Later in the year, Jane helped her nervous mare Hadibah deliver with great difficulty a tiny colt; 'like a little gazelle,' Jane said happily, though a filly would have been more valuable.

She spent only a few weeks in the desert that year and returned to

Damascus to hear at Christmas from Kenelm that his wife Caroline had died suddenly. At the same time she learned from the consul that she no longer enjoyed British protection. Both items of news were blows to her; but the latter, allied to her discovery that Rogers had accepted bribes from local businessmen in return for 'favours', decided her to leave Damascus. The house was offered for sale. The previous September she had written to Kenelm:

> We have not yet abandoned our [house] here for want of an adequate purchaser, but should we find one we intend to remove to Homs as a *pied-à-terre* [when we are not in the desert]. It is four days from Damascus, the same from Beyrout, on the borders of the desert, and the Sheikh has constant occupation there. Our tribe comes in the spring into the Aleppo, Tadmor and Homs deserts and remains there until October when they migrate again. All your family news is most interesting to me . . . and my *Bedouin* nephew Willy always interests me particularly.[21]

William, the younger son of Kenelm and Caroline, had emigrated and turned sheep-herder, escorting flocks of thousands of sheep across the deserts of Australia. He sent long letters to his parents describing his life which were sent on to Jane. 'Very like our life here; except for the raids,' Jane commented.

Medjuel bought a large plot of land adjoining the original house, and they began building a new house from her drawings. When Medjuel went back to the desert, leaving her to oversee the work, she wondered for the first time whether she had the enthusiasm and energy to start building all over again. Her sixtieth birthday in April 1867 marked the milestone of old age, she thought. And her age was brought home to her when a few weeks later she took a tremendous toss from her horse on some paving and tore all the sinews in one leg, which left her limping for months.

The lack of physical fitness for a woman of her energy was an annoyance but, worse, the accident made her nervous of riding and this irritated her more than anything else, for her horsemanship had always been a matter of pride to her. She expected Medjuel to return to her in mid-June, but as usual he was late, and meanwhile she had to deal with the building problems. Even in a small desert town over a century ago, planning permission was necessary: 'The building permission was granted for the garden wall and they began to build and repair it.'[22]

One evening she went to visit the missionary, Mr Lucas (who seems to have had a remarkable lack of tact), and in the course of their conversation the subject of Medjuel's frequent absences was raised again. Mr Lucas suggested yet again that Medjuel was unfaithful.

Thursday 20th. . . . he told me that Yusuf Redouan had told him of, and even shown him, a woman who he said was Medjuel's *wife* who he said Medjuel had married . . . and who he kept concealed among the Hessienne tribe when I came to this part of the country, and that he had seen her again this spring when he called one day at *our house*.

A clap of thunder would have startled me less. I sat *glacée*, and passed a most wretched night awaking with a fever in my veins and a throbbing head. In the afternoon I rode Eydah to the garden but felt reluctant to build, and repented ever having bought it. Oh, for Medjuel's speedy return to clear up the mystery.

Jane obviously called on Yusuf herself, for in her notebook she wrote down what he told her, 'Yusuf Redouan says she was at *their* house, and that Nehabi brought her to *ours*.'[23] For once Medjuel timed his return well, and only two days later the matter was resolved to Jane's satisfaction.

Saturday 22nd. Happiness inexpressible, and unknown but to those who are condemned to possess my ardent, ungovernable feelings; unchilled, untamed, unsubdued by age, experience of the world, [or] change of any kind! Dear Medjuel returned and in a long and serious conversation with Mr Lucas, in the presence of his wife, [and] Nehabi and myself, *solemnly* denied his having any other wife but me, since the day I married him up to the present time. Now twelve years ago! Oh, how time flies! It appears but the other day I gave Medjuel both heart and hand. The origin of all these evil and tormenting reports is the base jealousy and envy of Cheikh Faris el Meziad, who first spread the report six years ago, and his sister, Faddah, has since tried to make it true with her various intrigues – thank God, in vain!

There were more conversations with Mr Lucas, who promised 'for Medjuel's sake as much as my own' to try to trace the origin of the rumours and quash them. A week later Jane was able to record that Yusuf had confessed to Mr Lucas that 'the whole story was a fabrication of his and Faris el Meziad. What barefaced liars!'[24]

What Yusuf told Mr Lucas on this occasion may well have been the truth. But within a short time the rumours would start again from a different source; and from Medjuel, this time, there would come no comforting denial.

21

Challenge by Ouadjid
1867–1869

In August 1867 Jane received news of Steely's death. The influence Steely had in Jane's life was incalculable and Jane mourned her almost as deeply as she had mourned her mother; 'my firm, sincere and most devoted friend since I was 10 years of age,' she wrote, and indeed Steely had seen her through many a crisis that must have been abhorrent to her and her sister.[1]

As she recovered from this shock, Schebibb, her good-natured and intelligent stepson, came in from the desert ill. At first Jane was not unduly concerned; Medjuel often took such fevers in heavy hot weather. She nursed Schebibb, breakfasting with him each morning before she went off to oversee the building work. The new house had now risen almost to window height and she felt that the builders needed her guidance at every step. She also made a point of calling on several harems with whom she had developed a friendship. With her work in her tiny garden, and exercising and grooming the horses, her days were full. But she became uneasy when Schebibb made no progress, and she sent for Medjuel, who arrived home towards the end of September.

It was difficult to say what was wrong with the young man, for with the fever gone he should have started to gain in health, but rather he seemed to be wasting away.

Sunday, September 22nd. I passed the whole day reading . . . poor Schebibb's state is sad. He does not improve in strength as I would wish, and the poor fellow's patience under his confinement and enforced solitude is really edifying . . .

Wednesday 25th. A day of solemn event and awful trial. Poor Schebibb breathed his last this morning, a little after sunrise. I shall not easily forget the scene. After a short struggle . . . his young spirit fled in a gentle sigh.

Oh God have mercy upon him . . . and his dear Father, and to myself who was never before present at a death . . .

The day passed in various sad, very sad, offices; many of a superstitious and Bedouiny kind. In the afternoon I walked with Khadiqsh to the poor, dear boy's grave. It is now 12 years I have watched him growing into manhood, and at the early age of 20, full of hope and promise to his father, he sinks into the tomb . . .

Friday 27th. I rode again with dear Medjuel to the sealing of the tomb, that is putting the final headstone. The last token of love and honour was paid to poor Schebibb, a sheep sacrificed and given to the poor. The old Sheikhs chanted and read to his memory for the last time. All is over.

Jane had to go to Damascus a month later but did not press Medjuel, heartsick at the loss of his son, to accompany her. Instead he went into the desert promising he would not follow the tribe beyond Tadmor. He joined her in Damascus in February and in his company the depression she had felt since Schebibb's death lifted. All winter she had visited old friends and given dinners and attended weddings as guest of honour. She had plenty of occupation and did not lack for company, and she obtained much pleasure from her affectionate relationship with her animals, but it was only in Medjuel's company that she could enjoy life to the full. In writing to her brother she attributed her rising spirits to the season.

I cannot understand how and why, at each return of spring my whole being rises buoyantly and enjoying it, as though all the events which ought to crush me to dust have never been. I do *so* enjoy this beautiful world . . .

You may have heard from Theresa and Ed that we are thinking of changing our town residence to near Homs (the ancient Emesa) on the borders of the desert leading to Palmyra, on account of the Sheikh's business with the tribes, and more facility with his brothers. But even if this house is sold we intend making a pied-à-terre here of the stables, as a winter residence for 2 or 3 months. I have [now] very little enjoyment of the place when it is in its beauty in spring and summer, and have only the expense of keeping it up. The Sheikh has already a house outside the walls of Homs, with a garden he bought for the enormous sum of 5,000 piastres (£650), and that he intends making our domicile when not in the desert.[2]

Kenelm sent news of his children: Henry, whose career in the navy Jane had done much to promote, was touring Mexico on horseback, inspecting silver-mines; Willy in the Australian outback had bought land cheaply and was taming it into a ranch; Charlie, an Oxford graduate, was tutor to the children of the poet Tennyson in the Isle of Wight, and Emmie and Carrie, Kenelm's two elder girls, were both happily married with families. There was news, too, that King Ludwig had died at Nice in February. Poor Basily, Jane mourned. Lola Montez, in whom he believed he had found the all-encompassing love for which he had always longed, had wielded her power wilfully; through his loyal support of her, Ludwig lost his throne and, subsequently, Lola too. He spent the last years of his life wandering about the watering-spots of Europe in the way of deposed royalty, like a favourite old uncle.

Charles Venningen met his former king in November 1865 and wrote to tell Jane that Ludwig had asked after her: 'He is almost 80, but he remains as alert as ever. When we spoke of you he said he has always regretted what happened. "What a pity! What a shame!" he cried . . . but he takes comfort in thinking perhaps you were a little mad . . . !'[3] Excepting only Medjuel and her father, Jane regarded Basily as the kindest man she had known. Every other man she had loved had eventually betrayed her, but those three had never let her down.

Friday 3rd April 1868. My 61st birthday! An awful age . . . fast approaching that usually assigned to man as his span here, and yet here I am still wedded to life, and full of plans and projects, and hopes of enjoyment.

After another month of socialising in Damascus, which had apparently recovered all its *joie-de-vivre* despite the massacre eight years earlier, Jane returned to Homs. Medjuel had already returned to the tents, for ebn Merschid, allied with Hassan Bey, was attacking the summer encampments and plundering them. She seemed quite content working at the new house, trying to create a garden of sorts in the courtyard, though without the advantages of a direct feed of water as she had at Damascus. When the town was attacked by Hassan Bey and cannon and musketry were employed in its defence, she found the excitement enjoyable rather than frightening.

In October, Jane's life suddenly came off its tracks. Several things happened. First, Eugénie returned to Athens. She had been living at Jane's house for a year overseeing things as a friend, though latterly not as an employee. What happened to end the arrangement is not clear. Jane did not write of it and it would be five years before the two again made contact. In those five years Jane never even mentioned Eugénie's name in her diary. The large villa in Damascus was sold, although Jane retained the stable block and a plot of land upon which she planned to build a 'compact, new house'.

Jane was in Damascus, packing to move, when she heard – yet again – that Medjuel had another wife. Though she had never taken the stories of other women lightly (she cared for Medjuel too passionately to be complacent about any threat to their relationship), her first inclination was to place the latest rumours in the same category as the previous ones spread by Medjuel's enemies. But this time it was members of the tribe who reported to their *Sitt* with obvious reluctance that Medjuel had married another woman.

The woman was Ouadjid, they said, and she was twenty years younger than Medjuel. That made her forty years younger than Jane. 'A lifetime!' If what she was told *were* true, Jane agonised, this girl possessed all the things she could never bring to Medjuel: the freshness of youth, that inexplicable allure no mature women could manufacture no matter how beautiful or well preserved. A dusky beauty, of Medjuel's own culture and religions, Ouadjid undoubtedly knew all the womanly things that a bedouin wife should know. She could cook the foods that Medjuel liked, while she, Jane, did not care for cooking or housekeeping and whenever she could paid others to do such chores for her. But even worse was the thought that Ouadjid could bear Medjuel another son to take the place of Schebibb.

Nevertheless Jane could not wholly believe that Medjuel had broken his promises to her and betrayed the love he had not only professed but demonstrated in so many ways. When Medjuel returned, she told herself, he would answer in his gentle and serious manner that there had been no infidelity, no other marriage. She was sure of it. But still she was anxious and wrote, asking him to come to her at Damascus as soon as he could.

Wednesday 2nd December 1868. . . . On my return to the stable Beschir [a man from the tribe who looked after the horses] stopped me and said with an ominous and sepulchral voice that he wished to speak to me privately. I thought it was to beg some money, or some clothes and said '*Hakke*' [certainly].

Oh, that he had asked half my fortune! But no, it was to comfort me for Medjuel's dreadful, unheard of treachery!! Not one wife shares his couch and heart, but Mascha – the dead Mascha – still lives, has borne him two children since I married him, now fourteen years ago. Fourteen long, long years he has deceived me but to rob me according to Beschir. And now, now that he is rich, now that he no longer wants me he is ready to spurn me from him like a squeezed lemon!

It was the worst possible disaster that Jane could envisage happening to her. Could she believe Beschir? Yet why should he lie? But surely Medjuel would never deceive her; and Schebibb himself had told her of his mother's death many years ago. During the suspenseful wait she poured into her journal all the misery of suspicion and jealousy.

When Medjuel arrived he told her, with the honesty she had always admired in him, that Beschir's gossip about Mascha was not correct, but that it was true she was alive. The reports of her death were erroneous and when he had heard that Mascha still lived he and his sons decided to remain silent for Jane's peace of mind. But Mascha was married to someone in another tribe; he had not seen her in years and she had had no further children by him.[4]

However, it was true that he had married Ouadjid, though his involvement with this young woman, he stressed, had no bearing on his love for Jane. She was the daughter of Ali Ressoul, who had a garden in Homs where Faris el Meziad often stayed. Medjuel was unable to keep the lift out of his voice when he spoke of Ouadjid. Jane heard and felt it as a splinter of ice to the heart: 'the agony of hearing of his intense and passionate love for *another*! He, habitually so reserved in manner and speech. And all the world laughing at me for a miserable dupe! Oh, the unbearable agony.'[5]

They quarrelled bitterly; it was inevitable. Medjuel said he could not understand her distress; Ouadjid would never replace Jane – she was a passing desire and unimportant. In her anguish Jane said things that she later regretted, but she meant it when she said that she would not accept another wife. She would leave him and Syria unless he divorced Ouadjid.

Medjuel did not even unpack but left for Homs immediately, leaving Jane to torment herself with the belief that she had driven him back to Ouadjid. During the following days she suffered a turmoil of emotional stress. She could not sleep, could not eat, could not ride, could not read. She thought she would die of misery. She even wished to die, for Medjuel, she said, was her *entire reason* for living.

What I suffer . . . no words express! I know *all*, and I love him still. Wildly, madly, hopelessly! . . .

Project after project [to win him back] course each other through my brain in rapid succession. He promised to come and spend Ramadan with me, and now, *still* I cling to the wild hope that he will divorce her! The abhorred one. Ouadjid!! Oh God![6]

On the last day of the year, Medjuel returned as he had promised. Jane rode out to meet him, leading a fresh horse. 'Oh, that meeting!' she wrote, recalling the overwhelming moment when he came up to her with his eyes wary and full of hurt. All the love she had ever felt for him, all the passion and tenderness she had ever experienced, were still there. 'Why does my heart still beat with the feelings of youth when my head is tinged with the snows of age?'[7]

In the three weeks that he had been away from her she had considered the matter endlessly; she was prepared to listen to what he had to say. And Medjuel too had considered the matter. His culture allowed him to take Ouadjid as his wife with no disrespect to Jane; perhaps he thought he could keep his second marriage secret from her indefinitely. But now his new love for a young and beautiful girl put at risk his love for an older, also beautiful, woman whose wisdom and friendship had sustained him for nearly fourteen turbulent years. As before, when he had to choose, he decided in Jane's favour.

Sunday February 7th, 1869. I passed the day in deep and earnest conversation with dearest Medjuel, and in [his brother] Assaad's presence he promised to divorce Ouadjid on my arrival [at the tents]; and not to see her, or go to her tent till we go there together, and to cut out all the roots . . . and await my arrival at Homs.

Sunday 28th. Oh, morning never, *never*, to be forgotten! No, not if I live for a thousand years. I felt very unwell in the morning and could not get up. Dear Medjuel went and breakfasted alone, and then returned taking off his clothes again, and remained with me until dinner time! Can these delicious days, truly 'love's delight', last?

March 8th. I rode with Medjuel to el Khasseur and after receiving renewed promises of meeting again shortly, we parted. He again promised to divorce her, said he no longer loves her, that she is *cold* and avaricious etc., and that he would not see her again until I came to the tents.

For three weeks, until she was due to leave, Jane fretted that Medjuel would renege on his decision and send word telling her not to come to him. Meanwhile she packed all their possessions to send to Homs.

She had no qualms at leaving the house and garden in which she had invested so many years of hard work. With Fidayah her maid, little Fatmah her new slave, and her brother-in-law Redjib as guard, she set off for Homs via the desert and Baalbek, so that she could visit the ruins and do some sketching.

> *Monday 28th March.* Baalbek. With what different feelings I was there 16 years ago after my journey to Palmyra, and on my return to Greece previous to my journey to Bagdad. The road led through the domain of Emir Solyman. We slept at his home, the country lovely in parts and so we went on in peace until we came to the village of Khasseur.
>
> *Thursday April 1st.* Slept at Khasseur where I was horribly annoyed by the village Moslems asserting in the strongest manner that Medjuel was really married to 'Ressoul's girl', but that 'perhaps he has divorced her after three days?' What I suffer in addition to all the rest!
>
> *Friday 2nd April.* I arrived in Homs and the first person who came to salute me was 'Bint Ressoul'!! Ouadjid! I treated her as she merited!

She was irritated by Ouadjid's impudent greeting, until its significance burst into her consciousness like a sunbeam through clouds. It meant Medjuel had kept his promise. He was in the desert *without Ouadjid.*

> *Saturday April 3rd.* My birthday. Sixty-two years of age and an impetuous, romantic girl of 17 cannot exceed me in ardent and passionate feelings. I spent a week at Homs and left for Hamah on Thursday 8th.

At Hamah her stepson, Afet, whom she had coveted as a baby, came to meet her, accompanied by others from the tribe to escort her formally to the tents. Medjuel and another of his brothers, Telgarr, rode out to meet her as she arrived. As she dismounted, her stepdaughter Aafteh welcomed her warmly, and behind her the other women of the tribe stood in silent sympathy. When at last they were alone together, Medjuel once again promised to divorce Ouadjid. he said, however, that he was prevented from effecting it immediately because Arab law demanded that her father or brother be present at such a ceremony.

There was great fighting in the desert that year as the government attempted to confine the tribes to defined areas and thus keep them apart. Medjuel was badly wounded in a skirmish and therefore nothing could be done about the divorce. Then the Ressoul men could not get to them, it being too dangerous for them to travel. Consequently, it was September before Jane's purgatory was to end. That whole summer she spent at the tents, waiting. She could not bear to think that, even though Medjuel had no contact with Ouadjid, the girl was legally his wife. Many members of the tribe supported Jane, in particular her eldest brother-in-law, Sheikh Mohammed, who was concerned that Jane might seek a divorce. She had, after all, done a great deal for the tribe. But among all the flattery and sympathy there was gossip and innuendo, until she thought she would go mad.

> *Saturday September 25th.* A day never to be forgotten. A divan was assembled of 50 or 60 persons of different tribes, and Medjuel sent for Ouadjid in the midst of them, and firmly pronounced *'teleighu telaths cie tadjaret ha by telathe'* [I pronounce thee divorced three times]. She, Ouadjid, was firmly unflinching hearing the sentence.
>
> At Medjuel's request, or suggestion, I afterwards went and gave her my Sowali [probably a specific piece of jewellery, i.e. a silver bracelet]. What stupid weakness! But the awful fear of . . . his repenting and regretting her – even as a housekeeper – took possession of me and I recalled her, and permitted her to remain in my tent with the Binnaat [young girls]. Am I in my right mind?

On the following day, to the shrill joy-cries of the women's *zagharit*, Jane rode away from the tents to return to Homs, leaving Medjuel to follow several hours later. They settled in the new house and Jane worked hard to make it a home, but it was an unhappy period for them both. So many things lay between them, and each time people from the tribe came they sought to tell her things she would rather not know. In her notebook she made lists in Arabic and coded French of questions to ask Medjuel when he returned:

> Why were you so unhappy the day her brother came to the tents and you heard her? To be so unhappy you must have loved her *immensely*? Far more than you ever did me? And she must have seen it and known it.
>
> Is it true that Mohammed threatened to kill her if you did not divorce her? And *that* hurried the divorce at last?
>
> When Yusef Redouan asked, 'Is she divorced? how did you answer? As if you regretted her and had done it for my sake, or that *you* were tired of her?
>
> Why did you so *hurry* for me to give her my Sowali?
>
> You did not say anything to her to make her think you would take her back?
>
> . . . I do not think I want to live for long with this uncertainty and jealousy.

Jane suspected Medjuel had not forgotten Ouadjid, and she could not decide whether she was justified or whether her anxiety was the inevitable jealousy of an ageing woman for a much younger husband. In fact, it would transpire that Medjuel's feelings for Ouadjid ran deep, but fortunately Jane would never be sure of this, and after the divorce he never returned to Ouadjid.

In the winter of 1869 Jane and Medjuel moved to Damascus, where the 'compact new house' on a quiet tree-lined road next to an old mosque in the Khassab district was incomplete but ready for occupation.

22

The Burtons
1870–1871

Jane had not written to her family since the previous winter and when Kenelm wrote, concerned for her safety, she replied as though everything had been normal,

Damascus
1 February 1870

My dearest Kenelm,

Our *very* long stay in the desert last year, must in part account for my unusual silence. For 8 months we never put our foot in a town and the disturbed state of the desert, constant suspicion of treachery on the part of the Government, and feuds, and alerts among the Bedouin tribes have made the roads, and means of communication quite unsafe for the past year. Even now a plan of the government to circumscribe the Arabs within, or rather *without*, the boundaries of Tadmor and other frontiers of the Syrian Desert is, I think, useless and will not answer their expectations. In one of these feuds the Sheikh was wounded, and well nigh killed, but I am thankful to say his wound is healed . . .

The *large* house is no longer mine. The *kiosque* in which we now live here, is in the former stable yard . . . and not finished yet as to plastering and painting etc. I am quite vexed about it. Our new Consul here is Captain Richard Burton who went to Mecca, and his wife who is very agreeable. You know Eugénie has left me for good now and lives 'tired and drooping' in France? Her place is filled by [Marie] a Swiss German from Engadine of about 30; a good painstaking girl, but of course not so clever as Eugénie as to dressmaking etc.

I forgot whether I told you that the Sheikh has received an award from the Sultan, for his bravery and loyalty in the fight and capture of Hassan Bey [during] his attempt at insurrection last year but this is *all*; the long promised pecuniary indemnities for our, and our tribe's great losses are not yet forthcoming![1]

Shortly after this letter Edward and Theresa's daughter Lena visited Damascus on honeymoon after her marriage to Lord Ashburton, wishing to see the aunt about whom she had heard much. The desert was too dangerous to allow the couple to go to Palmyra but Lena was luckier than Emmie Buxton, for she met Medjuel and took home a favourable account of her aunt's exotic husband. She was the only member of the family ever to meet him. 'Carl Haag sent me the "illustrated" with Medjuel's portrait,' Jane wrote to her brother, 'but not a *bit* like, as Lena will tell you. He is, I think, much better looking.'[2]

The arrival in Damascus of Richard Burton, the renowned explorer, was of longer-term importance to Jane. He had arrived at the consulate on 1 October 1869 like a breath of fresh air. His adventurous and energetic wife Isabel bustled into the city three months later. It is to Isabel Burton's gossipy writing that we are indebted for the best description that exists of Jane and Medjuel's new home, the house that Jane had built in her former stableyard.

From another visitor we know that it was 'outside the town and surrounded by trees and gardens with narrow streams of running water, and paths full of old English flowers'. Like her former home, it was cool and green with pigeons and turtle doves fluttering about in the trees, and it was built in three wings around a courtyard like the one at Homs.[3] It had not, apparently, the spacious guest quarters of Jane's former house, but it was not inconsequential, which is the impression she conveys by the word *kiosque*.

the house is made noticeably by its projecting balcony-like windows and coloured glass. [At the] large wooden gateway, we are received by twenty or thirty Bedouins of the tribe of Mezrab, lounging in the archway, and a large Kurdish dog which knows its friends and will let me pass ... Downstairs a reception room is hung with arms and trophies; on the right ... are the stables.

The court presents a picturesque appearance with the thoroughbreds tethered here and there to the trees eating piles of cut grass. A fountain plays in the middle. On the other side is the reception house for any of the tribe who happen to come into the town, also the bath-house, the conservatory, and the house and playground for the fowls, amongst which

[are] curious snow-white geese with curling feathers, turkeys, ducks, poultry, pigeons, guinea hens and other pets. The whole is fronted and surrounded by a choice flower garden. Upstairs is a suite of apartments which is elegance itself. Family and home treasures and little reminiscences of European life, old china and paintings are mingled with Oriental luxury . . .

The master of the house, a Bedouin Sheikh, Sheikh Mijuel [*sic*], is a small man, with a most pleasing face, piercing black eyes, gentlemanly manners and a charming voice. He speaks the beautiful Bedouin-Arabic . . . these soft, guttural utterances are very attractive to those who admire the Eastern language.[4]

When the Burtons first arrived in Damascus, Jane was, said Isabel, the only other English resident of note in the city. Besides these three were Isabel's English maid and four British missionaries, and some thirty other Europeans attached to French, Italian and Russian embassies and missions. The two women took to each other and became friends, and when both were in Damascus they met regularly, but they each left it periodically for months at a time to go – as Isabel put it – 'gypsying'.

Isabel often called on Jane, bringing with her anyone she especially wished to impress. One of these was Amy Fullerton-Fullerton, who later wrote of her experiences in *A Lady's Ride through Palestine and Syria* and recalled meeting Jane (referred to as 'the Princess', Medjuel having been introduced to her as 'a Prince of the Desert'): 'We found the Princess in an English morning wrapper, just concluding her déjeuner . . . the Prince's manners were gentle and quiet.'[5]

As wife to the consul, Isabel held her weekly 'at home' every Wednesday, at their house in the foothills of the Jebel Kaysun at Salhiyeh rather than at the consulate. Most visitors would hurry away from Salhiyeh in the late afternoon, in order to be within the city wall by sunset when the gates were closed for the night; but Jane always remained, said Isabel, 'for she, like myself, lives without the gates, and she has no fear . . . though she has twice had a little skirmish going home . . . She helps me in the afternoon to receive, and dines afterwards, almost every Wednesday; that is my great intellectual treat.'[6]

There was another member of this party – Jane's friend Abd el Khader – who made up the foursome at a weekly rendezvous for dinner.

We would go up to the roof, where it was prepared and where the . . . cushions of our divan were spread about and have our evening meal. And after that we would smoke our narghiles and talk, and talk, and talk, far into the night . . . I shall never forget the scene on the housetop, backed as it was by the sublime mountain, a strip of sand between it and us, and on the other three sides was the view of Damascus, and beyond, the desert.

It was wild, romantic and solemn; and sometimes we would pause in our conversation to listen to the sounds around us – the last call to prayer on the minaret-top, the soughing of the wind through the mountain gorges, the noise of the water-wheel in the neighbouring orchard.[7]

The conversations – about philosophy and politics, history and travel – were conducted in many languages, for all were multilingual. Richard Burton said that Jane was 'out and out the cleverest woman' he ever met: 'there was nothing she could not do. She spoke nine languages perfectly, and could read and write in them. She painted, sculpted, was musical and her letters were splendid. And if on business there was never a word too much, or too little.'[8]

It was from Jane that Isabel learned a great deal about the lives of harem women, about which she wrote in her books, explaining coyly that she had abridged the information because on such a subject 'minute detail would not be suitable for English girls'.[9] Isabel's husband learned a great deal more. Richard Burton's experience of the East had enabled him to penetrate Mecca, but even he had not the facility of access to the closely guarded life of the harem. Nor indeed, in the eighteen months she spent there, had Isabel. Furthermore, though she casually boasted of spending two or three days at a time with a harem, she spoke only words and phrases in Arabic with extremely limited conversational facility, and no Turkish. In her book she admitted that when she visited harems she had to 'first obtain permission' to take her dragoman, Hannah Misk, with her, 'blindfolded, as translator'.[10] No harem woman would have discussed intimacies through a male interpreter, even one so old and venerable as Mr Misk.

But Jane, who was a constant friendly visitor to harems up and down the country, knew all there was to know. She not only lived among the women in the desert, she was a frequent house-guest at Turkish harems and those of high-ranking Arabs. She had travelled between Damascus and Homs with harems for safety and comfort, and needed no interpreter. Her diary reveals that she acted as a sympathetic listener and counsellor, attended weddings, births burials. She was distressed when young girls were sold into what she considered to be physical slavery for a few hundred pounds, sometimes to gain the favour of a social superior. She knew all the hopes, fears, jealousies and frustrations of the women, and the arts of love they used to maintain their status, and of which they spoke of freely to her, even – to Jane's disapproval – in front of their children.

Jane's knowledge of these 'arts of love', the sexual practices of Middle Eastern women about which Richard Burton questioned her at great length, provided a basis for his unique treatise on the sexual life and thought of the Muslim and formed part of his translation of the *Arabian Nights*, especially the most contentious 'Terminal Essay'. It also provided him with information used as footnotes in the controversial manual of sexual instruction, *The Perfumed Garden* (a translation of which he was working upon when he died). Burton's biographer remarked upon the relationship between Jane Digby and Richard Burton. They were, he said,

> unique, both of them in the history of adventurous travel. This artistic, independent woman, a brilliant linguist and musician . . . her knowledge of general Arab life almost equalled his own, her acquaintance with the female side far exceeded it and many were the evenings they spent on the leafy logia at Salhiyeh, talking under the stars . . . he questioning her on the female Arab customs, on the sex intimacies of the harem . . .
>
> How much of the knowledge of Moslem female sexual psychology which was later embodied in the famous Terminal Essay to the *Arabian Nights* came from the lips of Jane Digby one can only guess, but knowing the vigorous secrecy surrounding the harem . . . and remembering the minuteness of Burton's descriptions, we must conclude that it was much.[11]

Burton's monumental annotated translation of *Arabian Nights* was, not surprisingly given the date of its publication (sixteen volumes appeared between 1885 and 1888), printed 'for private subscribers only' to avoid prosecution, and was an immediate success. At the merest suggestion of the word 'pornography', Burton retaliated with the story of Dr Johnson's reply to the lady who complained that there were rude words in his dictionary: 'Madam, you must have been looking for them!' An emasculated 'library version' of the *Arabian Nights* (excluding the 'Terminal Essay') was published after Burton's death by Isabel. Among her husband's papers Isabel found the manuscript of *The Perfumed Garden* and immediately burned it, insisting that it was incomplete and that no one else was capable of completing it as her husband intended.[12]

The first summer of the Burtons' residency in Damascus, 1870, was full of incident. According to Isabel Burton, the desert was in an uproar, and they and their entourage were often attacked or menaced on their tours around the country. Her journal entries are borne out by Burton's businesslike reports to the Foreign Office. From Jane's diary it appears no worse than usual – constant raids and danger had become so commonplace to her that she only bothered to record detail if she or Medjuel was directly involved. Her comments were thus reduced to statements such as 'the roads are too dangerous for travel at present'.

The Mezrab tribe suffered losses of animals and tents after several raids in succession by the Mowali and Hadiden tribes, but these are recorded only in passing by Jane, and without descriptive comment. However, when the Mezrabs attempted to recover their property, they were driven back by the Weis Pasha and his army of 150 heavily armed soldiers, and to this Jane reacted indignantly. The encounter also entailed both Jane and Medjuel having to return to Homs by order of the Wali, for she was now seen as having as much responsibility for the Mezrabs in any formal negotiation as her husband.

The coolness following the divorce of Ouadjid had thawed, and once again Jane rode confidently at her husband's side. However, the rumours surrounding their relationship remained, for Isabel Burton heard them: 'Gossip said that he [Medjuel] had other wives, but she assured me he had not.'[13]

The couple remained in Homs negotiating terms for the tribe until Medjuel was arbitrarily arrested and flung into jail. Knowing she had no entitlement to official protection, Jane nevertheless called upon the assistance of Richard Burton, as a friend, to achieve Medjuel's release, and he complied. 'To my great delight,' she wrote, 'Medjuel returned here on August 4th, not having *been* even to his tent.' While Jane was at Homs, her new Swiss maid, Marie, contracted typhus in Damascus and died.

Sheikh Mohammed ebn Dukhi, who a decade earlier had robbed Jane of some £3,000 worth of camels and goods, and had subsequently been bankrupted in counter-raids, now embarked upon a series of plundering raids using connections in the corrupt Turkish administration to evade arrest. He attacked the Mezrabs and carried off tents and camels, as well as seven valuable mares. Medjuel led a retaliation raid, and while she waited for news of this in September Jane wrote to Kenelm, but as usual she never bothered her family with her anxieties:

I wished to answer your letter full of interesting family news, long ago, but I, and everyone here, have been literally prostrated by the heat which has been intense this year. Added to this we have had a vast deal of *disagreements* with the hostile tribes in the desert and with the new arrangements that the Ottoman Government are making with regard to the Arabs wishing to *fix* them, each tribe in a district and if possible to induce or force them to cultivate. For example they wished to transport us, the Mezrabs, bodily to the banks of the Euphrates, far beyond Tadmor. It was only by my begging and praying our Governor General Reschid Pacha, that we escaped, as we have properties at both Damascus and Homs.[14]

Medjuel recovered four of the seven precious mares, and in return for the remaining three – already disposed of by ebn Dukhi – he took a dozen others of inferior breeding, for with the loss of revenue from Palmyra the mares were vital to the trading economy of the tribe as breeding stock. But the stolen camels and tents had been sent off deep into the southern deserts. These too were of importance to the tribe, and Medjuel was grimly determined to retrieve them.

In November 1870 Isabel Burton attended the wedding of the Wali's daughter with Jane – looking, said Isabel, 'like a beautiful oriental queen' – and the wife of the Italian consul. All three wore European ball-gowns at the request of their hostess. Their hooped skirts, tiny nipped-in waists and off-the-shoulder sleeves trimmed with rosebuds and ribbons raised many questions by the women of the harem. 'Are you not cold being thus uncovered? Is it true that strange men dance with you one after another, and put their arms around your waist? Do you not feel dreadfully ashamed?' Jane had brought a cashmere shawl to cover her shoulders when the women joined the men, but her two younger companions had to don their capes in order not to shame the men by such a display of nakedness.[15]

So much was new and exciting to Isabel Burton that she was wide-eyed with enjoyment, as indeed Jane had been in her first months in Syria. But things had already started to go wrong for the Burtons, as a long letter from Jane to Isabel warning of the undercurrents of power within the city confirms. Jane had called the previous day at the house of a leading citizen. To her dismay she heard some fellow visitors, men known to her as usurers, boasting that they had arranged for Burton to be recalled and Richard Rogers reinstated as consul because he was happy to turn a blind eye to underhand dealings in return for a consideration.

You know that Sheikh Mohammed ebn Dukhi and Faris el Meziad openly say in the desert to those who ask them 'that they only owed having won the *camel* law suit I had with them, to the considerable sum they gave *Mr Rogers*, after he told me that I had won it; and this affair – as you know – involved the loss of my British Protection which is such a serious misfortune in this country . . .

> Yours most affectionately,
> Jane Digby el Mezrab[16]

In December, Medjuel fell seriously ill with an inflammation of the liver. He was almost two months in bed, nursed continuously by Jane. His anxiety over the tribe's property stolen by the Wuld Ali made him fretful, and he was still convalescent when, at Richard Burton's suggestion, Jane convened a council of war at their home on 4 February 1871 because Medjuel was still too weak to travel to the desert.

> There had been a fight, and ebn Dukhi had robbed the Mezrabs of camels, horses and everything. Captain Burton wanted, if possible, to obtain a part restoration, but ebn Dukhi was too slippery, and though everything was promised nothing was done. One point of honour, however, was religiously kept. When the time came to eat bread and salt together, he sprang into his saddle and rode away. By that we knew he did not mean friendship with the Mezrabs.[17]

Burton tried again to bring about a pact, but was told by ebn Dukhi that he was supported in his activities by the Turkish authorities. 'This was surely impolitic on the part of the authorities . . . for ebn Dukhi owed them no allegiance while the Mezrabs had been faithful allies,' said Isabel loyally standing by Jane.

> The Mezrabs were offered £10,000 to allow a certain renegade, O'Reilly, who called himself Hassan Beg, free passage in order to raise the Desert against the Turkish Government. The Mezrabs returned the blank cheque, and gave the Government warning, and Hassan Beg and his followers were captured.[18]

In March of that year two English visitors called at the consulate and Isabel took them to see Jane. Lord Stafford and Mr Barty Mitford, later Lord Redesdale, were duly introduced and from the latter there is a vignette of Jane. Mitford had heard of the infamous Lady Ellenborough. Indeed, he wrote,

> so many stories had been told about her and her strange life as the wife of an Arab chief, that I expected to see a grand and commanding figure like the Lady Hester Stanhope of *Eothen* and Lamartine; an imposing

personage, mystic, wonderful, half queen, half sybil; Semiramis and Meg Merrilies rolled into one, ruling by the force of the eye, a horde of ignoble, ragged dependants, trembling but voracious. No two people could be more unalike. I found Lady Ellenborough – Mrs Digby, as she now calls herself – living in a European house, furnished so far . . . as the rooms in which we were received were concerned, like those of an English lady; in the desert with the tribe she would be altogether Arab . . .

The owner was like her belongings; a [reminder] of the palmy days of Almack's; dressed in inconspicuous Paris fashion and very nice to look upon . . . she had the remainder of great good looks and the most beautiful and gracious old-world manners. She had been a great beauty, but in deference to the Arabs' superstitious fear of the evil eye, her hair and eyebrows were dyed black . . .

She asked after Lord Clanwilliam, grandfather of the present Earl. How was he? 'Wonderful,' I said, 'cutting us all out skating at Highclere two or three months ago.' Lady Ellenborough looked puzzled. 'But why should he not?' she asked. 'Well!' I answered. 'You must remember that he is past seventy years of age.' 'Dear me!' she replied. 'Is it possible? That handsome young man!' Her old friends remained in her mind just as she had known them – Lady Palmerston, Lady Jersey, Lady Londonderry – still reigning beauties, queens of Almack's.

It was strange to hear a delicately nurtured English lady talking of her life in the desert with 'her' tribe. She told us how, the summer before, a hostile tribe had raided them and stolen some of their mares, and how this next summer they must ride out to avenge the outrage and get back the lost treasures. There would be fierce fighting, she said, and she must be there to nurse the chief should anything happen to him. 'In fact,' she added, 'we have one foot in the stirrup, for we must start for the desert tomorrow morning . . .'[19]

Jane never explained why she dyed her hair black, though she had begun dyeing it when she found she was going grey, before she married Medjuel. However, even today, fair or blond hair is not welcomed among the bedouin, chiefly because it is regarded as so beautiful that it will attract bad luck.[20] Mitford found Medjuel, who was still convalescent, disappointing and ordinary-looking. 'Nevertheless, she seemed very fond and proud of him, and evidently in this wild nomadic life between the desert and Damascus, she had found a happy haven . . . after the adventures of her stormy youth.'[21]

That year marked Jane's sixty-fourth birthday. Isabel Burton wrote that she was still 'beautiful . . . commanding and queen-like, a *grande-dame* to her fingertips as [though] she had just left the salons of London or Paris . . . she looked splendid in oriental dress, and if you saw her as a Moslem woman in a bazaar you would have said she was not more than thirty-four years of age.'[22]

Several anecdotes concerning Jane during this period survive; they were recounted to E. M. Oddie in 1930. One visitor to the Mezrabs' house was extremely impressed with the exquisite taste of the furnishings. Not realising her hostess was within earshot, she said aloud, 'All this for a barbarian.' 'But he isn't a barbarian really,' Jane objected mildly behind her guest. 'He's just learning to use a knife and fork!'[23]

The other story illustrates Medjuel's sense of humour. Two missionaries, the Reverend Mott and the Reverend Parry, called on Jane. Mr Mott ran a mission in Beirut. Mr Parry had been the chaplain at Pisa; it was his assistant who was tutor to Leonidas at the time the child was killed, and Mr Parry had conducted the funeral. Now he was visiting Syria and was taken to visit Jane. As the men dismounted outside Jane's house Mr Mott noticed a bedouin standing in the gateway and, speaking in Arabic, called him over, ordering him to look after the horses while they visited the *Sitt*.

Mr Parry was extremely unhappy about this arrangement and, speaking in English, pointed out that they did not know who this Arab was, that the horses were valuable and the man might be a thief. Mott agreed it was perhaps not wise, but said it would appear discourteous to go back on his instruction. The two men called on Jane, and she and Mr Parry sat talking of Leonidas and mutual acquaintances in Italy. After a while an Arab came into the room and Jane introduced him to the men as her husband. To their consternation it was the Arab with whom they had left the horses. Speaking in English, Medjuel did not betray them, but smiled as he said: 'Gentlemen, I have handed your horses over to one of my servants. I assure you they will be quite safe!'[24]

In June 1871 Jane heard of her daughter-in-law's death. Charles Venningen had been concerned about Gabrielle's health ever since Heribert had married her. She had had three children, and her father-in-law had almost borne each one for the fragile girl. But her death was the result of an extraordinary accident: Gabrielle had slipped while walking downstairs carrying her knitting, and as she fell one of the knitting needles had pierced her spine. The sad news must have set Jane thinking about her own mortality, for on the following day, 15 June, she went to see Richard Burton about her will: 'I went to the Consulate and signed my will in the presence of Captain

Burton, and my good friends Mr Wright, and Mr Scott as witnesses.'

In July the temperature reached 170 degrees Fahrenheit, 105 degrees in the coolest shade. There was not a breath of air anywhere day or night, Isabel Burton wrote. The eyeballs seemed on fire, the tongue, throat and chest were parched, food or sleep was impossible. A pan of water set out in the sun was hot enough to boil an egg within a short time.[25] The Burtons went to Bludan in the mountains to escape the worst of it. Jane missed her friend but she had many things to occupy her mind: calling upon officials to try to obtain justice for the tribe over the Mohammed ebn Dukhi affair; the repurchase of some of the land she had sold with her large villa and 'the prettiest part of my old garden including the Sheikh's fountain. We began making a separating wall between our garden and the rest. The heat is intense just now, but we are well thank God. I am much, much too, occupied with my garden, building and improvements.'

Isabel Burton was warm-hearted, energetic, loyal and adventurous. She was also arrogant, pretentious, impulsive and capricious. She had the instinct of a present-day tabloid journalist when it came to gaining favour for her husband, and her pen was hardly ever still on his behalf. She was utterly besotted by and devoted to Richard Burton, and would have followed him into a volcano had he suggested it. Once when they were alone in the desert they were charged by a *ghazou* of a hundred horsemen, lances couched and pointed at them. Burton told her to sit tight and not flinch. 'They will stop two feet from you,' he told her. 'If you turn and run they will kill you, but if you face them with me they will say you have the heart of a lion.' She obeyed, glad that he had warned her. 'The whole tribe charged with their lances couched . . . we reined in and stood stock still. As soon as they got within a few yards . . . they lowered their lances and opened their ranks to enclose us, jumped off their horses, kissed our hands and galloped us in.'[26]

She endured every danger, every privation, every hardship Burton ever asked of her, and they were many, and she was pleased to do it for love of him. However, bolstered by Isabel's unqualified and continuous approval, Burton saw no reason to compromise. He ignored flattery and sycophants, and refused all gifts, even a basket of fruit for his wife. Many members of the Syrian community were adversely affected by Burton's Solomon-like judgements, especially those who held their rank by corruption and bribery. Even over-zealous missionaries felt the discomfort of his scathing remarks.

Consequently he made many powerful enemies. Though Burton's behaviour was moral, it was often undiplomatic, and it upset his senior colleague, the British consul-general in Beirut, a man of little ability but greater tact.

With his enemies, including Reschid Pasha, agitating for Burton's dismissal, it was inevitable that he would be recalled despite the loyal support of many upright citizens.[27] Burton had been travelling in the northern parts of his consular territory when he received his formal recall, and he left directly for Beirut and England to put his case. Isabel, left in Damascus, received the telegram famous for its brevity. 'I AM RECALLED PAY PACK AND FOLLOW.'[28] Jane was naturally upset. Burton was a good man to have in the consulate, from her point of view, and Isabel had been a good friend. On 18 August 1871 she wrote in her diary: 'The news is confirmed, and the Burtons go. This is very bad news for me, for they were most kind and sincere friends and many a pleasant hour have I passed in their society which I shall always remember.'

On hearing of Burton's departure, Medjuel wrote to him. It is the only known surviving letter by Medjuel, and it is noticeable that he uses the royal plural when referring to himself:

Jemadi 7 A.H. 1286

To His Excellency Captain Burton

After sending you most affectionate greetings, and the great affection we offer your Excellency, it was our misfortune that we did not see you when you came to our house, and we are very sorry for it. After we heard of your going to England, grief and sorrow came heavily upon us because we have never seen any one equal to your Excellency in this country.

All those related to England are deeply indebted to you – and all the denominations, Moslem and Christian, were fully satisfied with your Excellency; and they are all very sorry at your leaving. But we ask the Lord of Mercy to send you back to us in good health, and to let us meet you soon.

From us and our brothers who send their greetings, and from all the Bedouin who send their best salaams. Whatever you wish us to do, tell us to do it.

... Peace be with you.
Medjuel el Mezrab[29]

During the next three weeks Jane spent several days assisting Isabel, riding to Salhiyeh on Midjioumah to help her pack. On the

day of the sale of the Burtons' animals and effects Jane rode with
Isabel into the hills so that the younger woman would not have to
witness the break-up of her home.

> *Monday September 11th 1871.* Mrs Burton . . . came and breakfasted here
> and spent the day. How I regret their departure and how I shall miss
> her lively, friendly society.
> *Tuesday 12th.* I went and spent the day at Salhiyeh with Mrs Burton. My
> last day [with her], and at night we parted, probably never to meet again
> . . . notwithstanding her hopes of his return here as Consul-General.

Isabel decided to leave at night in order to avoid a rumoured demonstration of support by those who felt aggrieved at the treatment of
her husband. Abd el Khader and Jane were therefore the only two
people present at her secret departure:

> they accompanied me as far as the city gates where I bid them an affection-
> ate farewell. The parting with Lady Ellenborough affected me greatly. I
> was the poor thing's only woman friend. As she wrung my hand these
> were her last words. 'Do not forget your promise if I die and we should
> never meet again.' I replied, 'Inshallah, I shall soon return.' She rode a
> black thoroughbred mare, and as far as I could see anything in the moon-
> light, her large sorrowful blue eyes glistening with tears, haunted me . . .
> I stole away from Damascus an hour before dawn.[30]

Isabel's seemingly innocuous account of her parting with Jane
would later prove to be controversial. Jane was certainly present at
a night-time parting, according to her own diary, though a pedant
might cavil about the time, for the gates of the city were unlikely
to be open between dusk and dawn. She was undoubtedly riding
Midjioumah, her black, sure-footed, favourite mare. And it was more
than possible that at the loss of her friend she had tears in her eyes.
She shared with her mother, the handsome Lady Andover, an unusual
talent to shed large glittering tears, making her eyes appear even
more beautiful. But it was not this that would provoke indignation.
Nor would the statement 'I was the poor thing's only woman friend'.
In fact Jane was especially fond of Isabel because she was English,
but she had many other women friends, even if they were not English
and not of her rank; what Isabel really meant was that Jane was *her*
only woman friend. However, what caused the future controversy was
that curious final statement that Isabel attributed to Jane: 'Do not
forget your promise if I die . . .'

23

Untimely Obituary
1871–1878

The loss of the Burtons was sad but it made little difference to Jane's life. There were the same daily visits, the same members of Damascene society attended her European-style dinners; and when Medjuel entertained, which was far more often, it was in the Arab-style reception hall, with floor cushions and food served on large brass platters on low tables.

On those occasions Jane, veiled and dressed in bedouin clothes, would receive the guests, withdrawing to eat with any wives who had accompanied their husbands. She returned to pour water over the hands of Medjuel's guests between courses, and to serve coffee, sherbets and narghiles. The women might or might not join the men for conversation afterwards. Jane never attempted to impose European culture upon her guests, as Isabel Burton, confident that her way was best, had done. Isabel expected men to rise when she entered a room or stood up, to be waited upon with refreshments by men at dinner and could not resist telling Arab wives how 'it was done' in England. Eventually she was told courteously but firmly by a male visitor, 'Pray, Mrs Burton, do not teach our women things they do not know and never saw.'[1]

By October 1871 the extensions to Jane's house were complete. Additional fountains and a further piece of land extended the gardens around the house, which impressed a constant stream of visitors from Europe. She heard several times from the Burtons, with details of their new appointment in Trieste. But one letter brought back a ghost of the past.

Thursday 18th January 1872. I received a letter from Isabel confirming Lord Ellenborough's death on the 23rd December last, on dear Madre's birthday. She would have been 95 if still alive, and Lord Ellenborough was 82!!!! This news moved me with all kinds of sad remembrances. I felt sad and low as days and years long past, rose up before me . . .

In the late spring of 1872 Medjuel was summoned to Homs by the Wali but after several months of negotiations he was at stalemate. The Wali tore up a petition regarding territory that Medjuel, his brothers and several other sheikhs presented, although it had been at the Wali's instigation and invitation that they presented it. When, by August, the matter still detained Medjuel in Homs, Jane set off alone to join him. Better to face the danger of the roads in the heat of high summer than be parted from him, she concluded. He was at the tents near Hamah when she arrived at their house, but she sent a message and on 20 August he 'suddenly arrived back looking ill and worn, and his beard quite grey. Nothing is finished of his affairs with Daas and the Hessienne.'

Jane was annoyed when shortly afterwards the Wali, who had caused Medjuel such trouble, cast his eyes longingly upon Midjioumah. The mare was Jane's favourite horse, still one of the fastest horses in the desert, and showy. But a request from the Wali was almost a royal command, and Jane had no option but to treat with his dragoman for what was little more than an enforced sale at £120. 'Midjioumah, dear Midjioumah is gone! And for twenty pounds less than promised on account of her little spavin. I am very vexed.' A few days later, when the Wali summoned Medjuel, for the first time holding out hope that he might look upon Medjuel's tribal business with favour, Jane wrote resignedly that 'dear Midjioumah has accomplished her mission'. Some weeks later, when the Wali left for Constantinople, Midjioumah was part of his train, but Medjuel's problem was still not resolved.

It is not given to many to read their own obituaries, although there are several famous examples, but on Friday 14 March 1873 the *Morning Post* in London carried a story under the headline 'A Remarkable Career':

From a correspondent at Beyrout.
I met today an old acquaintance, the camel-driver Sheikh Abdul, and he told me that his wife had died. Abdul's wife was no common woman; her name was once known throughout Europe. Sheikh Abdul is the ninth husband of Lady Ellenborough, whom I met for the first time 30 years

ago in Munich, just after she had eloped with Prince Schwarzenberg from the residence of her first husband. She then went to Italy where . . . she got married six times in succession. All these unions were dissolved after a short duration.

In 1848 I met her at Athens where she concluded an eighth marriage with the Greek Colonel, Colonel Thodoki, however only for a short time. Her affections were now bestowed on an old Palikar chieftain, for whom she built a beautiful house at Athens. When her latest marriage was dissolved she went to the Levant. During a journey from Beyrout to Damascas she got pleased with the camel driver Sheikh Abdul and selected him for the ninth husband. She was married to him after the Arab fashion and . . .

There was more nonsense in a similar vein. Unfortunately, the story was picked up and reported by other papers including *The Times*, for Jane's name had appeared in the press on and off since the death of Lord Ellenborough fifteen months earlier. A new generation had taken an interest in the story of this 'wild and lovely creature' who had been once the 'exclusive Lady Ellenborough' and who now lived the exotic life of (depending on whose version one read) a camel driver's wife, a desert princess or an eccentric recluse similar to Hester Stanhope.

Jane had returned to Damascus on 12 December 1872. Had she been in the desert with the tribe, rumours of her death might have been understandable. But she had been going about in Homs and Damascus visiting people quite normally. She could only think that someone wished her ill when she first heard of the reports, thinking that they were a continuation of the stories run after Lord Ellenborough's death.

But her family, having not heard from her for some months, were anxious. Although they did not believe the reports and sent a notice to this effect to *The Times* pending definite information from Syria, there was no immediate way of verifying the report of her death. Her English friends such as Emily Beaufort, who had spent months in Damascus and gone to Palmyra with Jane in 1859, were equally concerned. Emily, now Lady Strangford, having married a noble reviewer of her book about Syria, wrote to Edward Digby for confirmation, or otherwise, of the report of Jane's death.

62 Montague Square
April 4th 1873

Dear Lord Digby,

You will probably be surprised at receiving this letter as you must long ago have forgotten the visit you and Lady Digby paid me in 1862 shortly after my marriage. I however, well remember the warm kindness with which you expressed yourselves regarding the pages I published about the excellent Arab gentleman (I might say nobleman) your sister had married . . .

I have just seen Mrs Burton's (well meant) letter in the Pall Mall Gazette in which I think *she* believes [the reports of Jane's death] to be a fact . . . When I first knew [your sister] I knew nothing whatsoever of her previous history – she herself told me of it before we parted. But by that time I had learned to love and admire her for what I saw her to be. She was in a difficult situation for one less unselfish, less devoted than she was, to fill worthily. How she *did* fill it, only a few people truly know.

She carried out a simple, unaffected, quiet, useful and beautiful life, finding happiness in doing good to all she came near, amply repaid by her husband's love and the affectionate respect of all who really knew her. I have heard of the lies told of her . . . and I know the value of each. I know too that some hurt her, and gently she bore them. Her grateful, loving friendship for those who loved and respected her was touching in its tenderness.[2]

The letter by Isabel Burton to which Emily Strangford referred had appeared in many leading newspapers and magazines throughout Europe, including *The Times* and *Pall Mall Gazette* in London. It was written from Trieste and dated 19 March, when reports of Jane's death reached Italy. Isabel had rushed to defend Jane, at the same time ensuring that she stamped her proprietorship on a sure-fire bestselling biography of a contemporary figure.

Sir,

Will you allow me to contradict the correspondent at Beyrout who writes concerning the late Lady Ellenborough? I scarcely know where to begin, but I must do it to keep my promise to her.

I lived for two years at Damascus while my husband, Captain Burton was Consul there and in daily intercourse with the subject of this paragraph. Knowing that after her death all sorts of untruths would appear in the papers, very painful to her family, she wished me to write her biography, and gave me an hour a day until it was accomplished. She did not spare herself, dictating the bad with the same frankness as the good. I was pledged not to publish this until after her death and that of certain relatives. But I am in a position to state that there is a grain of truth to a ton of falsehood in the paragraph from Beyrout, and inasmuch as Beyrout is only 72 miles from Damascus the writer must know that as well as I do. It must have come from a very common source when such English as this is used, 'Between Beyrout and Damascus she *got pleased* with the camel-driver'! It suggests a discharged Lady's maid.

I left Damascus just a year and a half ago, in the middle of the night, and she was the last friend to see me out of the city . . . her last words were 'Do not forget your promise if I die and we never meet again.' I cannot meddle with the past without infringing on the biography confided to me, but I can say a few words concerning her life dating from her arrival in the East about sixteen years ago, as told me by herself and those living there . . .

Lady Ellenborough arrived at Beyrout and went to Damascus, where she arranged to go to Bagdad across the desert. A Bedouin escort for this journey was necessary and as the Mezrab tribe occupied the ground the duty of commanding the escort developed upon Sheikh Medjuel, a younger brother of Sheikh Mohammed . . . on the journey the young sheikh fell in love with this beautiful woman who possessed all the qualities that could fire the Arab imagination. Even two years ago she was more attractive than half the young girls of our time. It ended by his proposing to divorce his Moslem wives and to marry her; to pass half the year in Damascus (which to him was like London or Paris would be to us) for her pleasure, and half in the desert to lead his natural life.

. . . She was married in spite of all opposition made by her friends and the British Consulate . . . according to Mohammedan law, changed her name to the Honourable Mrs Digby el Mezrab and was horrified when she found she had lost her nationality by her marriage and had become a Turkish subject . . . In Damascus . . . we Europeans all flocked around her with affection and friendship. The natives the same. She only received those who brought a letter of introduction . . . but this did not stop every ill conditioned passer by from boasting of his intimacy with the House of Mezrab . . . to sell his book or newspaper at a better profit.

She understood friendship in its best and fullest sense and . . . it was a treat to pass the hours with her. She spoke French, Italian, German, Slav, Spanish, Arabic, Turkish and Greek as she spoke her native tongue . . . Her heart was noble, she was charitable to the poor . . . she fulfilled all the duties of a good Christian lady and an Englishwoman . . . She had but one fault (and who knows if it was hers?)

washed out by fifteen years of goodness and repentance. She is dead
. . . let us shame those who seek to drag up the adventures of her wild
youth to tarnish so good a memory . . .

Isabel Burton

Jane received anxious letters from her family at roughly the same
time that Isabel Burton's letter was brought to her attention. She was
annoyed for the sake of her brothers and their families but felt that
the damage was limited, for surely, she reasoned, no one could be
interested in such old history. But this letter by Isabel Burton was a
different matter. She wrote immediately to Isabel denying the reports
of her death, and requesting an explanation of the claim that Isabel
had been asked to write an official biography. And when she received
an answer she wrote to Edward's wife to explain:

Damascus
May 21st 73

My dearest Theresa
. . . You may conceive that I have been intensely annoyed . . . the
announcement of my death was nothing. I am not superstitious and
no newspaper will kill me a minute before the appointed time, but the
raking up of so much that is painful to all connected with me, so
uninteresting to the present generation . . . A general outcry against
the author (whoever he was) has been raised. Mr Green, the Consul,
receiving many letters from people of rank not personally known to
him expressing . . . indignation. I myself have received kind letters
from Lady Ely, Lord Howard de Walden and others.

Today I received one from Mrs Burton from Trieste, explaining the
reasons for her 'Defence; the keeping people at bay by telling them that
she possessed the real biography, and to prevent any more being said
upon the subject' . . . I certainly *always* deprecated every idea of pub-
lishing anything relating to myself or my former existence, as you can
easily believe, and I never spoke to her at all on the subject except to
answer some of her general queries as to what the world of that day
knew, positively denying some other histories that people have forged.
And as to *begging* her to remember her *promise* after my death of *justifying*
me, it is pure error; she knew the horror and aversion I have to this
kind of thing.

Isabel Burton suffered the embarrassment of a public denial of her
claim in the *Pall Mall Gazette* by William Wright, formerly one of
Richard Burton's greatest supporters. The Reverend Wright stated
that he had received a letter from Jane in her own handwriting,

categorically denying that she provided Mrs Burton with information for a biography or extracted any promise in this respect.[3]

All summer Jane was alone while Medjuel spent months in Homs negotiating with the new Wali. To her relief, however, compensation was agreed. She spent a great deal of time answering correspondence, since the newspaper stories provoked letters from many old acquaintances. Having been embarrassed, Isabel maintained silence until after Jane's death, and then – contrary to what she had written to Jane, that her claim had been an attempt to stop others writing lies – she insisted afresh that Jane *had* given her the story and *had* made her promise to write her biography.

With his affairs now reaching some semblance of good order Medjuel decided to sell one of his two houses at Homs. Once he had accomplished that, he began to spend far more time at Damascus with Jane. The pace of life began to slow and, now nearing seventy, Jane did not mind. She still loved to accompany Medjuel to the desert for three or four weeks in the spring and autumn, but remained wary of seeing Ouadjid. Despite this she felt sympathy for the girl when her brother died. 'Poor Ouadjid, her troubles are certainly great,' she wrote, imagining how she would feel had she received news of Kenelm's or Edward's death.[4]

In Damascus, Jane still rode around the city and worked in her garden. She was deeply attached to her little white lap-dog, Petit, and her two cats, the Persian Pitsch-Witsch and the grey Misky. Servants were constantly being reprimanded or dismissed, for laziness, dishonesty, lying or sexual indiscretion, and it is difficult to keep up with the recurring changes in her household that are detailed in her diary. Some retainers who had been with her from the start were becoming too old to work, and these were pensioned off. She frequently lamented having to train a new housekeeper, but no one would ever take the place of Eugénie.

There were family losses in the years that followed. Among the first was her sister-in-law Theresa, who had taken over from Steely in filling Jane's commissions, though the shopping lists had grown smaller over the years. Kenelm's delicate daughter Lucy died, but she had been so ill for years, Emmie wrote, that the poor girl was almost pleased to die.

Wednesday July 15th, 1874. I received a sad letter from Heribert with (to me) most melancholy intelligence of the Baron's sudden death on horseback in the Hofgarten at Munich ... on Wednesday 10th June at half past eight in the morning ... The place where we first met and where we so often rode together in long bygone days! How quickly life passes.

The baron had remained faithful to the last, writing regularly right up to his death, always keeping Jane up to date with the progress of their children. Bertha had deteriorated over the years and from the age of twenty-five was completely insane, spending the remainder of her life in an asylum with her own suite of rooms and personal servants. Yet of Heribert and his three children Charles was immensely proud. Though Jane's defection ruined his life, the baron remained loyal, courteous and affectionate. He never remarried and many times told Jane that were she in trouble he would come to her or she could come to him. It was difficult for Jane to imagine him as an old man; she had not seen him for over thirty years and the lasting image was, she wrote, of the handsome, sandy-haired cavalier who had wooed her with such serious ardour that she had finally married him despite herself.[5]

But there were happy memories too. In May 1874 Richard Wood, the British consul who had tried so hard to persuade Jane not to travel to Palmyra and not to marry Medjuel, came to visit her. They were both amused when they looked back twenty years. There was a new consul now, a Mr T. S. Jago, who admired Jane and respected her husband. In May 1876 she was delighted to receive a visit from an old friend. She had first met him as a young officer in her father's command; he had conveyed her by a Naval ship to Italy from Athens after Spiros' departure from her life, and he had – at her request, when she visited London in 1856 – found a place on one of his ships for her nephew Henry.

> dear, kind old friend Admiral Drummond, now in command of our squadron in the Mediterranean! I gave him a horse to ride, but it was all the civility I could show him, having no cook ... I enjoyed a long conversation and heard plenty of news, private and public. [He was] so serious, so sincere, so kindly ... I hope the Turkish crisis past he may come here again. How refreshing to see again kind, good friends.[6]

A few months later, there came an extraordinary visitor, perhaps fulfilling the prophecy by a fortune-teller in Paris forty years earlier that Jane would captivate three kings.

Friday 17th. The Emperor of Brazil called on me at the early hour of six in the morning! ... Of all the pleasantest royalties I have ever come across he is the pleasantest. We exchanged photographs at his request, but I rather regretted parting with the Cheikh's by Karl Haag, and hope I may replace it.

One visitor who would not be put off was a visiting diplomat, Sir Edwin Pears, who longed to see her and 'determined' to do so, having heard through Carl Haag of Jane and her unique marriage to Medjuel, who, the diplomat wrote, was 'utterly devoted to her service'.

The difficulty which I anticipated was in getting to see her. Happily I was well acquainted with [Mr Heald] the director of a bank who had to go twice a year from Beyrout to Damascus to pay her her private income of, I believe £3,000 a year. My friend . . . told me that she refused to see any European, and that she had even ceased going to the English Church Service . . . but he would do his best . . . [The] Bedouins were devoted to her, and she exercised remarkable influence over her husband and his men.[7]

Jane's banker Mr Heald, accompanied by his diplomat visitor, called on her, sending in his own name only. The two men were shown into the drawing-room but when Jane came in she was affronted to see an unannounced visitor. Mr Heald explained that it was his friend's first visit to the city and that he could hardly leave him waiting in the street. With her permission, he suggested, Sir Edwin would wait at the other end of the room while they conducted their business. Sir Edwin was a watercolour artist and happily spent the time looking at Jane's pictures. Later when Jane came to join him out of courtesy, he chatted to her, praising one of the pictures, saying that the artist had caught the atmosphere of the desert.

She was interested in my criticism and recognising that I knew something of the subject informed me that the picture in question was painted by her. That broke the ice. We got into an interesting conversation, which ended by her stating that she would have tea on the table every day at 5 o'clock and would be very pleased to see me any day during the week I proposed to spend in Damascus. She then sent for her husband and introduced us. We became excellent friends and by this means I was able to get into various mosques and see other sights which I should not have seen but for his assistance.

I found her a close observer, an excellent talker, with keen flashes of insight and wit, and what interested me most of all, with an experience of harem life of which she spoke frankly, of quite an exceptional character. The women of the harem, said she, had about them the delightfulness of children, their employments were simple but genuine. Their passionate love of flowers constantly appealed to her, but there was another side to their character. There was the childishness of children which became imbecility ... sudden bursts of anger, swift reconciliation, passionate affection and even hate.

The worst part of their character related to their sensuality. They had no pleasures corresponding to those in Europe, no music, no literature, no social intercourse with others. The result ... was a gross sensuality which showed itself in the language even [superior] ladies would employ. Subjects were spoken of even in the presence of children, about which all Christian races agree to be silent.

He asked her about the Mezrabs and she recounted a recent occasion when the entire tribe had descended on her in Damascus, believing Medjuel had summoned them. They filled the house sleeping on the stairs and in all the rooms, she said, intending to amuse him. He asked her if she had not been afraid.

She immediately retorted that she was greatly alarmed, but not as I appeared to think, at anything her husband's tribe would do. Her fear was that some of the many Turkish soldiery near her house would make some remark derogatory to her, in which case, she said, not a Turk in the neighbourhood would have been left alive.

On mentioning this story to my friend he said he entirely believed it because the attachment of the Bedouins to her was passionate, and each would have been ready to die for her. She was the only woman whom the Arabs would permit to ride upon a horse ... I gained the impression that under different circumstances she might have exerted a most valuable influence in any society into which she had been thrown.[8]

Jane's stepson Afet often stayed at the house. He proudly owned Jane as his mother, and indeed described himself as half-English. He had three wives by the time he was twenty but the first, whom Jane thought the best, died young of some nameless illness in the desert. 'And now he has two, an increase and bother in every way. He has come with debts of £30 which he expects his father to pay,' Jane grumbled. But in fact she was very fond of him and fretted a great deal when he became ill, terrified that Medjuel would lose his remaining son. There are many references in her interminable lists to small gifts for Afet and his wives, and for Aafteh, Medjuel's daughter, who was married to the young Sheikh Meshur of the Gomussa tribe which, like the Mezrab, were allied with the Sebbah.

Age had scarcely diminished Jane's horsemanship. 'I rode Missouada to Salhiyeh at quite a canter. She is very pretty and has many good qualities as to character, but her legs and back are defective in strength which does not suit me and I fear I must try to get another,' she wrote at the age of seventy. The result was a pretty white mare, in foal and 'a bit frisky', which became for a while her favourite and named Nourah in honour of a previous good horse.

Mr Jago, the consul, and his wife became good friends of Jane's and took over the ordering of commissions from Europe which they shipped through the consulate. Nothing seemed too much trouble for them. Privately Jane was not impressed with the new-style dresses that arrived, with narrow underskirts and horse-hair bustles with demi-trains. 'I think the present fashions detestable from their expense and heaviness, and they are impractical into the bargain,' she wrote.

In January 1878 a young English couple came to Syria to locate the best Arab horses for an Arabian stud. They were Mr Wilfred Scawen Blunt and his lovely, intelligent wife Lady Anne, who were making an extended honeymoon tour. Anne Blunt was the only grand-daughter of the poet Byron, and in common with Jane she had a great knowledge of, and affinity with, horses. Her husband, a mesmeric personality, was a poet; he was also a womaniser and eventually made his wife's life deeply unhappy.

The Blunts' strategy for obtaining breeding stock was to go into the desert to buy from the bedouins who bred the horses. They wished to acquire the original old blood-lines with a provenance beyond dispute. In March 1878 they were the guests of one of the Anazeh tribes of whom the chief was Jane's old rival, Mohammed ebn Dukhi. While travelling with ebn Dukhi's tribe the Wuld Ali towards Damascus, the Blunts came upon the Gomussa and Mezrab tents. Afet was with the tribe and in the belief that he was a British subject through his stepmother naturally introduced himself to his compatriots, and invited them to stay with his parents in Damascus.[9] It was not the first time the Blunts had heard of Jane. Several weeks earlier they had found a young boy, the son of a sheikh, playing with an exquisitely decorated gun; he told them he had been given it by the Sitt el Mezrab.

> we have constantly heard her spoken of in the desert, and always in terms of respect . . . Medjuel himself is talked of as a supremely fortunate man, the possessor of boundless wealth, though some think his marriage a *mésalliance* as the lady is not of Arab blood and therefore not *asil*.[10]

A week later they arrived in Damascus and met Medjuel and Jane while they were visiting Abd el Khader. Medjuel, who was aged about fifty at the time, was described as 'a slight man . . . with extremely small hands and feet . . . carefully well dressed and has extremely good manners'. Of Jane, who had decided that the latest fashions were not for her and dressed in a simple though old-fashioned style, Lady Anne wrote:

> Mrs Digby has the traces of great beauty and now, even with the most unfavourable style of dress, she appears a person of distinction. She makes the great mistake of adopting the Arab fashion of blacking the rim all round the eyes and darkening the eyebrows, and I believe dying her hair . . . black. She wore a cap with some lilac and white flowers . . . and a dress of ecru-coloured soft silk with bows of its own shade, and with an underskirt of dark plum colour. In the street she wears a black lace Spanish veil over her head.
>
> Her manner is perfectly quiet, dignified and unassuming and I found her extremely amiable and even cordial . . . she invited me to her house tomorrow to see her drawings of Palmyra and other places. We had much interesting conversation.[11]

Jane told Anne Blunt a great deal about Arab life and customs, as well as describing the Governor Midhat Pasha's behaviour within his harem – 'depravities,' wrote Lady Anne, 'things that cannot be written, and of the generally rotten state of Moslem society as far as women are concerned'.[12] Jane had never been able to accept the lot of women in harems, who were kept in ignorance and fear in an unhappy hothouse of sexual rivalry.

The Blunts spent just over two weeks in Damascus. When the time came for them to leave, Jane and Anne were already starting to become fast friends. Lady Anne visited Jane and Medjuel's house frequently during their time in Damascus, and was always received in the pretty drawing-room. Her marriage to Blunt was to be a disaster and she was envious of the obviously tender relationship between Jane and Medjuel, marvelling at how 'he appeared to me, to pay great attention to her smallest wish and this without any particular show, noticing what she wanted before she asked for it'.[13] After viewing Jane's Palmyra sketches 'we went down to the yard and saw the pelican, which has lived there for three years, feeding on liver. It is not winged or clipped but never tries to go away and is in capital plumage.'[14]

The Blunts also interrogated Medjuel, drawing heavily on his comprehensive knowledge of the history of Arab horses and of the bedouin tribes – information that was subsequently used by the Burtons in several books. The pedigree of the old breeds were passed from generation to generation in oral form; there was no other record. Medjuel gave them 'a great deal of valuable advice' and is acknowledged as a major source in the magnum opus of the Blunts' daughter (Judith, Lady Wentworth), *The Authentic Arabian Horse*. Anne Blunt saw and respected in Medjuel the qualities that had caught Jane's interest. She commented that his build was that of a desert nobleman: 'the Bedouin Arab of pure blood is seldom more than five feet six inches high'.

> Desert matters occupy all his thoughts, and are of course to us of all important interest at the moment . . . I understand he is so much disgusted by the course of tribal politics . . . that he might resign in favour of his son Afet. In that case they might continue, as now, living partly at Damascus and partly in tents, and always a providence to their tribe whom they supply with all the necessities of Bedouin life, and guns, revolvers, and ammunition besides. The Mezrab, therefore, though [a small tribe] are always well mounted and better armed than any of their fellows, and can own their own in all the war-like adventures of the Sebbah.[15]

When the Blunts left it was with the reluctance of parting friends. But they left a promise that they would return to Damascus at the end of the year when they intended to make a longer journey around the desert.

24

Sunset Years
1878–1881

Jane's letters to her family are packed with chatty information. She wrote of the tribe, the desert politics that were so annoying to Medjuel, gardening matters and riding, threats of plague or cholera which were an annual worry, and European politics in which she took an intelligent interest.

These had become the fabric of her life. She no longer joined the tribe for the long winter *scherrak* [trek into the Baghdad desert], even though she was still reasonably fit and upright. In the desert she had always made a point of eating and drinking only when the bedouin did. During Ramadan this entailed no food or drink between sunrise and sunset. At other times she lived for weeks on irregular meals of camel's milk, rice and dates, tasting meat only on the rare occasion when an animal was slaughtered for a celebration, or to welcome visitors. But though she enjoyed camel's milk it is a purgative, and her constitution could no longer function for long periods on this diet, to which the bedouin with their evolutionary inheritance were tolerant. Occasionally the old rumours of Medjuel having another wife resurfaced and when he was away on business and the tribe were in their summer encampment, still the spectre of Ouadjid worried Jane.

> *Friday May 14th, 1878.* The post came but there was no letter for me. Medjuel has not received my last letter on account of the post being robbed. An abyss of jealousies pass through my head, with Ouadjid . . . so near Homs!

Her passionate love for Medjuel was undiminished by the years and on the day after this diary entry the jealousy she was never able to control soared to a crescendo. She learned from Afet that, before Medjuel's marriage to Ouadjid, Schebibb had quarrelled with his father, saying he thought it was not right for Medjuel to marry Ouadjid without first telling Jane. As a result Medjuel had 'cursed poor Schebibb and even wished him dead!' Many in the tribe had heard the quarrel. Medjuel's guilt after the death of his son must have been great, for curses are highly regarded by the bedouin. But Jane's mind ran on a single track where Medjuel was concerned, despite the fact that the younger woman had been divorced in Jane's favour. 'All this proves to me how he, Medjuel, must have loved her!!! I sent him a telegram today, half maddened by suspicion and jealousy.'[1]

To crown the misery she was feeling, Anton, her French gardener, seeing her upset and guessing because of the servants' gossip that it was because of Medjuel, suddenly declared he was madly in love with her. 'Preposterous and ridiculous!' Jane exploded in her diary. 'His head has been turned by novel-reading! I earnestly pray that God will take this trial from me.' It did not occur to her to regard the declaration as a compliment; she merely worried that a difficult situation was now bound to occur between her and the best gardener she had had for many years.[2] In fact Anton remained in her employment until her death.

Despite Jane's angry cable, Medjuel was away for a further three months, and his late return in mid-September was only partly explained by a fever he had caught in August. He was nursed on that occasion by a Scottish missionary friend of Jane's, Mary Mackintosh, who wrote that he had been desperately ill when he came to her for help *en route* to Damascus. Prior to that date, he explained, tribal business and ophthalmia had delayed his return.

That year, 1878, was the most bloodthirsty anybody would remember, and Afet took an active part in the fighting. At one point in a battle the chief of one of the noblest families in the desert, Sheikh ebn Jendall of the Roallah tribe, hereditary enemies of the Sebbah, was pursued by Mohammed ebn Dukhi's men into a group of tents commanded by Afet. As there was a blood feud between the Jendall and Dukhi families, his case was desperate. However, according to bedouin tradition, a man can yield honourably and ask an enemy for asylum, and ebn Jendall knew Afet to be of an old and honourable family who would respect the old traditions. Afet immediately accepted the man's surrender and covered him with his cloak to indicate that ebn Jendall was his prisoner and under his protection. But, to the great horror of everyone, one of Mohammed Dukhi's sons decided that in a blood feud no asylum was sacred. He dragged ebn Jendall out of the tent and slew him before Afet's eyes. It was undoubtedly cold-blooded murder and the tribes were outraged and apprehensive at the indifference towards the code of honour of ebn Dukhi's men.[3]

Medjuel's own part in these battles left him tired and ill. Even so, Jane worried that he had been seeing Ouadjid. Why else, she asked herself, should he not have sent for her when he knew he was going to be apart from her for such a long period?[4] It did not occur to her, apparently, that Medjuel may have thought a desert war conducted in summer temperatures of up to 140 degrees Fahrenheit was beyond his seventy-year-old wife. In fact Medjuel was still ill with fever when he arrived in Damascus and Jane had to send for a doctor. In his company and his loving attentiveness her fears subsided, and the following weeks were as delightful as ever, Medjuel escorting her to Saliyeh to visit friends, look at gardens, or offer veterinary advice.

In December 1878 the Blunts returned to Syria. During the journey to Damascus, Anne read Isabel Burton's book, *The Inner Life of Syria, Palestine and the Holy Land*. Jane knew of this book, which had been published in 1875, and indeed had written to Isabel several times during its gestation, prior to the cooling of their friendship. Possibly she had even approved what was said about herself, for these passages were considerably more restrained than Isabel's subsequent recollections of Jane. It was, and remains, a fascinating account of life in Damascus lived by a European woman at that time. 'There is much of interest [in it],' wrote Anne Blunt, 'but it is all coloured by the constant fulsome praise of Captain Burton, his wisdom and courage, all of which must have done his prospects harm rather than good.'[5]

The Blunts reached Damascus on 6 December and stayed at Demetri's hotel. Medjuel called on them almost immediately, riding his lovely white mare. 'He gave us a message from Mrs Digby who is as anxious to see us as we are to see her.'[6] The next week was spent in constant visits between the two couples, and by the end of it the Blunts had acquired further invaluable material for their book. Wilfred suggested buying a house in Damascus as a base for future explorations of the country. As things stood they had to make a camp in Damascus in one of the many 'gardens' available for travellers, so that their camels and horses could graze and their attendants had accommodation. In the winter months this made a dreary base.

When Jane and Medjuel mentioned that a small house next door to them was for sale for £350, Anne Blunt wrote, 'we all looked over the wall by means of a ladder . . . at the little house just mentioned . . . it has a good piece of ground at the back, and is . . . modest and suitable.'[7] Wilfred Blunt was fired with enthusiasm, and the decision was made to buy it. Jane was delighted at her new neighbours. 'I enjoy her energy and horsemanship and nerve,' she wrote of Anne Blunt, who reminded her of a much younger Jane Digby.[8]

During their long conversations, Medjuel advised them that for the journey they planned to make, through the western side of the desert, the best person to deal with was Mohammed ebn Dukhi. It was Wuld Ali territory, and ebn Dukhi would be sure to give them the most accurate information regarding grazing and wells. Jane grimaced at placing her new and valued friend in the hands of her old enemy, but Medjuel thought ebn Dukhi would honour important European travellers under his protection. Jane warned Anne that ebn Dukhi was clever, but not to be trusted – information which Anne subsequently found to be sound advice.

Medjuel provided letters of introduction to all the sheikhs they were likely to encounter, placing himself in their debt if they would assist his great friends the Blunts. 'Both of us are struck by his intelligence and way of putting things, besides his refinement and good-breeding equal to the best of any of the noble families,' Anne Blunt wrote. 'I remark this particularly because it has often been said that Medjuel was a camel-driver, and nothing more, and Mrs Digby enriched him and made him a Sheikh. Whereas it is really a fact that he is of an ancient family . . . one of the oldest tribes.'[9]

All too soon the visit to Damascus was over and the Blunts left on 13 December. However, Anne suggested that they write to each other, and through these long and detailed letters we know more of the final years of Jane's life than from her diary, entries in which from this point become intermittent.

A French visitor who called on Jane at this time reported that Jane looked no more than sixty, and was still a remarkable rider. She remained elegant and charming, indeed, 'still resembled the portrait Lawrence made of her when she was called Lady Ellenborough, which was recently disposed of at the sale of the Wilson collection'.[10] On her table she had current European newspapers and reviews, and she questioned the visitor closely about the Parisian theatre, authors and politicians.

Another visitor, Sir Valentine Chirol, met her briefly and commented that, though Jane was ageing,

> so long as her Turkish yashmak concealed the lower part of her face, her ivory white and almost unwrinkled brow, her luminous eyes and the fine line of her aquiline nose still preserved traces of the beauty which had captured so many hearts in many lands and in the highest places.
>
> Not only was she well-read, but the world had been to her a strangely interesting book, of which she seemed to enjoy turning the pages, with a disarming simplicity, as if they belonged not to her own, but to someone else's life. She also had a keen sense of humour, and when I once suggested to her that she ought to write her Memoirs, she replied with a chuckle that she was afraid they would be 'a rather naughty edition of the *Almanach de Gotha*', and then added rather primly that a prayer book was more suitable to her declining years.[11]

The summer of 1879 was the last Jane would spend in the desert. She did not record that she met Ouadjid, only that she felt more than previously the effects of the great heat. There was a good deal of fighting, but because in general the tribe were the victors she did not worry unduly about it. As usual she felt a surge of spiritual renewal in the harsh purity of bedouin life. She was still able to ride well and hard, considering her age, but during that summer she contracted ophthalmia, forcing her early return to Damascus. Medjuel was kindness itself, always riding ahead to ensure their camping site was set up and made comfortable for her arrival.

Because of her eye problems she did not keep her diary for a while, except to make a monthly summary of her life. In November she was annoyed because 'my eyes are again much inflamed and have been for some time, and for so long with few exceptions, I have not been out of the house; although more exercise, I think, would do me good.'[12] She received a letter from Anne Blunt, enclosing some manuscript pages of Anne's book in which Jane and Medjuel were mentioned. Knowing how Jane had been upset by Isabel Burton she wrote asking for permission to publish, but it was some time before Jane could answer.

Damascus
December 3, 1879

My dear Lady Anne,
    I cannot say how delighted I was to receive your last letter about a

317

month ago, nor how impatient I have been to answer it in detail as my heart always burns at everything relating to the Desert – but the whole summer, which was extra hot, I have been suffering more or less, with my eyes, but am now right of vision, and accordingly take up my pen. What a journey! But still a most satisfactory one to look back upon and I am very glad you are going to publish it; those parts are so little known.

In answer to what you say about mentioning *us* in your next work, we can have no objection, for we know that we are in friendly truthful hands, and what you say of our tribes etc. is perfectly correct, but as you allow me to offer a *hint* of what I should like *altered* in any way you like it, the sentence in which you say 'It is also easy to see that his *heart* remains in the Desert, and whence he succeeds to the Sheykhat [head of the tribe] – etc. etc., – I think he will hardly be able to spend even a part of his time in Damascus.' The first part of the sentence I think might easily be misconstrued by ill-natured persons, of whom I have met with my share. The latter part, relating to the Sheykhych [sheikhdom], has often been discussed between ourselves, but of late years he has been much disgusted with many things such as the differentiation of the tribe in various quarters – some were not able, or willing, to follow him as usual in the Desert – he would most likely resign in favour of Afet. But I hope all this may be still in the future and we are looking forward to being there in early spring. *Inshallah!* I hope you quite understand the little womanly feeling that suggests these changes of phrase as you think fit.[13]

She wrote to Kenelm to tell him of good rains over Christmas and the New Year, always welcomed by the bedouin for its promise of good grazing, and 'we are in hopes of a good white truffle year [manna]. They stand us instead of potatoes which have failed everywhere.'[14] In the spring of 1880 she suffered from a lung infection which left her weakened; however, she had recovered by April and as a birthday gift Medjuel gave her a new mare. 'My seventy-third birthday! . . . Medjuel has brought me the most beautiful mare I have ever had! A pure Seglawi, quite thoroughbred, and in foal. If she does not suit me I shall never get a horse that does.'[15] A few weeks later the lovely mare, called Ferah, produced a colt. 'Of course I should have preferred a filly,' Jane wrote in her diary, 'particularly such a beauty as the colt, whose sire is also a Seglawi.'

To her disappointment, Anne Blunt wrote to say their visit planned for the autumn was postponed until the spring. Jane's reply is an eight-page letter cataloguing the continuing desert warfare, fascinating gossip and horse news.[16]

At the same time, there again began to appear in her diary seeds of doubt regarding Medjuel's love for her. Throughout almost twenty-five years of marriage, their sex-life had been a great joy to Jane. The single exception had been during Ouadjid's brief reign. Now Jane wrote in puzzlement, and in code, 'Medjuel is obviously not well, and I cannot understand the mystery of his not lying with me! Oh, may there be no second Ouadjid as a reason for this extraordinary conduct. And yet he is so kind, so attentive to me.'[17] It was during the first week in August that she heard news which shocked her.

Medjuel told me that Ouadjid was dead. She died in the Arak desert . . . Medjuel must have heard it almost a month ago, and yet he has never told me.

I am thankful, now that she is gone, that I never voiced the wish or hope that it might be so. I am jealous of her memory for she proved herself a bright woman to Medjuel, though she cast a great gloom over my life . . . twelve years ago. A strange feeling, of pity and of thankfulness, came over me rather than one of hatred gratified . . . She can do me no further injury. But oh, that I could see what passes in *his* heart at this news . . . I long to see someone who will give me some *true* details. Medjuel is not well and appears depressed; is it on account of her?[18]

During the next months her diary entries detail the ebb and flow of her daily round. 'Poor Misky, my favourite grey cat, was found dead this morning, so handsome and fond in its way to me . . . the cannon sounded in the evening; the first evening of Ramadan.'[19] 'Midhat Pacha left for Constantinople . . . I wish it had been before many picturesque bits of old Damascus were destroyed. I rode Ferah up to Salhiyeh to see M. de Savoye, the mare is handsome and pleasant but frisky if horses come coursing up behind.'[20]

Through the daily trivia runs a constant underlying theme, that of Medjuel's lack of libido. He had not made love to her for months. She sometimes thought he might have become impotent and, on her worst days, that she was now so old and unattractive that he no longer desired her.[21] He remained as kind and attentive to Jane as ever, and appeared contented in her company, yet the old spark seemed lacking. When she gently raised the matter with him she ascribed his problem to 'a weakness in the back'.[22] She was not convinced. 'I cannot understand it . . . *Why*? Another Ouadjid? God forbid!' She found his lack of sexual desire strange, given his unabated ardour right up to the last time they made love, just prior to Ouadjid's death. Since then, she wrote, he had been in low spirits. But Medjuel's behaviour was symptomatic of depression and was almost certainly due to Ouadjid's illness and death. It was not until Jane started to make plans to accompany him to the desert in the spring that he cheered up.

A letter from Anne Blunt gave hope of another visit and Jane replied on New Year's Day 1881 with all her news, thanking her for sending a magnifying lens which had helped her to read more easily. 'I am very grateful and my eyes – I am happy to say – are better this year. I am much obliged to you for your promised book. Everything relating to the Desert and the Bedouin is of the greatest interest to me ... what a pleasure it will be to us to see you and Mr Blunt.'

In March the Blunts arrived for their third visit to Damascus and rode their camels straight to Jane's house – or, to be more precise, Medjuel's, since the previous month Jane had sold it to him for a peppercorn sum with no comment in her diary as to why. They were welcomed as old friends and their baggage camels, made to kneel in the courtyard, were unloaded and fed and watered. Jane had sent for the key to the Blunts' house, and, after they had all breakfasted, 'to our great satisfaction we found the house and garden in fairly good order and very much larger and nicer than expected ... our garden is full of almonds, apricots and pomegranates', Lady Anne recorded.

During the two weeks that the Blunts were in Damascus the two couples saw each other frequently; for Jane there were long and intellectually stimulating conversations, the like of which she had not been able to enjoy since the Burtons left, on wide-ranging subjects and in several languages. But Anne noticed a change in her friend: 'She has been suffering from weakness and seems to me feeble in health, though as young as ever in mind.'[23]

A great deal of the time was spent in Jane's stable and discussing horses. The Crabbett Arabian Stud in England was already established and flourishing, and would eventually become a world-famous institution under Anne's skilful direction, but these were early days. Lady Anne was still learning and absorbed what Jane told her like a sponge, recognising that Jane's knowledge came from her long experience in the desert where she 'fed foals on cornflour mixed very thick with camel's milk' to supplement their diet when there was poor grazing for the mare. A milk camel was allotted to the owner of every pregnant mare by the sheikh, Jane said, for the sole use of the mare and foal. The ears of a new-born foal were pierced and joined with twine, a process which caused no discomfort and ensured that the ears grew with the inward curving points so valued in the best types; the tiny hooves were lightly pared within a day of their birth and rubbed with salt to toughen the horn.[24]

Wilfred, meanwhile, spent a great deal of time with Medjuel, discussing the latest developments in guns, a subject which interested them both a good deal, and promised to send Medjuel a new type of rifle.

On 24 March the Blunts went on their way, promising to return at the end of the year. A month later Jane and Medjuel were delighted to hear that following an attack in the desert, from which they emerged unscathed, the Blunts had met Afet and stayed with him. Before they parted Wilfred Blunt and Afet had 'made a brotherhood.'

25

Funeral in Damascus
1881

Jane celebrated her seventy-fourth birthday shortly after the Blunts departed. She was physically tired and, as Anne Blunt had remarked, appeared weak despite her mental alertness. This frailty is reflected in her diary. The usual details of calls and visits, concern for her animals, and occasional visits to church are still her daily currency, but there is no further mention of exercising the horses as she had done even in the last months of the previous year. Nor did she visit the desert that spring.

The days when she rode at Medjuel's side were gone for ever, and she appears to have accepted the new phase of their relationship with grace. Medjuel was as considerate and caring of her as she could ever wish; few women of any age enjoy the loving attentions (noted enviously by Anne Blunt) that Medjuel lavished upon Jane. She had always marvelled, and in a sense been humbled by, Medjuel's attention to her smallest requirement, and his manner when, at times, he waited on her. He was never servile but offered his services as a gift.

A matter which caused her anxiety was an orphaned child. Jane had befriended a poor Circassian couple, Hanifeh and Ahmed. One Sunday in April Hanifeh died 'shortly after seven in the evening, her husband just arriving in time to hear her last adieu!' As 'her mother's last legacy to me', Jane acquired the mixed blessing of the couple's small daughter Fatmah, the father having no ability to bring up a girl child. Having already raised one orphan girl successfully, Jane sent the child to Mrs Mackintosh's missionary school, with high hopes for 'her good, present and future', and made adequate financial provision for her. Many poor families had reason to be grateful to Jane, who tried to demonstrate through genuine kindness and caring the basic tenent of Christianity. But she was not gullible. Her last diary entry was made on 15 July 1881.

Wednesday July 15th 1881. I answered poor Mr Lucas's letter requesting a second loan of a hundred pounds to be enabled to trade corn . . . I was obliged to refuse with regret for though I do not doubt his worth, he now owes Medjuel a heavy loan of £200 and me a hundred.

These were large sums for the time. Jane, though renowned for her generosity, was never a fool with her money. She liked Lucas, and over a decade she made several loans to him which he had until recently repaid. But the outstanding loans to which she referred dated back three years, and it is obvious that he was sinking deeper and deeper into debt. During the last years of her life, owing to many inroads on her capital for building projects and expensive gifts to the tribe and to Medjuel, Jane's income had fallen, according to Lord Redesdale, who had enquired about Jane's safety and been told that her income was about £1,500. But it was still, he was told by Sir Richard Burton, 'a fortune' in Damascus.

At the hottest time of the year, Jane contracted a form of fever and dysentery. She had suffered similar symptoms many times; all residents, especially Europeans, were familiar with them. She began to feel ill during the first week in August and Medjuel, concerned, called in Mrs Reichardt whom Jane had known, through the little mission church, for seven years. Jane disliked herself for sometimes thinking uncharitably of Mrs Reichardt; her poverty of spirit alienated Jane and never allowed a close friendship. Nevertheless, when Medjuel sent for her, the missionary's wife went to Jane's house and took over the nursing.

Later, Mrs Reichardt would write to Emmie Buxton, always Jane's favourite niece, that Jane had 'been growing weaker and weaker for the last three years, and gradually getting weaned from the things she loved so well, her garden, her animals, that is to say her cats and dogs and poultry, but not least her horses'. When the final illness struck, Jane had no physical resources to fight, and she died in a matter of days.

She was very fond of Damascus, and often assured me that the part of her life spent here was by far the happiest . . . She was loved and respected by all who knew her, especially the Arabs and Moslems to whom her kindness and charity were unlimited . . .

On the Sunday morning as I sat by her bedside, fanning her, she asked me the time. I told her it was after eleven. It was our church time and she knew our service had begun . . . she said 'They are praying for me', and then seeming to forget who she was speaking to, added, 'Mrs Reichardt has only gone to church, she will come back afterwards, she will not leave me.'

[Later] she rallied somewhat, and seemed to enjoy very much talking of *home* and her dear mother; and the pleasant time she had spent with her in Switzerland during her last visit to that place. She also liked to speak of English food, and when I mentioned one or two dishes her eyes brightened and she said with a longing accent, 'Oh, they make that so nicely at home, it was *particularly* good.'

Her death was peaceful; like a tired child falling asleep in its mother's arms. Content to the last, and for several days conscious that she was dying . . . she spoke sometimes in one language, sometimes in another . . . her love for her husband, and her anxiety for his happiness was beautiful to see . . . [As she died] such a sweet, happy and contented expression came over her face that we all simultaneously remarked upon it, and I could not help [remarking] that she was gone . . . from a word where I sincerely believe she was more sinned against than sinning.[1]

Another report was sent by Mrs Suzette Smith, a missionary from the Lebanon who called on Jane during the last days of July: 'It seems that she has generally suffered from diarrhoea but this being an exceptionally hot season proved fatal. She had no European [servants] about her, but I believe Mrs Reichardt was most kind and attentive to her. Mr Jago our Consul assured me your Aunt died in her arms.'[2]

In the first biography of Jane, E. M. Oddie recounted the story that, over fifty years, had passed into Damascus folklore. It told how Medjuel, as the chief mourner, was placed alone and reluctant in a black carriage behind the hearse, and how halfway to the cemetery his bedouin instincts could not tolerate the confinement.

He jumped from the moving carriage, and like a man pursued by a thousand devils, fled in the opposite direction to the funeral procession. It was disconcerting for the unfortunate clergyman who was to take the service, and for the few formal mourners who were neither kith nor kin to the dead woman. But still more disconcerting was Medjuel's dramatic return. In triumph he galloped back to the cemetery on Jane's lovely Saklowyek [Seglawi] mare, and he was there at the graveside with her favourite horse when they committed her body to the dust.

... He watched them while they buried ... the queer sweet woman who had loved him. Then he galloped back to the desert where he belonged, to mourn her after his own fashion among the tribes who had loved her ... and to sacrifice in her memory the finest of the camels which had been her gift to him.[3]

The reality is quieter, though no less dramatic in its way, according to a previously unpublished, eye-witness account by Roland Mitchell:

The death of the Hon. Mrs Digby took place at 6.30 on Thursday August 11th, and she was buried on the following day. At 3.30 pm on August 12th I rode to the house in the North-East quarter of Damascus to attend the funeral.[4]

Mitchell was shown upstairs to the English sitting-room where Jane's body lay on a bier, with fresh flowers from her garden wreathed around her head and scattered upon her body. Legend says that she was dressed in her bedouin 'fantasia'. Medjuel received him and he was introduced to a number of mourners already present: Medjuel's nephew, Mrs Reichardt and her two daughters, Jane's doctor and his wife and daughters, several members of the French community and a representative of the British consulate. There were few Europeans in Damascus, for most, like Mr Jago and his wife, had gone to the mountains of the Anti-Lebanon to escape the worst of the heat. Mr Jago set out for Damascus on hearing how ill Jane was, but arrived too late owing to 'an immensely hot wind' which obliged him to rest his horses.

At a quarter to five, when the air began to cool, Mr Reichardt – the officiating minister – arrived. The coffin was carried out and placed 'with careful hands' in the first of the carriages drawn up in front of the house. Immediately behind, on magnificent desert horses which carried their tails like plumes, rode Sheikh Medjuel in his scarlet and gold robes, his nephew and a number of bedouins forming a 'respectful and picturesque group'. Medjuel led Jane's white Seglawi mare. The young man Mr Mitchell identified as Medjuel's nephew led Jane's white mule.[5]

Some half-dozen carriages made up the cortège, which proceeded slowly along the road bordered by shady gardens and trees. All was quiet except for the jingle of a harness, the hollow echo of hooves, and the rattle of carriage wheels on the dusty roadway. The procession crossed the wooden bridge over the Barada River, and through the ancient Bab Tuma, where once a younger, still beautiful, Jane had eagerly ridden for the first time into Damascus, accompanied by Medjuel. They passed into the shadow of the minaret of the Great Mosque, and through the north-eastern Christian quarter of the city, where Jane had walked fearlessly after the massacre to see what help she could bring to the victims. And they left the walled city by Bab Kisan, near 'the quiet little Protestant cemetery where the body was laid in its resting place.'

Jane would have appreciated the bedouin guard of honour, ranged behind her coffin and led by her adored sheikh, and the presence of her favourite horse and the gentle mule as her body was lowered into the ground. It was as dramatic as the legend, but perhaps there was greater dignity.

Some time later a tombstone was erected over the grave under the trees. It was organised by Mr Jago in consultation with Medjuel, following correspondence with Edward Digby. It is an unexceptional, formal design that would not be out of place in any English country churchyard, except that the shape is more typical of that given to an old warrior. The slightly raised dais with a flat cross upon it is carved from grey granite. Along the side is written in English 'Jane Elizabeth Digby, daughter of Admiral Sir Henry Digby GCB. Born April 3rd, 1807. Died August 11th 1881.'

Resting across the foot of the gravestone, as a slightly incongruous addition, is a large block of pink desert limestone brought from Palmyra, where Jane had spent the happiest days of her life. It was Medjuel's parting gift to her. On it he carved her name in his own hand, in bedouin Arabic characters – 'Madame Digby el Mezrab'.[6]

Medjuel never remarried.

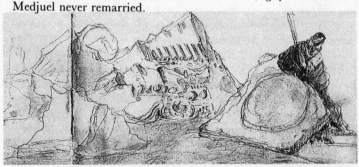

Jane's sketch of Medjuel sitting on fallen masonry at Palmyra.

Epilogue

On Sunday 14 August 1881 Lady Anne Blunt was at her country
house in Sussex when she received a telegram from Mr Jago which
said simply, 'Mrs Digby died on Thursday.'[1] By coincidence Anne
Blunt's guest that day was a friend of Edward Digby's, who left at
once to break the news to the Digby family.

It was a few weeks before the news appeared in the newspapers;
perhaps on this occasion they ascertained that Jane was dead before
printing. The obituaries were much the same as those which appeared
erroneously in 1873, the same old stories with the same errors. 'Jane's
many, many friends in this country' were deeply angry, according to
Edward Digby,[2] who had to call on some of them and persuade them
not to write to the press contradicting the 'base calumnies heaped
upon poor Jane in *The Times*'. Such a thing, he assured them, would
be most painful to her family.

Among these were Lady Strangford, the former Miss Emily Beaufort, who regarded Jane as her role model. Emily had been an adventurous girl when she made the trip to Palmyra and had now achieved
fame in her own right in the field of nursing. William Wright, a retired
missionary whom Jane had befriended in Damascus, had once before
written to the press about Jane following Isabel Burton's 'defence' of
her and was eager to do so again. An amateur archaeologist with
limited funds, with Jane's help he had been able to visit Tadmor.[3]
He subsequently produced an authoritative book on Palmyra and
Queen Zenobia in which he attributed much of his basic knowledge
to Jane, who 'knew more about the site than any other European'.[4]

'He told me', said Edward after meeting Wright, 'lots of anecdotes of her great kindness to the poor people . . . how wisely she dispensed her charity, and was looked up to, beloved and almost worshipped by them all.'[5]

In the following spring Jane's will was proved and her English estate valued at some £6,000. Much of the capital upon which Jane drew income during her life had been left in trust and, like the allowance paid by the Ellenborough estate, terminated on her death. This figure did not include the house in Damascus, which she had already sold to Medjuel for a peppercorn sum prior to her death, nor her effects which she had bequeathed directly to him.

After paying Heribert's legacy of £1,000 (see the Appendix), a sum of just over £5,000 remained. This was sent to Medjuel through Mr Jago, under the consular seal. It was delivered to him in packets of 500 gold sovereigns. Characteristically indifferent to Jane's money after her death as he was during it, he opened one or two of the packets to buy camels, but it is said that when he died most of the packets were under his pillow, still unopened.[6]

Medjuel had no use for the house without Jane. He let it for a short time to the Reverend J. Segall and then to the Dickson family, who were attached to the British consulate.[7] Mrs Dickson was the mother of a baby boy who, as the family arrived in Damascus, looked to have a slim chance of survival when his mother's milk failed. Hearing of this through Mr Jago, Medjuel provided one of the nursing women of his tribe as wet-nurse for the child, who later wrote: 'A Bedouin girl was duly produced, and according to my mother's testimony I drank her milk for several weeks. This in the eyes of the Bedawin entitles me to a "blood affinity" with the Anazeh, for to drink a woman's milk in the desert is to become a child of the foster-mother.'[8] In the following year the Dickson family became Medjuel's tenants and the boy, H. R. P. Dickson, grew up 'rambling about the old garden that had once been the pride and happiness of Lady Digby. At an early age I was given my first camel ride by Sheikh Medjuel's grown up son Sheikh Afet.' 'Afet . . . still clearly remembers the incident,' Dickson wrote in 1936.[9]

Consul Jago helped Medjuel to settle Jane's sundry bequests. With typical generosity he sent many items of jewellery and valuables to her family, in addition to those Jane had formally bequeathed. Perhaps she had asked him verbally to do so. To Edward went all her family portraits, papers and photographs; one of the portraits Edward later sent to Jane's illegitimate daughter Didi, as a memento of the mother she had never known. Among Jane's papers were over 200 letters from Felix Schwarzenberg and hundreds more from other correspondents. To Kenelm, Medjuel sent Jane's paintings, not just those she mentioned in her will but those of Switzerland and Greece, as well as some other items including a silver muff chain which is still used today as a necklace by a descendant in New Zealand.[10]

All of the remainder of Jane's jewellery, and there was a great deal, Medjuel gave away to her friends or sold along with furniture and contents when the house was let. Items worth a king's ransom were said to have been sold for the same price as Jane's silver bedouin bracelets; Medjuel never learned the English conception of values, but it is fair to say that Jane herself would probably have valued her bridal gift of silver bracelets more highly than any other item in her ample jewel case. Several pieces were bought by Mr Jago on behalf of Lady Anne Blunt, who requested some remembrance of her friend: a gilded and bejewelled 'fantasia' bridle; a silver bedouin necklace, and the gold and turquoise bracelet inset with a miniature of King Ludwig that Jane always referred to in her inventories as 'the King's bracelet'. Anne Blunt later gave the latter two items to her daughter Judith, Lady Wentworth, but Judith died childless and the family have now lost track of them.[11]

Edward, Lord Digby died in 1889, and Kenelm two years later in 1891. Their deaths ended the pained silence maintained by Isabel Burton since the public embarrassment she suffered after her 'defence' of Jane in 1873. Shortly before her death in 1896, Isabel, now Lady Burton, dictated her story to W. H. Wilkins, and a two-volume biography of her duly appeared. In it Isabel went further than referring to Jane as a friend. She dug into her own antecedents and found a distant relative married to a distant cousin of Jane's. On this tenuous relationship she claimed kinship with Jane.

Lady Ellenborough . . . was the most romantic and picturesque personality . . . she had married Lord Ellenborough, Governor-General of India, a man much older than herself when she was quite a girl. She was unhappy with him and ran away with Prince Schwarzenberg when she was only nineteen and Lord Ellenborough divorced her. She lived with Prince Schwarzenberg for some years and had two or three children by him, and then he basely deserted her. I am afraid after that she led a life for a year or two over which it is kinder to draw a veil.

She then tired of Europe and conceived the idea of visiting the East

. . . and went to Damascus, where she arranged to go to Bagdad, across the desert. For this journey a Bedouin escort was necessary, and as the Mezrab tribe occupied the ground, the duty of commanding the escort devolved upon Sheikh Medjuel, a younger brother of the chief of this tribe. On the journey the young Sheikh fell in love with this beautiful woman, and she fell in love with him. The romantic picture of becoming a queen of the desert, suited her wild and roving fancy. She married him in spite of all opposition, according to Mohammedan law.

At the time I came to Damascus she was living half the year in a house just outside the city gates; the other half of the year she passed in the desert in the tents of the Bedawin tribe, living absolutely as a Bedawin woman. When I first saw her she was a most beautiful woman, though sixty-one years of age. She wore one blue garment, and her beautiful hair was in two long plaits down to the ground.

When she was in the desert, she used to milk the camels, serve her husband, prepare his food, wash his hands, face and feet, and stood and waited on him while he ate, like any Arab woman, and gloried in doing so. But at Damascus she led a semi-European life. She blacked her eyes with kohl, but otherwise she was not in the least extraordinary. But what was incomprehensible to me was how she had given up all she had in England to live with that dirty little black – or nearly so – husband.

I went to see her one day, and when he opened the door to me I thought at first he was a native servant. I could understand her leaving a coarse, cruel husband, much older than herself who she never loved (every woman has not the strength of mind and the pride to stand by what she has done); I could understand her running away with Schwarzenberg; but the contact with that black skin I could not understand. Her Sheikh was very dark, darker than a Persian, and much darker than an Arab generally is. All the same he was a very intelligent and charming man in any light but as a husband. That made me shudder.

It was curious how she had retained the charming manner, the soft voice and all the graces of her youth. You would have known her at once to be an English lady, well born and bred, and she was delighted to meet in me one of her own order. We became great friends and she dictated to me the whole of her biography, and most romantic and interesting it is. I took a great interest in the poor thing. She was devoted to her Sheikh whereat I marvelled greatly. Gossip said he had other wives, but she assured me that he had not, and that both her brother Lord Digby and the British Consul required a legal and official statement to that effect before they were married. She appeared to be quite foolishly in love with him (and I fully comprehend any amount of sacrifice for the man one loves – the greater the better), though the object of her devotion astonished me.

Her eyes often used to fill with tears when talking of England, her people and old times; and when we became more intimate, she spoke to me of every detail of her erring but romantic career. It was easy to see that Schwarzenberg had been the love of her live, for her eyes would light up with a glory when she mentioned his name with bated breath. It was his defection that wrecked her life. Poor thing! She was far more sinned against than sinning . . .

. . . After I left [Syria] a report came home that she was dead. I answered some unpleasant remarks in the press about her, throwing a halo over her memory, in which I stated that I being the possessor of the biography, no one had any right to say anything about her except myself. She appeared again, having only been detained in the desert by fighting of the tribes. Her relatives attacked her for having given me the biography, and she, under pressure denied it in print through one of the missionaries, and then she wrote and asked me to give it back to her; but I replied that she should have it with the greatest pleasure, only 'having given me the lie' in print, I was obliged for my own sake to keep it, and she eventually died. I have got it now, but I shall never publish it.[12]

Elsewhere in the book, to illustrate the 'massive support' for her late husband, Isabel published a highly edited version of Jane's letter to her in November 1870 warning of a plot against Burton. She had no qualms about changing Jane's greeting from 'My Dear Mrs Burton' to 'My dear Isabel'. And Jane's letter which actually ended 'Yours most affectionately' appeared in Isabel's book as 'Your affectionate cousin'.[13]

Given Burton's reputation, and the public nature of the accusations and counter-accusations, a biographer must ask, 'Who is telling the truth?' It is obvious from at least one entry in Jane's diaries that she was occasionally given to talking about her past – witness her annoyance over her confidence to Madame Heuguard in November 1862: 'I was vexed with myself for speaking to them of bye-gone days. *Why*? I neither did the noble-minded Baron justice, nor the love I bear to the dear Sheikh.'

But the information published by Isabel is riddled with errors of fact. Moreover, except for her own eye-witness experiences, in everything she wrote about Jane (not all reprinted in this book) nothing appeared that was not already available in the public domain or that Isabel could not have observed for herself in Damascus. She offered nothing new to Jane's history, despite her claims that Jane unburdened herself 'daily' to Isabel over a period of many weeks.

Surely an authorised biographer would know the precise number of children Jane had by Schwarzenberg had she been given Jane's complete and unexpurgated version of the story, as Isabel claims? Short of her eyes filling with tears when she mentioned Schwarzenberg in her later years, Jane wrote of him quite unemotionally in her diary on several occasions after meeting former friends of his who called on her in Damascus. And the meeting with Medjuel, the *real* love of Jane's life, occurred not on the trip to Baghdad, which she made with Barak, but during her trip to Palmyra a year earlier.

It clearly suited Isabel's notions of what was acceptable to promote Felix as Jane's lifelong love, rather than Medjuel, whose black skin made Isabel 'shudder'. In her defence of Jane in 1873 Isabel referred to Medjuel divorcing his 'wives . . . to marry her'. At the time Medjuel married Jane he had only Mascha as a wife; Jane would never have *exaggerated* Medjuel's marital commitment; rather she consistently played it down. As for the supposed insistence on a pre-nuptial document by the British consul and Lord Digby, to verify that Medjuel had no other wives, about which Isabel claims to have been told by Jane, Jane had not corresponded with either of her brothers for some years before she married Medjuel. They were, as she put it, 'estranged'.

But Isabel went further than mere error; she knowingly stretched facts. Her actual eighteen months in Damascus became 'two years of . . . daily intimacy' with Jane. She deliberately altered parts of a letter of Jane's to substantiate her claim. The original of Jane's letter, sent to the Foreign Office by Burton as evidence, survives today, to reveal Isabel's small deceit.

Having read all the material written by Isabel (who in fact was as remarkable and extraordinary as Jane in her way), I prefer to accept Jane's mild comment (in her letter of 21 May 1873) to her sister-in-law as being the truth of the matter:

> I certainly always deprecated every idea of publishing anything relating to myself or my former existence . . . I never spoke to her at all on the subject except to answer some of her general queries as to what the world of that day knew, positively denying some other histories that people have forged. And as to *begging* her to remember her *promise* after my death of *justifying* me, it is pure error; she knew the horror and aversion I have to this kind of thing.

This does not have the desperate ring of someone caught in an untruth, as Isabel's statement does. Given the friendship the women shared, it is a pity that the relationship ended as it did. No one ever saw the biographical material in question. Isabel claimed she still had it in 1896 but her co-biographer Mr Wilkins did not mention seeing it – which, given its importance to Isabel, is surprising. An eye-witness would have clinched her case without her having to defend it so vigorously. It was not among Isabel's surviving papers, though this in itself is not conclusive, for, like her husband's, many were burned at her own request.

Medjuel was dead by 1904 when Lady Anne Blunt visited Damascus. His son, Afet, is said to have joined the Arabs who fought alongside T. E. Lawrence for the recapture of Damascus from the Turks during the First World War. He was still alive in September 1936, according to Colonel H. R. P. Dickson, and since he was born in 1854 he lived well into his eighties, old for a bedouin.

APPENDIX

Last Will and Testament of the Hon. Jane Digby

I, Jane Elizabeth Digby el Mezrab, of Damascus in Syria declare this to be my Last Will and Testament. I give to my husband, as a token of my respect and regard, my house, stables, garden and premises situated near the Bab Menzel Khassabb in the City of Damascus, together with all furniture, plate, linen, coppers, carpets, saddlery and household goods, my horses, dromedaries and other livestock, my gold watch and chain, large ruby ring, and Arab ornaments, belt and jewellery in gold or silver and my silver gilt headpiece, breast ornament and bridle studded with coral, and my silver gilt ewer basin, together with the sum of one thousand pounds (being a moiety of the legacy of two thousand pounds bequeathed to me by my dear mother).

I bequeath the sum of one thousand pounds (being the other moiety of the said legacy), my diamond necklace and earrings, my emerald and diamond bracelet and my silver gilt dressing box to my son, Heribert, Baron de Venningen, Ulner, and I bequeath my coloured diamond sprig for the head, and ear-rings and my crysolite necklace, together with the portraits of my dear father and mother, and the miniature of my brother Lord Digby, to my said brother, Lord Digby. And I give to my brother Kenelm Henry, in token of my affection my large turquoise ring, my silver and gilt inkstand and my coloured sketches in Switzerland and Palmyra.

I give and bequeath all the residue of my estate and effects whatsoever after payment thereout of my just debts and testamentary expenses, unto my said husband absolutely. And I appoint my said brother Lord Digby Executor of this my Will. In witness whereof, I, the said Jane Elizabeth Digby el Mezrab, the Testatrix, have, to this my last Will and Testament, set my hand, this fifteenth day of June, in the year of our Lord, one thousand eight hundred and seventy-one.

Jane Elizabeth Digby el Mezrab

Witnessed by: (Signed): William Wright AB
                (Signed): James Orr Scott MA

Corrected and Registered by me: Richard F. Burton –
                                   H.M. Consul Damascus

Notes

ABBREVIATIONS AND SOURCES

ABBREVIATIONS USED FOR NAMES

CD	Caroline Digby
CV	Baron Carl ('Charles') Venningen
ESD	Edward, Lord Digby
JED	Jane Elizabeth Digby
KD	Reverend Kenelm Digby
LA	Lady Andover
MS	Margaret Steele

ABBREVIATIONS USED FOR SOURCES

MH   *Minterne House Collection*

MH/01   Summary of Jane's life between 1807 and 1846 compiled from papers subsequently destroyed by a member of the family.

MH/02   December 1853–May 1854. Soft-covered notebook containing pencil-written diary of Baghdad trip.

MH/03   Journal inscribed 'Ianthe, Athens, 1841'. Diary 1841 to December 1855. All pages prior to September 1854 were cut out and destroyed after Jane's death.

MH/04   Bound diary covering period September 1855 to July 1881.

MH/05   Pencil-written diary from November 1858 to March 1859. Loose-leaf pages sewn together; a fair-copy edited version of this draft is incorporated into MH/04.

MH/06   Poetry written 1824–34.

MH/07   Letters 1856–73 between JED and ESD and Lady Digby.

MH/08   December 1853–April 1868. Leather-bound pocket notebook containing working sketches, sundry memoranda and accounts.

MH/09   (a) JED to Lady Andover, *c.* 1815.
(b) JED to Admiral Digby, *c.* 1820.

MH/10   Diary of Lady Andover, 1840–42.

MH/11   Letters to Edward Digby from Lady Strangford, 1873, and 'Didi' Selden Diebitsch, 1883.

MH/12   Letters 1875–80 from Heribert Venningen to JED.

MH/13   Letters 1839–65, from Baron Carl Venningen to JED.

MH/14   Sundry items including will, paintings, etc.

RB   *Roz Broadmore Collection, New Zealand*

RB/01   Letters June 1856–January 1880. Large tranche of correspondence between JED and KD; CD; LA; MS; others.

PRO   *Public Record Office at Kew*

FO78   Foreign Office correspondence from HBM Majesty's Consul in Damascus concerning JED. Ditto between JD and Isobel Burton.

PRO30/12   The Ellenborough Papers; private papers and correspondence of Lord Ellenborough.

Parliamentary Papers
House of Commons Sessions 1830, vol. 10, no. 214; Second Reading, vol. 10, no. 36. House of Lords: Ellenborough Divorce Minutes of Evidence.

SCA   *Sheffield City Archives*
Papers of the Spencer-Stanhope family.

Keele   *Keele University*
Papers of Mr Ralph Sneyd.

BHM   *Bayerisches Hauptsarchiv, Munich*
Wittelsbach archives. Papers of King Ludwig I of Bavaria. Specifically, correspondence between JED and King Ludwig 1831–8, and CV and King Ludwig 1824–60.

BL   *British Library, Manuscript Department*
Wentworth Collection: papers of Lady Anne Blunt. Lieven, Princess Dorothea de: papers and correspondence. Joseph Jekyll (Holland Correspondence), MS 51594.

OTHER ARCHIVE SOURCES CONSULTED

Royal Geographical Society library.
Bank of England, Research Section HO–M.
Victoria and Albert Museum, National Art Library – Haag research.
The Royal Archives, Windsor Castle – diaries of Edward VII.
Digby Stuart College, Roehampton – Ellenborough's home.
Royal Commission on Historical Monuments Library

Chapter 1   Golden Childhood

1 SCA, box 1 (a) 60599.
2 Thomas Coke's first wife; also (and confusingly) named Jane, miscarried her only male child because of fright when a mouse got into her nightcap.
3 According to the daughter of Elizabeth Coke, the three girls were given dowries ranging between £20,000 and £50,000. See E. Spencer-Stanhope, *The Letter-Bag of Lady Elizabeth Spencer-Stanhope*, p. 19.
4 A. M. W. Stirling, *Coke of Norfolk and his Friends*, p. 443.

5 Ibid., p. 428.
6 Sir Henry Keppel, *A Sailor's Life under Four Sovereigns* (edited by Sir A. West, 1905), p. 98.
7 According to *Equivalent Values of the Pound; Historical Series 1270 to 1994*, produced by the Bank of England, £57,000 in 1805 has a value today of approximately £1.5 million.
8 Hugh Montgomery-Massingberd, *Great British Families* (Michael Joseph, 1988), p. 92.
9 A. M. W. Stirling, *Diaries of Dummer* (Unicorn Press, 1934), p. 105.
10 Stirling, *Coke of Norfolk and his Friends*, p. 246.
11 Ibid.
12 Stirling, *Diaries of Dummer*, p. 105.
13 Keppel, *A Sailor's Life under Four Sovereigns*, pp. 11 and 12.
14 Thornton Hall, *Romances of the Peerage*, p. 65.
15 SCA, 60599/1, bundle B22(a).
16 MH/04, diary entry, 24 July 1863.
17 RB/01, JED to KD, 18 May 1867.
18 MH/09(a).
19 Stirling, *Coke of Norfolk and his Friends*, p. 428.
20 MH/09(b).
21 RB/01; JED to KD 31/3/1868. Caroline Boyle later became lady-in-waiting to Queen Adelaide, wife of William IV.
22 JED's 'secret code' referred to in later chapter.
23 Edmond About, *La Grèce contemporaine*, p. 100.
24 RB/01, JED to KD, 17 July 1859.
25 Hall, *Romances of the Peerage*, p. 64.

Chapter 2   The Débutante

1 SCA, file 60612, Mary Spencer Stanhope's daughter-in-law, Eliza, née Coke.
2 SCA, file 60612, 2 April 1824.
3 Stella Margetson, *Leisure and Pleasure in the Nineteenth Century*, p. 27.
4 Ibid., p. 28.
5 Ibid., p. 29.
6 SCA, file 60598, 16 March 1824.
7 Thornton Hall, *Romances of the Peerage*, p. 65.
8 Ibid.
9 Ibid.
10 Keele, SC12/11, G. Agar Ellis to Ralph Sneyd.
11 *The Times*, 13 March 1819, p. 5.
12 *Chambers's Biographical Dictionary*, vol. 1, p. 238.
13 Keele, SC5/210.
14 E. M. Oddie, *A Portrait of Ianthe*, and

Margaret Fox Schmidt, *Passion's Child*, have both written full-length biographies of Jane, based on original research. Many potted biographies exist within anthologies; the best of these is Lesley Blanch, *The Wilder Shores of Love*, and the most biased is Irving Wallace's *Nymphos and Other Maniacs*. None of the above is thoroughly sourced.

15 Oddie, *Portrait of Ianthe*, p. 35.
16 MH/06, Lord Ellenborough, undated, probably May 1824.
17 Ibid.
18 Byron, *Don Juan*, 15th canto, v. 43.
19 Oddie, *Portrait of Ianthe*, p. 37.
20 SCA, file 60612, 2 April 1824.
21 Now the site of the Roehampton Institute.
22 E. Spencer-Stanhope, *The Letter-Bag of Lady Elizabeth Spencer-Stanhope*, pp. 51–2. Note: The treatise written by Lady Andover was included in this privately printed book as a curiosity from a previous century.
23 F. Bamford and Duke of Wellington, *Journal of Mrs Arbuthnot*, p. 336.
24 Sir H. Maxwell, *The Creevey Papers*, 7 September 1824.
25 Lady Elizabeth Holland, *Lady Holland, to her Son*, p. 30.
26 Keele, SC8/129, G. Agar Ellis to Ralph Sneyd, 14 September 1828.
27 Lord Ellenborough, *Political Diaries*, vol. 2, p. 68.
28 PRO, Chancery Lane, p. 226 of the register.
29 MH/03, diary entry, 27 February 1855.

Chapter 3 Lady Ellenborough

1 Henry Spencer Law in evidence to the House of Lords, p. 5.
2 Butler's statement in evidence to House of Commons.
3 Joseph Jekyll, *Correspondence with Lady Sloane Stanley*, p. 148.
4 Ibid., p. 213.
5 Lord Ellenborough, *Political Diaries*, Preface, p. x.
6 MH/06, dated '1825', no specific date given.
7 A. M. W. Stirling, *Coke of Norfolk and his Friends*, p. 348.
8 MH/04, diary entry, 12 November 1855. 'Dear Medjuel gave me my silver bracelets [see explanation in later chapter]. How I value this proof of his affection far more than the costly gifts I used to receive from Lord Ellenborough!!'

9 MH/06, dated '1825', no specific date given.
10 *The Age*, 14 March 1830, p. 85, col. 1.
11 Jekyll, *Correspondence*, p. 152.
12 SCA, Mary Spencer-Stanhope to Eliza, 19 April 1826.
13 F. Bamford and Duke of Wellington, *Journal of Mrs Arbuthnot*, p. 23.
14 SCA, Mary Spencer-Stanhope to Eliza, 19 April 1826.
15 *Dictionary of National Biography* (Smith Elder, 1908).
16 Bamford and Wellington, *Journal of Mrs Arbuthnot*, p. 167.
17 SCA, G. Agar Ellis to Ralph Sneyd, SC8/134, 1 April 1819.
18 Sir H. Maxwell, *The Creevey Papers*, pp. 247 and 415.
19 Bamford and Wellington, *Journal of Mrs Arbuthnot*, p. 244; also JD801, letters to Eliza Spencer-Stanhope.
20 Bamford and Wellington, *Journal of Mrs Arbuthnot*, p. 175.
21 Maxwell, *Creevey Papers*, p. 247; Bamford and Wellington, *Journal of Mrs Arbuthnot*, p. 167.
22 MH/06; poem dated 23 September 1826.
23 Keele, Sneyd Collection, SC8/115, George Agar Ellis to Ralph Sneyd, 22 November 1828.
24 The Cottage Clique had as its members the King; the Lievens; the Hanoverian Ambassador, Count Munster; the Esterhazys (she was a distant cousin of the King); the King's current mistress, Lady Conyngham; and the Duke of Wellington. For further information, see Alan Palmer, *George IV* (Weidenfeld & Nicholson and Book Club Associates), 1972, p. 199.
25 *The Times*, transcript of the Ellenborough divorce hearing, 2 April 1830, p. 1.
26 Ibid.
27 Ibid.
28 MH/01, p. 1.
29 Harriet, Countess Granville, *Letters 1810–1845*, vol. 1, p. 183.
30 Keele, SC8/115 and 129.
31 Ibid.
32 *The Times*, 6 April 1830, p. 3; *The Age*, 4 April 1930, p. 106.
33 The third son born to Mr Thomas Coke and his wife Anne in January 1827.
34 Diary of Sir F. Madden, Bodleian Library, Oxford, MS. Eng. hist. C147, 14 March 1827.
35 Ibid., 16 and 17 March 1827.
36 Ibid., 18 March 1827.

37 Ibid., 20–22 April, 1827.

38 Ibid., 24 April 1827. Against lingering parental opposition, after gaining a post at the British Museum, Madden married Mary. As she was a small woman, her doctors warned her against having children. She ignored them, and complications developed during the birth of a much-longed-for child. Both mother and son died. Madden mourned for years, racked with guilt. Each daily entry mentioned her: 'Oh, my poor Mary. Oh, that dear child', etc. In 1831 he became Assistant Keeper of the MSS Department at the British Museum (his portrait still dominates the reading room of the Manuscripts Department), subsequently rose to become Keeper and was knighted by Queen Victoria. He eventually remarried, but he never again mentioned Jane in his diaries.

39 MH/o6, poem dated 19 March 1827, Holkham.

40 Ibid., poem dated 15 April 1827.

41 RB/o1, JED to KD, 1 February 1870.

42 MH/o6, poem dated 23 May 1827.

43 Keele, SC8/31, G. Agar Ellis to Ralph Sneyd, 16 March 1829.

Chapter 4   A Dangerous Attraction

1 MH/o6, poem annotated 'Cowes, August 19th 1827'.

2 Ibid., 23 August 1927.

3 Letter from Lady Anne Coke to Lady Ellenborough: 'Now you, dear Jane, have had your first experience of motherhood, while I am somewhat ahead of you with my three small sons.'

4 Joseph Jekyll, *Correspondence with Lady Sloane Stanley*, p. 176.

5 Keele, Lord Clare to Ralph Sneyd, SC6/142, 21 January 1828.

6 Princess Dorothea Lieven, *Correspondence with Earl Grey*, 20 January 1828.

7 Lord Ellenborough, *Extracts from his Papers*, 15 February 1828.

8 Margaret Fox Schmidt, *Passion's Child*, p. 47.

9 RB/o1, JED to KD, 18 May 1867.

10 MH/o6, poem annotated 'Paris December 29th, 1830'.

11 MH/o6, poem annotated 'April 5th 1828'.

12 Adolph Schwarzenberg, *Prince Felix zu Schwarzenberg*, p. 11.

13 Ibid., p. 5.

14 Ibid., p. 11.

15 Count Rodolphe Apponyi, *Vingt-cinq ans à Paris*, p. 33.

16 Schwarzenberg, *Prince Felix zu Schwarzenberg*, p. 1.

17 Irving Wallace, *Nymphos and Other Maniacs*, p. 140.

18 Ibid.

19 Apponyi, *Vingt-cinq ans à Paris*, p. 33.

20 Schwarzenberg, *Prince Felix zu Schwarzenberg*, p. 13.

21 Evidence given in Ellenborough Divorce Case, *Second Reading of the Bill*, House of Commons, 1 April 1830, p. 44.

22 Dietrichstein eventually became Austrian Ambassador to London.

23 Facts taken from evidence given at the divorce hearings in Parliament in 1830; House of Lords, *Minutes of Evidence Taken at the Second Reading of the Bill*, 15 March 1830; House of Commons, 1 April 1830.

24 MH/o6, poem annotated 'JE 11th December 1828'.

25 Apponyi, *Vingt-cinq ans à Paris*, p. 134.

26 Facts taken from evidence given at the divorce hearings in Parliament in 1830; House of Lords, *Minutes of Evidence Taken at the Second Reading of the Bill*, 15 March 1830; House of Commons, 1 April 1830. See also Apponyi, *Vingt-cinq ans à Paris*, pp. 138–40.

27 Apponyi, *Vingt-cinq ans à Paris*, pp. 138–40.

28 *The Age*, 21 March 1830, p. 91.

29 MH/o6, sundry notes on undated page in notebook.

30 Evidence given in House of Commons, 1 April 1830, by both grooms.

31 Ibid.

32 Keele, Sneyd Collection, SC8/115, G. Agar Ellis to Ralph Sneyd, 22 November 1828.

33 Evidence given in House of Commons hearing on the Ellenborough Divorce Bill, 1 April 1830.

34 Ibid., evidence of Margaret Steele, p. 37.

35 MH/o6, poem dated 22 December 1828.

36 F. Bamford and Duke of Wellington, *Journal of Mrs Arbuthnot*, p. 350.

37 Keele, SC8/115.

38 Jekyll, *Correspondence*, p. 187.

39 SCA, sundry correspondence of Mary Spencer-Stanhope.

40 JD802, SC8/115, G. Agar Ellis to Ralph Sneyd, 22 November 1828.

41 Poem, undated but written at Holkham, c. 1829.

42 Keele, SC8/31, G. Agar Ellis to Ralph Sneyd, 22 November 1828.

43 JED to Lord Ellenborough dated 6 February 1829. Presented in evidence at House of Commons hearing on Ellenborough Divorce Bill, 1 April 1830.

Chapter 5   Assignation in Brighton

1 Unless otherwise stated, all the details given in this chapter of Jane's rendezvous in Brighton and the letters quoted are contained in the Minutes of Evidence of either/both the House of Lords Papers, 1830, vol. 16, no. 36, pp. 333 ff.; and the House of Commons Sessional Papers (7), 1830, vol. 10, no. 214, p. 51 and pp. 867–918. The three letters from Jane to Lord Ellenborough quoted in this chapter were offered in evidence. (The page no's which follow are those in the individual reports.)

2 House of Lords *Minutes of Evidence* given by William Walton, p. 8 of report.

3 Sir H. Maxwell, *The Creevey Papers*, p. 308.

4 Margaret Steele's evidence to House of Commons, p. 41.

5 MH/01, p. 1.

6 Margaret Steele's evidence to House of Commons, pp. 36–1 of report.

7 F. Bamford and Duke of Wellington, *Journal of Mrs Arbuthnot*, pp. 276–7.

8 MH/01, pp. 1–2.

9 Margaret Steele's evidence to House of Commons, pp. 36–1 of report.

10 House of Commons, Minutes of Evidence, p. 48 of report.

11 MH/01, pp. 1–2.

12 SCA, Mary Spencer-Stanhope to Eliza, 60612, 5 June 1829.

13 Keele, SC3/60, G. Agar Ellis to Ralph Sneyd, 29 June 1829.

14 Ibid., SC8/129, 14 September 1829.

15 PRO 30/12, Ellenborough Papers, box 1(5), 7 September 1829.

16 MH/01, p. 1.

17 PRO, 30/12, Ellenborough Papers, Mrs Mowcock to Lord Ellenborough, 27 January 1830.

18 Ibid., Mr March to Lord Ellenborough, 29 January 1830.

19 PRO 30, box 7 (6–9), Ellenborough Papers housed in the Public Record Office at Kew.

20 MH/01, p. 2.

Chapter 6   A Fatal Notoriety

1 This paragraph and the quotations from witnesses that follow are extracted from the Minutes of Evidence of both the House of Lords Papers, 1830, vol. 16, no. 36, pp. 333 ff.; and the House of Commons Sessional Papers (7), 1830, vol. 10, no. 214, p. 51 and pp. 867–918.

2 *The Times*, 2 April 1830, p. 2, col. 3.

3 Ibid., opinion column, p. 3.

4 Ibid.

5 Ibid., 20 March 1830, p. 2, col. 6.

6 *The Age*, 14 March 1830, p. 107.

7 Ibid., 21 March 1830, p. 91.

8 Horace Wyndham, *Judicial Dramas*, p. 194.

9 *The Times*, leader, 7 April 1830, p. 5.

10 Ibid., 2 April 1830, p. 2, col. 3.

11 Count Rodolphe Apponyi, *Vingt-cinq ans à Paris*, p. 155.

12 Keele, Lord Clare to Ralph Sneyd, SC7/13, 5 April 1830.

13 E. M. Oddie, *A Portrait of Ianthe*, p. 98.

14 PRO 30/12, box 1(7), Ellenborough Papers, 16 April 1867, to Mrs Pembroke (governess to his daughters) 'The future of my daughters when I am no longer here to protect them has long been a matter of great anxiety to me . . . [I intend to make] a provision with a view to leaving them . . . in comfort and advantage when I am gone . . . I remember with gratitude the zeal you have had for their instruction and the indulgence with which you have treated their occasional waywardness.'

15 Will of Lord Ellenborough, Somerset House, London.

16 MH/01.

17 Ibid.

18 Apponyi, *Vingt-cinq ans à Paris*, p. xxv of Introduction.

19 MH/01 p. 2; quotes letter written by Felix Schwarzenberg on 31 December 1830.

20. Ibid.

21 MH/06, poem entitled 'To Felix' (her dead child), dated Paris, 29 December 1830.

22 Letter from FS to JED, dated 31 December 1830; quoted in MH/01, p. 2.

Chapter 7   Jane and the King

1 Harriet Countess Granville, *Letters 1810–1845*, January 1831, p. 76.

2 Count Rodolphe Apponyi, *Vingt-cinq ans à Paris*, pp. 423 ff.

3 MH/01, pp. 2–4.

4 MH/06, poem written by JED in Paris, undated, 1831.

5 Apponyi, *Vingt-cinq ans à Paris*, p. 423.

6 MH/01, letter quoted from FS to JED, 31 December 1830.

7 MH/01, letter from FS to JED, 20 June 1831.

8 MH/01, p. 3.

9 Adolph Schwarzenberg, *Prince Felix zu Schwarzenberg*, p. 11.

10 Elizabeth Holland, *Lady Holland to her Son*, 17 March 1830.

11 MH/04, diary entry, 15 December 1856; and BHM, JED to King Ludwig, 27 February 1836.

12 Sir H. Maxwell, *The Creevey Papers*, 21 April 1823 *et seq.*; and E. M. Oddie, *A Portrait of Ianthe*, p. 119.

13 Oddie, *Portrait*, p. 119.

14 Henry Channon, *The Ludwigs of Bavaria*, p. 29.

15 Ludwig's father Maximilian I was the first King of Bavaria, having been elevated from the status of Prince Elector by Napoleon.

16 Channon, *The Ludwigs of Bavaria*, p. 29.

17 Prince Leopold, widower of Princess Charlotte, who died in childbirth, and to whom Britain felt a moral responsibility, was a leading contender for the Greek throne but withdrew from the lists, having had a better offer from Belgium.

18 He was christened Louis after his godfather Louis XVI of France. 'Ludwig' is the German equivalent of 'Louis'. Charles Venningen always referred to King Ludwig as 'King Louis' in his letters to Jane, e.g. MH/13, CV to JED, 4 November 1865.

19 BHM, JED to King Ludwig, 26 October 1831. Jane met the King on 7 and 8 October. In his diary he describes her as twenty-one years old and says he paid his first visit to her home on 13 October; three days later he wrote a poem to her; Gerard Hojer, *Die Schönheitsgalerie König Ludwigs I* (Schnell & Steiner), 1990, p. 72.

20 Ibid., 20 October 1831.

21 MH/01, p. 3.

22 BHM, JED to King Ludwig, 30 October 1831.

23 At the Bayerisches Hauptsarchiv, Munich there are seventy-five letters from Jane Digby to King Ludwig. The first is dated 18 October 1831, the last 19 January 1838.

24 BHM, 24 July 1832.

25 Irving Wallace, *Nymphos and Other Maniacs*, p. 140.

26 BHM, JED to King Ludwig, 30 October 1831.

27 Poem entitled 'He comes not . . .', dated 3 November 1831.

28 Today this collection of portraits is displayed at Nyphenburg Palace, once King Ludwig's summer palace outside Munich but now within the city limits.

29 BHM, JED to King Ludwig, 11 November 1831.

30 MH/01, p. 3.

31 BHM, JED to King Ludwig, undated, c. 15 December 1831.

32 Ibid., 8 February 1832.

33 BHM, JED to King Ludwig, 25 March 1832.

34 Ibid., 10 November 1832.

35 Margaret Fox Schmidt, *Passion's Child*, p. 106.

36 Ibid.

37 BHM, JED to King Ludwig, 10 November 1832.

38 MH/01, p. 3.

39 BHM, JED to King Ludwig, 10 November 1832.

40 Ibid., 13 July 1832.

41 Ibid., 24 July 1832.

42 Ibid., 11 September 1832.

43 Ibid., 21 October 1832.

44 MH/01, p. 3.

45 BHM, JED to King Ludwig, 12 December 1832.

46 Ibid.

47 BHM, JED to King Ludwig, 1 January 1833.

48 MH/13, letter from CV to JED, 6 February 1861. De Laurin, the Austrian consul at Palermo, had personally registered the birth of Heribert to LJD [Lady Jane Digby], knowing her true identity. When Heribert grew up it was vital in order to claim the Venningen inheritance to prove his parentage. At Charles's request Jane sent a full statement to de Laurin and a request that he would confirm the real facts. De Laurin complied, and Charles wrote to her that their son was now safe, 'due to you. Without the different documents which you were good enough to send . . . it would have been difficult if not impossible to prove that he is the same person born to L.J.D., on January 27th 1833. Thanks to you we are able to prove it.'

49 BHM, JED to King Ludwig, 6 January 1833.

50 Ibid., 8 March 1833.

51 MH/04, diary entry, 12 May 1854.

52 MH/11, letter from Didi to Lord Edward Digby in 1883.

53 MH/01, p. 3.

54 Ibid.

55 BHM, JED to King Ludwig, undated, c. 6 July 1833, written at Kehl.

56 Ibid., 28 August 1833.
57 MH/01, p. 3; and H. J. Hunt, *Balzac and Lady Ellenborough*, French Studies (Oxford University Press, 1963), p. 255.
58 Princess Dorothea Lieven, *Correspondence with Earl Grey*, 10 October 1833.
59 Princess Dorothea Lieven, *Correspondence with Palmerston*, p. 154.
60 BHM, JED to King Ludwig, 28 August 1833.

Chapter 8 Ianthe's Secret

1 BHM, CV to King Ludwig, 26 October 1833. This was possible because the baron had property in the Duchy of Hessen as well as in that of Baden.
2 MH/01, p. 3.
3 BHM, JED to King Ludwig, 27 November 1833.
4 Ibid., 13 October 1833.
5 Letters from Charles Venningen to King Ludwig; Bayerisches Hauptsarchiv, No. NL Ludwig, I, C10 dated 26 October 1833 and 9 November 1833.
6 Ibid., and JED to King Ludwig, 8 September 1833.
7 Ibid.
8 These letters were destroyed after her death by a member of the Digby family in England; however, a summary was first made of the contents; see MH/01.
9 BHM, JED to King Ludwig, 26 October 1833.
10 Ibid., letter 48, undated, December 1833.
11 The Venningens' home at Weinheim is now the town hall.
12 BHM, JED to King Ludwig, undated, December 1833.
13 Ibid., undated, February 1834, headed 'Saturday morning'.
14 Sir Henry Keppel, *A Sailor's Life under Four Sovereigns*, p. 339. (It was generally but wrongly believed that Lord Ellenborough was over seventy when Jane married him; see *Die Schönheits-Galerie*, p. 72.)
15 Ibid., p. 342.
16 MH/13, CV to JED, 16 February 1839. 'Mazeppa' by Lord Byron was published in 1819.
17 BHM, JED to King Ludwig, undated, February 1834, headed 'Saturday'.
18 Ibid., 22 April 1834.
19 Ibid., 23 May 1834.
20 Ibid., 18 August 1834.
21 Ibid.
22 Ibid., 12 July 1834.
23 Conversation between Lord Digby and the author, Minterne House, 15 April

1993. It is a historical fact that several of Ludwig's children and grandchildren suffered mental illnesses ranging from mild eccentricity to complete insanity. His grandson Ludwig II, builder of the ethereal-looking castles, was suspected of madness prior to his mysterious death, in the lake at Berg in 1886. The next brother in line, King Otto I, had to be removed from the throne in 1913 because of insanity.
24 BHM, JED to King Ludwig, 8 February 1832.
25 Ibid., 10 November 1832.
26 MH/13, CV to JED, 16 February 1839.
27 Ibid.
28 BHM, JED to King Ludwig, undated, July 1834.
29 Ibid., 27 June 1835.
30 Honoré de Balzac, *Lily of the Valley*, Heron Books edition, pp. 287–8.
31 See Honoré de Balzac, *Lettres à l'étrangère*, 15 May 1840; also H. J. Hunt, 'Balzac and Lady Ellenborough', *French Studies* (1963), Bodleian Library, Oxford University. The original letter JED to Balzac, dated 19 July 1835, is archived at the Musée Balzac, Chantilly, France. See also Balzac, *The Love Letters of Honoré de Balzac 1833–1842*, vol. 2, p. 63.
32 Balzac, *Lily of the Valley*, p. 414.
33 Ibid., pp. 356–7.
34 JED to Balzac, 19 July 1835, Musée Balzac, Chantilly, France.
35 BHM, JED to King Ludwig, 23 July 1835.
36 Ibid., JED to King Ludwig, 21 September 1835.
37 BHM, JED to King Ludwig, undated, October 1835.
38 Ibid. The whereabouts of this portrait are unknown.
39 Ibid., undated, October 1835, headed 'Tuesday morning'.

Chapter 9 A Duel for the Baroness

1 MH/13, CV to JED, 16 February 1839.
2 Honoré de Balzac, *The Love Letters*, vol. 2, p. 346, and *Lettres à l'étrangère*, January 1836.
3 Count Rodolphe Apponyi, *Vingt-cinq ans à Paris*, p. 159.
4 MH/13, CV to JED, 16 February 1839.
5 Count Rodolphe Apponyi, *Vingt-cinq ans à Paris*, p. 159.
6 BHM, JED to King Ludwig, 27 February 1836.

7 BHM, JED to King Ludwig, 22 December 1836.
8 MH/13, CV to JED, 16 February 1839.
9 BHM, JED to King Ludwig, 18 July 1837.
10 RB/01, JED to KD, 1 February 1870.
11 BHM, JED to King Ludwig, 19 January 1838.
12 Ibid., and CV to Edward Digby, 25 March 1839.
13 MH/13, CV to ESD, 25 March 1839.
14 Ibid., CV to JED, 16 February 1839.
15 Ibid., CV to ESD, 25 March 1839.
16 Ibid.
17 Ibid., CV to JED, 16 February 1839.
18 Ibid., CV to JED, 27 June 1847.
19 Ibid.
20 MH/04, diary entry, 22 January 1857.

Chapter 10   False Colours

1 MH/10, Lady Andover's diary, 17 August 1840.
2 Ibid., 12 September 1840.
3 Ibid., 19 September 1840.
4 Ibid., 2 November 1840.
5 E. M. Oddie, *A Portrait of Ianthe*, p. 150.
6 BHM, Bavarian Consul in Athens to CVV, 17 January 1842, ref. NL Ludwig I, 90-1-2; and, Edmond About, *La Grèce contemporaine*, 8th French edition, p. 104.
7 Alexandre Buchon, *Premier Voyage dans les Cyclades* (Émile Paul, Paris 1911), pp. 7-8.
8 MH/02. This diary has survived only partially. All the pages from October 1841 to November 1854 have been cut out close to the binding, and were destroyed by Jane's nieces after her death. The contents of the surviving pages are covered in a later chapter. Fortunately, on several journeys JED recorded her day-to-day experiences in draft form, to transfer to the formal diary, and these have survived intact.
9 Harriet, Countess of Granville, *Letters 1810–1845*, p. 335.
10 BHM, Bavarian consul in Athens to CVV, 17 January 1842, ref. NL Ludwig I, 90-1-2.
11 E. M. Oddie, *A Portrait of Ianthe*, pp. 153-4.
12 SCA, JED to KD, 19 September 1841.
13 PRO, Chancery Lane, London, D 11 1979, Last Will and Testament of Admiral Sir Henry Digby, p. 312.
14 MH/10, Lady Andover's diary, 10 December 1842.
15 Oddie, *Portrait of Ianthe*, pp. 158-9.

16 Ibid., pp. 161-2; and Margaret Fox Schmidt, *Passion's Child*, p. 149.
17 Schmidt, *Passion's Child*, p. 149.
18 MH/04, diary entry, 12 December 1856.
19 MH/14, Mathilde Diebitsch to Lord Digby, March 1883.
20 MH/01, p. 5, and MH/04, diary entry dated 15 August 1859.
21 Ibid.
22 Schmidt, *Passion's Child*, p. 151.
23 Oddie, *Portrait of Ianthe*, p. 162.

Chapter 11   The Queen's Rival

1 E. M. Oddie, *A Portrait of Ianthe*, p. 162.
2 Ibid.
3 Horace Wyndham, *The Magnificent Montez* (Hutchinson, 1935), pp. 108-17.
4 MH/13, CV to JED, 27 June 1868.
5 Ibid.
6 MH/01; also MH/03, 22 November 1854.
7 MH/04, October 1856.
8 MH/08, notes in sketchbook.
9 Irving Wallace, *Nymphos and Other Maniacs* (Simon & Schuster, NY), pp. 158-9. No source is given for this story.
10 Edmond About, *La Grèce contemporaine*, 8th French edition (Hachette et cie, Paris, 1854), p. 104.
11 MH/01, p. 5.
12 This was a well-ingrained habit with JED, and a useful 'footprint' for researchers. A great number of these lists and accounts survive within the papers in the possession of the Digby family in Minterne.
13 MH/04, diary entry, 27 November 1855.
14 About, *La Grèce contemporaine*, 8th French edition, p. 104.
15 Lesley Blanch, *The Wilder Shores of Love*, p. 158.
16 Nassau Senior, *Journal Kept in Turkey and Greece 1857–58*, 20 November 1857.
17 Blanch, *The Wilder Shores of Love*, p. 159.
18 Oddie, *Portrait of Ianthe*, p. 327.
19 About, *La Grèce contemporaine*, 8th French edition, p. 105.
20 Ibid., pp. 31-2.
21 MH/03, diary entry, 4 January 1854.
22 MH/05, 8 May 1853.
23 About, *La Grèce contemporaine*, p. 106.
24 Oddie, *Portrait of Ianthe*, p. 171.
25 MH/02, diary entry, 8 May 1853.
26 Oddie, *Portrait of Ianthe*, p. 165.
27 The sketch upon which JED was working when this incident occurred still exists, dated 23 and 25 February 1852; MH/14.
28 About, *La Grèce contemporaine*, p. 394.
29 Ibid., p. 96.

30 Ibid., pp. 99, 107.
31 W. H. Wilkins, *The Romance of Isabel, Lady Burton*, p. 395.
32 About, *La Grèce contemporaine*, p. 109.
33 MH/08, 17 September 1852.
34 *La Grèce contemporaine*, p. 109.
35 MH/02, diary entry, 8 May 1853.

Chapter 12 The Road to Damascus

1 Edmond About, *La Grèce contemporaire*, French 1st edition (1854), p. 109.
2 Emily Beaufort, *Egyptian Sepulchres and Syrian Shrines*, p. 158. This is a contemporary description, written six years after Jane arrived there, in 1859.
3 Some of the sketches and a formal landscape survive: MH/08, 'Off Carpha', June 1853.
4 MH/03, diary entry, 6 May 1854.
5 MH/04, diary, Thursday 14 March 1855.
6 Several sketches of Jerusalem survive: see notebook MH/08.
7 Letter to the author from Lear's biographer, Valerie Noakes, August 1994.
8 MH/04, diary entry, 6 January 1855.
9 Nassau Senior, *Journal Kept in Turkey and Greece 1857–58* (Longmans 1959), p. 145.
10 Beaufort, *Egyptian Sepulchres and Syrian Shrines*, pp. 331–2.
11 Bayard Taylor, *Lands of the Saracen*, p. 76.
12 Visitors are still shown this view today. It is believed also to be the site where Cain slew Abel.
13 This description is an amalgam of the books of several contemporary writers, including Isabel Burton and Anne Blunt. The Barada River (said to be the ancient Abana mentioned in the Bible) is no longer clear as then, and its abundant fast-flowing muddy waters are confined in a concrete canal during its passage through the city centre.
14 Taylor, *Lands of the Saracen*, p. 123. This description was written six months before Jane stayed at the hotel and in the absence of her own words suffices to give an impression of what she found.
15 Acts 9: 1–25.
16 All these bazaars still exist, and still provide some of the most exciting shopping in the world. When I visited Damascus in 1993 and walked alone among the crowds in the souk I saw only two other Europeans, and they were members of the party with which I travelled out. Apart from the invention of electricity, the area is probably exactly as it was in Jane's day.

17 Beaufort, *Egyptian Sepulchres and Syrian Shrines*, vol. 1, p. 325.
18 MH/03, 25 December 1853.
19 Beaufort, *Egyptian Sepulchres and Syrian Shrines*, p. 326.
20 Much of the description used here is an amalgam of Jane's diaries and the account of Emily Beaufort, who six years later went to Palmyra with Medjuel and Jane and wrote a colourful description of the trip. See chapter 17.
21 MH/02, Jane diaries, 4 April 1854.
22 Mary Mackintosh, *Damascus and its People*, p. 222.
23 Beaufort. *Egyptian Sepulchres and Syrian Shrines*, vol. 1, p. 346.
24 *The Times*, obituary, 4 September 1881, p. 11, col. 4.
25 E. M. Oddie, *A Portrait of Ianthe*, pp. 190–1.
26 Lady Anne Blunt, *Journalists and Correspondence 1878–1917*, pp. 62–3.
27 1 Kings 9: 18.
28 Beaufort, *Egyptian Sepulchres and Syrian Shrines*, p. 369.
29 Ibid. p. 377.
30 MH/04, diary entry, 20 May 1855: 'Khan el Arrouss ... it was here, a year ago, that Medjuel wished to take me on his Hadjin.'
31 Isabel Burton, *The Inner Life of Syria, Palestine and the Holy Land*, p. 238.
32 MH/04, diary entry, 23 October 1857.
33 All unattributed information in this chapter is taken from Jane's diaries and sketchbooks, or from the first-hand accounts of travellers in Syria who were contemporaries of Jane and who had relevant experiences.

Chapter 13 Arabian Nights

1 MH/08, coded notes in JED's pocket sketchbook.
2 MH/07, 8 October 1866.
3 MH/02, 2 November 1853.
4 MH/03, 26 November 1853.
5 MH/02, 19 December 1853.
6 Ibid., 21 December 1853.
7 Ibid., 19 December 1853.
8 Isabel Burton *The Life of Sir Richard Burton*, p. 493v.i.
9 MH/02, 26 December 1854.
10 Ibid.
11 MH/02, 28 January 1854.
12 MH/02, 4 January 1854.
13 Ibid., 5 January 1854.
14 Ibid., 9 January 1854.
15 MH/04, 1 January 1855.

16 Sir Henry Rawlinson (1810–95) was a noted oriental scholar. As a young army officer he was sent to Persia in 1833 to reorganise the Shah's army. In his spare time he studied undeciphered cuneiform texts. It was he who translated the triple texts of Behistun, providing the foundation of all our knowledge of ancient Babylon and Assyria.

17 MH/08, from notes and sketches in pocket notebook.

18 MH/08, sketch in pocket notebook entitled 'Messoul March '54'.

19 MH/02, 5–7 April 1854.

20 Ibid., 4 May 1854.

21 Ibid., 21 April 1854.

22 Ibid., 19 April 1854.

23 Ibid., 6 May 1854.

24 Ibid., 8 May 1854.

25 Ibid., 14 May 1854.

26 Ibid., 21 May 1854.

27 Ibid., 22 May 1854.

28 Ibid. This was the final entry in a soft notebook of the type Jane sometimes used to make *aides-mémoire* which would later be transferred into a diary in a 'fair hand'. This book contained the entire record of her Baghdad trip, much of it written in tiny cramped handwriting in pencil, often by the aid of firelight in camp, and sometimes as she rode along on her camel.

Chapter 14 Honeymoon in Palmyra

Note: The primary source for this chapter, and for most of the quotations, is JED's diary. Where the quote is an obvious diary entry and/or the date is given in the text, separate citations have been omitted.

1 Edmond About, *La Grèce contemporaine*, 1st French edition, pp. 110–11.

2 MH/03, 23 October 1857.

3 About, *La Grèce contemporaine*, p. 111.

4 MH/03, 19 November 1854.

5 Ibid., 22 November 1854.

6 Ibid., 2 December 1854.

7 MH/03, 19 January 1855.

8 Richard Wood was wrong in this assertion. Though they may not instigate or refuse a divorce, bedouin women have considerable rights in the event they are divorced (and Islam itself gives women the right to divorce). See H. R. P. Dickson, *The Arab of the Desert*, pp. 106–7.

9 MH/03, 26 February 1855.

10 Ibid., 27 March 1855.

11 Ibid.

12 Emily Beaufort, *Egyptian Sepulchres and Syrian Shrines*, p. 386. Emily Beaufort undoubtedly had this information from Medjuel and Jane during her journey with them to Palmyra in 1859.

13 Ibid., vol. 1, pp. 329 and 342. When the slave children grew up they were usually given their freedom, according to Emily Beaufort's research. Some, however, remained in the household of the former master 'on an equality with the rest of the people and the fact of being a slave [is] no social disadvantage'. See Lady Anne Blunt, *Journals and Correspondence 1878–1917*, p. 75.

14 MH/03, 20 March 1855.

15 Ibid., 31 December 1856.

16 Ibid., 22 March 1855.

17 Ibid., undated, July 1855.

18 Ibid., 15 August 1855.

19 Ibid., 25 August 1855.

20 Ibid.

Chapter 15 Wife to the Sheikh

Note: Because many of the extracts from Jane's diary are identified and dated as such within the text I have not sourced every extract. Those separately identified here are those where the text may not make the precise source or date clear.

1 BL, Lady Anne Blunt's diaries, 10 April 1881.

2 MH/04, diary entry, 12 November 1855.

3 MH/04, diary entry, 18 November 1855.

4 A. M. W. Stirling, *Coke of Norfolk and his Friends*, p. 350.

5 The description of Jane's house and garden is taken from various entries by Jane, and the journals of many visitors to the house.

6 RB/01, JED to KD, 15 October 1862.

7 MH/04, 24 November 1855.

8 Ibid., 7 December 1855.

9 MH/04, 5 March 1856.

10 These drawings and watercolours still exist in the possession of Lord Digby at Minterne House, Dorset.

11 MH/04, 16 February 1856.

12 Ibid.; also Emily Beaufort, *Egyptian Sepulchres and Syrian Shrines*, p. 374.

13 MH/04, 14 April 1856.

14 Ibid., 21 April 1856.

15 RB/01, JED to KD, 22 June 1856.

16 Through marriage the estates subsequently passed to the Wingfield Bakers.

17 RB/01, JED to KD, 22 June 1856.

18 MH/04, diary entry, 14 September 1856.

19 Sir Horace Rumbold, *Final Recollections of a Diplomatist*, pp. 36–8.

20 MH/04, 3 December 1856.
21 See chapter 14: 'Frangya' was an affectionate corruption of the bedouin word for western Europeans, Ferengi (Franks), still in use today.

Chapter 16   Return to England

1 Jane had spent some summers in Tunbridge Wells at the house of Countess Huntington when she was a boarder at school.
2 MH/04, 28 December 1856.
3 Ibid., 3 January 1857.
4 Ibid., 24 March 1857.
5 RB/01, JED to KD, 15 July 1857.
6 MH/04, 25 August 1857.
7 Lieutenant-Colonel R. W. C. Charlton (Rtd), who spent many years serving in the East and in Syria, told me that one year in India his regiment had produced a cartoon Christmas card showing an 8th Hussar trooper cutting off the head of the Rani of Jhansi. 'Months later,' he said, 'I was sitting with the Roalla tribe, well east of Aqaba, when a song was sung to the *rushaba* (the bedouin single-string violin) about the Ferengi cutting off the head of the Queen of the Jhansi. The song had travelled from India across the deserts . . . On that occasion only, I did not mention my regiment!' Letter to author 20 March 1994.
8 A. M. W. Stirling, *Coke of Norfolk and his Friends*, p. 351.
9 RB/01, 5 February 1858.
10 MH/04, 2 May 1858.
11 RB/01, JED to KD, 17 July 1859.
12 Ibid., 30 June 1858.
13 MH/13, CV to JED, 7 November 1858.
14 RB/01, JED to KD, 7 November 1858.

Chapter 17   Alone in Palmyra

1 MH/08, draft in JED's notebook, translated by Jehan Rajab.
2 MH/03, 1 January 1859.
3 Ibid., Monday 24 January 1859.
4 Ibid., 17 February 1859. The chief purpose of the search by the old man was, of course, for jewellery, which the women of the desert greatly prized, but of almost equal importance was the gummy cloth close to the bodies valued by the bedouin men for the treatment of splints and sprains in horses. See also Emily Beaufort, *Egyptian Sepulchres and Syrian Shrines*, vol. 1, p. 382.
5 MH/03, 20 February 1859.
6 Laudanum, a tincture of opium, was used

extensively in the eighteenth and nineteenth centuries as a painkiller and powerful analgesic.
7 A. M. W. Pickering, *Memoirs of A. M. W. Stirling*, p. 194.
8 MH/03, 19 March 1859.
9 Isabel Burton, *Life of Sir Richard Burton*, p. 486.
10 MH/13, CV to JED, 7 August 1859.
11 Beaufort, *Egyptian Sepulchres and Syrian Shrines*, vol. 1, pp. 324–6.
12 Ibid., p. 331.
13 Ibid., pp. 351–75.
14 The splendid portraits of Jane and Medjuel reproduced elsewhere in this book are the property of Mr and Mrs Tareq Rajab of the TSR Museum in Kuwait, and by whose kind permission they are included. Carl Haag's work has not received the recognition today that it undoubtedly deserves, as the works owned by the Victoria and Albert Museum, London, readily reveal.
15 RB/01, JED to KD, 1 January 1860.
16 Isabel Burton, *The Inner Life of Syria, Palestine and the Holy Land*, vol. 1, pp. 125–6.

Chapter 18   The Massacre

1 Isabel Burton, *The Inner Life of Syria*, p. 68.
2 T. E. Lawrence wrote of similar doors in his desert fortress at Azrak: 'The door was a poised slab of dressed basalt, a foot thick, turning on pivots of itself, socketed into threshold and lintel. It took a great effort to start swinging and at the end went shut with a clang and a crash, which made tremble the west wall of the old castle.' See *Seven Pillars of Wisdom* (Reprint Society, 1939, p. 445.
3 Burton, *The Inner Life of Syria*, vol. 2, p. 68.
4 MH/04, 14 May 1860.
5 RB/01, JED to KD, 30 July 1860.
6 William G. Palgrave, *Four Lectures on the Syrian Massacre*, pp. 11–44.
7 Charles H. Churchill, *The Druzes and the Maronites*, p. 210.
8 Burton, *The Inner Life of Syria*, p. 109.
9 MH/04, 9 July 1860.
10 RB/01, JED to KD, 30 July 1860.
11 MH/04, 10 July 1860. Mr Graham was a missionary whom Jane had befriended. He had provided her with a supply of Arabic primers so she could teach the bedouin children to read.
12 RB/01, JD to KD, 30 July 1860.
13 MH/04, 11 July 1860.

14 RB/01, JED to KD, 30 July 1860.
15 MH/04, 21 July 1860.
16 MH/13, CV to JED, 6 February 1861.
17 RB/01, JED to KD, 9 September 1867.
18 E. M. Oddie, *A Portrait of Ianthe*, p. 250.
19 MH/04, 10 October 1860.
20 Ibid., 1 December 1860. Dibs are sun-dried grapes dipped in a sweet coating. They are mentioned several times in the Bible.
21 Ibid., 18 December 1860.
22 Ibid., 24 December 1860.
23 Ibid., 13 January 1861.
24 RB/01, JED to KD, 21 March 1861.
25 MH/04, 21 March 1864.
26 RB/01, letter from Mrs Charlton to Theresa Buxton (granddaughter of Kenelm Digby), February 1956.

Chapter 19   Visitors from England

1 BL, Wentworth Bequest no. 53892, Lady Anne Blunt, diary, 8 April 1878.
2 Isabel Burton, *The Inner Life of Syria*, p. 109.
3 Details of Jane's life in camp are taken from a number of sources, chiefly her diary, her letters home; from the diaries, journals and correspondence of Richard and Isabel Burton; and from those of Lady Anne Blunt.
4 E. M. Oddie, *A Portrait of Ianthe*, p. 234.
5 MH/04, 8–10 March 1862.
6 Isabel Burton, *Life of Sir Richard Burton*, p. 512.
7 RB/01, JED to KED, 19 March 1862. Kenelm was Rector of Tittleshall, a village near Holkham in Norfolk, the living of which was in the gift of his uncle the Earl of Leicester (i.e. Thomas Coke's son by his second wife).
8 MH/04, 7 April 1862.
9 RB/01, Caroline Digby to JED, 19 February 1862.
10 Royal Archives, diary of HRH Edward Prince of Wales, 29 April 1862. Included by gracious permission of Her Majesty the Queen.
11 Valerie Noakes, *Edward Lear* (Collins, 1968), p. 164.
12 PRO, FO78/1686, Consul Rogers to FO, 25 February 1862.
13 MH/04, 23 August 1862.
14 RB/01, JED to KD, and JED to Caroline Digby Watson, 15 October 1862.
15 PRO, FO78 1751, Consul Rogers to FO, XC 11848.
16 Ibid.

17 Ibid.
18 MH/04, 26 October 1862.
19 Ibid., Thursday 6 November 1862.

Chapter 20   The Sitt el Mezrab

1 MH/13, CV to JED, 28 March 1865.
2 RB/01, JED to KD, 1 July 1863.
3 MH/04, 15 July 1863.
4 Ibid., 24 July 1863.
5 Ibid., 5 August 1863.
6 Ibid., 12 October 1864.
7 MH/13, CV to JED, 27 August 1863 and 28 March 1865.
8 MH/07, JED to Theresa, Lady Digby, 8 October 1866. A point of particular interest in this letter to her sister-in-law is Jane's unselfconscious use of the code she used often in her diary. Clearly she knew that her brother would also understand it.
9 MH/04, 9 July 1864.
10 PRO, FO78 1751, XC 11848 1863.
11 Ibid.
12 MH/04, 12–24 September 1864.
13 Ibid., 24 September 1864.
14 MH/07, JED to Theresa, Lady Digby, 22 April 1865.
15 MH/04, 16 March 1866.
16 Ibid., 13 July 1865.
17 Ibid., 27 September 1865.
18 Ibid., 6 September 1865.
19 RB/01, JED to KD, 27 September 1866.
20 MH/04, 11 January 1866.
21 Ibid., 27 September 1866.
22 Ibid., 20 June 1867.
23 MH/08, pocket sketchbook, 1867, p. 50.
24 MH/04, 5 July 1867.

Chapter 21   Challenge by Ouadjid

1 MH/04, 10 August 1867.
2 RB/01, JED to KD, 31 March 1868.
3 MH/13, CV to JED, 4 November 1865.
4 This was subsequently confirmed in the diaries of Lady Anne Blunt, BL MS Dept, Wentworth Bequest, 53892 22 April 1878. Note that Jane saw Mascha several times over the next decade; Mascha always made a point of calling on her to pay her respects.
5 MH/04, 2 December 1868.
6 Ibid., 19 December 1868.
7 Ibid., 31 December 1868.

Chapter 22   The Burtons

1 RB/01, JED to KD, 1 February 1870.
2 RB/01, JED to KD, 9 September 1870.
3 BL, MS Dept, Wentworth Bequest

53892, Anne Blunt, Journals, 7 December 1878.

4 Isabel Burton, *The Inner Life of Syria, Palestine and the Holy Land*, pp. 126–7.

5 Amy Fullerton-Fullerton, *A Lady's Ride through Palestine and Syria*, p. 335.

6 Burton, *Inner Life of Syria*, p. 136.

7 W. H. Wilkins, *The Romance Isabel, Lady Burton*, p 396.

8 Isabel Burton, *Life of Sir Richard Burton*, p. 486.

9 Burton, *Inner Life of Syria*, p. 3.

10 Ibid., p. 293.

11 Sefton Dearden, *The Arabian Knight* (Arthur Barker), 1936, p. 288.

12 See *The Perfumed Garden*, translated by Sir Richard Burton, with an Introduction by Alan Hull Walton (Panther Books, 1963). Isabel's act caused a furore among scholars (and probably voyeurs) since a great deal of new and academic thought on pederasty was known to have been included by Burton following a lifetime's academic interest in the subject. A draft translation of the original Arabian script discovered in Algeria in 1850 had been made by Burton some years previously in co-operation with an Oxford scholar. But a second translation was eagerly awaited, for it was known to include an additional new chapter on homosexuality, many unpublished notes and annotations made by Burton over several decades of travel in Arabia and the East, and other information that was stored in his brain. The first translation with chapter headings such as, 'Prescriptions for increasing the Dimensions of Small Members, and for making them Splendid, 'Everything that is favourable to the Act of Coition', as well as helpful information such as the 'Deceits and Treacheries of Women', guaranteed sales in any case. A version published in French had already enjoyed remarkable success, but it was generally conceded that Burton's knowledge of the culture and Arabic language was vastly superior, and would have provided a unique opus.

13 Wilkins, *The romance of Isabel, Lady Burton*, p. 395.

14 RB/01, JED to KD, 9 September 1870.

15 Burton, *Inner Life of Syria*, vol. 2, p. 3.

16 Isabel printed an abridged version of this long letter, altering Jane's address of 'My dear Mrs Burton' to 'My dear Isabel', and the ending to read 'Your affectionate cousin' (see *Life of Sir Richard Burton*,

p. 539), to support her claim of close relationship. Mr Rogers would certainly have had grounds for suing Isabel had she not abridged it, for Jane was open in her remarks about his corruption.

17 Burton, *Inner Life of Syria*, vol. 2, pp. 12–13.

18 Ibid., p. 13. Medjuel received a decoration from the Sultan for his part in the capture of Hassan Beg.

19 Lord Redesdale, *Memories*, p. 564.

20 Jehan Rajab, Kuwait, private correspondence with author, June 1994.

21 Redesdale, *Memories*, p. 564.

22 Burton, *Life of Sir Richard Burton*, p. 486.

23 E. M. Oddie, *A Portrait of Ianthe*, p. 280.

24 Ibid. Although Oddie does not provide any date for this incident, Mott and his wife were partially responsible for the dismissal of Burton, and Jane never received them after June 1871.

25 Burton, *Inner Life of Syria*, p. 267.

26 Burton, *Life of Richard Burton*, p. 512.

27 Fifty-eight letters of protest from Syrian residents still survive in the Foreign Office files at Kew – see PRO, FO78/2259–2681.

28 Burton, *Life of Sir Richard Burton*, p. 512.

29 PRO, FO78/2259. Note the dates by the Muslim calendar.

30 Burton, *Inner Life of Syria*, p. 270.

Chapter 23 Untimely Obituary

1 Isabel Burton, *The Inner Life of Syria*, p. 134.

2 MH/11, Lady Strangford to Lord Digby, 4 April 1873.

3 Isabel Burton, *Life of Sir Richard Burton*, p. 487.

4 MH/04, 16 July 1871.

5 MH/12, Heribert to JED, 28 March 1875.

6 MH/04, May 1876. Admiral Murray was five years younger than Jane. He was C.-in-C. Mediterranean 1874–77; and Gentleman Usher of the Black Rod from 1883 until his death in 1887.

7 Sir Edwin Pears, *Forty Years in Constantinople*, pp. 71–4.

8 Ibid.

9 BL, Wentworth Bequest, 53892, Anne Blunt's diary, 8 April 1878.

10 Lady Anne Blunt, *Bedouin Tribes of the Euphrates*, p. 108. Anne Blunt spells Medjuel as Mijuel, but as elsewhere I have changed it in her narrative to avoid confusion.

11 BL, Wentworth Bequest, 53892, Anne Blunt's Journal, 22 April 1878.
12 Ibid.
13 Ibid., 23 April 1878.
14 Ibid.
15 Ibid.

Chapter 24 Sunset Years

1   MH/04, 15 May 1878.
2   Ibid., 18 May 1878.
3   BL MSS Dept, 53892, Wentworth Bequest, Anne Blunt's diary, 12 December 1878.
4   MH/04, several entries during May 1878.
5   BL MSS Dept, 53892, Wentworth Bequest, Anne Blunt's diary, 5 December 1878.
6   Ibid., 6 December 1878.
7   Ibid.
8   MH/04, 8 December 1878.
9   BL, Wentworth Bequest, Anne Blunt's diary, 12 December 1878.
10 *The Times*, 4 September 1881, p. 11.
11 Sir Valentine Chirol, *Fifty Years in a Changing World*, p. 81.
12 MH/04, 7 November 1879.
13 BL, ADD 54146, Wentworth Bequest, JED to Anne Blunt.
14 RB/01, JED to KD, 12 January 1880.
15 MH/04, 3 April 1880.
16 BL, ADD 54146, Wentworth Bequest, JED to Anne Blunt.
17 MH/04, 20 June 1880.
18 Ibid., 3 August 1880.
19 During Ramadan the cannon sounded to mark the end of the fast at sunset each evening.
20 MH/04, 4 September 1880.
21 Ibid., 5 September 1880.
22 Ibid., 27 November 1880.
23 BL, MSS Dept, 53892, Wentworth Bequest, Anne Blunt's diary, 17 March 1881.
24 Ibid., 21 March 1881.

Chapter 25 Funeral in Damascus

1   RB/01, letter from Mrs Reichardt to Emmie Buxton and Hon. Rev. Kenelm Digby, September 1881.

2   RB/01, Suzette H. Smith, Mt Lebanon, to Mrs E. N. Buxton, undated.
3   E. M. Oddie, *A Portrait of Ianthe*, pp. 322–3.
4   RB/01, appendix to letters, pp. 117–18: 'Account Written by Roland L. N. Mitchell'. The entire report of Jane's funeral, which follows in the text, is taken from this eye-witness account.
5   When I read about this nephew I wondered if Mr Mitchell had been mistaken and that the young man was Afet, who was very attached to Jane. But Medjuel had many nephews, the sons of his eight brothers, and Afet spent most of his time in the desert, so he was probably not contactable.
6   Hussein Hinnawi to author, 20 August 1993; see also Charles Glass, *Tribes with Flags* (Atlantic Press, NY, 1990), p. 244.

Epilogue

1   BL, MSS Dept, 53912, Wentworth Bequest, Anne Blunt diaries.
2   RB/01, 'Edward Digby, Written Account', appendix notes, p. 114.
3   Ibid. William Wright was also a witness to Jane's will.
4   William Wright, *Zenobia and Palmyra*.
5   RB/01, appendix notes, p. 114.
6   E. M. Oddie, *A Portrait of Ianthe*, p. 325.
7   Mr Dickson succeeded T. S. Jago and HBM Consul at Damascus.
8   Colonel H. R. P. Dickson, *The Arab of the Desert* (Allen & Unwin, 1949), Preface (written 26 September 1936), p. xiii. Colonel Dickson was subsequently a member of the British Political Agency, and played a significant part in the discovery of Kuwait's oilfields.
9   Ibid.
10 Roz Broadmore, New Zealand, in telephone conversation with the author, May 1994.
11 BL, Wentworth Bequest, diary entry 5 September 1905; also letter to the author from the Earl of Lytton, 11 August 1993.
12 W. H. Wilkins, *The Romance of Isabel, Lady Burton*, p. 539.
13 Ibid.

Bibliography

(All titles published in London unless otherwise stated)

About, Edmond. *La Grèce contemporaine*. Hachette, Paris, various editions, 1855–1907.

Apponyi, Count Rodolphe. *Vingt-cinq ans à Paris*. 4 vols, Daudet, Paris, 1913.

Balzac, Honoré de. *Lily of the Valley*. Heron Books, 1990.

—— *Correspondence*, trans. C. Lamb Kenney. 2 vols, 1878.

—— *The Love Letters of Honoré de Balzac 1833–1842*, trans. D. F. Hanningan. 2 vols, Downey, 1901.

—— *Lettres à l'étrangère*, 2 vols.

Bamford, F., and Wellington, Duke of. *Journal of Mrs Arbuthnot*. Macmillan, 1950.

Beaufort, Emily. *Egyptian Sepulchres and Syrian Shrines*. 2 vols, Longman, 1874.

Blanch, Lesley. *The Wilder Shores of Love*. Murray, 1954.

Blessington, Lady Marguerite. *The Idler in Paris*. 2 vols, Colburn, London, 1841.

Blunt, Lady Anne. *Bedouin Tribes of the Euphrates*. 2 vols, Murray, 1879.

—— *Pilgrimage to Nejd*. 2 vols, John Murray, 1879.

—— *Journals and Correspondence 1878–1917*, ed. Rosemary Marcher and James Fleming. Heriot, 1986.

Blunt, Wilfred Scawen. *My Diaries*. Martin Secker, 1922.

Buchon, Alexandre. *Voyage dans l'Eubée, les Iles Ioniennes et les Cyclades en 1841*. Paul, Paris, 1911.

Burton, Isabel. *Life of Sir Richard Burton*. 2 vols, Chapman & Hall, 1893.

—— *The Inner Life of Syria, Palestine and the Holy Land*. 2 vols, H. S. King, 1875.

Burton, J. *Life of Lady Burton*. Harrap, 1942.

Channon, Henry. *The Ludwigs of Bavaria*. Methuen, 1934.

Chirol, Sir Valentine. *Fifty Years in a Changing World*. 1927: BL shelf mark 010855 eee23.

Churchill, Charles H. *The Druzes and the Maronites*. Bernard Quaritch, 1862.

—— *Abd el Khader*. Chapman & Hall, 1867.

Dickson, H. R. P. *The Arab of the Desert*. Allen & Unwin, 1983.

Ellenborough, Lord. *Political Diaries 1828–1830*, Lord Colchester. Bentley, 1881.

—— *Extracts from his Papers*. A. Law, 1926.

Floyd, Juanita Helm. *Women in the life of Balzac*. Holt, NY, 1921.

Fullerton-Fullerton, A. *A Lady's Ride through Palestine and Syria*. Partridge & Co., 1872.

Glass, Charles. *Tribe with Flags*. Atlantic Monthly Press, NY, 1990.

Gore, John. *Life and Times of Creevey*. Murray, 1937.

Granville, Harriet Countess. *Letters 1810–1845*, ed. F. Leveson-Gower. 2 vols, Longman, 1894.

—— *Letters*. Unwin, 1924.

—— *The Greville Diary*. Heinemann, 1927.

Haag, Carl. *Catalogue of the Pictures and Drawings of Egyptian Life*. Fine Arts Society, London [undated].

Hall, Thornton. *Romances of the Peerage*. Holden & Hardinge, 1914.

Holland, Elizabeth. *Lady Holland to her Son*. Murray, 1946.

Hudson, Marianne (née Stanhope). *Almack's*. 3 vols, Saunders & Otley, 1887.

Jekyll, Joseph. *Correspondence with Lady Sloane Stanley*. Murray, 1894.

Keppel, Sir Henry. *Memoirs*, ed. Sir A. West. Macmillan, 1905.

Lieven, Princess Dorothea. *Correspondence with Earl Grey*. Bentley, 1891.

—— *Letters from London*. Bentley, 1902.

—— *Unpublished Diary* (p. Murray 1925).

—— *Correspondence with Palmerston*. Murray, 1943.

MacGregor, John. *The Rob Roy on the Jordan*. John Murray, 1876; 1904.

MacInlay, Leila. *Unwise Wanderer*. Ward, Locke & Co., 1951.

Mackintosh, Mary. *Damascus and its People*. Seeley & Co., 1883.

Margetson, Stella. *Leisure and Pleasure in the Nineteenth Century*. Cassell, 1969.

Maxwell, Sir H. *The Creevey Papers*. Murray, 1903.

Murray's *Handbook to Syria and Palestine*. Murray, 1858.

Nevill, Lady. *The Reminiscences of Lady Dorothy Nevill*. Thos. Nelson, 1906.

Oddie, E. M. *A Portrait of Ianthe*. Cape, 1935.

Palgrave, William G. *A Year's Journey through Central and Eastern Arabia 1862–1863*. Richardson, 1965.

—— - *Four Lectures on the Syrian Massacre*. Richardson, 1861.

Parry. *The Correspondence of Lord Aberdeen and Princess Lieven*. 1939.

Pears, Sir Edwin. *Forty Years in Constantinople*. Jenkins, 1916.

Pickering, Anna Maria W. *Memoirs of A. M. Stirling*. Privately published, 1904.

Porter, J. L. *Five Years in Damascus*. Murray, 1855.

Quennel, Peter. *Private Letters of Princess Lieven to Metternich*. Murray, 1937.

Redesdale, Lord. *Memories*. 2 vols, Hutchinson, 1915.

—— *Letters*. Houston, 1891.

Roget. *History of the Watercolour Society*. Longman, 1891.

Rumbold, Sir Horace. *Final Recollections of a Diplomatist*. 2 vols, Edward Arnold, 1905.

Schmidt, Margaret Fox. *Passion's Child*. Hamish Hamilton, 1977.

Schwarzenberg, Adolph. *Prince Felix zu Schwarzenberg*. Columbia University Press, NY, 1946.

Senior, Nassau W. *Journal Kept in Turkey and Greece 1857–58*. Longman, 1859.

Spencer-Stanhope, E. *The Letter-Bag of Lady Elizabeth Spencer-Stanhope*, ed. A. M. Stirling. 2 vols, John Lane, 1912.

Stirling, A. M. W. *Coke of Norfolk and his Friends*. 2 vols, Bodley Head, 1912.

Stisted, Georgiana. *The True Life of Richard Burton*. Nichols, 1896.

Taylor, Bayard. *Lands of the Saracen*. G. P. Puttnam, NY, 1855.

Tuckerman, Charles. *Recollections*. 2 vols, 1872.

Vandam, Albert Dresden. *An Englishman in Paris*. Ivers & Co., NY, 1892.

Wallace, Irving. *Nymphos and Other Maniacs*. Simon & Schuster, NY, 1971.

Wilberforce, Edward. *Social Life in Munich*. London, 1864.

Wilkins, W. H. *The Romance of Isabel, Lady Burton*. 2 vols, Hutchinson, 1897.

Wright, William. *Zenobia and Palmyra*. Thos. Nelson, 1895.

Wyndham, Horace. *Judicial Dramas*. Fisher Unwin, 1927.

Acknowledgements

While I was researching this book many people provided help in a variety of guises ranging from time and hospitality, to information, documentation and expertise.

My chief acknowledgement must go, with my grateful thanks, to Lord and Lady Digby who so kindly entrusted me with precious family documents including Jane's diaries, papers and art work. They also gave me gracious hospitality when I worked at Minterne House, and allowed me to organise a photo-shoot of family portraits.

In Syria, Hussein Hinnawi was tremendously important in the search for traces of Jane Digby and her life there. Not only was Hussein extraordinarily helpful as guide and interpreter during my own visit to Syria, but after I returned to England he continued to work out of his own interest in the project, refusing any reward. All previous biographers stated that Jane's house in Damascus had been destroyed to make a tramway in the 1930s. But we now know, thanks to Hussein's untiring research, that the house – or a major part of it – survives and that the original decorations are surprisingly intact although some thirty families now live in the flats into which the original villa has been converted.

It lies just outside the old walls of the city, next to the mosque in the old Khassab quarter, and Hussein was able to photograph the interior and interview at length one of the occupants whose parents bought the property from Medjuel's son, Afet. Although the fountains and trees are long gone, and the aqueducts which carried the water from the River Barada to Jane's gardens and orchard are now covered, the old man showed Hussein the base of what Jane used to call 'the Sheikh's fountain, in the prettiest part of the garden' in what remains of the courtyard.

In a piece of research which particularly pleases me, I traced a branch of

Jane's family to New Zealand. Subsequently, Ros Broadmore (whose father is a direct descendant of Jane's brother Kenelm) wrote and later telephoned to say that her family had many mementoes (such as Jane's silver inkwell, and her silver bejewelled muff chain, which are still used by the family today, the latter as a necklace). More importantly they had a large collection of Jane's papers, including all the letters written to Kenelm and other family members during her years in the desert. Such moments in research are even more satisfying than the publication of a book.

At the Victoria and Albert Museum's National Art Library, with assistance from Antonia Leak, I was able to trace the works of Carl Haag, the artist who made a trip to Palmyra with Jane in 1859. Surely, I reasoned, he could not have resisted painting her? As a result of my research there I made contact in Kuwait with Jehan Rajab, who owns the wonderful paintings by Carl Haag of both Jane and Medjuel at Palmyra. Jehan, an Englishwoman, is a writer and teacher married to a Kuwaiti scholar, Tareq Rajab. She had long been interested in Jane's story.

During the Iraqi occupation of Kuwait in 1990, Jehan hid many artefacts behind false wooden panels she had erected in the museum that she and her husband own. These treasures included the Haag paintings, and it is no exaggeration to state that they survived at great personal risk to Jehan. Her book *Invasion Kuwait* (published in 1993) about her horrific experience as an ordinary housewife and mother, under siege for six months from August 1990, oppressed by an army as brutish as Hitler's, should be compulsory reading for every Western politician.

In the archives of Bavaria's royal family, the House of Wittelsbach, in Munich, I was able – thanks to the assistance of Dr Hans Puchta and Peter Kastner – to transcribe seventy-five letters and notes written by Jane to King Ludwig between 1831 and 1838 when she was his closest confidante and, for a time, his mistress. At the Nymphenburg Palace I was helped by Dr Gerhard Hojer and his staff to trace various likenesses of Jane commissioned by King Ludwig I; and by Dr Christoph Heilmann at the Neue Pinakothek to research King Ludwig. Herr Kleefoot, Oberbürgermeister (Mayor) of the town of Weinheim, kindly provided a photograph of Jane's former home there – it is now the town hall.

At Holkham Hall in Norfolk, Christine Hiskey helped me to find my way through the relevant archives of the Earl of Leicester and the Coke family. There I was able to see in full flight the neo-classic architectural style that Jane adopted in all her building projects. I also walked the wide clean beaches and pinewoods that had been Jane's playground as a child. It was a long way, I decided, from Holkham to Damascus.

I should also like to thank the following individuals who helped me in various ways: Rosemary Archer; R. W. C. Charlton; the late Miss Fiona Digby; Simon Digby; Maldwin Drummond; Angela Hurrell; Lord Lytton;

Costas Manolis and Denis Minotos at the National Historical Museum, Athens; Spiros Mouzakitis; Vivien Noakes; Bernadette Rivett; Nicola Soana; George Theotoky.

In translating Jane's diaries and other documentation I was ably assisted by: Janet Dubois (French); Alan Keenan (German); Jehan and Tareq Rajab (Arabic); Louise H. Watts and Mark Wazir (French).

Many archives, libraries and organisations were consulted. At each one staff were unfailingly kind and generous with their time and expertise. They were:

In and around London: The Bank of England (Mr Philip Davies, Museum and Historical Section); British Library, Gt Russell St Reading Room, Manuscripts Department (Martin Harris) and Department of Prints and Drawings (Jessica White); BL Newspaper Library, Collindale; Courtauld Collection (Sarah Wimbush and Barbara Hilton-Smith); House of Lords Library (Mr Michael Troke); National Portrait Gallery (Jo Copeland); National Register of Archives; Public Record Office, Kew; Public Record Office, Chancery Lane; St Catherine's House; The Royal Archives, Windsor (Miss Frances Dimond); the Royal Geographical Society (Fiona Catherines and the Librarian); Society of the Sacred Heart at the Roehampton Institute (Sister M. Coke, Provincial Archivist); Somerset House.

Regional: Ashmolean Library, Oxford (Corinne Cherrad-Marshall); the Bodleian Library, Oxford (staff of the lower reading room, and Michael Webb, Assistant Librarian, Dept of Western Manuscripts); Bristol Museum (Sheena Stoddard – Assistant Curator, Fine Art); Farquarson & Murless (photographers); the Fitzwilliam Museum, Cambridge (Ms Margaret Clarke); Keele University Library (Mr Martin Phillips); Sheffield City Archives (Ms Julie Hibberd); Sotheby's (Mrs Jackie Rees); St Anthony's College, Oxford (Dianne King); Colin Wakeham (photographer); East Sussex Library Service (Hilary Woodard); Wiltshire County Record Office.

My special thanks to Heather Screen and Gaynor Myers of Lydney Library in West Gloucestershire for the cheerful efficiency with which they dealt with my frequent requests for long-out-of-print books which they sometimes obtained in spite of all odds.

I should also like to thank my long-suffering family. No one should have to live in the same household as a writer trying to meet a deadline. And finally I should like to thank Richard Cohen (editor and publisher), Linden Stafford (copy editor), Margaret Fraser (designer) and Robert Ducas (my agent) who are all part of the team who brought this book into print.

Illustrations in this book appear courtesy of the copyright holders, as follows: Ashmolean Museum: frontispiece

Courtauld Collection: plate 1
Photographed at Minterne House: plates 2, 5, 11, 17, 20, 24, 27, 29–31, 35, 41, 52; illustrations on pages 200, 214, 255, 326
Jasper Books: plates 3, 4, 43–8
British Library: plate 9
National Portrait Gallery: plates 7, 8, 18
Society of the Sacred Heart, Roehampton: plate 6
British Museum: plates 10, 12
E. M. Oddie: plates 13, 21–3
East Sussex Library Service: illustration on page 62
Bayerstaatsgemäldesammlungen, Munich: plates 14–16, 25
Herr Kleefoot, Oberbürgermeister of Weinheim: plate 19
J. Allen & Co.: plates 32–3, 50, 51
St Anthony's College, Oxford: plate 34
Tareq and Jehan Rajab: plates 36–9
Royal Archives (by gracious permission of HM the Queen): plates 40, 49
Hussein Hinnawi: plate 42
National Historical Museum, Athens: plate 26

Index

Abdallah, Munni 192, 229, 231, 233, 235
About, Edmond 137–8, 148, 185–6; on Jane
  and Xristos 140, 141; meets Jane 145–7;
  La Grèce contemporaine 185–7
Achmed Pasha 246, 250, 251
Albania 139
Albert, Prince 258, 259
Almack's 12–13, 14, 26, 27, 218
Almack's (Spencer-Stanhope) 28, 71
Amalie, Queen of Greece 128, 182, 265;
  dislikes Jane 129–30, 139, 170; jealous of
  Jane and Xristos 140, 141–3, 144
Amherst, Mr and Mrs 269
Anazeh tribe 155, 165–6, 192
Andover, Lady Jane Digby (née Coke;
  mother) 1, 6–7, 77–8, 118–19, 121–2,
  132; introduces Jane to society 14–15;
  distraught over end of Jane's marriage
  54–5; asks Steely to testify 68; continuing
  affection for Jane 123–4; death of
  husband 127–8; Jane's last visit 215–18;
  death of 266
Anson, Lady Anne (née Coke; aunt) 1–2, 9,
  30; tries to mend Ellenborough marriage
  52, 53–4
Anson, Fanny (later Isted; cousin) 3, 218,
  222, 234
Anson, George (cousin) 9, 24, 199; affair
  with Jane 26–30, 33–5; end of affair
  35–7, 40; father of child 35–7; death of
  brother 47; escapes divorce case 70;
  marriage to Isabella Forrester 74–5; later
  life 170; death of 222
Anson, Henry (cousin) 3, 182; death from
  plague 46–8
Anson, Isabella (née Forrester) 74–5, 75, 234

Anson, Lord (uncle) 3
Anson, William 75
Anton (gardener) 314
Apponyi, Count Rodolphe 40, 42–3, 72, 76,
  96; duel between Charles and Spiros
  109–11
Arabian Nights, The (Burton) 290
Arbuthnot, Harriet 19, 27, 55
Ashburton, Lady Lena (niece) 288
Athens, Greece 129, 130; Otto's court
  139–40
Authentic Arabian Horse, The (Wentworth) 312

Babylon 180
Baghdad 179–80
Balzac, Honoré de 103–5, 109; *Le Lys dans la
  vallée* 103; *Comédie humaine, La* 104
Bandel, Josef 187
Barak, Sheikh 188, 191, 192; journey to
  Baghdad 174–84; becomes a nuisance
  198–90
'Basily' *see* Ludwig I of Bavaria
Beaufort, Emily (later Lady Strangford)
  192–3, 237–40; *Egyptian Sepulchres and
  Syrian Shrines* 239–40; concerned about
  Jane's reported death 302–3; Jane as role
  model 327
bedouins *see also* Mezrab, Sheikh Medjuel el:
  Saleh's caravan 152–4; enemy tribes of
  Anazeh and Shemmar 155; rival tribes
  165–6; Jane's introduction 177; marriage
  customs 192; slaves 192–3; women
  195–6, 197–8; tents and status 202;
  marriage customs 203; desert warfare
  229–30, 235, 292–3, 314–15; reaction to
  European dress 293

Beirut 149, 172-3
Bey, Hassan 280, 288
Bibichi the highwayman 145
Blunt, Lady Anne 310-12, 315-16, 320-1
Boyle, Caroline 8
Brighton 48-51, 56-7, 70
Buchon, Alexandre 124, 125
Buffet, Madame 227
Burton, Isabel 278-95; parting from Jane
   298-9; unrelentingly European 300;
   upsets Jane with proposed biography
   303-6, 317; *The Inner Life of Syria, Palestine
   and the Holy Land* 315; erroneous biography
   of Jane 329-33
Burton, Sir Richard 168, 175, 278-95, 315,
   331; *The Arabian Nights* 290; *The Perfumed
   Garden* 290; Jane as source for sexual
   knowledge 290; political rumblings 293,
   297-8; dismissed as consul 298-9
Buxton, Edward 257, 259-61
Buxton, Emmie (née Digby; niece) 257-8,
   259-61, 280, 323
Byron, Lord (George Gordon); *Don Juan* 18

Cabouly Effendi 269
Cadlands (racehorse) 41, 46, 79
Caroline of Brunswick 16, 58, 70-1
Carpenter, William 44, 57, 65
Castlereagh, Lord (Robert Stewart) 15-16,
   29
Charles X of France 74
Chirol, Sir Valentine 317
Christians: massacred in Syria 244-53; Jane
   supports community in Damascus 251-2
Churchill, Charles 240, 246
Clare, Lord 72
Coke, Anne *see* Anson, Lady Anne
Coke, Edward 4
Coke, Elizabeth *see* Spencer-Stanhope,
   Elizabeth
Coke, Thomas (later Lord Leicester of
   Holkham; grandfather) 1-2, 3-5, 9, 256;
   new family 8-9, 20, 30; manuscript
   collection 30; Jane never sees again 113;
   death of 127
Comédie humaine, La (Balzac) 104
Creevey, Thomas 19-20, 27, 30
Crystal Palace 217-18

Dalkeith, Lord 160
Damascus 156-9, 168-70; Jane's house
   203-6, 210, 220, 224-5, 227-8, 240,
   253-4, 265; social life 236-41, 280, 306;
   massacre of Christians 244-53; Jane's
   disillusionment 251, 260; Jane sells house
   265
Demetri (Damascus hotelier) 156, 161, 174,
   315

Dickson, H. R. P. 328, 333
Dietrichstein, Count Moritz 41, 44-5
Digby, Caroline (sister-in-law) 259, 276
Digby, Carrie (niece) 280
Digby, Charles (nephew) 280
Digby, Lord Edward (brother) 3, 55, 558,
   122-3, 263, 326; marriage 113; Charles
   confides in 117-18; death of father
   127-8; becomes Lord Digby 211; distance
   from Jane 215-16; receives news of Jane's
   death 327; inheritance from Jane 328-9,
   334; death of 329
Digby, Emmie *see* Buxton, Emmie
Digby, Admiral Sir Henry (father) 2-3, 7-8,
   55; remains friendly with Ellenborough
   58-9, 71; tries to persuade Felix to marry
   Jane 73; approves marriage to Charles
   97, 98; welcomes Spiros and Leonidas
   120-2; ill-health 123-4; death of 127-8
Digby, Henry (nephew) 258
Digby, Jane Elizabeth: appearance when
   young 1, 14-15, 51, 86-7; early
   childhood 1, 5-10; education 6-8, 12, 82;
   débutante 11-16; courtship with
   Ellenborough 15-20; marries
   Ellenborough 20-6; marriage to
   Ellenborough breaks up 23-6, 42-3, 46,
   51-7; affair with George 26-30, 33-7, 40,
   41-2, 44; affair with Madden 30-2, 33-4;
   birth of Arthur 35-9; affair with Felix
   39-46, 48-52, 57-60, 76-9, 90-5;
   pregnant by Felix 51, 56, 66-7;
   Ellenborough considers divorce 57-61;
   birth of Mathilde 60; notorious divorce
   63-73; family embarrassment 73, 97, 105,
   113, 122-3; Felix unable to marry 73-5;
   birth and death of son Felix 75
   move to Munich 78-80; friendship with
   King Ludwig 82-4, 88-94, 99-101,
   105-6, 130, 280; affair with Charles
   83-95; pregnant by Charles 89; marries
   Charles 90-4, 96-9; birth of Heribert 92;
   gives up little Mathilde to Felix's sister 93;
   as Charles's wife 101-2; birth of Bertha
   101-2; portrayed by Balzac 103-4;
   portrayed in *Two Friends* 105; affair with
   Spiros 106-12; financial provision from
   Ellenborough 113-14; elopes with Spiros
   115-19; birth of Leonidas 119-20; happy
   family life with Spiros 120-7, 128-9; last
   visit to England 121-2; marries Spiros
   123; investigates history of Tinos 124-5;
   disliked by Queen Amalie 129-30; rift in
   marriage to Spiros 132; death of Leonidas
   132-3, 134-5; end of marriage to Spiros
   134-5; travels after Spiros 136-8;
   ill-health 137, 151, 181; settlement for
   Spiros 138-9; affair with Xristos 139-48,

150, 154; betrayed by Xristos to Queen 143; annulment of marriage to Spiros 144, 146; meets Edmond About 145–7; appearance when older 146, 295–6, 311, 316–17

leaves Greece for Syria 147–9; travels in Jordan 151–5; affair with Saleh 152–4; visit to Palmyra 155–70; easy comradeship with Medjuel 156; visit to Palmyra 166–8; return to Damascus 171–3, 218–20; Medjuel proposes marriage 173–4, 183–4; journey to Baghdad with Barak 175–84; held for ransom 176–7; story of the horse and the sheikh 185–6; terms for marriage to Medjuel 186–91; honeymoon with Medjuel 191–200; relationship to bedouin women 194–8; gloomy about rumours 201, 208; married life with Medjuel 201–12, 220–7, 266–77, 306, 310–11, 313–15, 322; visit to England 213–18; family tree for Heribert 217; return to Damascus 218–20; escorts Englishmen to Palmyra 223–4; ill-health 227, 270, 276, 317–18; reflection on children 227; alone in Palmyra 229–35; social life in Damascus 236–41, 307–12; emissary for tribe to sheikh assembly 243–4; role during the massacre of Christians 244–51; becomes churchgoer 251–2; nicknamed 'Umm el Laban' 255; acceptance by tribe 255–7; most important European in Syria 257; social life in Damascus 258–60; tries to recover camels from ebn Dukhi 261–5; loses British nationality 271, 276; worry about cholera 273; worried by remours of another wife 274, 277; friendship with Burtons 278–95, 315; hurt by Medjuel's marriage to Ouadjid 281–6; described by Mitford 294–5; false report of death 301–6; whole tribe sleeps in house 309; friendship with Blunts 310–12, 315–16, 320–1; sexual relationship with Medjuel 319–20; death and funeral 322–6; erroneous obituaries 327–8; estate and will 328–9, 334; Isabel Burton's erroneous biography 329–33
Digby, Kenelm (brother) 3, 122, 280; Vicar of Tittleshall 113; meets Jane and Spiros in Paris 118–19; letter from Damascus 210–11; good nature 216–17; becomes Honourable 235; wife dies 276; death of 329; inheritance from Jane 329, 334
Digby, Lena (niece) 288
Digby, Lord 211
Digby, Lucy (niece) 306
Digby, Theresa (sister-in-law) 122, 306
Digby, William (nephew) 276, 280

Don Juan (Byron) 18
Doukades, Corfu 125
Drummond, Admiral 307
Drummond, Mr (banker) 201
Druses 150, 240, 244, 263
Dufferin, Lord 251, 258
Dukhi, Sheikh Mohammed ebn 229, 232, 243–4, 257, 271; steals Jane's camels 261–5; raids and counter-raids 292–3; refuses friendship 294; sons murder ebn Jendall 314–15; recommended escort 316

Edward, Prince of Wales 259
Egyptian Sepulchres and Syrian Shrines (Beaufort) 239–40
Ellenborough, Lord Edward (Law) 82, 199, 329; politics 15–16; courtship of Jane 15–20; marries Jane 20–6; first marriage 23; marriage breaks up 28, 42–3, 46, 51–7; politics 37–8; affairs 43, 70; considers divorce 57–61; death of Arthur 60–1; notorious divorce 63–73; affairs 70; later life 72–3; financial provisions for Jane 113–14; death 300–1
Ellenborough, Lady Octavia 15–16, 23
Erskine, Lord 79
Esterhazy, Prince Paul Anton 46, 52
Esterhazy, Princess 28, 29, 72, 82, 89–90
Eugénie (maid) 120, 141, 219, 228, 261; nurses Jane through malaria 137; devotion 138, 208; affair with Xristos 147–8, 150, 212; in Damascus 159, 187, 192, 198, 205; trip to Palmyra 161–2; journey to Baghdad 174–5, 176; prickly in Baghdad 179–80, 181; Jane leaves for Medjuel 183; resigns 199, 201, 216, 221; devotion 208; hopes for marriage disappointed 213; quarrels with Jane 236, 240; returns to Athens 242–3, 278, 280–1; re-employed 269
Euphrates (river) 177–8
Exclusives, The (anonymous novel) 71

Fares, Sheikh of Tadmor 206–7; marriage tease 254–5
Fatmah (orphan) 322
Feisal, Sheikh 243, 244, 250, 265
Ferhan, Sheikh 179
Feydan, Sheikh 232
Fidayah (maid) 252, 253, 284
Florenzi, Marchesa Marianna 87, 88, 101
Fox Lane, Mrs 27, 29
Fox Strangways, John 46–7
Fuad Pasha 253, 258
Fullerton-Fullerton, Amy: *A Lady's Ride through Palestine and Syria* 289

George III 114
George IV 14, 15, 38; Crown property 16, attempt to divorce 58, 70–1
Gomussa, Sheikh Meshur el 309
Graham, Mr 245, 248
Grèce contemporaine, La (About) 185
Gronow, Captain 13
Grove, Anna 48

Haag, Carl 237, 239, 288, 308
Hadji-Petros, Eirini 140–1, 143, 211–13, 216
Hadji-Petros, Xristodolous 153–4, 170, 182, 186–7, 197, 199; affair with Jane 139–48, 150, 154; denounces love for Jane to Queen 143; affair with Eugénie 147–8; Jane visits 211–13
Hamwoya 230–1
Hanska, Evaline 103, 104
harems 240–1, 290–1, 308–9
Hatzfeld, Madame 76
Heald, Mr (banker) 308
Hebron 172
Hedeb, Sheikh Faris ebn 176–7
Hepple, Robert 50–1, 52, 56–7, 64–5
Hessienne tribe 254–5, 257
Heuguard, Monsieur and Madame 263, 265, 331
Holkham Hall, Norfolk 2, 3–5, 258; Ellenborough visits 18; Jane's last visits 30, 34–5; after death of Henry Anson 47–8; taste similiar to King Ludwig's 81; Jane's model in Greece 125
Holland, Lady 20, 72
Holmes, James 51
Homs 261; second home 251, 252–3, 266, 279, 283–5; description of house 288–9
Hume, Joseph 65–6

'Ianthe' nickname 82
Inner Life of Syria, Palestine and the Holy Land, The (Burton) 315
Islam 156–7; Ramadan observance 164, 169
Isted, Fanny *see* Anson, Fanny

Jaffa 149–50
Jago, T. S. 307, 310, 324, 325, 326, 328
Jekyll, Joseph 22, 43, 46
Jendall, Sheikh ebn 314–15
Jerhan, Sheikh 180
Jerusalem 151–2
Jesus Christ: Jordanian places 154; Muslim reverence for 156–7
Jordan 151–5

Kane, Edward 68
Keppel, Lady Anne (later Coke) 9

Khader, Emir Abd el 236, 289; Jane visits harem 240–1; protects Christians from massacre 246, 247–9, 250; Jane's contact 257
Kissini, Mr 182
Kurds 247, 251, 253–4

Labuteau, Monsieur 76–7, 96
Lady's Ride through Palestine and Syria, A (Fullerton-Fullerton) 289
Lamia 141
Law, Arthur Dudley (son) 38; paternity 48; ill in Brighton 48–9; death of 60–1
Law, Charles 18
Law, Edward *see* Ellenborough, Lord
Law, Elizabeth 18
Law, Henry 18, 51, 54–5
Lawrence, T. E. 333
Lear, Edward 151, 260
Leicester of Holkham, Lord *see* Coke, Thomas
Lely, Sir Peter 86
Le Roy, Monsieur 249, 250
Lieven, Princess Dorothea 28, 29, 53, 72; on Ellenborough's politics 37–8; Jane corresponds with 82
Little Sisters of Charity 245
Londonderry, Lady 18, 42
Londonderry, Lord 42, 82, 113, 218
Lucas, Mr 274, 275, 276–7, 323
Ludwig I of Bavaria 79–82, 199; hopes for reunion between Jane and Felix 83–4, 85–6, 92–3; friendship with Jane 88–94, 99–100, 105–6, 130; brings Jane and Charles into court life 97–8; and Jane's fifth child 100–1; silent after Spiros affair 111–12; rumours in London 114; and Lola Montez 135, 280; last years 280
Lys dans la vallée, Le (Balzac) 103

Mackintosh, Mary 314, 322
Madden, Frederick 30–2, 33–4, 199
Mannheim 115
Marguerite, Countess of Blessington: *The Two Friends* 105
Maronites 240
Mecca 168
Medjuel el Mezrab *see* Mezrab, Sheikh Medjuel el
Merschid, Sheikh Beteyen ebn 254, 257; raids on Mezrab tribe 280
Meschaka, Dr 251–2
Metternich, Prince Klemens 39–40, 52; selects Prince Otto for Greece 82
Meziad, Sheikh Faris el 229, 243–4, 271–2; complains to authorities about Medjuel 257; rumours of Medjuel's other wife 277
Mezrab, Aafteh el (stepdaughter) 284, 309

Mezrab, Afet el (stepson) 208, 284, 309, 310, 328, 333; desert warfare 314–15
Mezrab, Endaya el 209
Mezrab, Joffell el 207
Mezrab, Manah el 208, 250, 262
Mezrab, Mascha el 332; divorce 118–91, 192, 208–9; meeting after marriage 194–5; circumcision of son 196–7; Jane's guilt feelings 203; rumour of remarriage to Medjuel 233–5; death of 244; alive after all 282
Mezrab, Sheikh Medjuel el: conducts Jane through Syria 155–70; easy comradeship with Jane 156; appearance 161–2, 189, 288, 294; invites Jane to Mecca 168; asks Jane to marry him 173–4, 183–4; other wives 174, 225–6, 233–5, 274–5, 281–6, 292, 313–15; tries to meet Jane's terms for marriage 186–91; honeymoon with Jane 191–200; married life with Jane 201–12, 220–7, 266–77, 310–11, 322; personality 225–6, 296, 316; trip to Beirut– 242–3; sends Jane as emissary because of ill-health 243–4; protects Jane from massacres 244–9; Shemmar attack on tribe 250–1; thrown into jail 257, 292; in trouble with authorities 258, 261, 262–5, 267; ill-health 267–8, 294, 314, 315; letter to Burton 298; political negotiations 301; Anne Blunt writes about 317–18; depression and lack of libido 319–20; friendship with Blunts 321; Jane's funeral 324–6; inheritance from Jane 328, 334; Isabel Burton's erroneous biography 330, 332; death 333
Mezrab, Sheikh Mohammed el 155, 200, 262; opposed to Medjuel's marriage to Jane 189; meeting after marriage 194; tent 202; marries again 226; Jane presents women's grievances to 256; concerned about Jane leaving tribe 285
Mezrab, Ouadjid el 306; Medjuel's marriage to 281–6; argument between Medjuel and Schebibb 313–14; death of 319–20
Mezrab, Schebibb el (stepson) 208, 226, 275; circumcision feast 196–7; death of mother 244; illness and death 278–9; death of 314; father's curse 314
Mezrab, Telgarr el 284
Mezrab tribe 165, 207, 232; escort duties 155–6; Sehmmar attacks 250–1; acceptance of Jane 255–7; inter-tribal raids 292–3; faithful to government 294; devotion to Jane 309; well equipped 312
Miguel, Maria Evarist, King of Portugal 40
Misk, Hannah 205, 264, 290
Mitchell, Roland 325

Mitford, Barty (later Lord Redesdale) 294–5
Mohammed, Prophet 157
Montez, Lola 135, 280
Mott, Reverend 296
Munich 79–82, 101, 102, 105
Murray, Sir Patrick 269
M'wayaja tribe 176, 230

Nazareth 154
Nicorat, Dr 227–8
Noel, Roden 237
Noeys, Mr 269
Norfolk Hotel, Brighton 48–51, 56–7, 64–5

Oddie, E. M. 126–7, 165, 296, 324–5
Otto, King of Greece 82, 107–8, 199, 265; friendship with Jane 128–30, 139; and Amalie 142; relieved of power 182
Oudenarde, Madame d' 76

Palikares (Albanian mercenaries) 139, 141
Palmyra 156, 206, 220, 237–40, 269–70; rival tribes 155; history 159–60; Jane advised against visiting 160–1; visit to the sheikh 167–8; Jane and Medjuel's honeymoon 193–4; Jane's gravestone 326
Parry, Mr 296
Paumgarten, Countess Gabrielle de see Venningen, Gabrielle
Payen, Catherine 273
Pears, Sir Edwin 308
Pedro II of Brazil 307–8
Pennant, Mr 22
Perfumed Garden, The (Burton) 290
Pinakothek, Munich 81–2
Plaisance, Duchesse de (Sophie de Barbe-Marbois) 139, 144–5, 147, 170, 213; tells story of Jane and the sheikh 185–6

Radcliffe, Ann 7
Radcliffe, Mr 222
Ralley, Mr 222
Rawlinson, Sir Henry 179, 218
Redouan, Yusuf 277
Reichardt, Mrs 323–4, 325
Reschid Pasha 298
Ressoul, Ali 282
Revolution of 1830, The (Schwarzenberg) 74
Roallah tribe 314–15
Robson, Dr 245, 252
Roehampton 22–3, 27, 45
Rogers, Richard 257, 263, 264, 293; can't offer protection 271, 276; wife dies of cholera 273
Rome (ancient): and Palmyra 160

Roseby, Lady 218
Rutland, Duchess of 27, 29

St Antonio, Countess 43, 45, 72
Saleh (bedouin host) 152–4, 172–3, 199
Salim, Sultan 243
Schönberg-Hartenstein, Prince Alfred de 103, 109
Schönheits-Galerie 86–7
Schwarzenberg, Field Marshal Karl Philipp 39
Schwarzenberg, Mathilde 'Didi' (daughter) 77, 79, 227, 329; birth 60, 62; meets Jane 131–2
Schwarzenberg, Prince Felix Ludwig 114, 199, 329; affair with Jane 39–46, 76–9, 83–6, 90–5; nicknamed Cadlands 41, 46, 79; Brighton meeting 48–52; sent away from Jane 52, 55; urges Jane to join him in Austria 57–8; feelings changed 60–1; Ellenborough divorce case 63–73; unable to marry Jane 69, 73–5; *The Revolution of 1830* 74; death of son 75; posted to Berlin 80; mystical powers 85; approves Jane's marriage to Charles 89, 96–8; later life 95, 103; meets Jane later in Naples 131–2; death of 146; Isabel Burton claims was Jane's lasting love 331–2
Schwarzenberg, Princess Aloyse 103
Schwarzenberg, Princess Mathilde 77; adopts little Mathilde 93
Schwarzenberg, Princess Pauline 39
Sclamya 197
Sebbah tribe 155
Segall, Rev. J. 328
Selaine, Sheikh 150–1, 153, 155, 170, 172–3
Seminary for Young Ladies 8
Senior, Nassau 142, 153–4
Seyd, Sheikh 205
Sehmmar tribe 155, 179, 225; attacks on Mezrab tribe 250–1
Solomon, King 166
Solyman, Emir 284
Spencer-Stanhope, Elizabeth (née Coke; aunt) 1–2, 9, 14, 30
Spencer-Stanhope, John 9
Spencer-Stanhope, Marianne: *Almack's* 28, 71
Stafford, Lord 294
Stanhope, Lady Hester 159–60
Steele, Jane 7, 9, 121, 215, 275
Steele, Margaret 6–7, 11–12, 77–8, 94, 118–19, 132, 188, 208; warns Jane 24, 26, 27–8; approaches Lord Ellenborough 51; supports Jane at end of Ellenborough marriage 54–6; testifies in divorce court 66–8; disapproves of Medjuel 199, 205,

216; lives with Lady Andover 215; death of 278
Stieler, Josef 86–7
Stirling, A. M. 165
Strangford, Emily *see* Beaufort, Emily
Syria *see also* bedouins; Damascus; Homs: Henry Anson's death in 46–7; massacre of Christians 244–53

Tadmor *see* Palmyra
Tappenden, Mrs 240, 242, 243, 253; unsatisfactory as maid 250, 252, 261, 269
Theotoky, Leonidas Jean Henry (son) 119–20, 216, 296; death of 132–3, 134–5
Theotoky, Spiridon 199; affair with Jane 106–12; duel with Charles 109–10; elopes with Jane 115–19; charms Jane's family 118–19; happy family life 120–7, 128–9; end of marriage 132, 134–5; financial settlement 138–9; later life 140; end of marriage 144, 146; financial settlement 147
Theresa, Princess of Saxe-Hildburghausen 81
Tinos, Greece 124–5
Turkey 245, 246, 247, 250, 294
Two Friends, The (Marguerite, Countess of Blessington) 105

Vaudeuil, Madame la 95
Venningen, Baron Carl (Charles) 199; marriage to Jane 90–4, 96–9, 101–2; in love with Jane 83–95; and Jane's affair with Spiros 106, 108–12; duel with Spiros 109–10; financial troubles 114–15; end of marriage 116–19; divorce 119, 120–1, 123; lifelong affection for Jane 120–1, 123, 125–6; reaction to Jane's separation from Spiros 135–6; worries about children and Jane 228–9; praise for Jane's bravery 249; on death of Lady Andover 266; death 306–7
Venningen, Baroness (mother-in-law) 100
Venningen, Bertha (daughter) 100–1, 117, 128, 136, 227; asks to live with Jane in Damascus 216; insanity 228, 236, 307
Venningen, Gabrielle (née Countess de Paumgarten) 268–9, 272; death of 296
Venningen, Heribert (son) 101, 111, 128, 136, 227, 236, 334; birth 92; need for family proof 217, 228–9, 235; marries Countess Gabrielle de Paumgarten 268–9; wife dies 296; family life 307
Venningen, Philip 105
Victoria, Queen 114, 122, 239, 271

Waldkirk, Mimi 100
Walton, William 51, 56–7

Ward, John 65
Wellington, Duke of (Arthur Wellesley) 13, 20
Wentworth, Lady Judith 329; *The Authentic Arabian Horse* 312
William IV 114

Wood, Richard 160–1, 190, 198 307
Wright, Rev. William 305–6, 327

Zappani, Countess 95
Zenobia, Queen of Palmyra 160. 327

All Fourth Estate books are available at your local bookshop or newsagent, or can be ordered direct from the publisher.

Indicate the number of copies required and quote the author and title.

Send cheque/eurocheque/postal order (Sterling only), made payable to Book Service by Post, to:

Fourth Estate Books
Book Service By Post
PO Box 29, Douglas
I-O-M, IM99 1BQ.

Or phone: 01624 675137

Or fax: 01624 670923

Alternatively pay by Access, Visa or Mastercard

Card number:

Expiry date ....

Signature ....

Please allow 75 pence per book for post and packing in the UK. Overseas customers please allow £1.00 per book for post and packing.

Name ....
Address ....
....
....

Please allow 28 days for delivery. Please tick the box if you do not wish to receive any additional information. ☐

Prices and availability subject to change without notice.